Realism

Modern Literatures in Perspective

General Editor:

Seán Hand, University College of Wales, Aberystwyth

Published Titles:

Lilian R. Furst, *Realism*

REALISM

Edited and Introduced by

LILIAN R. FURST

LONGMAN

LONDON AND NEW YORK

Longman Group UK Limited,
Longman House, Burnt Mill,
Harlow, Essex CM20 2JE, England
and Associated Companies throughout the world.

Published in the United States of America
by Longman Publishing, New York

First published 1992

British Library Cataloguing-in-Publication Data
A catalogue record for this book is
available from the British Library

Library of Congress Cataloging-in-Publication Data
Realism / edited and introduced by Lilian R. Furst.
        p.   cm. – (Modern literatures in perspective)
    Includes bibliographical references and index.
    ISBN 0-582-08532-2 – ISBN 0-582-08531-4 (pbk.)
    1. Criticism.   2. Realism in literature.   I. Furst, Lilian R.
II. Title.   III. Series.
PN98.R4R43   1992
809'.912 — dc20   91–42452
                                                                              CIP

Set by 9AA in 9/11½ pt Palatino
Produced by Longman Singapore Publishers (Pte) Ltd.
Printed in Singapore

Contents

Contents

General Editor's Preface

Modern Literatures in Perspective is a series of collected critical essays on post–1800 European-language authors, works or concepts. It is designed to help the reader study these literatures in isolation and in context by selecting and presenting the most representative and inspiring reactions to the works in question from the time of their first appearance to the present day.

A crucial feature of the series' approach is its open recognition of the critical revolution which has taken place this century and in particular in the last thirty years. Marxist, structuralist, psychoanalytical, deconstructionist and feminist theories have utterly transformed our assessment of literature. *Modern Literatures in Perspective* takes full account of the general issues raised by the revolution in theory, together with the practical effects which these theories have on the reading of the literary canon.

Recognising the need for direction within this plural field of perspectives, each volume offers a high degree of critical guidance and advice in addition to presenting its subject in a methodical and accessible manner.

A substantial introduction outlines the historical and cultural contexts within which the literature in question was produced. It explores and explains the conflicting critical reactions to the literature in perspective and suggests ways in which these critical differences may be put to work. Each essay is prefaced by an introductory headnote setting forth the significance of the piece. A glossary of critical terms and cultural references provides further background information.

Modern Literatures in Perspective offers much more than textual analysis, therefore. It openly examines the relationship between literature and a range of wider issues. At the same time, its approach is more concrete than any history of literature. Rather than impose a synthesis or single methodology, the volumes in this series bring the reader into the heart of a crucial critical debate.

New critical insights, teaching practices and reading publics continue to transform our view of modern European-language writings. *Modern Literatures in Perspective* aims to contribute to this continuous transformation by disseminating and analysing the best modern criticism on the best modern literatures.

Acknowledgements

We are grateful to the following for permission to reproduce copyright material:

Cambridge University Press for the chapter 'The Reality Effect' by Roland Barthes from *French Literary Theory Today* edited by Tzvetan Todorov, translated by R. Carter (1982); Columbia University Press for the chapter 'The Play of the Text' by Wolfgang Iser from *Languages of the Unsayable* edited by S. Budick and W. Iser (1989), copyright © 1989 Columbia University Press; Editions du Seuil for an extract from the article 'Un discours contraint' by Philippe Hamon from *Poetique*, 16 (1973); the Hemingway Foreign Rights Trust for the story 'Cat in the Rain' by Ernest Hemingway from *In Our Time* (1925); Little, Brown & Company for extracts from the chapter 'Realism and the Fear of Desire' from *A Future for Astyanax* by Leo Bersani (1969), copyright © 1969, 1974, 1975, 1976, by Leo Bersani; The Merlin Press Ltd for extracts from the chapter 'Balzac's *Lost Illusions*' from *Studies in European Realism* by Georg Lukács, translated by Edith Bone (1950); Oxford University Press and Alfred A. Knopf, Inc. for an extract from the chapter 'Repetition, Repression, and Return: The Plotting of *Great Expectations*' from *Reading for the Plot* by Peter Brooks (1984), copyright © 1984 by Peter Brooks; Princeton University Press for an extract from the chapter 'In the Hotel de La Mole' from *Mimesis* by Erich Auerbach, translated by Willard R. Trask (1953); Random Century Group and the University of California Press for the chapter 'Realism and the Novel Form' from *The Rise of the Novel: Studies in Defoe, Richardson, and Fielding* by Ian Watt (1957), © 1957 Ian Watt; Routledge for the chapter 'Analysis and Interpretation of the Realist Text: Hemingway's *Cat in the Rain*' from *Working with Structuralism* by David Lodge (Routledge and Kegan Paul, 1981) and extracts from the chapter 'Balzac's *Les Paysans*: A Disparate Text' from *A Theory of Literary Production* by Pierre Macherey, translated by Geoffrey Wall (Routledge and Kegan Paul, 1978); Routledge and the author's agent for the chapter 'The Rhetoric of *Hard Times*' from *The Language of Fiction* by David Lodge (Routledge and Kegan Paul/ Columbia University Press, 1966); University of California Press for extracts from the chapter 'The Fiction of Realism: *Sketches by Boz, Oliver Twist* and Cruikshank's Illustrations' by J. Hillis Miller from *Dickens Centennial Essays* edited by Ada Nisbet and Blake Nevius (1971), copyright © 1971 The Regents of the University of California; University of Michigan, Department of Romance Languages, for an extract from the article 'Appreciating Fiction: Suspending Disbelief or Pretending Belief?' by Kendall L. Walton from *Dispositio*, Vol. V. nos 13–14 (1983); Verso for the chapter 'Realism and the Ends of Feminism' by Penny Boumelha from *Grafts: Feminist Cultural Criticism* edited by Susan Sheridan (1988).

Preface

This volume presents a series of extracts from criticism about realism written between the mid 1830s and the late 1980s. The principle underlying the selection is to illustrate the diversity and multiplicity of the modes of reading realism. The extracts are not arranged in strictly chronological order, although one of the purposes of this collection is to show the changes and development of perceptions of realism over the past hundred and fifty years. For this reason contemporary views and reviews are given first as a backcloth to later readings. Part Two is concerned with the humanist readings which appeared in roughly the fifteen years after the end of World War II. The third and largest part is devoted to the past thirty years when a plethora of new approaches has come into prominence to enrich the study of realism. British, American and European critics have been juxtaposed to illustrate the confluences and divergences, but the emphasis is on a typology of critical approaches, not on national distinctions.

Key concepts and major theoreticians, highlighted in bold type when they first occur, are annotated in the Glossary at the end of the volume.

I would like to express my deep gratitude to the General Editor of this series, Dr Seán Hand, for his careful reading of my first draft, for his many constructive suggestions and for his generosity with advice and guidance. He was also my co-translator of the essay by P. Hamon. All other translations from the French are mine. I want to thank, too, the Institute for the Arts and Humanities at the University of North Carolina at Chapel Hill for a summer fellowship in 1990 which enabled me to start on this project. I am much indebted to my capable research assistants, Eric Iversen and Laura Via, who served as such willing legs. Finally, I would like to record my thanks to the Stanford Humanities Center for the courtesy so graciously extended to me in the use of its facilities in the final stages.

Chapel Hill, North Carolina, May 1991

Introduction

Realism has recently been described as 'a monster with many heads desperately in need of disentangling'.[1] This is an apposite but frightening image which evokes memories of that mythological beast the hydra, which grew two heads for every one that was cut off. In many ways 'realism', as used in literary criticism, seems like a hydra, for it opens up further vistas with each new exegesis. Yet even though it may be tempting to shy away from it, we cannot in practice evade it because it has become, and will continue to be, a staple of our critical vocabulary. Broadly speaking, realism denotes an illustrious body of texts which form the core of the latter half of nineteenth-century literature and related arts, and which have both earlier antecedents and later descendants. As an artistic movement realism is the product and expression of the dominant mood of its time: a pervasive rationalist **epistemology** that turned its back on the fantasies of Romanticism and was shaped instead by the impact of the political and social changes as well as the scientific and industrial advances of its day. To disentangle the monster's many heads is the purpose of this volume by tracing the kaleidoscopic variety of interpretations it has been given by writers and critics over the past century and a half.

Early theories of realism

One of the primary difficulties in dealing with realism is the absence of an organised corpus of theory such as the Romantics, the Naturalists or the Surrealists, for instance, produced in their manifestos. The realist writers handled the business of self-definition with a curious casualness that can perhaps best be explained by their desire to eschew the grandiloquence of their predecessors, and deliberately to present their enterprise in a low-key manner. Their pronouncements about their ideals

1

and their practices are scattered in prefaces, letters and occasional essays, and also interpolated in their fictions.

The earlier history of realism as a critical concept has been tracked by René Wellek in his article 'The Concept of Realism in Literary Scholarship',[2] which follows the word from its origins in late eighteenth-century philosophy through its changing usages in the nineteenth century. The realists' encompassing motto is succinctly summarised in Balzac's claim at the beginning of *Le Père Goriot* that '*All is true*',[3] which echoes the definition given in the *Mercure de France* of 1826: '*la littérature du vrai*' ('the literature of the true'). The appearance of new literary ideals from the 1830s onwards reflects and corresponds to the changing face and spirit of Europe politically and socially. The revolution in France in 1830, which led to the abdication of Charles X in favour of Louis-Philippe, the 'Citizen-King', prefigures the more violent uprising of 1848 which brought Louis Napoléon to power and with his coup d'état in 1852 ushered in the Second Republic (1852–70). The turbulence echoed throughout Europe in 1848 with rebellions in Vienna, Berlin, Venice, Milan and Prague. Though temporarily quelled, these insurrections were early manifestations of the widespread growth of national consciousness, which resulted in the 1870s in the unification of Germany and Italy as independent states and later in the formation of democratic nation states in Poland, Hungary and the Balkans.

This political restructuring was in turn fostered by social factors such as the spread of literacy and, especially, the increasing power of the bourgeoisie as it became enfranchised to vote (for example in England through a series of Parliamentary Reform Acts) and as it gained in economic stature as a result of commercial and industrial growth, which created greater affluence for it and greater hardships for the exploited labourers. A vivid picture of working conditions in the mid to later nineteenth century is given in such realist novels as Elizabeth Gaskell's *Mary Barton* (1848), Dickens' *Hard Times* (1854) and Zola's *Germinal* (1885). The opening of the first railway lines from Liverpool to Manchester in 1830, from St Etienne to Andrézieux in 1832, from Zurich to Baden in 1847, the improvement in roads, the spread of gas lighting, such changes as the invention of Nasmyth's steam hammer in 1842, the sewing machine in 1846, the introduction of electric telegraph in 1837 – all these advances made life more comfortable for the middle classes. The bourgeoisie were the primary readers of realist writing, whose tone and content were geared to appeal to an audience convinced of its capacity to master the physical world. Of particular significance for the evolution of realism was the Daguerre-Niepce method of photography, presented in 1839, which facilitated a more exact reproduction of reality.

It was in keeping with this mood that the realists placed truth-telling at the core of their beliefs, implying thereby a certain directness, simplicity and unadorned artlessness well attuned to the mid nineteenth-century preference for sober factuality. The reiterated emphasis on truth is the central motif of all contemporary views and reviews, even though the exposition of its meaning undergoes modification between the early 1830s and the late 1880s. As shown by the extracts in this volume, the notion of truthfulness was taken most literally by Balzac, who liked to cast himself in the role of recording secretary to the nineteenth century, and by the minor novelist and journalist Edmond Duranty, who adopted 'truth' as the dominant slogan of his short-lived journal *Réalisme* (1856–7), and who upheld sincerity, modernity and prose, along with truthfulness, as the distinguishing features of realism, in contrast to the idealisation, historical remoteness and verse typical of Romanticism. George Lewes, too, in his review of contemporary German fiction, makes truth a cornerstone of his principles when he asserts that 'Art always aims at the **representation** of Reality, i.e. of Truth'.[4] Lewes goes to the extreme of trying to subsume all art under realism on the grounds that 'its antithesis is not **Idealism**, but *Falsism*'. Truth to life denoted for Lewes, as for Balzac and Duranty, comprehensiveness, a willingness on the artist's part to extend his vision to include the commonplace, the everyday, essentially the ordinary lives of humble people. The elitist aestheticism of the Romantics is here replaced by a popularism more in consonance with the political trends of the nineteenth century.

This simplistic theory of art as merely truth-telling soon came to be qualified in the writings of some of the great realists themselves as they realised its intrinsic shortcomings. George Eliot, for example, in Chapter XVII of *Adam Bede*, declares her desire 'to give a faithful account of men and things as they have mirrored themselves in my mind'[5]; yet she immediately concedes: 'The mirror is doubtless defective; the outlines will sometimes be disturbed, the reflection faint or confused.' Eliot is already conscious of the crucial quandary of literary realism, which has become the fulcrum of present-day examination of its writing, *viz*, how to translate an allegedly true (but necessarily subjective) vision into words. She comments on the ease of describing an imaginary griffin ('the longer the claws, and the larger the wings, the better') as against the perplexity of depicting 'a real unexaggerated lion'. Then she adds a warning that will reverberate throughout later criticism of realism: 'Examine your words well, and you will see that even when you have no motive to be false, it is a very hard thing to say the exact truth, even about your own immediate feelings – much harder than to say something fine about them which is not the exact truth' (p. 173). What Eliot here adumbrates is precisely the problem that continues to preoccupy critics in our age: the realisation that realism saw its mission as telling the truth about ordinary life, but that it is extremely difficult, perhaps hardly possible, to achieve this aim in the medium of words because they are so laden with associations and sometimes open to a spectrum of **denotations**.

To find the appropriate but not banal words, phrases and rhythms to convey the mediocrity of bourgeois life and love is the problem with which Flaubert wrestles in the composition of *Madame Bovary*. His letters to his friend and fellow writer Louise Colet are a running commentary on his poignant struggles to give artistic form to his commonplace subject matter, whose vulgarity often disgusts him. Flaubert believes that ordinary topics are just as admissible in art as exotic ones ('Yvetot is just as good as Constantinople' he maintains in the letter of 25 June 1853, a part of which is reprinted in this volume) because it is the manner of narration and the style that are the crucial criteria for a work of art. For this reason he forces himself to endless revisions in his endeavour to avoid both triteness and lyricism. Reading Flaubert's often agonised letters, from which several excerpts are included in this anthology, it becomes abundantly apparent that realism is by no means the simple, artless form it had originally announced itself as being. Both Guy de Maupassant and Henry James subscribe likewise to the essential artfulness of realist fiction, while at the same time insisting on its fundamental commitment to truth-telling, as is discussed in the headnotes to the section 'Contemporary Views and Reviews'. Maupassant, in a salient amendment of the realist posture, chooses to underscore the artist's personal vision. He is also categoric in distinguishing realist art from mere photography, and reaches the important conclusion that the realists ought rather to designate themselves 'illusionists' since to tell the truth is in effect to give the illusion of complete truthfulness. The 'air of reality' propounded by Henry James and defined as 'solidity of specification'[6] runs parallel to Maupassant's belief that it is 'the illusion of life' that is captured by realism. Compared to Balzac and the early exponents of realism, James plays down the notion of actual truth in favour of **verisimilitude**. What is more, as the title of his essay 'The Art of Fiction' implies, he envisages the novel, like Flaubert whom he so admired, not as a random imitation of life but as an art in its own right.

Even this brief survey of contemporary views and reviews shows how rapidly the concept of realism became both increasingly complex and sophisticated. The call for truth to life was amended to the prescript of verisimilitude, plausibility, life-likeness, while the necessity for a shaping vision and artistic skill in presentation were openly acknowledged, although these latter elements were supposed to remain subservient to the observation of reality, and as far as possible concealed from readers. Perhaps it is a measure of realism's success in attaining its objectives that academic critics persisted, for almost a century, in perpetuating a series of clichés that derive largely from the early advocates of realism such as

Duranty, and that patently have little foundation in the texts themselves.[7] Misconceptions, including the realists' total objectivity and absence from the text, the simplicity of their language and the artlessness of their narrative techniques, resulted in a condescending image of realism as a naive genre. That cosy but utterly mistaken view of realism has been decisively dispelled by the close critical analysis of realist texts from diverse angles over the past forty years. The more carefully realism has been scrutinised, the more its subtleties – and contradictions – have come to be uncovered, and the more intriguing it has become to discern the artfulness it contains beneath its facade of simplicity.

Form versus content: realism reassessed

The revival of interest in realism as a serious genre was sparked by a remarkable book which first appeared in German in Switzerland in 1946 and was before long translated into several languages, including English: *Mimesis* by Erich Auerbach. Subtitled 'Represented Reality', it consists of twenty chapters each devoted to a simultaneously meticulous and imaginative analysis of textual passages from Homer, Petronius, Ammanius Marcellinus, St Augustine, Gregory of Tours, *The Song of Roland*, Chrétien de Troyes, Dante, Boccaccio, Rabelais, Montaigne, Shakespeare, Cervantes, Molière, Racine, the Abbé Prévost, Schiller, Stendhal (reprinted in this volume), Edmond and Jules de Goncourt, Zola and Virginia Woolf. This hardly constitutes a conventional list of realists, nor did Auerbach intend it as such. A Romance philologist by profession, exiled from Germany to Istanbul by the Nazis, with no scholarly library at his disposal, Auerbach worked on the canonical texts of world literature at hand, with a preference for the earlier period, which was his field of specialisation. The outcome is a book of startling freshness, devoid of traditional academic apparatus and opinions, whose conclusions are drawn exclusively from the evidence of the texts. Working deductively, Auerbach postponed any theory or definition of realism until the 'Epilogue', where he puts forward the hypothesis that the essence of realism lies in its complete emancipation from the classical doctrine of levels of representation.

> When Stendhal and Balzac took random individuals from daily life in their dependence upon current historical circumstances and made them the subjects of serious, problematic, and even tragic representation, they broke with the classical rule of distinct levels of style, for according to this rule, everyday practical reality could find a place in literature only within the frame of a low or intermediate kind

5

of style, that is to say, as either grotesquely comic or pleasant, light, colorful, and elegant entertainment. They thus completed a development which had long been in preparation (since the time of the comedy of manners and the *comédie larmoyante* of the eighteenth century, and more pronouncedly since the *Sturm und Drang* and early romanticism). And they opened the way for modern realism, which has ever since developed in increasingly rich forms, in keeping with the constantly changing and expanding reality of modern life.[8]

Through this emphasis on the flexibility and mingling of modes, Auerbach in effect shifted the criterion for realism from its subject matter to its literary treatment. He also underscored the importance to realism of both the political framework of the action and the social stratification of the figures. In conclusion, Auerbach put forward his theory that realism denotes above all the serious portrayal of everyday occurrences among the lower social strata at a specific moment in the history of their time.

Auerbach's **humanist**, sociological reading of realism was refined some ten years later in another study that has become a classic: Ian Watt's *The Rise of the Novel* (Berkeley and London: University of California Press, 1957). Although Watt's primary focus is on the eighteenth-century novel (Defoe's *Robinson Crusoe* and *Moll Flanders*, Richardson's *Pamela* and *Clarissa Harlowe*, and Fielding's *Tom Jones*), his two introductory chapters, 'Realism and the novel form' (pp. 9–34) and 'The Reading public and the rise of the novel' (pp. 35–59), map the foundations of nineteenth- as much as of eighteenth-century fiction. Watt builds Auerbach's insistence on the need to heed the 'social base' into a coherent theory. Realism presents a concrete, individualised figure embedded in the context of a particular place at a particular time. The impression of fidelity to life which it creates stems above all from the individualisation and particularisation of the figures. By establishing the salient underlying features of realism in socio-historical terms distinct from the realists' own claims, Watt provides a sound workable basis for the identification of realist works.

While Watt's readings rest on a sociological approach to literature, they are free of any overt political ideology, although in their emphasis on individuality they subsume certain middle-class assumptions. In this respect they differ from those of the Marxists whose impetus comes from a conscious and systematic socio-political world view which they apply to the interpretation of texts. **Marxism** has its roots in nineteenth-century thought through its filiation from Marx and Engels, but its primary propagator in literary criticism is the Central European Georg (György) Lukács, who wrote in both Hungarian and German. His writings on realism were not widely disseminated in English-speaking countries until the publication in translation in England in 1950 and in the United States

in 1964 of his *Studies in European Realism*, a collection of essays dating
from 1935–9. Lukács' work has exerted a widespread and potent
influence on many modernist critics, but it still derives largely from the
humanist tradition insofar as the work of art is perceived as stemming
directly from a pre-existent order of reality. Lukács repeatedly reiterates
the fundamental Marxist belief that literature reflects a social reality,
whose phenomena serve as a model for the work of art. Because of its
aptitude for capturing the relations between human beings and their
world, between life and literature, realism is the favourite field for
Marxist critics. Society at any given historical moment is conceived as
preformed raw material available for examination in the realist novel,
which is cast as 'the privileged instrument of the analysis of reality'.[9] So
Lukács argues that the realist gives a complete and correct account of an
observed social reality.

> The transformation of literature into a commodity is painted by Balzac
> in great detail. From the writer's ideas, emotions and convictions to the
> paper on which he writes them down, everything is turned into a
> commodity that can be bought and sold. Nor is Balzac content merely
> to register in general terms the ideological consequences of the rule of
> capitalism – he uncovers every stage in the concrete process of
> 'capitalization' in every sphere (the periodical press, the theatre, the
> publishing business, etc.) together with all the factors governing the
> process.[10]

What evidently fascinates Lukács in Balzac, whom he deemed the
greatest of the realists because of his 'inexorable veracity' (p. 22), is his
capacity for insight into the mechanisms of capitalist society. Unlike Zola,
who merely describes, Balzac offers an adequate reflection of the true
nature of society, and so continues the great tradition of epic. For the
record of the average social reality represents only the surface
appearance of things, whereas the great realist has the insight to
transcend the immediate so as to uncover the driving forces of history
and to articulate the principles governing social change. According to
Lukács, this is precisely what Balzac is able to achieve through his
instinctive grasp of the interaction of various social pressures in post-
revolutionary France; he shows how the ubiquitous decline in idealism
leads inevitably to the loss of the individual's illusions as he is ground
down by the totality of the socially decisive forces which come
increasingly to determine every life. It is the broad sweep of the plot of
Lost Illusions that lends universality to Balzac's understanding of social
and political processes. For Lukács this parallels Marx's differentiation
between the material transformation of the economic conditions of
production and the ideological ways in which one becomes conscious of

a conflict and fights it out. This is the sense in which Balzac represents for Lukács the most consummate realist writer. Lukács has left a strong imprint on many critics of realism including those, for example, who have more recently examined the role of money and the language of exchange in nineteenth-century writing.

In defending realism Lukács puts less emphasis on the points made by Auerbach and Watt about the method of realist fiction and more on the nature and dynamics of its content and its particular historical role and origins. In so doing he was influenced by early reflectionist Marxist theories of the representation of reality. Later Marxist critics have been more sophisticated in characterising the relationship between the realist tradition and what it represents. Among the later generation of Marxist critics the most subtle and original is Pierre Macherey, who has written a stimulating study of Balzac's *Les Paysans*, parts of which are included in this anthology. Macherey argues that Balzac himself accepted the need for a novelist to be not only an historian but also an ideologue, undertaking to 'say *two things at once*, which cannot be taken for each other: on the one hand, he must tell the truth, he must know and he must display this knowledge; on the other hand, he must select and propagate a decorous fiction, that Monarchy and Catholicism alone can ensure the future of French society' (p. 113). As a result of this dualism, the Balzacian novel, far from being simple and unified, is uneven and disparate, containing a double meaning that makes possible a double reading. Macherey is more discerning than Lukács and the early Marxists in conceiving the realm of the fiction not only as a reflection of the real universe but also as constituting its own system of reality. In his echo of Barthes in the phrase 'the effect of reality' (p. 118), Macherey reveals the extent to which he has absorbed some of the main tenets of **structuralism** too. It is this daring fusion of Marxism with structuralism that gives Macherey's work its special place insofar as it confronts the aesthetic complexity of a work of art, accommodating it to his modified Marxist position.

The dominance of form: structuralist and rhetorical approaches

Macherey is certainly not the only critic to draw on Marxism and structuralism simultaneously; Roland Barthes is another striking example. However, the combination is a precarious one because the two schools hold potentially divergent views on the relationship between life and literature. On the whole, the sociologically oriented Marxists tend to read the literary work as a reflection of an actual situation at a given historical moment, and hence to espouse a broadly mimetic approach.

The structuralists, on the other hand, are essentially verbal in thrust, deriving their inspiration from such linguists as Ferdinand de Saussure and Roman Jakobson.

Saussure's revolutionary contribution to the study of language lies in his substituting for the historical model of linguistic change current in his day an approach from a wholly different angle. In his *Cours de linguistique générale* (1915; *Course on General Linguistics*), a series of lectures delivered at the University of Geneva between 1906 and 1911, he asserts that language should also be studied **synchronically**, i.e. ahistorically in terms of the relationships between its parts. He thus envisages language as a self-sufficient system structured in recognisable patterns, foremost among which is that of binary oppositional pairs. This relational, structural view, together with the idea of binary pairs, was to be of utmost importance to the structuralists, who applied Saussure's perception of the workings of language to the workings of texts.

Saussure's ideas are seminal to the **Prague School** and the **Russian Formalists** who were interested in reading literary texts in the light of structural linguistics.[11] The dominant figure was that of Roman Jakobson, whose short theoretical essay 'On Realism in Art'[12] is an early key example of a structuralist, relational approach. Written in Czech in 1921, it squarely acknowledges the ambiguity of the term 'realism' and outlines five defining characteristics: a conscious awareness by both author and reader of a particular mode; its success; a stylistic preference for metonymic devices in which images are closely related in time and space to the things they describe (as opposed to metaphor, which links otherwise different things); the presence of 'redundancies', i.e. elements not essential to the advancement of the plot but necessary as tokens of what Barthes was later to term 'the reality effect' (see pp. 135–41); and finally, the consistency of the prevailing mode and its realisation in the appropriate poetic devices. Jakobson's essay is a landmark in the history of realism as the first attempt at a systematic understanding of its formal features.

These beginnings of structuralism in Russian formalism were subsequently developed in the 1960s and early 1970s primarily by a coterie of French critics such as Roland Barthes, **Gérard Genette** and **Tzvetan Todorov** (a Bulgarian resident in Paris). On the whole, the structuralists were more attracted to other kinds of writing, notably the chiaroscuro of the fantastic and the gamesmanship of the **self-reflexive** novel. They tended to regard realist writing as too transparent, too readily intelligible, too 'readerly', to use the term coined by Barthes in his dichotomisation of texts into the relatively straightforward 'readerly' and the more demanding and exciting, irreducibly plural 'writerly'.[13] Nevertheless, by exploring alternative strategies of textual analysis, the structuralists introduced innovative ways of reading realist texts. They

rejected the **referential** analysis followed by Marxist critics because they
perceived narrative as a largely self-contained hierarchy of systems
governed by artifice in construction, not oriented towards any postulated
external reality but woven out of a web of **intertextual** allusions to
previous literary texts. This marks a decisive watershed in critical
approaches to realism: instead of looking back to life as the source of the
fiction, the structuralists from Jakobson on focus exclusively on the text
itself. The reading of texts turns into a study of the **semiotic** process in
the creation and organisation of **signs** to produce a world charged with
significance intelligible to a reader competent in the modes of ordering.
The transaction takes place on the linguistic plane; tensions arise
between ease of intelligibility and the problematics of reading occasioned
by uncertainties, ambivalencies, contradictions and internal subversions.
In such a hermetic **hermeneutic** system there is no place for any appeal
to an extraneous order of knowledge or of being.

Once literature is seen in this way as a means to structure and
communicate discrete entities and not to apprehend and interpret a
cohesive reality, let alone to tell the truth about it, writing becomes a
highly ritualised activity that pivots on certain conventions recognised by
writer and reader alike. When this conception of the literary act is
applied to realism, its aspiration to true representation has to be
dismissed as mere posture. 'The writing of Realism,' Barthes maintains in
Writing Degree Zero, 'is far from being neutral, it is on the contrary loaded
with the most spectacular signs of fabrication.'[14] Those 'signs of
fabrication', which the writer is at pains to conceal but which the reader
may nevertheless discover, betray the complicated double-dealing in
which the realist text is actually engaged: 'a formal dialectics which
clothes an unreal fact in the garb first of truth and then of a lie
denounced as such'.[15] So realist fiction, by purporting to offer a faithful
account of the empirical world, attempts to lend to the imaginary the
guarantee of the real; in so doing, however, through its necessary
recourse to the signs of language, it unintentionally unmasks its own
pretence. For 'as nothing exists outside the text',[16] there can be no
question of referentiality, nor for that matter of a stable, whole, finite
work amenable to a reading resulting in a closed interpretation. Instead,
all texts, including the realist, are envisaged as **'code upon code'** (p. 55)
so that reading them becomes a 'cubist' exercise in which the meanings
are 'cubes, piled up, altered, juxtaposed, yet feeding on each other'
(p. 61). Only in a certain descriptive residue, as Barthes argues in his
article 'The Reality Effect',[17] for instance in the items in a description of
an interior not integrable into the thematic or symbolic code, is the text
creating 'the reality effect', which must be read precisely as an *effect*, not
as substance. The example that Barthes cites is the notation of the
presence of a barometer in the description of Mme Aubain's room in

Flaubert's story *Un Coeur simple* (*A Simple Heart*). The barometer has no function whatsoever to fulfil in the plot; it is mentioned purely to create 'the reality effect' by furnishing the room with credible objects.

This fundamental structuralist premise, that writing is *all* style, is a forceful challenge to the traditional view of realism. Realism cannot, any more than any other kind of writing, vouchsafe access to an innocent, uncoded or objective experience of an independently existing real world. Through the work notably of Barthes, it has come to be recognised as itself a code or mode of writing. It is different from other modes (e.g. the fantastic, the Romantic) by its deliberate endeavour to present itself as a continuous, univalent whole, a true and faithful record of reality. This is in itself a simulation, or, as Hillis Miller will deem it, a 'fiction' (see pp. 287–318), into which it attempts to draw the reader as its accomplice.

By uncovering the systems prevailing within texts, structuralism has provided stimulating models for new ways of reading realism. Foremost among them is *S/Z* by Barthes, in which he turns his attention to Balzac's tale *Sarrasine* and creates a radically different mode of reading through his probing of the very processes of reading. Proceeding 'in the manner of a minor earthquake',[18] Barthes divides the short narrative **diachronically** into 561 fragments called 'lexias', and synchronically into five voices or codes: the 'hermeneutic', which is concerned with distinguishing enigmas of the plot; the 'semantic', which contains indications of themes; the 'symbolic', which is the locus of multivalence and reversibility; the 'proairetic', which deals with actions; and the 'cultural', which refers to science or a body of knowledge (pp. 19–20). Each fragment or 'lexia' is then described according to the codes it comprises. This transforms the text into a choral network with a succession of entrances and exits, and disrupts the natural flow of reading in which blocks of material are assimilated sequentially. By fragmenting and interrupting the text Barthes makes space for a flood of associations, connections and tangents, crisscrossing the text beneath any conventional and illusory narrative order. The emphasis is thereby shifted from any final retrieval of a signification on to the means used to achieve signification. The text is endowed with an often dazzling multiplicity of dimensions as it is turned into 'a galaxy of **signifiers**, not a structure of **signifieds**' (p. 5). Though fundamentally structuralist in method, *S/Z* already sets in motion a deconstruction, transcending itself, as it were, and pointing forward to post-structuralism.

The structuralists' innovative methods have greatly enriched the reading of realism, not least by indicating a path that bypasses the entire vexed question of referentiality. On the other hand, this approach brings its own peculiar difficulties, above all in the resolute dissociation from any link to a reality. Because the text is a purely verbal structure, it runs the risk of becoming depersonalised and dehumanised into a self-serving play of figures and codes. David Lodge's 'Analysis and Interpretation of the Realist Text: Hemingway's "Cat in the Rain"' illustrates, however, that these dangers can be avoided. While concerned primarily with analysis of the story's structure, Lodge also engages in interpretation of the protagonists' actions and their potential meanings. Taking the problem of interpretation as its starting point, Lodge's piece explores various possibilities to end with a classically bi-polar paradigm: 'Loving (Joy) : Quarrelling (Ennui) :: stroking a cat (Non-joy, a giving but not a receiving of pleasure) : reading a book (Non-ennui)' (p. 157). This allows the reader to envisage the text in relation to a set of oppositional clusters, at the heart of which lies a contrast between culture and nature.

One of the most positive by-products of structuralism, through its own almost hypnotised attachment to the verbal texture, has been to encourage greater attention to the linguistic aspects of the text and the effect of its rhetoric. Rhetorical approaches have been fostered, too, by the impact of post-war inquiries in the philosophy of language. For realism one of the most interesting impetuses in this area comes from Chapter VII of J. L. Austin's *Sense and Sensibilia* (Oxford: Clarendon Press, 1962, pp. 62–77). Austin was a philosopher of language who focused on the speech act. He believed that concepts could be properly elucidated only by paying meticulous attention to the words used to express them. So he went right back to the word 'real' and subjected it to scrutiny. He begins with two apparently contradictory assertions: '"Real" is an absolutely *normal* word, with nothing new-fangled or technical or highly specialised about it. It is, that is to say, already firmly established in, and very frequently used in, the ordinary language we all use every day' (p. 62). Yet at the same time: '"real" is *not* a normal word at all, but highly exceptional; exceptional in this respect that, unlike "yellow" or "horse" or "walk", it does not have one single, specifiable, always-the-same *meaning*' (p. 64). This basic observation helps in grappling with some of the confusions surrounding realism. Austin cites a number of telling examples of the variety of meanings with which the word may be endowed in differing contexts; on the affirmative side it is frequently aligned with such words as 'proper', 'genuine', 'live', 'true', 'authentic' and 'natural', while its negatives may comprise 'artificial', 'fake', 'false', 'bogus', 'makeshift', 'dummy', 'synthetic', 'toy' (p. 71). Having underscored the multiplicity of potential meanings, Austin concludes that 'there are no criteria to be laid down *in general* for distinguishing the real from the not real. How this is to be done depends on *what* it is with respect to which the problem arises in particular cases' (p. 76). Transferred to 'realism', Austin's persuasive arguments strongly suggest that instead of seeking a single denotation we should be endeavouring to grasp the spectrum of features it encompasses.

An attempt to do just this is represented by Philippe Hamon's 'A

Constrained Discourse', the opening article in a special issue of *Poétique* (**16**, 1973) devoted to realist **discourse**. Hamon's essay is a wide-ranging and highly technical analysis of the assumptions and definitions concerning realist discourse. For the specific purposes of this volume I undertook to edit and translate this essay, in collaboration with Seán Hand, in order to isolate and elucidate the central points of a difficult but rewarding thesis that assumes a familiarity with structural linguistics. Like the structuralists, Hamon is totally opposed to the notion of realism as a copy of reality, and envisages literary forms as essentially modes of discourse. He aims to outline the hallmarks not of realism *per se*, but of realist discourse, doing for it what Todorov had done for fantastic discourse in his monograph *Introduction à la littérature fantastique* (1970; *The Fantastic*, trans. Richard Howard, Ithaca and London: Cornell University Press, 1975). After devoting considerable space to his preparatory clearing of the ground, Hamon offers an inventory of fifteen salient procedures of realist discourse: the flash-back, the memory, the return to the past or the projection into the future, which may take the familiar form of heredity and the generational chronicle; the cohesiveness of the psychological motivation; the presence of what Hamon denotes as a parallel intertext, by which he means allusions to Biblical or other previous narratives, as a tacit model for the plot; the systematic use of the names of protagonists and of places; the overloading of the text with detail, which leads to its character as a paraphrasable discourse; a potent strain of erudition, very likely authorial in origin but frequently disguised as emanating from one or other of the protagonists, manifest too in descriptions and technical vocabulary, and transmitted to the reader by indirect avenues, which Hamon schematises in a series of diagrams; a marked excess of information, referred to as 'redundancy', together with foreseeability of content; the delegation of the act of narration to a fictional persona; the absence of reference to the act of story-telling in order to maintain the appearance of a transparent mode of writing, dominated by the transmission of information, although in practice the author must intervene in an oblique manner to assure the credibility of the information; the problem of the hero, who must not be so inflated as to reintroduce romance, yet who must command interest despite the setbacks he suffers; the *'monosemesis'*, i.e. unambiguity of the text with its preference for such precise facts as numbers and for technical language; the avoidance of discrepancies between essence and appearance; the 'hurriedness' of the text in its haste to fulfil the reader's horizon of expectations; a tendency to cyclical alternations of high and low, of conjunction and disjunction; and the belief that the world is amenable to description and denomination. Hamon admits that these elements of realist discourse are enumerated in no particular order, and that further ones might be added. Finally, he raises two issues: whether description occupies a privileged place in realist discourse, and whether it carries demarcational signs to enframe it. Even this cursory summary of Hamon's far-ranging exploration reveals the extraordinary richness and complexity of his conceptualisation of realism. By way of conclusion he identifies some of its internal contradictions, such as that between the use of technical terms and the aim of easy readability, which prove that it is a discourse far more constrained than it appears. In Hamon's discourse analysis the perception of realism has reached the opposite pole to the early views of it as a simple and artless mode.

That is also the upshot of David Lodge's examination of 'The Rhetoric of *Hard Times*'. Taking *Hard Times* 'as a polemical work, a critique of mid-Victorian industrial society dominated by materialism, acquisitiveness, and ruthlessly competitive capitalist economics',[19] Lodge shows how intimately connected the persuasiveness of its argument is to the success of its rhetorical strategies. That the characters are incapable of change is indicated by the language in which they are embodied and which 'fixes them in their "given" condition' (p. 202). The rhetoric in fact functions here as the inferred carrier of the novel's meaning. Lodge's scrupulous analysis of a single text is a fine complement to Hamon's enveloping overview. Interestingly, heterogeneous though their methods are, they both stress that realism achieves its ends 'by means of a complex verbal activity that is far from simple' (p. 192).

Readers' responses and writers' motivations: the individual and realism

Rhetoric must by its nature entail an acute sense of the audience as well as of the process of communication. So the rhetorical approaches favoured by the structuralists and the post-structuralists lead logically to a **reader-oriented** criticism which posits as its central question: how do readers construct the text? For realism this question assumes increasing importance with the passage of time, for what was at the period of writing a segment of commonplace everyday experience neither long ago nor far away to contemporary readers has, after more than a century, become *de facto* historical fiction that requires an additional effort of empathetic and informed comprehension on the part of today's readers. The 'return of the reader' to a key role in the literary act has been ably mapped by Elizabeth Freund in her monograph of that title (London and New York: Methuen, 1987) which surveys the various directions taken by what is generally known as 'reader-response' criticism.[20] Among the earliest and leading exponents of this style of criticism is Wolfgang Iser, whose books *The Implied Reader: Patterns of Communication from Bunyan to*

Beckett (Baltimore and London: Johns Hopkins University Press, 1974)
and *The Act of Reading: A Theory of Aesthetic Response* (Baltimore and
London: Johns Hopkins University Press, 1978) were instrumental in
laying the foundations for this now common methodology. As Iser
points out at the beginning of his recent essay, 'The Play of the Text',
reprinted in its totality in this volume:

> It is reasonable to presuppose that author, text, and reader are closely
> interconnected in a relationship that is to be conceived as an ongoing
> process that produces something that had not existed before. This view
> of the text is in direct conflict with the traditional notion of
> representation, insofar as mimesis entails reference to a pregiven
> 'reality' that is meant to be represented.[21]

This is an unequivocal declaration of war on conventional attitudes to
realism. In place of the old closed system that gave priority to
representation as mimesis, Iser proposes an open system that privileges
the performative, i.e. the enactment of a transaction between text and
reader. At the heart of the performative, according to Iser, lies play. He
therefore regards the literary text 'as a playground between author and
reader' (p. 209), and argues that the space may be filled by four different
types of game, which he names *argon*, *alea*, *mimicry* and *ilinx* (p. 212). The
forms of play, corresponding to Iser's terminology, are: a fight or a
contest, when the text centres on conflicting norms and values; the
intervention of chance, which results in making things strange and
unfamiliar; a pattern designed to generate illusion (i.e. as in realism); and
the practice of subverting and undercutting successive situations as they
are played off against one another. The outcome of such games is a
process of transformation, which moves from absence to presence in 'the
"supplement" that the reader has added onto the text' (p. 215). In other
words, through the transformations resulting from play and through
their own active participation, readers can **'objectify'** a text.

The idea of play also predominates in Kendall L. Walton's
'Appreciating Fiction: Suspending Disbelief or Pretending Belief?'. As a
philosopher, whose field is aesthetics, Walton is interested in the
representational arts as a genre, in the visual arts (painting, sculpture
and film) as well as in literary texts. He concentrates less on specific
techniques than on the larger implicit issue: how does the work of art
induce the reader to believe that it is an image of reality? In contrast to
Iser, whose formulations tend towards abstraction sometimes to the
point of opacity, Walton addresses fundamental theoretical questions in a
direct, refreshingly down-to-earth manner. His major hypothesis is that
readers do not temporarily suspend disbelief in facing fiction, as
Coleridge had supposed, but that they are drawn into an active state of

pretending belief. To illustrate this, Walton uses a cast of characters in certain situations, such as Henry leaping on to the stage to save a heroine in danger,[22] and Charles feeling *'really terrified'* at a horror film as the green slime oozes out to engulf him (p. 224). Both Henry and Charles know that they are watching a spectacle (for which they have paid admission!), but the persuasive force of the fiction is so great that they forget, for the moment, the barrier between the real and the fictional realms as they become involved in the happenings of the fiction. Walton proposes the existence of a fictional truth, similar and parallel to real truth, yet distinct from it. Readers/viewers enter into the world of the fiction by the extension of their beliefs through pretence.

> Fictionally we do believe that Huck Finn floated down the Mississippi; we know that he did. And fictionally we have various feelings or attitudes about him and his adventures. Rather than somehow fooling ourselves into thinking fictions are real, we become fictional. So we end up 'on the same level' with fictions. And our presence there is accomplished in the extraordinarily realistic manner that I described. This enables us to comprehend our sense of closeness to fictions, without attributing to ourselves patently false beliefs.
>
> (p. 15)

Walton's ingenious and original speculations are valuable in affording a better understanding of the impact of realism on readers and their reactions to it. In place of the 'suspension of disbelief' vis-à-vis a fiction, traditional since Coleridge, Walton suggests that readers adopt the posture of pretending belief. This changes the fundamental attitude with which we approach a realist text, and helps to foster acceptance of its credibility.

Psychoanalytic approaches

Curiously, the interaction of text and reader has elicited little interest in psychoanalytic criticism. It has mostly been concerned with the application of psychoanalytic insights and techniques to the realm of the fiction. There are long-standing precedents for this in **Freud**'s (1970) discussion of delusions and dreams in W. Jensen's story *Gradiva*, and in the analysis of Hamlet's character and situation by Freud's British disciple and biographer Ernest Jones in *Hamlet and Oedipus* (1949). The tendency of early psychoanalytic criticism was to treat the fictional figure as if he or she were an actual patient, surmising subconscious motivations from the evidence of overt actions or statements. While this can in some instances elucidate the behaviour of characters in fiction, its main drawback lies in the limitations imposed by the availability of data, which make it hardly possible to probe a fictional psyche beyond a certain point. Of greater importance for literary criticism in the long run was Freud's interest in the uses of language, particularly in such minor psychopathologies as slips of the tongue, puns, and the verbal mechanism of jokes.[23] Structural psychoanalysis, which takes the psyche as text, and post-structural psychoanalysis, which conversely takes the text as psyche, evolved in France by Jacques Lacan and Jacques Derrida in the 1970s and early 1980s, both grew out of Freud's awareness of the cardinal role of language in the economy of the psyche.[24] The free association of ideas, which is the controlling principle of psychoanalysis, can be fruitfully manipulated in a corresponding inquiry into the associative potential of the words and patterns in a text.

The two examples of psychoanalytic criticism reprinted here represent respectively the two main lines of approach. Leo Bersani, in parts of his chapter on 'Realism and the Fear of Desire' from *A Future for Astyanax: Character and Desire in Literature*, focuses on the protagonists within the fiction. Challenging Freud's theory of sublimation, he reads a variety of texts as covertly or openly resisting Oedipal structures by disturbing the traditionally unified images of character and identity. In realist fiction in particular Bersani sees the convention of a compulsive pursuit of significant design. But, he argues that the realistic novel questions existing orders more seriously by working within a certain field of agreement about the shape of the self. He points to *Middlemarch* as a striking example of an ambivalent attitude towards the prospect of establishing connections in experience (p. 248ff), and to Balzac's *Peau de chagrin* as interpreting the containment of desire as a triumph for social stability (p. 253ff). Bersani's wide-ranging comparative consideration of English, French and American novels offers a provocatively different angle from which to read familiar fictions by making the notion of desire the fulcrum of our readings.

Like Bersani, Peter Brooks in *Reading for the Plot* uses the concept of desire as a central thread, but he applies it not to the characters but to the progress of the plot. In taking the text as psyche, he engages in a series of close analyses of individual and related clusters of texts by Stendhal, Balzac, Flaubert, Dickens, Conrad and Freud himself. The theoretical basis is laid in Chapter Four, 'Freud's Masterplot' (pp. 90–112). Brooks envisages the plot as though it were a human being, moving from a sense of beginning through variable phases of transformation, quiescence, deviance, postponement, compulsions to repetition, repressions, recapitulation and returns to abut in an ending that may ultimately subvert the very notions of beginning and end. This dynamic, energetic model of plot structure is tested in relation to the shape of *Great*

Expectations. In mapping the underlying schema of the plot, Brooks places the text in a new context which enables us to see it as an independent aesthetic artifact determined by its own inner laws.

Undoing the text: postmodern realism

While psychoanalytic readings are carried by a methodology, postmodern criticism is generally inspired by an ideology of one kind or another. To this extent it is a deliberate attempt to move beyond formalism, although postmodern criticism has also clearly appropriated elements from structuralist, rhetorical and reader-oriented approaches. The major manifestations of **postmodernism** are **deconstruction** and **feminism**, which are separate though interrelated, as is illustrated in the section 'Reading as a Woman' in Jonathan Culler's *On Deconstruction: Theory and Criticism after Structuralism* (Ithaca and London: Cornell University Press, 1982, pp. 43–64). For deconstruction the prime formative influence emanates from the French thinker Jacques Derrida, who refuses to grant either philosophy or language the privileged standing they have customarily held in Western thought.[25] Because of its awareness of the ways in which language deflects, complicates and betrays thought, deconstruction is strongly drawn to the paradoxes and contradictions, the gaps, blanks and indeterminacies latent in the text. These form the starting point for readings which show that the text is in fact quite other than what it appears to be.

For realism this has very important implications insofar as deconstruction completes the undoing of the simple image that the realists had tried to project of their writing. Thus J. Hillis Miller entitles his study of Dickens' *Sketches by Boz* and *Oliver Twist* 'The Fiction of Realism', allying realism with a term that suggests its non-existence. He begins by positing

the disintegration of the paradigms of realism under the impact of structural linguistics and the renewal of rhetoric. If meaning in language rises not from the reference of signs to something outside words but from differential relations among the words themselves, if 'referent' and 'meaning' must always be distinguished, then the notion of a literary text which is validated by its one-to-one correspondence to some social, historical, or psychological reality can no longer be taken for granted. No language is purely mimetic or referential, not even the most utilitarian speech. The specifically literary form of language, however, may be defined as a structure of words which in one way or another calls attention to this fact, while at the same time allowing for its own inevitable misreading as a 'mirroring of reality.'[26]

Miller sets out to prove these contentions in connection with *Sketches by Boz*. His choice of example is at first glance surprising because the *Sketches* are, as he himself admits, 'an unpromising text for such [i.e. deconstructive] study' (p. 287). This choice is in itself an act of defiance. It is all too tempting to read the sequence of scenes from London life presented by Boz, the 'speculative pedestrian',[27] as a record of actual experience. The journalistic model is the habitual narrative structure of the *Sketches*, and its status as a 'mirroring of reality' is reinforced by the frequent references to well-known, named streets and places. The *Sketches*, Miller comments, 'seem firmly attached to the social facts of London in 1836' (p. 289), carrying out the promise of their subtitle to be 'Illustrative of Every-day Life and Every-day People'. This subtitle has provided the cue for criticism of the *Sketches* from 1836 to the present, thereby affording 'an excellent example of the fallacy in realism at its most straightforward' (p. 290).

Miller's reading is in effect a rebuttal of the traditional approach. He sees London as a set of signs, a text for the young Dickens in his disguise as Boz to interpret, searching for patterns dispersed in the multiplicity of the city in the same way as Miller himself does with Dickens' text. He shows that the characteristic progression in the *Sketches* is imaginative, and that the **metonymic** reciprocity (i.e. adjacency) between persons and their surroundings forms the basis for **metaphorical** (i.e. transformative) substitutions. Tracing persistent repetitions, similar to those noted by Peter Brooks in *Great Expectations*, and noting the ubiquity of theatrical images, Miller argues that: 'What had seemed "realistic" comes to be seen as **figurative**, and the radically fictive quality of the *Sketches* as a whole comes into the open. . . . The *Sketches* are not *mimesis* of an externally existing reality, but the interpretation of that reality according to highly artificial schemas inherited from the past' (p. 309). Particularly in their use of a language which exposes its own rhetorical devices and assumptions, and thus reveals the fictitiousness of the fictive, the *Sketches* are a narrative fiction. Miller rejects the traditional polarity between seeing literature as either a realistic representation or the creation of a self-contained subjective realm. He proposes instead a more complex and mobile model, whose beginning, medium and end are all a play of language.

> The *Sketches* are not a mirror of reality, but interpretation of interpretation, and the critic's discourse about the *Sketches* may be defined as interpretation of interpretation of interpretation. This chain of substitutions and transformations creates illusion out of illusion and

the appearance of reality out of illusion, in a play of language without beginning, end, or extra-linguistic foundation.

(p. 309)

By centring attention on the figurative patterns and rhetorical ploys immanent in the *Sketches*, Miller deconstructs its conventional acceptance as a copy of a specific reality, and underscores its quintessentially literary nature.

Like deconstruction, feminism has as its aim 'the unmaking and remaking of knowledges'.[28] Feminists are impelled to their task by the recognition that reading, because it has been 'sex-coded and gender-inflected',[29] is a political act. To read as a woman is, therefore, not merely to avoid reading as a man, but to identify the distortions of male readings and to provide a corrective counter-reading. Such a critical mode, again like deconstruction, goes against the hitherto normative grain, being '*ex*propriative' insofar as it 'works to undo the ownership of a text by a consortium of patriarchal vested interests' (Boumelha, p. 320). In its political dimension feminism necessarily privileges gender in a way which has analogies with the class-based analysis of the Marxist critics Lukács and Macherey.

Some of these theoretical bases of feminism are adduced by Penny Boumelha at the opening of her piece 'Realism and the Ends of Feminism'. While eschewing 'the rapturous instability' (p. 323) provoked by deconstruction, she argues for the need for a revisionary gendered reading, adding, however, that it must be grounded in an awareness of the historical and formal possibilities of reading and writing if it is genuinely to explore the relation between the work and the society that produces it and its reading. In this respect feminism is an alliance of cultural and literary criticism. Boumelha illustrates the potential of feminist readings in relation to George Eliot's novels because they are generally regarded as examples of '"classic realism"' (p. 324), although she points out that they are far from conforming wholly to the accepted model. The primary focus of her critique is the novels' endings, which have frustrated and even enraged some feminists. Eliot, she maintains, 'displays the injustices and abuses that press upon the lives of her women and then seems to refuse the logic of the insight offered by her own texts, apparently resolving the conflict between romantic, individualist rebellion and the power of community morality all too easily in favour of the latter' (p. 325). Thus the options for the female protagonists are reduced to either marriage or death, forms of closure which not only reproduce but indeed reinforce the impoverished opportunities that the social order of nineteenth-century Britain afforded actual historical women of the middle class. The dilemma recurs in all of Eliot's major novels, which 'bring into fiction the collision of the unsatisfied, perhaps even illimitable, desire of her heroines with the restricted possibilities of the world as it could be imagined by realism' (p. 332). By envisaging the figures within their social context and by emphasising its determining importance, feminism marks a reprise too of humanist, sociological readings, though applied above all to one group of characters and supported by an active ideology of opposition.

The future of realism

In conclusion, then, we can see clearly that, from the beginning, the reflections entertained by the realists themselves betrayed fundamental tensions within the concept of realism. On the one hand, they put forward views in opposition to Classical and Romantic ideals, seeing the content of realism as a concern with the particular and the ordinary, with the ways contemporary heroines and heroes function in and are determined by their social context. On the other hand, they were gradually forced to realise the insuperable difficulty of capturing the nature of reality through the medium of language, and equally to acknowledge the role of form in creating an 'air of reality' and endowing a work with aesthetic and philosophical significance.

Since then the debate on realism has focused on these two aspects of content and form. The humanist readings of Auerbach and Watt, the Marxism of Lukács and Macherey, and the feminism of Boumelha have sought in part to categorise and criticise the content of realist novels, emphasising their relationship to and determination by previous traditions and contemporary social forces. Other critics have concentrated their attention at the level of the individual, charting the ways the unconscious determines the writer's construction of a fictional 'reality' and the way the reader enters into the game to endow that reality with the illusion of truth. Yet other strands of criticism, while both implicated in the analyses and operating parallel to them, centre less on the content of realist novels, their relationship to the individual and society, than on the internal mechanics of realism as a form. Rhetorical and deconstructionist critics have done much to unlock the numerous strategies which coalesce to create the illusion of truth within a realist text, together with the tensions and ambiguities which undermine that truth.

Aspects of all these approaches take us forward from earlier notions of realism as a direct and uncomplicated reporting of the truth of everyday life to a more differentiated understanding of the writer's partial relationship to his or her world, to the complexities, constraints and artifices involved in trying to depict it, including the role of literary form in determining a writer's options, and the dynamics of readers' responses to those strategies.

One issue which was raised at the beginning of this Introduction, but which has received surprisingly little attention, is the sheer variety of meanings encompassed by the very term realism. To recall that realism has been taken to epitomise authors as diverse as Balzac, Eliot, Dickens and James is to realise the fluidity of the term as a historical category and its many local variations across time and between writers. Realism can be seen both as a specific historical moment and as a far broader technique that plays a role, in different ways, in most narratives. As we have seen, the philosopher of language J. L. Austin has shown the wide range of meaning the word itself has. Here is, arguably, an agenda for the future, in which we pay less attention to realism than to realisms. Much of this complexity has been illustrated in the work collected in this volume, but there are many heads of the hydra still to discover.

Notes

1. KENDALL L. WALTON, *Mimesis as Make-Believe: On the Foundations of the Representational Arts* (Cambridge, MA.: Harvard University Press, 1990), p. 328.

2. *Neophilologus* **44** (1960); reprinted in *Concepts of Criticism*, ed. Stephen J. Nichols Jr. (New Haven and London: Yale University Press, 1963), pp. 222–55.

3. *La Comédie humaine*, ed. Marcel Bouteron (Paris: Gallimard, 1956), vol. II, p. 848.

4. 'Realism in Art: Recent German Fiction', *Westminster Review* **70** (1858), p. 493.

5. *Adam Bede* (London: Dent, 1966), p. 171.

6. *The Art of Fiction* (London and New York: Oxford University Press, 1948), p. 11.

7. Even as recently as 1967 in 'Realism: A Symposium' in *Monatshefte* **59**, 2 and, though to a lesser extent, in 'A Symposium on Realism' in *Comparative Literature* **3**, 3 (summer 1951), the majority of the contributors were content to repeat standard platitudes without examining the extent to which they were borne out by the actual practices in the texts. The notable exception was Harry T. Levin.

8. *Mimesis*, trans. Willard R. Trask (Princeton, NJ: Princeton University Press, 1953), p. 489.

9. FREDRIC JAMESON, *Marxism and Form* (Princeton, NJ: Princeton University Press, 1971), p. 195.

10. *Studies in European Realism*, trans. Edith Bone (London: Hillway, 1950), p. 49.

11. One of the earliest examples is Boris Eichenbaum's 'The Structure of Gogol's *The Overcoat*', which dates from 1918 (trans. Beth Paul and Muriel Nesbitt, *Russian Review* **22** (1963), pp. 377–99). Eichenbaum's article first examines

separately the basic narrative devices in the tale and then goes on to delineate the system whereby they are linked.

12. In *Readings in Russian Poetics*, ed. Ladislav Matejka and Krystyna Pomorska (Cambridge, MA.: MIT Press, 1978), pp. 38–46.

13. *S/Z*, trans. Richard Miller (New York: Hill & Wang, 1974), pp. 4–6.

14. *Writing Degree Zero*, trans. Annette Lavers and Colin Smith (New York: Hill & Wang, 1967), pp. 67–8.

15. *Writing Degree Zero*, p. 33.

16. *S/Z*, p. 6.

17. In *French Literary Theory Today*, ed. Tzvetan Todorov, trans. R. Carter (Cambridge and New York: Cambridge University Press, 1982), pp. 11–17.

18. *S/Z*, p. 13.

19. *The Language of Fiction* (London: Routledge & Kegan Paul, and New York: Columbia University Press, 1966), p. 145.

20. In preference to 'reader-response', which suggests and indeed often consists of subjective, affective, personal readings, I use the term 'reader-oriented' because it denotes readings that remain within the domain of public, widely recognisable parameters.

21. *The Languages of the Unsayable*, ed. S. Budick and W. Iser (New York: Columbia University Press, 1989), p. 325.

22. *Dispositio, Revista Hispánica de Semiótica Literaria* 5 (Department of Roman Languages, University of Michigan, 1983), p. 5.

23. SIGMUND FREUD, *Jokes and their Relation to the Unconscious*, trans. James Strachey (New York and London: Norton, 1960).

24. See ELIZABETH WRIGHT, *Psychoanalytic Criticism: Theory in Practice* (London and New York: Methuen, 1984).

25. For a clear, brief introduction see CHRISTOPHER NORRIS, *Deconstruction: Theory and Practice* (London and New York: Methuen, 1982).

26. *Dickens Centennial Essays*, ed. Ada Nisbet and Blake Nevius (Berkeley: University of California Press, 1971), pp. 85–6.

27. CHARLES DICKENS, *Sketches by Boz* (London: Oxford University Press, 1966), p. 190.

28. PENNY BOUMELHA, 'Realism and the Ends of Feminism' in *Grafts: Feminist Cultural Criticism*, ed. Susan Sheridan (London and New York: Verso, 1988), p. 77.

29. ANNETTE KOLODNY, 'Reply to Commentaries: Women Writers, Literary Historians, and Martian Readers', *New Literary History* 11 (1980), p. 588.

Part One

Contemporary Views and Reviews

Introduction

Unlike the Romantics, the naturalists or the surrealists, the realists did not present a systematic theory in the shape of manifestos or treatises. Their views have, mostly, to be gleaned from scattered comments in their fictions or in prefaces, reviews and letters. The two notable exceptions are Edmond Duranty, a journalist and minor novelist, who issued proclamations in his short-lived journal *Réalisme* (1856–7), and Henry James, who gave sustained thought to the writing of narrative in his *Art of Fiction* (1884).

The tone is set by Honoré de Balzac in his Preface (1834) to his collected novels under the title *La Comédie humaine*, where he casts himself in the role of 'secretary' to the nineteenth century, registering good and ill as the faithful painter of human life. At the opening of *Le Père Goriot* (1834, *Old Goriot*), he claims that 'All is true.' Edmond Duranty, too, adopted truth as the pervasive slogan for the theories in *Réalisme*. And George Lewes, in his review 'Realism in Art: Recent German Fiction' in the *Westminster Review* (**70**, 1858, pp. 488–518), writing of Gustav Freytag's novel *Soll und Haben* (1855), asserts that 'Art always aims at the representation of Reality, i.e. of Truth.'

This simplistic projection of realism was gradually refined in the latter half of the nineteenth century, mainly as the writers themselves came to realise its inherent inadequacy. George Eliot, in Chapter Seventeen of *Adam Bede* (1859), while expressing the desire 'to give a faithful account of men and things as they have mirrored themselves in my mind', is none the less already aware of the central difficulty of realism, namely how to translate a true (but necessarily subjective) vision into words. This is the problem with which Gustave Flaubert wrestles throughout the years (1851–7) of the composition of *Madame Bovary*, lamenting in his letters to his friend and fellow writer, Louise Colet, the virtual impossibility of finding appropriate words for his commonplace subject, avoiding the poles of triteness or lyricism.

Unlike the earlier writers, Flaubert makes no attempt to conceal the essential artfulness of realist fiction despite the ordinariness of its topics. Both Guy de Maupassant in the Preface to his novel *Pierre et Jean* (1888) and Henry James in *The Art of Fiction* (1884) seek to combine the ideals of truth and artfulness. Maupassant suggests that the realists should call themselves 'illusionists' since to tell the truth is in effect to give the illusion of truthfulness, while Henry James favours verisimilitude: an 'air of reality' and an 'impression of life'. Although there is no radical departure from the tenet of truth during the course of the century, it becomes attenuated by the recognition of the artistic demands of writing.

1 Balzac on his Role as Secretary to Society*

Chance is the greatest novelist in the world: in order to be productive, one has only to study it. French society was to be the historian, I had merely to be its secretary. By setting up an inventory of vices and virtues, by gathering the principal facts of the passions, by portraying characters, by choosing the major events of Society, by composing types through an amalgam of the traits of several homogeneous characters, perhaps I could manage to write the history forgotten by historians, that of manners. With much patience and courage I would actualise for nineteenth century France that book which, to the great regret of us all, Rome, Athens, Tyrrhe, Memphis, Persia, India unfortunately failed to leave us about their civilisations. . . .

This work in itself was nothing yet. By keeping to rigorous reproduction, a writer could become a more or less faithful, more or less felicitous, patient or courageous painter of human types, the narrator of the dramas of intimate life, the archaeologist of social property, the namer of professions, the registrar of good and ill; but in order to deserve the praise to which every artist should aspire, ought I not to probe the reasons or the reason for these social manifestations, unveil the hidden meaning in this immense collection of figures, passions, and events. Finally, having sought, and I do not say found, this reason, this social motor agent, should one not meditate on natural principles, and see how Societies move further from or closer to the eternal rule, to the true and the beautiful.

---

* From the Preface (1842) to *The Human Comedy*, Marcel Bouteron (Paris: Gallimard, 1951), Vol. I, p. 7.

2　Balzac Addresses the Reader about Truth*

You, who hold this book in your white hands, as you sit comfortably ensconced in a soft armchair, you will show the same insensitivity as you say to yourself: 'Perhaps this will amuse me.' After you have read of the secret sorrows of old Goriot, you will have a fine appetite at dinner, and you will blame your callousness on the author, accusing him of exaggeration and of poetic licence. But mark this well: this drama is neither a fiction nor a romance. *All is true*,† so true that each one of you can recognise its elements in his or her own home, maybe even in his or her own heart.

---

* From *Le Père Goriot* in *La Comédie humaine* (*The Human Comedy*), ed. Marcel Bouteron (Paris: Gallimard, 1956), vol. II, p. 848.
† This phrase is in English and italicised in the French text.

3 Duranty on the Principles of Realism*

Summary of the Preceding Issue

Since certain people who never understand have not understood what
was written, it is good to make them notice that the following has been
very clearly established:

That Realism bans the *historical* in painting, the novel, and the theatre
so that no lie may creep in and the artist cannot borrow knowledge from
others;

That Realism demands of artists only the study of their period;

That in this study of their period it asks them not to distort anything,
but to keep everything in its exact proportions;

That the best way not to err in this study is to think always of the idea
of representing the *social* side of man, which is the most visible, the most
comprehensible and the most varied, and to think also of the idea of
reproducing the things affecting the lives of the greatest number, which
happen often in the realm of instincts, desires, and passions;

That Realism thereby attributes to the artist a philosophical, practical,
useful aim, and not that of amusement, and consequently raises him up.

That, in demanding of the artist useful *truth*, it demands of him
particularly the intelligent feeling and observation which *sees* a lesson, an
emotion in a spectacle at any level, low or high, according to convention,
and which always extracts this lesson, this emotion from the spectacle,
knowing how to represent it *completely*, and to embed it in its social
cadre.

That the public was the final judge of the *sentiments* studied in a work,
because the crowd is as open to pity, to misfortune, to anger, etc. as the
writer addressing it; – That every man *popular* for thirty years has a real
value, and every man *popular* for over fifty years is a great artist; – That
all celebrity established by the tradition of scholars, professors, colleges is

---

* From *Réalisme* 2, 15 December 1856.

dubious, and that intelligent criticism would have to make a drastic choice among them.

It was announced that we would apply these principles by active criticism of contemporary and older works.

It is possible to find more fair those who say that beauty is the splendour of truth, that the ideal is everywhere, and that one must know how to discover it.

Yes, here are the clear minds that must be listened to; but those flat writers who speak to us of commonplace happenings are excessively disdained for the weakness of their imagination and their claim to draw attention to these beautiful ideas.

When it is said: 'beauty is the splendour of truth', here are agreeable, pleasing, and exalting words which immediately make one think of some well dressed courtesan, of the illuminations on the Champs Elysées, of the Venus of Medici, of Raphaël's pictures, of English horses, and 'the splendour of the truth' is instantly understood. Whereas those coarse realist natures want to lower people to commonplace things. But they come in a thousand variants and many very lowly. Every night one puts on a cotton bonnet to sleep, that's something that happens often. Those realists are truly idiots or mystificators if they try to be interesting with such nonsense.

It is not surprising that such things are said.

We are almost alone up against a large number of people: the enemy because we do not fraternise with their laziness, their lack of intelligence, and their bad faith; other adversaries because they have accepted ready made ideas without reflection and no longer want to have the courage of a conversion; the mass, disinterested, but prepared, conditioned by the literary systems between 1830 and 1848, curious and disturbed rather than sympathetic.

To undertake anything with the fidelity of a conviction is very rare these days. To say simply simple but specific things perhaps does not suffice: one is read but not heeded. Hardly fifty people, I don't say will give admittance to, but merely take notice of this journal. Nevertheless, if I am not mistaken on the spirit of the age, *people will become accustomed to it.*

4 George Lewes on Realism in Art*

One feels that there is a great deal of merit in Freitag's book, and that it contains matter which a more artistic hand would have fashioned into enduring forms; but it is a work to read, not to re-read. This is felt by some German critics also who, now they have recovered from their surprise at having been really interested in a work which, after all, leaves behind it no enduring impression, attribute this failure to produce a deep impression to what they call the author's 'realism'. According to them, Freitag's work fails, because it moves amid the prosaic realities of life, telling us of merchants and shopkeepers, such as may be found behind many a counter; men honourable, indeed, and honoured in their circle, but having no care or thought of art, philosophy, and the higher aims of life. It is this want of the 'ideal element' which makes 'Soll und Haben', according to the critics, a work of the day; which gives it a temporary success, 'because our age is realistic', and because the bourgeoisie loves to see itself represented in fiction; but which inevitably condemns it to oblivion. Were this criticism well-founded, the consequence to be drawn from it would be that novelists should care little about reality, and much about ideal subjects: a conclusion which renders the dearth of good novels somewhat inexplicable, seeing that already the libraries swarm with works having but the faintest possible relation to any form of human life, and the strongest infusion of what is considered the 'ideal element'. The hero is never a merchant, a lawyer, an artisan – *Gott bewahre!* He must have a pale face and a thoughtful brow; he must be either a genius or a Herr Baron. The favourite hero is a poet, or an artist, often a young nobleman who has the artistic nature; but always a man of genius; because prose can be found at every street-corner, and art must elevate the public by 'beautifying' life.

This notion of the function of Art is widely spread. It has its advocates in all countries, for it is the natural refuge of incompetence, to which men fly, impelled by the secret sense of their inability to portray Reality

---

* Reprinted from *The Westminster Review* 70 (1958), pp. 492–3, 495–6.

so as to make it interesting. A distinction is drawn between Art and
Reality, and an antithesis established between Realism and Idealism
which would never have gained acceptance had not men in general lost
sight of the fact that Art is a Representation of Reality – a Representation
which, inasmuch as it is not the thing itself, but only represents it, must
necessarily be limited by the nature of its medium; the canvas of the
painter, the marble of the sculptor, the chords of the musician, and the
language of the writer, each bring with them peculiar laws; but while
thus limited, while thus regulated by the necessities imposed on it by
each medium of expression, Art always aims at the representation of
Reality, i.e. of Truth; and no departure from truth is permissible, except
such as inevitably lies in the nature of the medium itself. Realism is thus
the basis of all Art, and its antithesis is not idealism, but *Falsism*. When
our painters represent peasants with regular features and irreproachable
linen; when their milkmaids have the air of Keepsake beauties, whose
costume is picturesque, and never old or dirty; when Hodge is made to
speak refined sentiments in unexceptionable English, and children utter
long speeches of religious and poetic enthusiasm; when the conversation
of the parlour and drawing-room is a succession of philosophical
remarks, expressed with great clearness and logic, an attempt is made to
idealise, but the result is simple falsification and bad art. To misrepresent
the forms of ordinary life is no less an offence than to misrepresent the
forms of ideal life: a pug-nosed Apollo, or Jupiter in a greatcoat, would
not be more truly shocking to an artistic mind than are those senseless
falsifications of nature into which incompetence is led under the pretence
of idealising, of 'beautifying' nature. Either give us true peasants, or
leave them untouched; either paint no drapery at all, or paint it with the
utmost fidelity; either keep your people silent, or make them speak the
idiom of their class.

In like manner the novelist (to return to the point from which we started)
expresses his mind in his novels, and according as his emotional
sympathy is keen and active, according to his poetic disposition, will the
choice and treatment of his subject be poetical: but it must always be real
– true. If he select the incidents and characters of ordinary life, he must
be rigidly bound down to accuracy in the presentation. He is at liberty to
avoid such subjects, if he thinks them prosaic and uninteresting (which
will mean that he does not feel their poetry and interest), but having
chosen, he is not at liberty to falsify, under pretence of beautifying them;
every departure from truth in motive, idiom, or probability, is, to that
extent, a defect. His dressmaker must be a young woman who makes
dresses, and not a sentimental 'heroine', evangelical and consumptive;
she may be consumptive, she may also be evangelical, for dressmakers
are so sometimes, but she must be individually a dressmaker. So also the

merchant must have an air of the counting-house, an ostler must smell of the stables. To *call* a man a merchant, and tell us of his counting-house, while for anything else we might suppose him to be a nobleman, or an uncle from India, is not Art, because it is not representation of reality. If the writer's knowledge or sympathies do not lead him in the direction of ordinary life, if he can neither paint town nor country, let him take to the wide fields of History or Fancy. Even there the demands of truth will pursue him; he must paint what he distinctly *sees* with his imagination; if he succeed, he will create characters which are true although ideal; and in this sense Puck, Ariel, Brutus, and Falstaff are as real as Dick Swiveller or Tom Jones.

To accuse 'Soll und Haben' of 'realism' would in our eyes be the highest of compliments, because the book undertakes to represent the life of the bourgeoisie in Germany; and although it may not be so great an achievement to represent such a form of life as to represent the life of a poet, an artist, a thinker, or a statesman, it would be a greater achievement to represent the ordinary life truly than the extraordinary life incompletely.

5 George Eliot on Truthfulness*

In which the story pauses a little

'This Rector of Broxton is little better than a pagan!' I hear one of my
readers exclaim. 'How much more edifying it would have been if you
had made him give Arthur some truly spiritual advice. You might have
put into his mouth the most beautiful things – quite as good as reading a
sermon.'

Certainly I could, if I held it the highest vocation of the novelist to
represent things as they never have been and never will be. Then, of
course, I might refashion life and character entirely after my own liking; I
might select the most unexceptionable type of clergyman, and put my
own admirable opinions into his mouth on all occasions. But it happens,
on the contrary, that my strongest effort is to avoid any such arbitrary
picture, and to give a faithful account of men and things as they have
mirrored themselves in my mind. The mirror is doubtless defective; the
outlines will sometimes be disturbed, the reflection faint or confused; but
I feel as much bound to tell you as precisely as I can what that reflection
is, as if I were in the witness-box narrating my experience on oath.

Sixty years ago – it is a long time, so no wonder things have changed –
all clergymen were not zealous; indeed, there is reason to believe that the
number of zealous clergymen was small, and it is probable that if one
among the small minority had owned the livings of Broxton and
Hayslope in the year 1799, you would have liked him no better than you
like Mr Irwine. Ten to one, you would have thought him a tasteless,
indiscreet, methodistical man. It is so very rarely that facts hit that nice
medium required by our own enlightened opinions and refined taste!
Perhaps you will say, 'Do improve the facts a little, then; make them
more accordant with those correct views which it is our privilege to
possess. The world is not just what we like; do touch it up with a tasteful

---

* Reprinted from *Adam Bede* (London: Dent, 1906), Book Second, Chapter XVII,
pp. 171–5.

pencil, and make believe it is not quite such a mixed entangled affair. Let all people who hold unexceptionable opinions act unexceptionably. Let your most faulty characters always be on the wrong side, and your virtuous ones on the right. Then we shall see at a glance whom we are to condemn, and whom we are to approve. Then we shall be able to admire, without the slightest disturbance of our prepossessions: we shall hate and despise with that true ruminant relish which belongs to undoubting confidence.

But, my good friend, what will you do then with your fellow-parishioner who opposes your husband in the vestry? – with your newly-appointed vicar, whose style of preaching you find painfully below that of his regretted predecessor? – with the honest servant who worries your soul with her one failing? – with your neighbour, Mrs Green, who was really kind to you in your last illness, but has said several ill-natured things about you since your convalescence? – nay, with your excellent husband himself, who has other irritating habits besides that of not wiping his shoes? These fellow-mortals, every one, must be accepted as they are: you can neither straighten their noses, nor brighten their wit, nor rectify their dispositions; and it is these people – amongst whom your life is passed – that it is needful you should tolerate, pity, and love: it is these more or less ugly, stupid, inconsistent people, whose movements of goodness you should be able to admire – for whom you should cherish all possible hopes, all possible patience. And I would not, even if I had the choice, be the clever novelist who could create a world so much better than this, in which we get up in the morning to do our daily work, that you would be likely to turn a harder, colder eye on the dusty streets and the common green fields – on the real breathing men and women, who can be chilled by your indifference or injured by your prejudice; who can be cheered and helped onward by your fellow-feeling, your forbearance, your outspoken, brave justice.

So I am content to tell my simple story, without trying to make things seem better than they were; dreading nothing, indeed, but falsity, which, in spite of one's best efforts, there is reason to dread. Falsehood is so easy, truth so difficult. The pencil is conscious of a delightful facility in drawing a griffin – the longer the claws, and the larger the wings, the better; but that marvellous facility which we mistook for genius is apt to forsake us when we want to draw a real unexaggerated lion. Examine your words well, and you will find that even when you have no motive to be false, it is a very hard thing to say the exact truth, even about your own immediate feelings – much harder than to say something fine about them which is *not* the exact truth.

It is for this rare, precious quality of truthfulness that I delight in many Dutch paintings, which lofty-minded people despise. I find a source of delicious sympathy in these faithful pictures of a monotonous homely existence, which has been the fate of so many more among my fellow-mortals than a life of pomp or of absolute indigence, of tragic suffering or of world-stirring actions. I turn, without shrinking, from cloud-borne angels, from prophets, sibyls, and heroic warriors, to an old woman bending over her flowerpot, or eating her solitary dinner, while the noonday light, softened perhaps by a screen of leaves, falls on her mob-cap, and just touches the rim of her spinning-wheel, and her stone jug, and all those cheap common things which are the precious necessaries of life to her; – or I turn to that village wedding, kept between four brown walls, where an awkward bridegroom opens the dance with a high-shouldered, broad-faced bride, while elderly and middle-aged friends look on, with very irregular noses and lips, and probably with quart-pots in their hands, but with an expression of unmistakable contentment and goodwill. 'Foh!' says my idealistic friend, 'what vulgar details! What good is there in taking all these pains to give an exact likeness of old women and clowns? What a low phase of life! – what clumsy, ugly, people!'

But bless us, things may be lovable that are not altogether handsome, I hope? I am not at all sure that the majority of the human race have not been ugly, and even among those 'lords of their kind', the British, squat figures, ill-shaped nostrils, and dingy complexions are not startling exceptions. Yet there is a great deal of family love amongst us. I have a friend or two whose class of features is such that the Apollo curl on the summit of their brows would be decidedly trying; yet to my certain knowledge tender hearts have beaten for them, and their miniatures – flattering, but still not lovely – are kissed in secret by motherly lips. I have seen many an excellent matron, who could never in her best days have been handsome, and yet she had a packet of yellow love-letters in a private drawer, and sweet children showered kisses on her sallow cheeks. And I believe there have been plenty of young heroes, of middle stature and feeble beards, who have felt quite sure they could never love anything more insignificant than a Diana, and yet have found themselves in middle life happily settled with a wife who waddles! Yes! thank God; human feeling is like the mighty rivers that bless the earth: it does not wait for beauty – it flows with resistless force and brings beauty with it.

All honour and reverence to the divine beauty of form! Let us cultivate it to the utmost in men, women, and children – in our gardens and in our houses. But let us love that other beauty too, which lies in no secret of proportion, but in the secret of deep human sympathy. Paint us an angel, if you can, with a floating violet robe, and a face paled by the celestial light; paint us yet oftener a Madonna, turning her mild face upward and opening her arms to welcome the divine glory; but do not impose on us any æsthetic rules which shall banish from the region of Art those old women scraping carrots with their work-worn hands, those heavy clowns taking holiday in a dingy pot-house, those rounded backs and stupid weather-beaten faces that have bent over the spade and done the rough work of the world – those homes with their tin pans, their brown pitchers, their rough curs, and their clusters of onions. In this world there are so many of these common coarse people, who have no picturesque sentimental wretchedness! It is so needful we should remember their existence, else we may happen to leave them quite out of our religion and philosophy, and frame lofty theories which only fit a world of extremes. Therefore let Art always remind us of them; therefore let us always have men ready to give the loving pains of a life to the faithful representing of commonplace things – men who see beauty in these commonplace things, and delight in showing how kindly the light of heaven falls on them. There are few prophets in the world; few sublimely beautiful women; few heroes. I can't afford to give all my love and reverence to such rarities: I want a great deal of those feelings for my everyday fellow-men, especially for the few in the foreground of the great multitude, whose faces I know, whose hands I touch, for whom I have to make way with kindly courtesy. Neither are picturesque lazzaroni or romantic criminals half so frequent as your common labourer, who gets his own bread, and eats it vulgarly but creditably with his own pocket-knife. It is more needful that I should have a fibre of sympathy connecting me with that vulgar citizen who weighs out my sugar in a vilely-assorted cravat and waistcoat, than with the handsomest rascal in red scarf and green feathers; – more needful that my heart should swell with loving admiration at some trait of gentle goodness in the faulty people who sit at the same hearth with me, or in the clergyman of my own parish, who is perhaps rather too corpulent, and in other respects is not an Oberlin or a Tillotson, than at the deeds of heroes whom I shall never know except by hearsay, or at the sublimest abstract of all clerical graces that was ever conceived by an able novelist.

6 Flaubert on Writing *Madame Bovary**

Letter to Louise Colet, 15 January 1853 (p. 238)

I have spent *five days doing one page!* What bothers me in my book is the
element of *amusement*, which is meagre. It lacks happenings. I believe
that *ideas* are happenings. It is harder to arouse interest with them, I
know, but then the fault lies in the style. I now have fifty pages in a row
without a single happening. It is the continuous picture of a bourgeois
life and of a sluggish love affair, a love affair all the more difficult to
portray because it is at once timid and deep, but alas! without commotion
because my man is of a temperate nature. – I already had something
similar in the first part. My husband loves his wife in much the same
way as my lover. They are two mediocrities, in the same environment,
and yet they must be differentiated. If it succeeds, it will be very
powerful because it is putting shade on shade without distinctive colours
(which is easier). – But I am afraid that all these subtleties will be boring,
and that the reader will want to see more action. – However, it must be
carried out as it was conceived. If I were to put action into it, I would
conform to an expectation and spoil everything. – One has to sing in
one's own voice, and mine will never be dramatic or engaging. – I am
convinced that it is all a matter of style, or rather of turn of phrase and
perspective.

Letter to Louise Colet, 25 June 1853 (p. 362)

If the book that I am writing with so much trouble turns out well, I will
have established, merely by executing it, these two truths, which are
axiomatic for me, namely: first, that poetry is purely subjective, that
there are not in literature beautiful artistic subjects, and that Yvetot is

---

* From *Correspondance*, ed. Jean Bruneau (Paris: Gallimard, 1980), vol. II.

therefore just as good as Constantinople; and consequently that one can write just as well about anything, no matter what it is.

Letter to Louise Colet, 12 July 1853 (p. 382)

The whole past week has been bad. . . . The vulgarity of my subject sometimes makes me feel nausea, and the difficulty of writing well so many commonplace things still in prospect horrifies me. I am now labouring over one of the simple scenes: a blood-letting and a fainting. It is terribly hard. And what saddens me is to realise that, even if it is done to perfection, it cannot be more than passable and will never be beautiful on account of its subject matter.

Letter to Louise Colet, 14 August 1853 (p. 392)

Everything that one invents is true, you can be sure of that. Poetry is as precise as geometry. Inference is as good as deduction, and then after a certain point there is no mistaking what goes on in the soul. My poor Bovary is doubtless suffering and weeping in twenty French villages at this very moment.

Letter to Louise Colet, 12 September 1853 (p. 429)

What I am up against are commonplace situations and trivial dialogue. To write the *mediocre* well and to see that it maintains at the same time its appearance, its rhythm, its words is really a diabolical task, and I now see ahead of me thirty pages at least of this kind. Style is hard won! I am beginning over again what I did last week.

Letter to Louise Colet, 19 March 1854 (p. 536)

My work is progressing, though slowly and with many corrections and re-writes. In July I'll see the end, at one go, I hope. – But it is an atrocious task! The order of the ideas is the greatest difficulty. – And then, since my subject is always the same, and takes place in the same environment, now that I am two-thirds of the way through it, I no longer know how to avoid repetitions. The simplest phrase like 'he closed the door', 'he went out', etc requires incredible artistic ingenuity! It's a matter of constantly varying the sauce with the same ingredients. – I cannot save myself by fantasy because there is not in this book *a single* move in my name, and the author's personality is *completely* absent.

7   Henry James on the Art of Fiction*

It is still expected, though perhaps people are ashamed to say it, that a production which is after all only a 'make-believe' (for what else is a 'story'?) shall be in some degree apologetic – shall renounce the pretension of attempting really to represent life. This, of course, any sensible, wide-awake story declines to do, for it quickly perceives that the tolerance granted to it on such a condition is only an attempt to stifle it disguised in the form of generosity. The old evangelical hostility to the novel, which was as explicit as it was narrow, and which regarded it as little less favourable to our immortal part than a stage-play, was in reality far less insulting. The only reason for the existence of a novel is that it does attempt to represent life. . . .

The characters, the situation, which strike one as real will be those that touch and interest one most, but the measure of reality is very difficult to fix. The reality of Don Quixote or of Mr Micawber is a very delicate shade; it is a reality so coloured by the author's vision that, vivid as it may be, one would hesitate to propose it as a model: one would expose one's self to some very embarrassing questions on the part of a pupil. It goes without saying that you will not write a good novel unless you possess the sense of reality; but it will be difficult to give you a recipe for calling that sense into being. Humanity is immense, and reality has a myriad forms; the most one can affirm is that some of the flowers of fiction have the odour of it, and others have not; as for telling you in advance how your nosegay should be composed, that is another affair. . . .

I am far from intending by this to minimise the importance of exactness – of truth of detail. One can speak best from one's own taste, and I may therefore venture to say that the air of reality (solidity of specification)

* Reprinted from *The Art of Fiction and Other Essays* (New York: Oxford University Press, 1948), pp. 4–5, 10, 11–12, 16–17.

seems to me to be the supreme virtue of a novel – the merit on which all its other merits. . . helplessly and submissively depend. If it be not there they are all as nothing, and if these be there, they owe their effect to the success with which the author has produced the illusion of life. . . .

Catching the very note and trick, the strange irregular rhythm of life, that is the attempt whose strenuous force keeps Fiction upon her feet. In proportion as in what she offers us we see life *without* rearrangement do we feel that we are touching the truth; in proportion as we see it *with* rearrangement do we feel that we are touching the truth; in proportion as we see it *with* rearrangement do we feel that we are being put off with a substitute, a compromise and convention. It is not uncommon to hear an extraordinary assurance of remark in regard to this matter of rearranging, which is often spoken of as if it were the last word of art. Art is essentially selection, but it is a selection whose main care is to be typical, to be inclusive. For many people art means rose-coloured window-panes, and selection means picking a bouquet for Mrs Grundy. They will tell you glibly that artistic considerations have nothing to do with the disagreeable, with the ugly; they will rattle off shallow commonplaces about the province of art and the limits of art till you are moved to some wonder in return as to the province and the limits of ignorance. It appears to me that no one can ever have made a seriously artistic attempt without becoming conscious of an immense increase – a kind of revelation – of freedom. One perceives in that case – by the light of a heavenly ray – that the province of art is all life, all feeling, all observation, all vision.

8 Maupassant on Realism as 'Illusionism'*

So, after the literary schools which wanted to give us a distorted, superhuman, poetic, touching, charming or proud vision of life, the realist or naturalist school came, which sought to show us the truth, nothing but the truth and the whole truth.

These very different theories of art must be admitted with equal standing, and the works they produce must be judged solely for their artistic value with an *a priori* acceptance of the general ideas from which they may spring.

To contest the writer's right to create a poetic or a realistic work is to want to force him to modify his temperament, to object to his originality, not to allow him to use the eye and the intelligence that nature has given him.

To reproach him for seeing beautiful or ugly, slight or epic, pleasing or sinister things is to reproach him for being conformist in one way or another and for not holding a vision in concordance with our own.

Let us leave him free to understand, to observe, to conceive as he wishes, provided he is an artist. Let us become poetically exalted to judge an idealist, and let us prove to him that his dream is mediocre, banal, not sufficiently magnificent. But if we judge a naturalist, let us show him how truth in life differs from the truth in his book.

It is obvious that schools so different had to use radically opposite methods of composition.

The novelist who transforms the constant, brutal, disagreeable truth in order to make of it an exceptional and seductive adventure must, without exaggerated care for verisimilitude, manipulate happenings according to his wishes, prepare and arrange them to please, move, or touch his readership. The plan of his novel is merely a series of ingenious combinations leading adroitly to the dénouement. The incidents are disposed and heightened towards the culminating point, and the effect of the ending, which is a major and decisive happening, satisfies all the

---

* From 'The Novel', Preface to *Pierre et Jean* (1888).

curiosity aroused at the beginning, putting an end to the readers' interest, and so completely terminating the narrated story that one no longer has the desire to know what will happen the next day even to the most attractive figures.

On the other hand, the novelist who seeks to give us an exact image of life must take care to avoid any sequence of happenings that could appear exceptional. His aim is not to tell us a story, to amuse or to touch us, but to force us to think, to understand the profound and hidden meanings of the happenings. As a result of having seen and meditated, he looks at the universe, things, facts, and human beings in a certain way peculiar to him, the outcome of the combination of his observations and reflections. It is this personal vision of the world that he tries to communicate to us by reproducing it in a book. In order to move us, as he himself has been by the spectacle of life, he must reproduce it before our eyes in a scrupulous resemblance. He will have to compose his work in so skilful and so concealed a manner, with such apparent simplicity as to make it impossible to perceive and indicate its plan, to uncover its intentions.

Instead of fiddling an adventure and unfurling it in such a way as to make it interesting up to the dénouement, he will take his figure or figures at a certain phase of their lives and will lead them, by natural transitions, to the following phase. By this means he will show how minds are modified under the influence of surrounding circumstances, how feelings and passions develop, how people love and how they hate, how there is strife at all social levels, how bourgeois interests, money interests, family interests, political interests are locked into combat.

The virtue of his plan will thus not consist in its emotion or charm, nor in its engaging beginning or its moving catastrophe, but in the adroit grouping of successive small happenings, from which the work's overall meaning will become apparent. If he encompasses in three hundred pages ten years of a life in order to show its particular and characteristic significance amidst all the surrounding beings, he must know how to eliminate from among all the innumerable minor daily occurrences all those that are useless to him, and to illuminate in a special way all those which would have remained unnoticed by observers with less insight and which give his book its import, its total value.

Obviously such a manner of composition, so different from the old procedure visible to every eye, often disorients critics; they do not discover all the fine, hidden, almost invisible threads used by certain modern artists in place of the single string that had the name: Plot.

To summarise: if yesterday's novelists chose and narrated life's crises, the soul's and the heart's acute states, today's novelist writes the story of the heart, the soul, and the mind in their normal state. In order to produce the effect he seeks, that is to say, the sense of simple reality, and in order to bring out the artistic lesson he wants to draw from it, that is to say, the revelation of what contemporary man really is in his eyes, he must use only the facts of an irrefutable and consistent truth.

But even while espousing the point of view of these realist artists, it is necessary to discuss and contrast their theory, which seems apt to be resumed in these words: 'Nothing but the truth and the whole truth'.

Since their intention is to disengage the philosophy of certain constant and current events, they will often have to correct happenings for the sake of verisimilitude and to the detriment of truth for:

The true can sometimes not seem plausible.

The realist, if he is an artist, will seek not to show us the banal photograph of life, but to give us a more complete, more striking, more probing vision of reality itself.

To narrate everything would be impossible for it would require at least a volume per day to enumerate the multitude of insignificant incidents which fill our existence.

A choice is therefore imposed – and this is the first strike against the theory of the whole truth.

Besides, life is composed of the most different, the most unforeseen, the most contrary, the most disparate things; it is brutal, devoid of succession or sequence, full of inexplicable, illogical, contradictory catastrophes which must be classified under the heading of *faits divers* (disparate happenings).

That is why the artist, having chosen his theme, will take from this life encumbered with chance and futility only the characteristic details useful to his subject, and will reject all the rest, all the peripheral incidentals.

One example among a thousand:

The number of people who die accidentally every day on this earth is considerable. But can we make a tile drop on the head of the principal figure, or throw him under the wheels of a carriage, in the middle of a narrative, on the grounds that accident must be given its due?

Life leaves everything on the same level, precipitates things or lets them drag on indefinitely. Art, by contrast, consists of invoking precautions and preparations, of setting up clever and hidden transitions, of fully illuminating, simply by the skill of the composition, the essential events and giving all the others the degree of prominence they deserve according to their importance in order to produce the profound sensation of the special truth one wants to show.

To do the true consists therefore of giving the complete illusion of the true, following the ordinary logic of facts, and not in servilely transcribing them in the confusion of their successive appearance.

I conclude from this that the talented realists ought rather to call themselves Illusionists.

Part Two

Humanist Readings

Introduction

'Humanists' concern themselves with common human needs and the rational (rather than supernatural) way in which progressive intellectual beings look to solve problems.

'Humanists' concern themselves with common human needs and the rational (rather than supernatural) way in which progressive intellectual beings look to solve problems. This is a pervasive, indeed 'classic' reading of realism because we assume (and realism assumed) that this same attitude and intellectual approach is at the very heart of the nature of realism itself. Humanist readings thus suppose that the realist work is a reflection of the social reality of its time, and examine how this is translated into literary texts.

'In the Hôtel de la Mole' is Chapter 18 of Erich Auerbach's famous book *Mimesis*, originally published in German in 1946 and translated since into several languages, including into English in 1953 by Willard R. Trask for Princeton University Press. This chapter begins with discussion of Stendhal's *Le Rouge et le noir* (1830, *The Red and the Black*), but also moves on to Balzac's *Le Père Goriot* (1834, *Old Goriot*) and Flaubert's *Madame Bovary* (1857). Auerbach underscores the importance for realism of both the political framework and the social stratification of the protagonists. He therefore emphasises the specific context in which the characters are acting out their lives. He also believes that nineteenth-century realism brought about an expansion of literature's social horizon to include the portrayal of the middle and lower strata not merely as comic adjuncts but as central protagonists.

Like Auerbach, Ian Watt in *The Rise of the Novel*, which first appeared in 1957, sees specificity of time as one of the distinguishing hallmarks of the realist mode as against the generality favoured by neo-classicism. But he also adds specificity of place and of characterisation. In the opening chapter, 'Realism and the Novel Form', Watt builds Auerbach's insistence on the necessity of heeding the social background into a coherent theory. However, in contrast to Auerbach, Watt asserts that 'the novel's realism does not reside in the kind of life it portrays, but in the way it presents it'. Watt's approach complements Auerbach's insofar as both dwell on the importance of the characters' social embedment, but while Auerbach concentrates more on the actual content, Watt focuses on the formal too, on the ways in which specificity is created.

9   Erich Auerbach on Stendhal, Balzac, and Flaubert*

Julien Sorel, the hero of Stendhal's novel *Le Rouge et le Noir* (1830), an ambitious and passionate young man, son of an uneducated petty bourgeois from the Franche-Comté, is conducted by a series of circumstances from the seminary at Besançon, where he has been studying theology, to Paris and the position of secretary to a gentleman of rank, the Marquis de la Mole, whose confidence he gains. Mathilde, the Marquis's daughter, is a girl of nineteen, witty, spoiled, imaginative, and so arrogant that her own position and circle begin to bore her. The dawning of her passion for her father's *domestique* is one of Stendhal's masterpieces and has been greatly admired. One of the preparatory scenes, in which her interest in Julien begins to awaken, is the following, from volume 2, chapter 14:

Un matin que l'abbé travaillait avec Julien, dans la bibliothèque du marquis, à l'éternel procès de Frilair:
   – Monsieur, dit Julien tout à coup, dîner tous les jours avec madame la marquise, est-ce un de mes devoirs, ou est-ce une bonté que l'on a pour moi?
   – C'est un honneur insigne! reprit l'abbé, scandalisé. Jamais M. N. . . l'académicien, qui, depuis quinze ans, fait une cour assidue, n'a pu l'obtenir pour son neveu M. Tanbeau.
   – C'est pour moi, monsieur, la partie la plus pénible de mon emploi. Je m'ennuyais moins au séminaire. Je vois bâiller quelquefois jusqu'à mademoiselle de la Mole, qui pourtant doit être accoutumée à l'amabilité des amis de la maison. J'ai peur de m'endormir. De grâce, obtenez-moi la permission d'aller dîner à quarante sous dans quelque auberge obscure.
   L'abbé véritable parvenu, était fort sensible à l'honneur de dîner avec un grand seigneur. Pendant qu'il s'efforçait de faire comprendre ce sentiment par Julien, un léger bruit leur fit tourner la tête. Julien vit

---

* Reprinted from 'In the Hôtel de la Mole' in *Mimesis*, trans. Willard R. Trask (Princeton University Press, 1953), pp. 400–34.

mademoiselle de la Mole qui écoutait. Il rougit. Elle était venue chercher un livre et avait tout entendu; elle prit quelque considération pour Julien. Celui-là n'est pas né à genoux, pensa-t-elle, comme ce vieil abbé. Dieu! qu'il est laid.

A dîner, Julien n'osait pas regarder mademoiselle de la Mole, mais elle eut la bonté de lui adresser la parole. Ce jour-là on attendait beaucoup de monde, elle l'engagea à rester . . . .

(One morning while the Abbé was with Julien in the Marquis's library, working on the interminable Frilair suit:

'Monsieur,' said Julien suddenly, 'is dining with Madame la Marquise every day one of my duties, or is it a favor to me?'

'It is an extraordinary honor!' the Abbé corrected him, scandalized. 'Monsieur N., the academician, who has been paying court here assiduously for fifteen years, was never able to manage it for his nephew, Monsieur Tanbeau.'

'For me, Monsieur, it is the most painful part of my position. Nothing at the seminary bored me so much. I even see Mademoiselle de la Mole yawning sometimes, yet she must be well inured to the amiabilities of the guests of this house. I am in dread of falling asleep. Do me the favor of getting me permission to eat a forty-sou dinner at some inn.'

The Abbé, a true parvenu, was extremely conscious of the honor of dining with a noble lord. While he was trying to inculcate this sentiment into Julien, a slight sound made them turn. Julien saw Mademoiselle de la Mole listening. He blushed. She had come for a book and had heard everything; she began to feel a certain esteem for Julien. He was not born on his knees, like that old Abbé, she thought. God, how ugly he is!

At dinner Julien did not dare to look at Mademoiselle de la Mole, but she condescended to speak to him. A number of guests were expected that day, she asked him to stay. . . .)

The scene, as I said, is designed to prepare for a passionate and extremely tragic love intrigue. Its function and its psychological value we shall not here discuss; they lie outside of our subject. What interests us in the scene is this: it would be almost incomprehensible without a most accurate and detailed knowledge of the political situation, the social stratification, and the economic circumstances of a perfectly definite historical moment, namely, that in which France found itself just before the July Revolution; accordingly, the novel bears the subtitle *Chronique de 1830*. Even the boredom which reigns in the dining room and salon of this noble house is no ordinary boredom. It does not arise from the fortuitous personal dullness of the people who are brought together there; among them there are highly educated, witty, and sometimes important people, and the master of the house is intelligent and amiable.

Rather, we are confronted, in their boredom, by a phenomenon politically and ideologically characteristic of the Restoration period. In the seventeenth century, and even more in the eighteenth, the corresponding salons were anything but boring. But the inadequately implemented attempt which the Bourbon regime made to restore conditions long since made obsolete by events, creates, among its adherents in the official and ruling classes, an atmosphere of pure convention, of limitation, of constraint and lack of freedom, against which the intelligence and good will of the persons involved are powerless. In these salons the things which interest everyone – the political and religious problems of the present, and consequently most of the subjects of its literature or of that of the very recent past – could not be discussed, or at best could be discussed only in official phrases so mendacious that a man of taste and tact would rather avoid them. How different from the intellectual daring of the famous eighteenth-century salons, which, to be sure, did not dream of the dangers to their own existence which they were unleashing! Now the dangers are known, and life is governed by the fear that the catastrophe of 1793 might be repeated. As these people are conscious that they no longer themselves believe in the thing they represent, and that they are bound to be defeated in any public argument, they choose to talk of nothing but the weather, music, and court gossip. In addition, they are obliged to accept as allies snobbish and corrupt people from among the newly-rich bourgeoisie, who, with the unashamed baseness of their ambition and with their fear for their ill-gotten wealth, completely vitiate the atmosphere of society. So much for the pervading boredom.

But Julien's reaction, too, and the very fact that he and the former director of his seminary, the Abbé Pirard, are present at all in the house of the Marquis de la Mole, are only to be understood in terms of the actual historical moment. Julien's passionate and imaginative nature has from his earliest youth been filled with enthusiasm for the great ideas of the Revolution and of Rousseau, for the great events of the Napoleonic period; from his earliest youth he has felt nothing but loathing and scorn for the piddling hypocrisy and the petty lying corruption of the classes in power since Napoleon's fall. He is too imaginative, too ambitious, and too fond of power, to be satisfied with a mediocre life within the bourgeoisie, such as his friend Fouquet proposes to him. Having observed that a man of petty-bourgeois origin can attain to a situation of command only through the all-powerful Church, he has consciously and deliberately become a hypocrite; and his great talents would assure him a brilliant intellectual career, were not his real personal and political feelings, the direct passionateness of his nature, prone to burst forth at decisive moments. One such moment of self-betrayal we have in the passage before us, when Julien confides his feelings in the Marquise's

salon to the Abbé Pirard, his former teacher and protector; for the
intellectual freedom to which it testifies is unthinkable without an
admixture of intellectual arrogance and a sense of inner superiority
hardly becoming in a young ecclesiastic and protégé of the house. (In this
particular instance his frankness does him no harm; the Abbé Pirard is
his friend, and upon Mathilde, who happens to overhear him, his words
make an entirely different impression from that which he must expect
and fear.) The Abbé is here described as a true parvenu, who knows how
highly the honor of sitting at a great man's table should be esteemed and
hence disapproves of Julien's remarks; as another motive for the Abbé's
disapproval Stendhal could have cited the fact that uncritical submission
to the evil of this world, in full consciousness that it is evil, is a typical
attitude for strict Jansenists; and the Abbé Pirard is a Jansenist. We know
from the previous part of the novel that as director of the seminary at
Besançon he had had to endure much persecution and much chicanery
on account of his Jansenism and his strict piety which no intrigues could
touch; for the clergy of the province were under the influence of the
Jesuits. When the Marquis de la Mole's most powerful opponent, the
Abbé de Frilair, a vicar-general to the bishop, had brought a suit against
him, the Marquis had made the Abbé Pirard his confidant and had thus
learned to value his intelligence and uprightness; so that finally, to free
him from his untenable position at Besançon, the Marquis had procured
him a benefice in Paris and somewhat later had taken the Abbé's favorite
pupil, Julien Sorel, into his household as private secretary.

The characters, attitudes, and relationships of the dramatis personae,
then, are very closely connected with contemporary historical
circumstances; contemporary political and social conditions are woven
into the action in a manner more detailed and more real than had been
exhibited in any earlier novel, and indeed in any works of literary art
except those expressly purporting to be politico-satirical tracts. So
logically and systematically to situate the tragically conceived life of a
man of low social position (as here that of Julien Sorel) within the most
concrete kind of contemporary history and to develop it therefrom – this
is an entirely new and highly significant phenomenon. The other circles
in which Julien Sorel moves – his father's family, the house of the mayor
of Verrières, M. de Rênal, the seminary at Besançon – are sociologically
defined in conformity with the historical moment with the same
penetration as is the La Mole household; and not one of the minor
characters – the old priest Chélan, for example, or the director of the
dépôt de mendicité, Valenod – would be conceivable outside the particular
historical situation of the Restoration period, in the manner in which they
are set before us. The same laying of a contemporary foundation for events
is to be found in Stendhal's other novels – still incomplete and too
narrowly circumscribed in *Armance*, but fully developed in the later works:

in the *Chartreuse de Parme* (which, however, since its setting is a place not yet greatly affected by modern development, sometimes gives the effect of being a historical novel), as also in *Lucien Leuwen*, a novel of the Louis Philippe period, which Stendhal left unfinished. In the latter, indeed, in the form in which it has come down to us, the element of current history and politics is too heavily emphasized: it is not always wholly integrated into the course of the action and is set forth in far too great detail in proportion to the principal theme; but perhaps in a final revision Stendhal would have achieved an organic articulation of the whole. Finally, his autobiographical works despite the capricious and erratic 'egotism' of their style and manner, are likewise far more closely, essentially, and concretely connected with the politics, sociology, and economics of the period than are, for example, the corresponding works of Rousseau or Goethe; one feels that the great events of contemporary history affected Stendhal much more directly than they did the other two; Rousseau did not live to see them, and Goethe had managed to keep aloof from them.

To have stated this is also to have stated what circumstance it was which, at that particular moment and in a man of that particular period, gave rise to modern tragic realism based on the contemporary; it was the first of the great movements of modern times in which large masses of men consciously took part – the French Revolution with all the consequent convulsions which spread from it over Europe. From the Reformation movement, which was no less powerful and which aroused the masses no less, it is distinguished by the much faster tempo of its spread, its mass effects, and the changes which it produced in practical daily life within a comparatively extensive territory; for the progress then achieved in transportation and communication, together with the spread of elementary education resulting from the trends of the Revolution itself, made it possible to mobilize the people far more rapidly and in a far more unified direction; everyone was reached by the same ideas and events far more quickly, more consciously, and more uniformly. For Europe there began that process of temporal concentration, both of historical events themselves and of everyone's knowledge of them, which has since made tremendous progress and which not only permits us to prophesy a unification of human life throughout the world but has in a certain sense already achieved it. Such a development abrogates or renders powerless the entire social structure of orders and categories previously held valid; the tempo of the changes demands a perpetual and extremely difficult effort toward inner adaptation and produces intense concomitant crises. He who would account to himself for his real life and his place in human society is obliged to do so upon a far wider practical foundation and in a far larger context than before, and to be continually conscious that the social base upon which he lives is not constant for a moment but is perpetually changing through convulsions of the most various kinds.

We may ask ourselves how it came about that modern consciousness of reality began to find literary form for the first time precisely in Henri Beyle of Grenoble. Beyle-Stendhal was a man of keen intelligence, quick and alive, mentally independent and courageous, but not quite a great figure. His ideas are often forceful and inspired, but they are erratic, arbitrarily advanced, and despite all their show of boldness, lacking in inward certainty and continuity. There is something unsettled about his whole nature: his fluctuation between realistic candor in general and silly mystification in particulars, between cold self-control, rapturous abandonment to sensual pleasures, and insecure and sometimes sentimental vaingloriousness, is not always easy to put up with; his literary style is very impressive and unmistakably original, but it is short-winded, not uniformly successful, and only seldom wholly takes possession of and fixes the subject. But, such as he was, he offered himself to the moment; circumstances seized him, tossed him about, and laid upon him a unique and unexpected destiny; they formed him so that he was compelled to come to terms with reality in a way which no one had done before him.

When the Revolution broke out Stendhal was a boy of six; when he left his native city of Grenoble and his reactionary, solidly bourgeois family, who though glumly sulking at the new situation were still very wealthy, and went to Paris, he was sixteen. He arrived there immediately after Napoleon's *coup d'état*; one of his relatives, Pierre Daru, was an influential adherent of the First Consul; after some hesitations and interruptions, Stendhal made a brilliant career in the Napoleonic administration. He saw Europe on Napoleon's expeditions; he grew to be a man, and indeed an extremely elegant man of the world; he also became, it appears, a useful administrative official and a reliable, cold-blooded organizer who did not lose his calm even in danger. When Napoleon's fall threw Stendhal out of the saddle, he was in his thirty-second year. The first, active, successful, and brilliant part of his career was over. Thenceforth he has no profession and no place claims him. He can go where he pleases, so long as he has money enough and so long as the suspicious officials of the post-Napoleonic period have no objection to his sojourns. But his financial circumstances gradually become worse; in 1821 he is exiled from Milan, where he had first settled down, by Metternich's police; he goes to Paris, and there he lives for another nine years, without a profession, alone, and with very slender means. After the July Revolution his friends get him a post in the diplomatic service; since the Austrians refuse him an exequatur for Trieste, he has to go as consul to the little port of Cività Vecchia; it is a dreary place to live, and there are those who try to get him into trouble if he prolongs his visits to Rome unduly; to be sure, he is allowed to spend a few years in Paris on leave – so long, that is, as one of his protectors is Minister of Foreign

Affairs. Finally he falls seriously ill in Cività Vecchia and is given another leave in Paris; he dies there in 1842, smitten by apoplexy in the street, not yet sixty. This is the second half of his life; during this period, he acquires the reputation of being a witty, eccentric, politically and morally unreliable man; during this period, he begins to write. He writes first on music, on Italy and Italian art, on love; it is not until he is forty-three and is in Paris during the first flowering of the Romantic movement (to which he contributed in his way) that he publishes his first novel.

From this sketch of his life it should appear that he first reached the point of accounting for himself, and the point of realistic writing, when he was seeking a haven in his 'storm-tossed boat', and discovered that, for his boat, there was no fit and safe haven; when, though in no sense weary or discouraged, yet already a man of forty, whose early and successful career lay far behind him, alone and comparatively poor, he became aware, with all the sting of that knowledge, that he belonged nowhere. For the first time, the social world around him became a problem; his feeling that he was different from other men, until now borne easily and proudly, doubtless now first became the predominant concern of his consciousness and finally the recurring theme of his literary activity. Stendhal's realistic writing grew out of his discomfort in the post-Napoleonic world and his consciousness that he did not belong to it and had no place in it. Discomfort in the given world and inability to become part of it is, to be sure, characteristic of Rousseauan romanticism and it is probable that Stendhal had something of that even in his youth; there is something of it in his congenital disposition, and the course of his youth can only have strengthened such tendencies, which, so to speak, harmonized with the tenor of life of his generation; on the other hand, he did not write his recollections of his youth, the *Vie de Henri Brulard*, until he was in his thirties, and we must allow for the possibility that, from the viewpoint of his later development, from the viewpoint of 1832, he overstressed such motifs of individualistic isolation. It is, in any case, certain that the motifs and expressions of his isolation and his problematic relation to society are wholly different from the corresponding phenomena in Rousseau and his early romantic disciples.

Stendhal, in contrast to Rousseau, had a bent for practical affairs and the requisite ability; he aspired to sensual enjoyment of life as given; he did not withdraw from practical reality from the outset, did not entirely condemn it from the outset – instead he attempted, and successfully at first, to master it. Material success and material enjoyments were desirable to him; he admires energy and the ability to master life, and even his cherished dreams (*le silence du bonheur*) are more sensual, more concrete, more dependent upon human society and human creations (Cimarosa, Mozart, Shakespeare, Italian art) than those of the *Promeneur Solitaire*. Not until success and pleasure began to slip away from him, not until practical circumstances threatened to cut the ground from under his feet, did the society of his time become a problem and a subject to him. Rousseau did not find himself at home in the social world he encountered, which did not appreciably change during his lifetime; he rose in it without thereby becoming happier or more reconciled to it, while it appeared to remain unchanged. Stendhal lived while one earthquake after another shook the foundations of society; one of the earthquakes jarred him out of the everyday course of life prescribed for men of his station, flung him, like many of his contemporaries, into previously inconceivable adventures, events, responsibilities, tests of himself, and experiences of freedom and power; another flung him back into a new everyday which he thought more boring, more stupid, and less attractive than the old; the most interesting thing about it was that it too gave no promise of enduring; new upheavals were in the air, and indeed broke out here and there even though not with the power of the first.

Because Stendhal's interest arose out of the experiences of his own life, it was held not by the structure of a possible society but by the changes in the society actually given. Temporal perspective is a factor of which he never loses sight, the concept of incessantly changing forms and manners of life dominates his thoughts – the more so as it holds a hope for him: In 1880 or 1930 I shall find readers who understand me! I will cite a few examples. When he speaks of La Bruyère's *esprit (Henri Brulard*, Chapter 30), it is apparent to him that this type of formative endeavor of the intellect has lost in validity since 1789: *L'esprit, si délicieux pour qui le sent, ne dure pas. Comme une pêche passe en quelques jours, l'esprit passe en deux cents ans, et bien plus vite, s'il y a révolution dans les rapports que les classes d'une société ont entre elles.* The *Souvenirs d'égotisme* contain an abundance of observations (for the most part truly prophetic) based on temporal perspective. He foresees (Chapter 7, near the end) that 'at the time when this chatter is read' it will have become a commonplace to make the ruling classes responsible for the crimes of thieves and murderers; he fears, at the beginning of Chapter 9, that all his bold utterances, which he dares put forth only with fear and trembling, will have become platitudes ten years after his death, if heaven grants him a decent allowance of life, say eighty or ninety years; in the next chapter he speaks of one of his friends who pays an unusually high price for the favors of an *honnête femme du peuple,* and adds in explanation: *cinq cents francs en 1832, c'est comme mille en 1872* – that is, forty years after the time at which he is writing and thirty after his death.

It would be possible to quote many more passages of the same general import. But it is unnecessary, for the element of time-perspective is apparent everywhere in the presentation itself. In his realistic writings, Stendhal everywhere deals with the reality which presents itself to him:

Je prends au hasard ce qui se trouve sur ma route, he says not far from the
passage just quoted: in his effort to understand men, he does not pick
and choose among them; this method, as Montaigne knew, is the best for
eliminating the arbitrariness of one's own constructions, and for
surrendering oneself to reality as given. But the reality which he
encountered was so constituted that, without permanent reference to the
immense changes of the immediate past and without a premonitory
searching after the imminent changes of the future, one could not
represent it; all the human figures and all the human events in his work
appear upon a ground politically and socially disturbed. To bring the
significance of this graphically before us, we have but to compare him
with the best-known realistic writers of the pre-Revolutionary eighteenth
century: with Lesage or the Abbé Prévost, with the preeminent Henry
Fielding or with Goldsmith; we have but to consider how much more
accurately and profoundly he enters into given contemporary reality than
Voltaire, Rousseau, and the youthful realistic work of Schiller, and upon
how much broader a basis than Saint-Simon, whom, though in the very
incomplete edition then available, he read assiduously. Insofar as the
serious realism of modern times cannot represent man otherwise than as
embedded in a total reality, political, social, and economic, which is
concrete and constantly evolving – as in the case today in any novel or
film – Stendhal is its founder.

However, the attitude from which Stendhal apprehends the world of
event and attempts to reproduce it with all its interconnections is as yet
hardly influenced by Historism – which, though it penetrated into France
in his time, had little effect upon him. For that very reason we have
referred in the last few pages to time-perspective and to a constant
consciousness of changes and cataclysms, but not to a comprehension of
evolutions. It is not too easy to describe Stendhal's inner attitude toward
social phenomena. It is his aim to seize their every nuance; he most
accurately represents the particular structure of any given milieu, he has
no preconceived rationalistic system concerning the general factors which
determine social life, nor any pattern-concept of how the ideal society
ought to look; but in particulars his representation of events is oriented,
wholly in the spirit of classic ethical psychology, upon an *analyse du cœur
humain,* not upon discovery or premonitions of historical forces; we find
rationalistic, empirical, sensual motifs in him, but hardly those of
romantic Historism. Absolutism, religion and the Church, the privileges
of rank, he regards very much as would an average protagonist of the
Enlightenment, that is as a web of superstition, deceit, and intrigue; in
general, artfully contrived intrigue (together with passion) plays a
decisive role in his plot construction, while the historical forces which are
the basis of it hardly appear. Naturally all this can be explained by his
political viewpoint, which was democratic-republican; this alone sufficed

to render him immune to romantic Historism; besides which the emphatic manner of such writers as Chateaubriand displeased him in the extreme. On the other hand, he treats even the classes of society which, according to his views, should be closest to him extremely critically and without a trace of the emotional values which romanticism attached to the word people. The practically active bougeoisie with its respectable money-making, inspires him with unconquerable boredom, he shudders at the *vertu républicaine* of the United States, and despite his ostensible lack of sentimentality he regrets the fall of the social culture of the *ancien régime*. *Ma foi, l'esprit manque,* he writes in Chapter 30 of *Henri Brulard, chacun réserve toutes ses forces pour un métier qui lui donne un rang dans le monde*. No longer is birth or intelligence or the self-cultivation of the honnête homme the deciding factor – it is ability in some profession. This is no world in which Stendhal-Dominique can live and breathe. Of course, like his heroes, he too can work and work efficiently, when that is what is called for. But how can one take anything like practical professional work seriously in the long run! Love, music, passion, intrigue, heroism – these are the things that make life worthwhile . . .

Stendhal is an aristocratic son of the *ancien régime grande bourgeoisie*, he will and can be no nineteenth-century bourgeois. He says so himself time and again: My views were Republican even in my youth but my family handed down their aristocratic instincts to me (*Brulard*, Ch. 14); since the Revolution theater audiences have become stupid (*Brulard*, Ch 22); I was a liberal myself (in 1821), and yet I found the liberals *outrageusement niais* (*Souvenirs d'égotisme*, Ch. 6); to converse with a *gros marchand de province* makes me dull and unhappy all day (*Egotisme*, Ch. 7 and *passim*) – these and similar remarks, which sometimes also refer to his physical constitution (*La nature m'a donné les nerfs délicats et la peau sensible d'une femme, Brulard*, Ch. 32), occur plentifully. Sometimes he has pronounced accesses of socialism: in 1811, he writes, energy was to be found only in the class *qui est en lutte avec les vrais besoins* (*Brulard*, Ch. 2). But he finds the smell and the noise of the masses unendurable, and in his books, outspokenly realistic though they are in other respects, we find no 'people', either in the romantic 'folk' sense or in the socialist sense – only petty bourgeois, and occasional accessory figures such as soldiers, domestic servants, and coffee-house mademoiselles. Finally, he sees the individual man far less as the product of his historical situation and as taking part in it, than as an atom within it; a man seems to have been thrown almost by chance into the milieu in which he lives; it is a resistance with which he can deal more or less successfully, not really a culture-medium with which he is organically connected. In addition, Stendhal's conception of mankind is on the whole preponderantly materialistic and sensualistic; an excellent illustration of this occurs in *Henri Brulard* (Ch 26): *J'appelle* caractère *d'un homme sa manière habituelle*

d'aller à la chasse du bonheur, en termes plus claires, mais moins qualificatifs,
l'ensemble de ses habitudes morales. But in Stendhal, happiness, even
though highly organized human beings can find it only in the mind, in
art, passion, or fame, always has a far more sensory and earthy coloring
than in the romanticists. His aversion to philistine efficiency, to the type
of bourgeois that was coming into existence, could be romantic too. But a
romantic would hardly conclude a passage on his distaste for money-
making with the words: *J'ai eu le rare plaisir de faire toute ma vie à peu près ce
qui me plaisait (Brulard,* Ch. 32). His conception of *esprit* and of freedom is
still entirely that of the pre-Revolutionary eighteenth century, although it
is only with effort and a little spasmodically that he succeeds in realizing
it in his own person. For freedom he has to pay the price of poverty and
loneliness and his *esprit* easily becomes paradox, bitter and wounding:
une gaité qui fait peur (Brulard, Ch. 6). His *esprit* no longer has the self-
assurance of the Voltaire period; he manages neither his social life nor
that particularly important part of it, his sexual relations, with the easy
mastery of a gentleman of rank of the *ancien régime*; he even goes so far as
to say that he cultivated *esprit* only to conceal his passion for a woman
whom he did not possess – *cette peur, mille fois répétée, a été, dans le fait, le
principe dirigeant de ma vie pendant dix ans (Egotisme,* Ch. 1). Such traits
make him appear a man born too late who tries in vain to realize the
form of life of a past period; other elements of his character, the merciless
objectivity of his realistic power, his courageous assertion of his
personality against the triviality of the rising *juste milieu*, and much more,
show him as the forerunner of certain later intellectual modes and forms
of life; but he always feels and experiences the reality of his period as a
resistance. That very thing makes his realism (though it proceeded, if at
all, to only a very slight degree from a loving genetic comprehension of
evolutions – that is, from the historistic attitude) so energetic and so
closely connected with his own existence: the realism of this *cheval
ombrageux* is a product of his fight for self-assertion. And this explains the
fact that the stylistic level of his great realistic novels is much closer to the
old great and heroic concept of tragedy than is that of most later realists –
Julien Sorel is much more a 'hero' than the characters of Balzac, to say
nothing of Flaubert.

That the rule of style promulgated by classical aesthetics which
excluded any material realism from serious tragic works was already
giving way in the eighteenth century is well known; we have discussed
the matter in the two preceding chapters. Even in France the relaxation
of this rule can be observed as early as the first half of the eighteenth
century; during the second half, it was Diderot particularly who
propagated a more intermediate level of style both in theory and in
practice, but he did not pass beyond the boundaries of the bourgeois and
the pathetic. In his novels, especially in the *Neveu de Rameau*, characters

from everyday life and of intermediate if not low station are portrayed
with a certain seriousness; but the seriousness is more reminiscent of the
moralistic and satirical attitudes of the Enlightenment than of nineteenth-
century realism. In the figure and the work of Rousseau there is
unmistakably a germ of the later evolution. Rousseau, as Meinecke says
in his book on Historism (2,390), was able 'even though he did not attain
to complete historical thinking, to help in awakening the new sense of
the individual merely through the revelation of his own unique
individuality'. Meinecke is here speaking of historical thinking; but a
corresponding statement may be made in respect to realism. Rousseau is
not properly realistic; to his material – especially when it is his own life –
he brings such a strongly apologetic and ethico-critical interest, his
judgement of events is so influenced by his principles of natural law, that
the reality of the social world does not become for him an immediate
subject; yet the example of the *Confessions*, which attempts to represent
his own existence in its true relation to contemporary life, is important as
a stylistic model for writers who had more sense of reality as given than
he. Perhaps even more important in its indirect influence upon serious
realism is his politicizing of the idyllic concept of Nature. This created a
wish-image for the design of life which, as we know, exercised an
immense power of suggestion and which, it was believed, could be
directly realized; the wish-image soon showed itself to be in absolute
opposition to the established historical reality, and the contrast grew
stronger and more tragic the more apparent it became that the realization
of the wish-image was miscarrying. Thus practical historical reality
became a problem in a way hitherto unknown – far more concretely and
far more immediately.

In the first decades after Rousseau's death, in French pre-romanticism,
the effect of that immense disillusionment was, to be sure, quite the
opposite: it showed itself, among the most important writers, in a
tendency to flee from contemporary reality. The Revolution, the Empire,
and even the Restoration are poor in realistic literary works. The heroes
of pre-romantic novels betray a sometimes almost morbid aversion to
entering into contemporary life. The contradiction between the natural,
which he desired, and the historically based reality which he
encountered, had already become tragic for Rousseau; but the very
contradiction had roused him to do battle for the natural. He was no
longer alive when the Revolution and Napoleon created a situation
which, though new, was, in his sense of the word, no more 'natural' but
instead again entangled historically. The next generation, deeply
influenced by his ideas and hopes, experienced the victorious resistance
of the real and the historical, and it was especially those who had fallen
most deeply under Rousseau's fascination, who found themselves not at
home in the new world which had utterly destroyed their hopes. They

entered into opposition to it or they turned away from it. Of Rousseau they carried on only the inward rift, the tendency to flee from society, the need to retire and to be alone; the other side of Rousseau's nature, the revolutionary and fighting side, they had lost. The outward circumstances which destroyed the unity of intellectual life, and the dominating influence of literature in France, also contributed to this development; from the outbreak of the Revolution to the fall of Napoleon there is hardly a literary work of any consequence which did not exhibit symptoms of this flight from contemporary reality, and such symptoms are still very prevalent among the romantic groups after 1820. They appear most purely and most completely in Sénancour. But in its very negativeness the attitude of the majority of pre-romantics to the historical reality of their time is far more seriously problematic than is the attitude of the society of the Enlightenment. The Rousseauist movement and the great disillusionment it underwent was a prerequisite for the rise of the modern conception of reality. Rousseau, by passionately contrasting the natural condition of man with the existing reality of life determined by history, made the latter a practical problem; now for the first time the eighteenth-century style of historically unproblematic and unmoved presentation of life became valueless.

Romanticism, which had taken shape much earlier in Germany and England, and whose historical and individualistic trends had been long in preparation in France, reached its full development after 1820; and, as we know it was precisely the principle of a mixture of styles which Victor Hugo and his friends made the slogan of their movement; in that principle the contrast to the classical treatment of subjects and the classical literary language stood out most obviously. Yet in Hugo's formula there is something too pointedly antithetical; for him it is a matter of mixing the sublime and the grotesque. These are both extremes of style which give no consideration to reality. And in practice he did not aim at understandingly bestowing form upon reality as given; rather, in dealing both with historical and contemporary subjects, he elaborates the stylistic poles of the sublime and the grotesque, or other ethical and aesthetic antitheses, to the utmost, so that they clash; in this way very strong effects are produced, for Hugo's command of expression is powerful and suggestive; but the effects are improbable and, as a reflection of human life, untrue.

Another writer of the romantic generation, Balzac, who had as great a creative gift and far more closeness to reality, seized upon the representation of contemporary life as his own particular task and, together with Stendhal, can be regarded as the creator of modern realism. He was sixteen years younger than Stendhal, yet his first characteristic novels appeared at almost the same time as Stendhal's that is, about 1830. To exemplify his method of presentation we shall first give his portrait of the pension-mistress Madame Vauquer at the beginning of *Le Père Goriot* (1834). It is preceded by a very detailed description of the quarter in which the pension is located, of the house itself, of the two rooms on the ground floor; all this produces an intense impression of cheerless poverty, shabbiness, and dilapidation, and with the physical description the moral atmosphere is suggested. After the furniture of the dining room is described, the mistress of the establishment herself finally appears:

Cette pièce est dans tout son lustre au moment où, vers sept heures du matin, le chat de Mme Vauquer précède sa maîtresse, saute sur les buffets, y flaire le lait que contiennent plusieurs jattes couvertes d'assiettes et fait entendre son *ronron* matinal. Bientôt la veuve se montre, attifée de son bonnet de tulle sous lequel pend un tour de faux cheveux mal mis; elle marche en traînassant ses pantoufles grimacées. Sa face vieillotte, grassouillette, du milieu de laquelle sort un nez à bec de perroquet; ses petites mains potelées, sa personne dodue comme un rat d'église, son corsage trop plein et qui flotte, sont en harmonie avec cette salle où suinte le malheur, où s'est blottie la spéculation, et dont Mme Vauquer respire l'air chaudement fétide sans en être écœurée. Sa figure fraîche comme une première gelée d'automne, ses yeux ridés, dont l'expression passe du sourire prescrit aux danseuses à l'amer renfrognement de l'escompteur, enfin toute sa personne explique la pension, comme la pension implique sa personne. Le bagne ne va pas sans l'argousin, vous n'imagineriez pas l'un sans l'autre. L'embonpoint blafard de cette petite femme est le produit de cette vie, comme le typhus est la conséquence des exhalaisons d'un hôpital. Son jupon de laine tricotée, qui dépasse sa première jupe faite avec une vieille robe, et dont la ouate s'échappe par les fentes de l'étoffe lézardée, résume le salon, la salle à manger, le jardinet, annonce la cuisine et fait pressentir les pensionnaires. Quand elle est là, ce spectacle est complet. Agée d'environ cinquante ans, Mme Vauquer ressemble à toutes les femmes *qui ont eu des malheurs*. Elle a l'œil vitreux, l'air innocent d'une entremetteuse qui va se gendarmer pour se faire payer plus cher, mais d'ailleurs prête à tout pour adoucir son sort, à livrer Georges ou Pichegru, si Georges ou Pichegru étaient encore à livrer. Néanmoins elle est *bonne femme au fond*, disent les pensionnaires, qui la croient sans fortune en l'entendant geindre et tousser comme eux. Qu'avait été M. Vauquer? Elle ne s'expliquait jamais sur le défunt. Comment avait-il perdu sa fortune? 'Dans les malheurs,' répondait-elle. Il s'était mal conduit envers elle, ne lui avait laissé que les yeux pour pleurer, cette maison pour vivre, et le droit de ne compatir à aucune infortune, parce que, disait-elle, elle avait souffert tout ce qu'il est possible de souffrir.

(The room is at its brilliant best when, about seven in the morning, Madame Vauquer's cat enters before its mistress, jumps up on the buffet, sniffs at the milk which stands there in a number of bowls covered over with plates, and emits its matutinal purring. Presently the widow appears, got up in her tulle bonnet, from beneath which hangs an ill-attached twist of false hair; as she walks, her wrinkled slippers drag. Her oldish, fattish face, from the middle of which juts a parrot-beak nose, her small, plump hands, her figure as well filled out as a church-warden's, her loose, floppy bodice, are in harmony with the room, whose walls ooze misfortune, where speculation cowers, and whose warm and fetid air Madame Vauquer breathes without nausea. Her face, as chilly as a first fall frost, her wrinkled eyes, whose expression changes from the obligatory smile of a ballet-girl to the sour scowl of a sharper, her whole person, in short, explains the pension, as the pension implies her person. A prison requires a warder, you could not imagine the one without the other. The short-statured woman's blowsy *embonpoint* is the product of the life here, as typhoid is the consequence of the exhalations of a hospital. Her knitted wool petticoat, which is longer than her outer skirt (made of an old dress), and whose wadding is escaping by the gaps in the splitting material, sums up the drawing-room, the dining room, the little garden, announces the cooking and gives an inkling of the boarders. When she is there, the spectacle is complete. Some fifty years of age, Madame Vauquer resembles all women *who have had troubles*. She has the glassy eye, the innocent expression of a bawd who is about to make a scene in order to get a higher price, but who is at the same time ready for anything in order to soften her lot, to hand over Georges or Pichegru if Georges or Pichegru were still to be handed over. Nevertheless, she is a *good woman at heart*, the boarders say, and they believe, because they hear her moan and cough like themselves, that she has no money. What had Monsieur Vauquer been? She never gave any information about the deceased. How had he lost his money? 'In troubles,' she answered. He had acted badly toward her, had left her nothing but her eyes to weep with, this house for livelihood, and the right to be indulgent toward no manner of misfortune because, she said, she had suffered everything it is possible to suffer.)

The portrait of the hostess is connected with her morning appearance in the dining room; she appears in this center of her influence, the cat jumping onto the buffet before her gives a touch of witchcraft to her entrance; and then Balzac immediately begins a detailed description of her person. The description is controlled by a leading motif, which is several times repeated – the motif of the harmony between Madame Vauquer's person on the one hand and the room in which she is present, the pension which she directs, and the life which she leads, on the other;

in short, the harmony between her person and what we (and Balzac too, occasionally) call her milieu. This harmony is most impressively suggested: first through the dilapidation, the greasiness, the dirtiness and warmth, the sexual repulsiveness of her body and her clothes – all this being in harmony with the air of the room which she breathes without distaste; a little later, in connection with her face and its expressions, the motif is conceived somewhat more ethically, and with even greater emphasis upon the complementary relation between person and milieu: *sa personne explique la pension, comme la pension implique sa personne;* with this goes the comparison to a prison. There follows a more medical concept, in which Madam Vauquer's *embonpoint blafard* as a symptom of her life is compared to typhoid as the result of the exhalations in a hospital. Finally her petticoat is appraised as a sort of synthesis of the various rooms of the pension, as a foretaste of the products of the kitchen, and as a premonition of the guests; for a moment her petticoat becomes a symbol of the milieu, and then the whole is epitomized again in the sentence: *Quand elle est là, ce spectacle est complet* – one need, then, wait no longer for the breakfast and the guests, they are all included in her person. There seems to be no deliberate order for the various repetitions of the harmony-motif, nor does Balzac appear to have followed a systematic plan in describing Madame Vauquer's appearance; the series of things mentioned – headdress, false hair, slippers, face, hands, body, the face again, eyes, corpulence, petticoat – reveal no trace of composition; nor is there any separation of body and clothing, of physical characteristics and moral significance. The entire description, so far as we have yet considered it, is directed to the mimetic imagination of the reader, to his memory-pictures of similar persons and similar milieux which he may have seen; the thesis of the 'stylistic unity' of the milieu, which includes the people in it, is not established rationally but is presented as a striking and immediately apprehended state of things, purely suggestively, without any proof. In such a statement as the following, *ses petites mains potelées, sa personne dodue comme un rat d'église . . . sont en harmonie avec cette salle où suinte le malheur . . . et dont Mme Vauquer respire l'air chaudement fétide . . .* the harmony-thesis, with all that it includes (sociological and ethical significance of furniture and clothing, the deducibility of the as yet unseen elements of the milieu from those already given, etc.) is presupposed; the mention of prison and typhoid too are merely suggestive comparisons, not proofs nor even beginnings of proofs. The lack of order and disregard for the rational in the text are consequences of the haste with which Balzac worked, but they are nevertheless no mere accident, for his haste is itself in large part a consequence of his obsession with suggestive pictures. The motif of the unity of a milieu has taken hold of him so powerfully that the things and the persons composing a milieu often acquire for him a sort of second significance which, though different from that which reason can comprehend, is far more essential – a significance which can best be defined by the adjective demonic. In the dining room, with its furniture which, worn and shabby though it be, is perfectly harmless to a reason uninfluenced by imagination, 'misfortune oozes, speculation cowers.' In this trivial everyday scene allegorical witches lie hidden, and instead of the plump sloppily dressed widow one momentarily sees a rat appear. What confronts us, then, is the unity of a particular milieu, felt as a total concept of a demonic-organic nature and presented entirely by suggestive and sensory means.

The next part of our passage, in which the harmony-motif is not again mentioned, pursues Madame Vauquer's character and previous history. It would be a mistake, however, to see in this separation of appearance on the one hand and character and previous history on the other a deliberate principle of compositon; there are physical characteristics in this second part too (*l'œil vitreux*), and Balzac very frequently makes a different disposition, or mingles the physical, moral, and historical elements of a portrait indiscriminately. In our case his pursuit of her character and previous history does not serve to clarify either of them but rather to set Madame Vauquer's darkness 'in the right light,' that is, in the twilight of a petty and trivial demonism. So far as her previous history goes, the pension-mistress belongs to the category of women of fifty or thereabouts *qui ont eu des malheurs* (plural!): Balzac enlightens us not at all concerning her previous life, but instead reproduces, partly in *erlebte Rede*, the formless, whining, mendaciously colloquial chatter with which she habitually answers sympathetic inquiries. But here again the suspicious plural occurs, again avoiding particulars – her late husband had lost his money *dans les malheurs* – just as, some pages later, another suspicious widow imparts, on the subject of her husband who had been a count and a general, that he had fallen on LES *champs de bataille*. This conforms to the vulgar demonism of Madame Vauquer's character; she seems *bonne femme au fond*, she seems poor, but, as we are later told, she has a very tidy little fortune and she is capable of any baseness in order to improve her own situation a little – the base and vulgar narrowness of the goal of her egoism, the mixture of stupidity, slyness, and concealed vitality, again gives the impression of something repulsively spectral; again there imposes itself the comparison with a rat, or with some other animal making a basely demonic impression on the human imagination. The second part of the description, then, is a supplement to the first; after Madame Vauquer is presented in the first as synthesizing the milieu she governs, the second deepens the impenetrability and baseness of her character, which is constrained to work itself out in this milieu.

In his entire work, as in this passage, Balzac feels his milieux, different though they are, as organic and indeed demonic unities, and seeks to convey this feeling to the reader. He not only, like Stendhal, places the human beings whose destiny he is seriously relating, in their precisely defined historical and social setting, but also conceives this connection as a necessary one: to him every milieu becomes a moral and physical atmosphere which impregnates the landscape, the dwelling, furniture, implements, clothing, physique, character, surroundings, ideas, activities, and fates of men, and at the same time the general historical situation reappears as a total atmosphere which envelops all its several milieux. It is worth noting that he did this best and most truthfully for the circle of the middle and lower Parisian bourgeoisie and for the provinces; while his representation of high society is often melodramatic, false, and even unintentionally comic. He is not free from melodramatic exaggeration elsewhere; but whereas in the middle and lower spheres this only occasionally impairs the truthfulness of the whole, he is unable to create the true atmosphere of the higher spheres – including those of the intellect.

Balzac's atmospheric realism is a product of his period, is itself a part and a result of an atmosphere. The same intellectual attitude – namely romanticism – which first felt the atmospheric unity-of-style of earlier periods so strongly and so sensorily, which discovered the Middle Ages and the Renaissance as well as the historical idiosyncrasy of foreign cultures (Spain, the Orient) – this same intellectual attitude also developed organic comprehension of the atmospheric uniqueness of its own period in all its manifold forms. Atmospheric Historism and atmospheric realism are closely connected; Michelet and Balzac are borne on the same stream. The events which occurred in France between 1789 and 1815, and their effects during the next decades, caused modern contemporaneous realism to develop first and most strongly there, and its political and cultural unity gave France, in this respect, a long start over Germany; French reality, in all its multifariousness, could be comprehended as a whole. Another romantic current which contributed, no less than did romantic penetration into the total atmosphere of a milieu, to the development of modern realism, was the mixture of styles to which we have so often referred; this made it possible for characters of any station, with all the practical everyday complications of their lives – Julien Sorel as well as old Goriot or Madame Vauquer – to become the subject of serious literary representation.

These general considerations appear to me cogent; it is far more difficult to describe with any accuracy the intellectual attitude which dominates Balzac's own particular manner of presentation. The statements which he himself makes on the subject are numerous and provide many clues, but they are confused and contradictory; the richer he is in ideas and inspirations, the less is he able to separate the various elements of his own attitude, to channel the influx of suggestive but vague images and comparisons into intellectual analyses, and especially to adopt a critical attitude toward the stream of his own inspiration. All his intellectual analyses, although full of isolated observations which are striking and original, come in the end to a fanciful macroscopy which suggests his contemporary Hugo; whereas what is needed to explain his realistic art is precisely a careful separation of the currents which mingle in it.

In the *Avant-propos* to the *Comédie humaine* (published 1842) Balzac begins his explanation of his work with a comparison between the animal kingdom and human society, in which he accepts the guidance of Geoffroy Saint-Hilaire's theories. This biologist, under the influence of contemporary German speculative natural philosophy, had upheld the principle of typal unity in organization, that is, the idea that in the organization of plants (and animals) there is a general plan; Balzac here refers to the systems of other mystics, philosophers, and biologists (Swedenborg, Saint-Martin, Leibnitz, Buffon, Bonnet, Needham) and finally arrives at the following formulations:

Le créateur ne s'est servi que d'un seul et même patron pour tous les êtres organisés. L'animal est un principe qui prend sa forme extérieure, ou, pour parler plus exactement, les différences de sa forme, dans les milieux où il est appelé à se développer . . .

(The creator used but one and the same pattern for all organized cratures. The animal is a principle which takes its external form, or, to put it more precisely, the differences of its form, from the milieux in which it is called upon to evolve . . .)

This principle is at once transferred to human society:

La Société [with a capital, as Nature shortly before] ne fait-elle pas de l'homme, suivant les milieux où son action se déploie, autant d'hommes différents qu'il y a de variétés en zoologie?

(Does not Society make of man, according to the milieux in which his activity takes place, as many different men as there are varieties in zoology?)

And then he compares the differences between a soldier, a workman, an administrative employee, an idler, a scholar, a statesman, a shopkeeper, a seaman, a poet, a pauper, a priest, with those between wolf, lion, ass, raven, shark, and so on.

Our first conclusion is that he is here attempting to establish his views of human society (typical man differentiated by his milieu) by biological analogies; the word milieu, which here appears for the first time in the sociological sense and which was to have such a successful career (Taine seems to have adopted it from Balzac), he learned from Geoffroy Saint-Hilaire, who for his part had transferred it from physical science to biology; now it makes its way from biology to sociology. The biologism present in Balzac's mind, as may be deduced from the names he cites, is mystical, speculative, and vitalistic; however, the model-concept, the principle 'animal' or 'man,' is not taken as immanent but, so to speak, as a real Platonic idea. The various genera and species are only *formes extérieures*; furthermore, they are themselves given not as changing within the course of history but as fixed (a soldier, a workman, etc., like a lion, an ass). The particular meaning of the concept milieu, as he uses it in practice in his novels he here seems not to have fully realized. Not the word, but the thing – milieu in the social sense – existed long before him; Montesquieu unmistakably has the concept; but whereas Montesquieu gives much more consideration to natural conditions (climate, soil) than to those which spring from human history, and whereas he attempts to construe the different milieux as unchanging model-concepts to which the appropriate constitutional and legislative models can be applied, Balzac in practice remains entirely within the orbit of the historical and perpetually changing structural elements of his milieux; and no reader arrives unassisted at the idea which Balzac appears to maintain in his *Avant-propos*, that he is concerned only with the type 'man' or with generic types ('soldier,' 'shopkeeper'); what we see is the concrete individual figure with its own physique and its own history, sprung from the immanence of the historical, social, physical, etc. situation; not 'the soldier' but for example, Colonel Brideau, discharged after the fall of Napoleon, ruined and leading the life of an adventurer in Issoudun (*La Rabouilleuse*).

After his bold comparison of zoological with sociological differentiation, however, Balzac attempts to bring out the distinguishing characteristics of *la Société* as against *la Nature*; he sees them above all in the far greater multifariousness of human life and human customs, as well as in the possibility – nonexistent in the animal kingdom – of changing from one species to another ('the grocer . . . becomes a Peer of France, and the nobleman sometimes sinks to the lowest rank of society'); furthermore, different species mate ('the wife of a merchant is sometimes worthy to be the wife of a prince . . .; in Society, a woman does not always happen to be the female of a male'); he also refers to dramatic conflicts in love, which seldom occur among animals, and the different degrees of intelligence in different men. The epitomizing sentence reads: 'The social State has risks which Nature does not permit herself, for it is Nature plus Society.' Inaccurate and macroscopic as this passage is, badly as it suffers from the *proton pseudos* of the underlying comparison, it yet contains an instinctive historical insight ('customs, clothing, modes of speech, houses . . . change in accordance with civilizations'); there is much, too, of dynamism and vitalism ('if some scientists do not yet admit that Animality floods over into Humanity by an immense current of life'). The particular possibilities of comprehension between man and man are not mentioned – not even in the negative formulation that, as compared with man, the animal lacks them; on the contrary, the relative simplicity of the social and psychological life of animals is presented as an objective fact, and only at the very end is there any indication of the subjective character of such judgments: 'the habits of each animal are, to our eyes at least, constantly similar at all times.'

After this transition from biology to human history, Balzac continues with a polemic against the prevailing type of historical writing and reproaches it with having long neglected the history of manners; this is the task he has set himself. He does not mention the attempts at a history of manners which had been made from the eighteenth century on (Voltaire); hence there is no analysis setting forth the distinction between his presentation of manners and that of his possible predecessors; only Petronius is named. Considering the difficulties of his task (a drama with three or four thousand characters), he feels encouraged by the example of Walter Scott's novels; so here we are completely within the world of romantic Historism. Here too clarity of thought is often impaired by striking and fanciful formulations; for example *faire concurrence à l'Etat-Civil* is equivocal, and the statement *le hasard est le plus grand romancier du monde* requires some explanation if it is to tally with its author's historical attitude. But a number of important and characteristic motifs emerge successfully: above all the concept of the novel of manners as philosophical history, and, in general, Balzac's conception (which he upholds energetically elsewhere) of his own activity as the writing of history, to which we shall later return; also his justification of all stylistic genres and levels in works of this nature; finally his design of going beyond Walter Scott by making all his novels compose a single whole, a general presentation of French society in the nineteenth century, which he here again calls a historical work.

But this does not exhaust his plan; he intends also to render a separate account of *les raisons ou la raison de ces effets sociaux*, and when he has succeeded in at least investigating *ce moteur social*, his final intention is 'to meditate upon natural principles and see wherein Societies depart from or approach the eternal rule, the true, the beautiful.' We need not here discuss the fact that it was not given to him to make a successful theoretical presentation outside the frame of a narrative, that hence he could only attempt to realize his theoretical plans in the form of novels; here it is only of interest to note that the 'immanent' philosophy of his novels of manners did not satisfy him and that in the passage before us this dissatisfaction, after so many biological and historical expositions, induces him to employ classical model-concepts (*la règle éternelle, le vrai, le beau*) – categories which he can no longer utilize practically in his novels.

All these motifs – biological, historistic, classically moralistic – are in fact scattered through his work. He has a great fondness for biological comparisons; he speaks of physiology or zoology in connection with social phenomena, of the *anatomie du cœur humain*; in the passage commented on above he compares the effect of a social milieu to the exhalations which produce typhoid, and in another passage from *Père Goriot* he says of Rastignac that he had given himself up to the lessons and the temptations of luxury 'with the ardor which seizes the calix of a female date-palm for the fecundating dusts of its nuptials.' It is needless to cite historistic motifs, for the spirit of Historism with its emphasis upon ambient and individual atmospheres in the spirit of his entire work; I will, however, quote at least one of many passages to show that historical concepts were always in his mind. The passage is from the provincial novel *La vieille Fille*; it concerns two elderly gentlemen who live in Alençon, the one a typical *ci-devant*, the other a bankrupt Revolutionary profiteer:

Les époques déteignent sur les hommes qui les traversent. Ces deux personnages prouvaient la vérité de cet axiome par l'opposition des teintes historiques empreintes dans leurs physionomies, dans leurs discours, dans leurs idées et leurs coutumes.

(Periods rub off on the men who pass through them. These two personages proved the truth of this axiom by the contrast in the historical coloring imprinted upon their physiognomies, their talk, their ideas, and their clothes.)

And in another passage from the same novel, in reference to a house in Alençon, he speaks of the *archétype* which it represents; here we have not the archetype of a nonhistorical abstraction but that of the *maisons bourgeoises* of a large part of France; the house, whose piquant local character he has previously described, deserves its place in the novel all the more, he says, *qu'il explique des mœurs et représente des idées*. Despite many obscurities and exaggerations, biological and historical elements are successfully combined in Balzac's work because they are both consonant with its romantic-dynamic character, which occasionally passes over into the romantic magical and the demonic; in both cases one feels the operation of irrational 'forces.' In contrast, the classically moralistic element very often gives the impression of being a foreign body. It finds expression more especially in Balzac's tendency to formulate generalized

apophthegms of a moral cast. They are sometimes witty as individual
observations, but for the most part they are far too generalized;
sometimes too they are not even witty; and when they develop into long
disquisitions, they are often – to use the language of the vulgar – plain
'tripe'. I will quote some brief moralizing dicta which occur in *Père Goriot:*

Le bonheur est la poésie des femmes comme la toilette en est le fard. –
(La science et l'amour . . .) sont des asymptotes qui ne peuvent jamais se
rejoindre. – S'il est un sentiment inné dans le cœur de l'homme, n'est-ce
pas l'orgueil de la protection exercé à tout moment en faveur d'un être
faible? – Quand on connaît Paris, on ne croit à rien de ce qui s'y dit, et
l'on ne dit rien de ce qui s'y fait. – Un sentiment, n'est-ce pas le monde
dans une pensée?

(Happiness is the poetry of women as get-up is their rouge. – [Science
and love . . .] are asymptotes which can never meet. – If there is a
sentiment innate in the heart of man, is it not pride in protection
perpetually exercised on behalf of a weak creature? – When one knows
Paris, one believes nothing that is told there and tells nothing that is
done there. – Is not a sentiment a world in a thought?)

At best one can say of such apophthegms that they do not deserve the
honor bestowed upon them – that of being erected into generalizations.
They are *aperçus* produced by the momentary situation, sometimes
extremely cogent, sometimes absurd, not always in good taste. Balzac
aspires to be a classical moralist, at times he even echoes La Bruyère (eg,
in a passage from *Père Goriot* where the physical and psychological effects
of the possession of money are described in connection with the
remittance Rastignac receives from his family). But this suits neither his
style nor his temperament. His best formulations come to him in the
midst of narrative, when he is not thinking about moralizing – for
example when in *La Vieille Fille* he says of Mademoiselle Cormon, directly
out of the momentary situation: *Honteuse elle-même, elle ne devinait pas la
honte d'autrui.*

On the subject of his plan for the entire work, which gradually took
shape in him, he has other interesting statements, particularly from the
period when he finally saw it whole – in his letters of ca. 1834. In this
self-interpretation three motifs are especially to be remarked; all three
occur together in a letter to the Countess Hanska (*Lettres à l'Etrangère*,
Paris 1899, letter of Oct. 26, 1834, pp. 200–206), where (p. 205) we find:

Les Etudes de Mœurs représenteront tous les effets sociaux sans que ni
une situation de la vie, ni une physionomie, ni un caractère d'homme ou
de femme, ni une manière de vivre, ni une profession, ni une zone

sociale, ni un pays français, ni quoi que ce soit de l'enfance, de la
vieillesse, de l'âge mûr, de la politique, de la justice, de la guerre ait été
oublié.

Cela posé, l'histoire du cœur humain tracée fil à fil, l'histoire sociale
faite dans toutes ses parties, voilà la base. Ce ne seront pas des faits
imaginaires; ce sera ce qui se passe partout.

(The Studies of Manners will represent all social effects, without
forgetting a single situation in life, a physiognomy, a man's or woman's
character, a way of life, a profession, a social zone, a part of France, or
anything of childhood, old age, maturity, politics, law, war.

This established, the history of the human heart traced thread by
thread, social history set down in all its parts – there is the foundation. It
will not be imaginary facts; it will be what happens everywhere.)

Of the three motifs to which I have referred, two are immediately
apparent; first, the universality of his plan, his concept of his work as an
encyclopedia of life; no part of life is to be omitted. Second, the element
of random reality – *ce qui se passe partout*. The third motif lies in the word
histoire. This *histoire du cœur humain* or *histoire sociale* is not a matter of
'history' in the usual sense – not of scientific investigation of transactions
which have already occurred, but of comparatively free invention; not, in
short, of *history* but of *fiction*; is not, above all, a matter of the past but of
the contemporary present, reaching back at most only a few years or a
few decades. If Balzac describes his *Etudes de Mœurs au dix-neuvième siècle*
as history (just as Stendhal had already given his novel *Le Rouge et le Noir*
the subtitle *Chronique du dix-neuvième siècle*), this means, first, that he
regards his creative and artistic activity as equivalent to an activity of a
historical-interpretative and even historical-philosophical nature, as his
Avant-propos in itself makes it possible to deduce; secondly, that he
conceives the present as history – the present is something in the process
of resulting from history. And in practice his people and his
atmospheres, contemporary as they may be, are always represented as
phenomena sprung from historical events and forces; one has but to read
over, say, the account of the origin of Grandet's wealth (*Eugénie Grandet*),
or that of Du Bousquier's life (*La vieille Fille*) or old Goriot's, to be certain
of this. Nothing of the sort so conscious and so detailed is to be found
before the appearance of Stendhal and Balzac, and the latter far outdoes
the former in organically connecting man and history. Such a conception
and execution are thoroughly historistic.

We will now return to the second motif – *ce ne seront pas des faits
imaginaires; ce sera ce qui se passe partout*. What is expressed here is that the
source of his invention is not free imagination but real life, as it presents
itself everywhere. Now, in respect to this manifold life, steeped in

history, mercilessly represented wth all its everyday triviality, practical preoccupations, ugliness and vulgarity, Balzac has an attitude such as Stendhal had had before him: in the form determined by its actuality, its triviality, its inner historical laws, he takes it seriously and even tragically. This, since the rise of classical taste, had occurred nowhere – and even before then not in Balzac's practical and historical manner, oriented as it is upon a social self-accounting of man. Since French classicism and absolutism, not only had the treatment of everyday reality become much more limited and decorous, but in addition the attitude taken toward it renounced the tragic and problematic as it were in principle. We have attempted to analyze this in the preceding chapters: a subject from practical reality could be treated comically, satirically, or didactically and moralistically; certain subjects from definite and limited realms of contemporary everyday life attained to an intermediate style, the pathetic; but beyond that they might not go. The real everyday life of even the middle ranks of society belong to the low style; the profound and significant Henry Fielding, who touches upon so many moral, aesthetic, and social problems, keeps his presentation always within the satiric moralistic key and says in *Tom Jones* (Book 14, Chapter 1): '. . . that kind of novels which, like this I am writing, is of the comic class.'

The entrance of existential and tragic seriousness into realism, as we observe it in Stendhal and Balzac, is indubitably closely connected with the great romantic agitation for the mixture of styles – the movement whose slogan was Shakespeare vs Racine – and I consider Stendhal's and Balzac's form of it, the mixture of seriousness and everyday reality, far more important and genuine than the form it took in the Hugo group, which set out to unite the sublime and the grotesque.

The newness of this attitude, and the new type of subjects which were seriously, problematically, tragically treated, caused the gradual development of an entirely new kind of serious or, if one prefers, elevated style; neither the antique nor the Christian nor the Shakespearean nor the Racinian level of conception and expression could easily be transferred to the new subjects; at first there was some uncertainty in regard to the kind of serious attitude to be assumed.

Stendhal, whose realism had sprung from resistance to a present which he despised, preserved many eighteenth-century instincts in his attitude. In his heroes there are still haunting memories of figures like Romeo, Don Juan, Valmont (from the *Liaisons dangereuses*), and Saint-Preux; above all, the figure of Napoleon remains alive in him; the heroes of his novels think and feel in opposition to their time, only with contempt do they descend to the intrigues and machinations of the post-Napoleonic present. Although there is always an admixture of motifs which, according to the older view, would have the character of comedy, it remains true of Stendhal that a figure for whom he feels tragic sympathy, and for whom he demands it of the reader, must be a real hero, great and daring in his thoughts and passions. In Stendhal the freedom of the great heart, the freedom of passion, still has much of the aristocratic loftiness and of the playing with life which are more characteristic of the *ancien régime* than of the nineteenth-century bourgeoisie.

Balzac plunges his heroes far more deeply into time-conditioned dependency; he thereby loses the standards and limits of what had earlier been felt as tragic, and he does not yet possess the objective seriousness toward modern reality which later developed. He bombastically takes every entanglement as tragic, every urge as a great passion; he is always ready to declare every person in misfortune a hero or a saint; if it is a woman, he compares her to an angel or the Madonna; every energetic scoundrel, and above all every figure who is at all sinister, he converts into a demon; and he calls poor old Goriot *ce Christ de la paternité*. It was in conformity with his emotional, fiery, and uncritical temperament, as well as with the romantic way of life, to sense hidden demonic forces everywhere and to exaggerate expression to the point of melodrama.

In the next generation, which comes on the stage in the fifties, there is a strong reaction in this respect. In Flaubert realism becomes impartial, impersonal, and objective. In an earlier study, 'Serious Imitation of Everyday Life,' I analyzed a paragraph from *Madame Bovary* from this point of view, and will here, with slight changes and abridgements, reproduce the pages concerned, since they are in line with the present train of thought and since it is unlikely, in view of the time and place of their publication (Istanbul, 1937), that they have reached many readers. The paragraph concerned occurs in Part 1, Chapter 9, of *Madame Bovary*:

Mais c'était surtout aux heures des repas qu'elle n'en pouvait plus, dans cette petite salle au rez-de-chaussée, avec le poêle qui fumait, la porte qui criait, les murs qui suintaient, les pavés humides; toute l'amertume de l'existence lui semblait servie sur son assiette, et, à la fumée du bouilli, il montait du fond de son âme comme d'autres bouffées d'affadissement. Charles était long à manger; elle grignotait quelques noisettes, ou bien, appuyée du coude, s'amusait, avec la pointe de son couteau, de faire des raies sur la toile cirée.

(But it was above all at mealtimes that she could bear it no longer, in that little room on the ground floor, with the smoking stove, the creaking door, the oozing walls, the damp floor-tiles; all the bitterness of life seemed to be served to her on her plate, and, with the steam from the boiled beef, there rose from the depths of her soul other exhalations as it were of disgust. Charles was a slow eater; she would nibble a few hazelnuts, or else, leaning on her elbow, would amuse herself making marks on the oilcloth with the point of her table-knife.)

The paragraph forms the climax of a presentation whose subject is Emma Bovary's dissatisfaction with her life in Tostes. She has long hoped for a sudden event which would give a new turn to it – to her life without elegance, adventure, and love, in the depths of the provinces, beside a mediocre and boring husband; she has even made preparations for such an event, has lavished care on herself and her house, as if to earn that turn of fate, to be worthy of it; when it does not come, she is seized with unrest and despair. All this Flaubert describes in several pictures which portray Emma's world as it now appears to her; its cheerlessness, unvaryingness, grayness, staleness, airlessness, and inescapability now first become clearly apparent to her when she has no more hope of fleeing from it. Our paragraph is the climax of the portrayal of her despair. After it we are told how she lets everything in the house go, neglects herself, and begins to fall ill, so that her husband decides to leave Tostes, thinking that the climate does not agree with her.

The paragraph itself presents a picture – man and wife together at mealtime. But the picture is not presented in and for itself; it is subordinated to the dominant subject, Emma's despair. Hence it is not put before the reader directly: here the two sit at table – there the reader stands watching them. Instead, the reader first sees Emma, who has been much in evidence in the preceding pages, and he sees the picture first through her; directly, he sees only Emma's inner state; he sees what goes on at the meal indirectly, from within her state, in the light of her perception. The first words of the paragraph, *Mais c'était surtout aux heures des repas qu'elle n'en pouvait plus* . . . state the theme, and all that follows is but a development of it. Not only are the phrases dependent upon *dans* and *avec*, which define the physical scene, a commentary on *elle n'en pouvait plus* in their piling up of the individual elements of discomfort, but the following clause too, which tells of the distaste aroused in her by the food, accords with the principal purpose both in sense and rhythm. When we read further, *Charles était long à manger*, this, though grammatically a new sentence and rhythmically a new movement, is still only a resumption, a variation, of the principal theme; not until we come to the contrast between his leisurely eating and her disgust and to the nervous gestures of her despair, which are described immediately afterward, does the sentence acquire its true significance. The husband, unconcernedly eating, becomes ludicrous and almost ghastly; when Emma looks at him and sees him sitting there eating, he becomes the actual cause of the *elle n'en pouvait plus*; because everything else that arouses her desperation – the gloomy room, the commonplace food, the lack of a tablecloth, the hopelessness of it all – appears to her, and through her to the reader also, as something that is connected with him, that emanates from him, and that would be entirely different if he were different from what he is.

The situation, then, is not presented simply as a picture, but we are first given Emma and then the situation through her. It is not, however, a matter – as it is in many first-person novels and other later works of a similar type – of a simple representation of the content of Emma's consciousness, of *what* she feels *as* she feels it. Though the light which illuminates the picture proceeds from her, she is yet herself part of the picture, she is situated within it. In this she recalls the speaker in the scene from Petronius discussed in our second chapter; but the means Flaubert employs are different. Here it is not Emma who speaks, but the writer. *Le poêle qui fumait, la porte qui criait, les murs qui suintaient, les pavés humides* – all this, of course, Emma sees and feels, but she would not be able to sum it all up in this way. *Toute l'amertume de l'existence lui semblait servie sur son assiette* – she doubtless has such a feeling; but if she wanted to express it, it would come out like that; she has neither the intelligence nor the cold candor of self-accounting necessary for such a formulation. To be sure, there is nothing of Flaubert's life in these words, but only Emma's; Flaubert does nothing but bestow the power of mature expression upon the material which she affords, in its complete subjectivity. If Emma could do this herself, she would no longer be what she is, she would have outgrown herself and thereby saved herself. So she does not simply see, but is herself seen as one seeing, and is thus judged, simply through a plain description of her subjective life, out of her own feelings. Reading in a later passage (Part 2, Chapter 12): *jamais Charles ne lui paraissait aussi désagréable, avoir les doigts aussi carrés, l'esprit aussi lourd, les façons si communes . . .*, the reader perhaps thinks for a moment that this strange series is an emotional piling up of the causes that time and again bring Emma's aversion to her husband to the boiling point, and that she herself is, as it were, inwardly speaking these words; that this, then, is an example of *erlebte Rede*. But this would be a mistake. We have here, to be sure, a number of paradigmatic causes of Emma's aversion, but they are put together deliberately by the writer, not emotionally by Emma. For Emma feels much more, and much more confusedly; she sees other things than these – in his body, his manners, his dress; memories mix in, meanwhile she perhaps hears him speak, perhaps feels his hand, his breath, sees him walk about, good-hearted, limited, unappetizing, and unaware; she has countless confused impressions. The only thing that is clearly defined is the result of all this, her aversion to him, which she must hide. Flaubert transfers the clearness to the impressions; he selects three, apparently quite at random, but which are paradigmatically taken from Bovary's physique, his mentality, and his behavior; and he arranges them as if they were three shocks which Emma felt one after the other. This is not at all a naturalistic representation of consciousness. Natural shocks occur quite differently. The ordering hand of the writer is present here, deliberately summing up the confusion of the psychological situation in the direction toward which it tends of itself – the direction of 'aversion to Charles Bovary.' This ordering of the psychological situation does not, to be sure, derive its standards from without, but from the material of the situation itself. It is the type of ordering which must be employed if the situation itself is to be translated into language without admixture.

In a comparison of this type of presentation with those of Stendhal and Balzac, it is to be observed by way of introduction that here too the two distinguishing characteristics of modern realism are to be found; here too real everyday occurrences in a low social stratum, the provincial petty bourgeoisie, are taken very seriously (we shall discuss the particular character of this seriousness later); here too everyday occurrences are accurately and profoundly set in a definite period of contemporary history (the period of the bourgeois monarchy) – less obviously than in Stendhal or Balzac, but unmistakably. In these two basic characteristics the three writers are at one, in contradistinction to all earlier realism; but Flaubert's attitude toward his subject is entirely different. In Stendhal and Balzac we frequently and indeed almost constantly hear what the writer thinks of his characters and events; sometimes Balzac accompanies his narrative with a running commentary – emotional or ironic or ethical or historical or economic. We also very frequently hear what the characters themselves think and feel, and often in such a manner that, in the passage concerned, the writer identifies himself with the character. Both these things are almost wholly absent from Flaubert's work. His opinion of his characters and events remains unspoken; and when the characters express themselves it is never in such a manner that the writer identifies himself with their opinion, or seeks to make the reader identify himself with it. We hear the writer speak; but he expresses no opinion and makes no comment. His role is limited to selecting the events and translating them into language; and this is done in the conviction that every event, if one is able to express it purely and completely, interprets itself and the persons involved in it far better and more completely than any opinion or judgment appended to it could do. Upon this conviction – that is, upon a profound faith in the truth of language responsibly, candidly, and carefully employed – Flaubert's artistic practice rests.

This is a very old, classic French tradition. There is already something of it in Boileau's line concerning the power of the rightly used word (on Malherbe: *D'un mot mis en sa place enseigna le pouvoir*); there are similar statements in La Bruyère. Vauvenargues said: *Il n'y aurait point d'erreurs qui ne périssent d'elles-mêmes, exprimées clairement*. Flaubert's faith in language goes further than Vauvenargues's: he believes that the truth of the phenomenal world is also revealed in linguistic expression. Flaubert is a man who works extremely consciously and possesses a critical comprehension of art to a degree uncommon even in France; hence there occur in his letters, particularly of the years 1852–1854 during which he was writing *Madame Bovary (Troisième Série* in the *Nouvelle édition augmentée* of the *Correspondance, 1927)*, many highly informative statements on the subject of his aim in art. They lead to a theory – mystical in the last analysis, but in practice like all true mysticism, based upon reason, experience, and discipline – of a self-forgetful absorption in the subjects of reality which transforms them (*par une chimie merveilleuse)*) and permits them to develop to mature expression. In this fashion subjects completely fill the writer; he forgets himself, his heart no longer serves him save to feel the hearts of others, and when by fanatical patience, this condition is achieved, the perfect expression, which at once entirely comprehends the momentary subject and impartially judges it, comes of itself; subjects are seen as God sees them, in their true essence. With all this there goes a view of the mixture of styles which proceeds from the same mystical-realistic insight: there are no high and low subjects; the universe is a work of art produced without any taking of sides, the realistic artist must imitate the procedures of Creation, and every subject in its essence contains, before God's eyes, both the serious and the comic, both dignity and vulgarity; if it is rightly and surely reproduced, the level of style which is proper to it will be rightly and surely found; there is no need either for a general theory of levels, in which subjects are arranged according to their dignity, or for any analyses by the writer commenting upon the subject, after its presentation of the subject itself.

It is illuminating to note the contrast between such a view and the grandiloquent and ostentatious parading of the writer's own feelings, and of the standards derived from them, of the type inaugurated by Rousseau and continued after him; a comparative interpretation of Flaubert's *Notre cœur ne doit être bon qu'à sentir celui des autres*, and Rousseau's statement at the beginning of the Confessions, *Je sens mon cœur, et je connais les hommes*, could effectually represent the change in attitude which had taken place. But it also becomes clear from Flaubert's letters how laboriously and with what tensity of application he had attained to his convictions. Great subjects, and the free, irresponsible rule of the creative imagination, still have a great attraction for him; from this point of view he sees Shakespeare, Cervantes, and even Hugo wholly through the eyes of a romanticist, and he sometimes curses his own narrow petty-bourgeois subject which constrains him to tiresome stylistic meticulousness (*dire à la fois simplement et proprement des choses vulgaires)*; this sometimes goes so far that he says things which contradict his basic views: . . . *et ce qu'il y a de désolant, c'est de penser que, même réussi dans la perfection, cela [Madame Bovary] ne peut être que passable et ne sera jamais beau, à cause du fond même.* Withal, like so many important nineteenth-century artists, he hates his period; he sees its problems and the coming crises with great clarity; he sees the inner anarchy, the *manque de base théologique*, the beginning menace of the mob, the lazy eclectic Historism, the domination of phrases, but he sees no solution and no issue; his fanatical mysticism of art is almost like a substitute religion, to which he clings convulsively, and his candor very often becomes sullen, petty, choleric, and neurotic. But this sometimes perturbs his impartiality and that love of his subjects which is comparable to the Creator's love. The paragraph which we have analyzed, however, is untouched by such deficiencies and weaknesses in his nature; it permits us to observe the working of his artistic purpose in its purity.

The scene shows man and wife at table, the most everyday situation imaginable. Before Flaubert, it would have been conceivable as literature only as part of a comic tale, an idyll, or a satire. Here it is a picture of discomfort, and not a momentary and passing one, but a chronic discomfort, which completely rules an entire life, Emma Bovary's. To be sure, various things come later, among them love episodes; but no one could see the scene at table as part of the exposition for a love episode, just as no one would call *Madame Bovary* a love story in general. The novel is the representation of an entire human existence which has no issue; and our passage is a part of it, which however, contains the whole. Nothing particular happens in the scene, nothing particular has happened just before it. It is a random moment from the regularly recurring hours at which the husband and wife eat together. They are not quarreling, there is no sort of tangible conflict. Emma is in complete despair, but her despair is not occasioned by any definite catastrophe; there is nothing purely concrete which she has lost or for which she has wished. Certainly she has many wishes, but they are entirely vague – elegance, love, a varied life; there must always have been such unconcrete despair, but no one ever thought of taking it seriously in literary works before; such formless tragedy, if it may be called tragedy, which is set in motion by the general situation itself, was first made conceivable as literature by romanticism; probably Flaubert was the first to have represented it in people of slight intellectual culture and fairly low social station; certainly he is the first who directly captures the chronic character of this psychological situation. Nothing happens, but that nothing has become a heavy, oppressive, threatening something. How he accomplishes this we have already seen; he organizes into compact and unequivocal discourse the confused impressions of discomfort which arise in Emma at sight of the room, the meal, her husband. Elsewhere too he seldom narrates events which carry the action quickly forward; in a series of pure pictures – pictures transforming the nothingness of listless and uniform days into an oppressive condition of repugnance, boredom, false hopes, paralyzing disappointments, and piteous fears – a gray and random human destiny moves toward its end.

The interpretation of the situation is contained in its description. The two are sitting at table together; the husband divines nothing of his wife's inner state; they have so little communion that things never even come to a quarrel, an argument, an open conflict. Each of them is so immersed in his own world – she in despair and vague wish-dreams, he in his stupid philistine self-complacency – that they are both entirely alone; they have nothing in common, and yet they have nothing of their own, for the sake of which it would be worthwhile to be lonely. For, privately, each of them has a silly, false world, which cannot be reconciled with the reality of his situation, and so they both miss the possibilities life offers them. What is true of these two applies to almost all the other characters in the novel; each of the many mediocre people who act in it has his own world of mediocre and silly stupidity, a world of illusions, habits, instincts, and slogans; each is alone, none can understand another, or help another to insight; there is no common world of men, because it could only come into existence if many should find their way to their own proper reality, the reality which is given to the individual – which then would be also the true common reality. Though men come together for business and pleasure, their coming together has no note of united activity; it becomes one-sided, ridiculous, painful, and it is charged with misunderstanding, vanity, futility, falsehood, and stupid hatred. But what the world would really be, the world of the 'intelligent,' Flaubert never tells us; in his book the world consists of pure stupidity, which completely misses true reality, so that the latter should properly not be discoverable in it at all; yet it is there; it is in the writer's language, which unmasks the stupidity by pure statement; language, then, has criteria for stupidity and thus also has a part in that reality of the 'intelligent' which otherwise never appears in the book.

Emma Bovary, too, the principal personage of the novel, is completely submerged in that false reality, in *la bêtise humaine*, as is the 'hero' of Flaubert's other realistic novel, Frédéric Moreau in the *Education sentimentale*. How does Flaubert's manner of representing such personages fit into the traditional categories 'tragic' and 'comic'? Certainly Emma's existence is apprehended to its depths, certainly the earlier intermediate categories such as the 'sentimental' or the 'satiric' or the 'didactic,' are inapplicable, and very often the reader is moved by her fate in a way that appears very like tragic pity. But a real tragic heroine she is not. The way in which language here lays bare the silliness, immaturity, and disorder of her life, the very wretchedness of that life, in which she remains immersed (*toute l'amertume de l'existence lui semblait servie sur son assiette*), excludes the idea of true tragedy, and the author and the reader can never feel as at one with her as must be the case with the tragic hero; she is always being tried, judged, and, together with the entire world in which she is caught, condemned. But neither is she comic; surely not; for that, she is understood far too deeply from within her fateful entanglement – though Flaubert never practises any 'psychological understanding' but simply lets the state of the facts speak for itself. He has found an attitude toward the reality of contemporary life which is entirely different from earlier attitudes and stylistic levels, including – and especially – Balzac's and Stendhal's. It could be called, quite simply, 'objective seriousness.' This sounds strange as a designation of the style of a literary work. Objective seriousness, which seeks to penetrate to the depths of the passions and entanglements of a human life, but without itself becoming moved, or at least without betraying that it is moved – this is an attitude which one expects from a priest, a teacher, or a psychologist rather than from an artist. But priest, teacher, and psychologist wish to accomplish something direct and practical – which is far from Flaubert's mind. He wishes, by his attitude – *pas de cris, pas de convulsion, rien que la fixité d'un regard pensif* – to force language to render the truth concerning the subjects of his observation: 'style itself and in its own right being an absolute manner of viewing things' (*Corr.* 2, 346). Yet this leads in the end to a didactic purpose: criticism of the contemporary world; and we must not hesitate to say so, much as Flaubert may insist that he is an artist and nothing but an artist. The more one studies Flaubert, the clearer it becomes how much insight into the problematic nature and the hollowness of nineteenth-century bourgeois culture is contained in his realistic works; and many important passages from his letters confirm this. The demonification of everyday social intercourse which is to be found in Balzac is certainly entirely lacking in Flaubert; life no longer surges and foams, it flows viscously and sluggishly. The essence of the happenings of ordinary contemporary life seemed to Flaubert to consist not in tempestuous actions and passions, not in demonic men and forces, but in the prolonged chronic state whose surface movement is mere empty bustle, while underneath it there is another movement, almost imperceptible but universal and unceasing, so that the political, economic, and social subsoil appears comparatively stable and at the same time intolerably charged with tension. Events seem to him hardly to change; but in the concretion of duration, which Flaubert is able to suggest both in the individual occurrence (as in our example) and in his total picture of the times, there appears something like a concealed threat: the period is charged with its stupid issuelessness as with an explosive.

Through his level of style, a systematic and objective seriousness, from which things themselves speak and, according to their value, classify themselves before the reader as tragic or comic, or in most cases quite unobtrusively as both, Flaubert overcame the romantic vehemence and uncertainty in the treatment óf contemporary subjects; there is clearly something of the earlier positivism in his idea of art, although he sometimes speaks very derogatorily of Comte. On the basis of this objectivity, further developments became possible, with which we shall deal in later chapters. However, few of his successors conceived the task of representing contemporary reality with the same clarity and responsibility as he; though among them there were certainly freer, more spontaneous, and more richly endowed minds than his.

The serious treatment of everyday reality, the rise of more extensive and socially inferior human groups to the position of subject matter for problematic-existential representation, on the one hand; on the other, the embedding of random persons and events in the general course of contemporary history, the fluid historical background – these, we believe, are the foundations of modern realism, and it is natural that the broad and elastic form of the novel should increasingly impose itself for a rendering comprising so many elements. If our view is correct, throughout the nineteenth century France played the most important part in the rise and development of modern realism.

10 Ian Watt on Realism and the Novel Form*

There are still no wholly satisfactory answers to many of the general questions which anyone interested in the early eighteenth-century novelists and their works is likely to ask: Is the novel a new literary form? And if we assume, as is commonly done, that it is, and that it was begun by Defoe, Richardson and Fielding, how does it differ from the prose fiction of the past, from that of Greece, for example, or that of the Middle Ages, or of seventeenth-century France? And is there any reason why these differences appeared when and where they did?

Such large questions are never easy to approach, much less to answer, and they are particularly difficult in this case because Defoe, Richardson and Fielding do not in the usual sense constitute a literary school. Indeed their works show so little sign of mutual influence and are so different in nature that at first sight it appears that our curiosity about the rise of the novel is unlikely to find any satisfaction other than the meagre one afforded by the terms 'genius' and 'accident', the twin faces on the Janus of the dead ends of literary history. We cannot, of course, do without them: on the other hand there is not much we can do with them. The present inquiry therefore takes another direction: assuming that the appearance of our first three novelists within a single generation was probably not sheer accident, and that their geniuses could not have created the new form unless the conditions of the time had also been favourable, it attempts to discover what these favourable conditions in the literary and social situation were, and in what ways Defoe, Richardson and Fielding were its beneficiaries.

For this investigation our first need is a working definition of the characteristics of the novel – a definition sufficiently narrow to exclude previous types of narrative and yet broad enough to apply to whatever is usually put in the novel category. The novelists themselves do not help us very much here. It is true that both Richardson and Fielding saw

---

* Reprinted from 'Realism and the Novel Form' in *The Rise of the Novel* (Berkeley: University of California Press, 1957), pp. 9–18.

themselves as founders of a new kind of writing, and that both viewed their work as involving a break with the old-fashioned romances; but neither they nor their contemporaries provide us with the kind of characterisation of the new genre that we need; indeed they did not even canonise the changed nature of their fiction by a change in nomenclature – our usage of the term 'novel' was not fully established until the end of the eighteenth century.

With the help of their larger perspective the historians of the novel have been able to do much more to determine the idiosyncratic features of the new form. Briefly, they have seen 'realism' as the defining characteristic which differentiates the work of the early eighteenth-century novelists from previous fiction. With their picture – that of writers otherwise different but alike in this quality of 'realism' – one's initial reservation must surely be that the term itself needs further explanation, if only because to use it without qualification as a defining characteristic of the novel might otherwise carry the invidious suggestion that all previous writers and literary forms pursued the unreal.

The main critical associations of the term 'realism' are with the French school of Realists. '*Réalisme*' was apparently first used as an aesthetic description in 1835 to denote the '*vérité humaine*' of Rembrandt as opposed to the '*idéalité poétique*' of neo-classical painting; it was later consecrated as a specifically literary term by the foundation in 1856 of *Réalisme*, a journal edited by Duranty.[1]

Unfortunately much of the usefulness of the word was soon lost in the bitter controversies over the 'low' subjects and allegedly immoral tendencies of Flaubert and his successors. As a result, 'realism' came to be used primarily as the antonym of 'idealism', and this sense, which is actually a reflection of the position taken by the enemies of the French Realists, has in fact coloured much critical and historical writing about the novel. The prehistory of the form has commonly been envisaged as a matter of tracing the continuity between all earlier fiction which portrayed low life: the story of the Ephesian matron is 'realistic' because it shows that sexual appetite is stronger than wifely sorrow; and the fabliau or the picaresque tale are 'realistic' because economic or carnal motives are given pride of place in their presentation of human behaviour. By the same implicit premise, the English eighteenth-century novelists, together with Furetière, Scarron and Lesage in France, are regarded as the eventual climax of this tradition: the 'realism' of the novels of Defoe, Richardson and Fielding is closely associated with the fact that Moll Flanders is a thief, Pamela a hypocrite, and Tom Jones a fornicator.

This use of 'realism', however, has the grave defect of obscuring what is probably the most original feature of the novel form. If the novel were realistic merely because it saw life from the seamy side, it would only be an inverted romance; but in fact it surely attempts to portray all the varieties of human experience, and not merely those suited to one particular literary perspective: the novel's realism does not reside in the kind of life it presents, but in the way it presents it.

This, of course, is very close to the position of the French Realists themselves, who asserted that if their novels tended to differ from the more flattering pictures of humanity presented by many established ethical, social and literary codes, it was merely because they were the product of a more dispassionate and scientific scrutiny of life than had ever been attempted before. It is far from clear that this ideal of scientific objectivity is desirable, and it certainly cannot be realised in practice: nevertheless it is very significant that, in the first sustained effort of the new genre to become critically aware of its aims and methods, the French Realists should have drawn attention to an issue which the novel raises more sharply than any other literary form – the problem of the correspondence between the literary work and the reality which it imitates. This is essentially an epistemological problem, and it therefore seems likely that the nature of the novel's realism, whether in the early eighteenth century or later, can best be clarified by the help of those professionally concerned with the analysis of concepts, the philosophers.

I

By a paradox that will surprise only the neophyte, the term 'realism' in philosophy is most strictly applied to a view of reality diametrically opposed to that of common usage – to the view held by the scholastic Realists of the Middle Ages that it is universals, classes or abstractions, and not the particular, concrete objects of sense-perception, which are the true 'realities'. This, at first sight, appears unhelpful, since in the novel, more than in any other genre, general truths only exist *post res*; but the very unfamiliarity of the point of view of scholastic Realism at least serves to draw attention to a characteristic of the novel which is analogous to the changed philosophical meaning of 'realism' today: the novel arose in the modern period, a period whose general intellectual orientation was most decisively separated from its classical and mediaeval heritage by its rejection – or at least its attempted rejection – of universals.[2]

Modern realism, of course, begins from the position that truth can be discovered by the individual through his senses: it has its origins in Descartes and Locke, and received its first full formulation by Thomas Reid in the middle of the eighteenth century.[3] But the view that the external world is real, and that our senses give us a true report of it, obviously does not in itself throw much light on literary realism; since almost everyone, in all ages, has in one way or another been forced to some such conclusion about the external world by his own experience, literature has always been to some extent exposed to the same epistemological naïveté. Further, the distinctive tenets of realist epistemology, and the controversies associated with them, are for the most part much too specialised in nature to have much bearing on literature. What is important to the novel in philosophical realism is much less specific; it is rather the general temper of realist thought, the methods of investigation it has used, and the kinds of problems it has raised.

The general temper of philosophical realism has been critical, anti-traditional and innovating; its method has been the study of the particulars of experience by the individual investigator, who, ideally at least, is free from the body of past assumptions and traditional beliefs; and it has given a peculiar importance to semantics, to the problem of the nature of the correspondence between words and reality. All of these features of philosophical realism have analogies to distinctive features of the novel form, analogies which draw attention to the characteristic kind of correspondence between life and literature which has obtained in prose fiction since the novels of Defoe and Richardson.

(a)
The greatness of Descartes was primarily one of method, of the thoroughness of his determination to accept nothing on trust; and his *Discourse on Method* (1637) and his *Meditations* did much to bring about the modern assumption whereby the pursuit of truth is conceived of as a wholly individual matter, logically independent of the tradition of past thought, and indeed as more likely to be arrived at by a departure from it.

The novel is the form of literature which most fully reflects this individualist and innovating·reorientation. Previous literary forms had reflected the general tendency of their cultures to make conformity to traditional practice the major test of truth: the plots of classical and renaissance epic, for example, were based on past history or fable, and the merits of the author's treatment were judged largely according to a view of literary decorum derived from the accepted models in the genre. This literary traditionalism was first and most fully challenged by the novel, whose primary criterion was truth to individual experience – individual experience which is always unique and therefore new. The novel is thus the logical literary vehicle of a culture which, in the last few centuries, has set an unprecedented value on originality, on the novel; and it is therefore well named.

This emphasis on the new accounts for some of the critical difficulties which the novel is widely agreed to present. When we judge a work in another genre, a recognition of its literary models is often important and sometimes essential; our evaluation depends to a large extent on our analysis of the author's skill in handling the appropriate formal conventions. On the other hand, it is surely very damaging for a novel to be in any sense an imitation of another literary work: and the reason for this seems to be that since the novelist's primary task is to convey the impression of fidelity to human experience, attention to any pre-established formal conventions can only endanger his success. What is often felt as the formlessness of the novel, as compared, say, with tragedy or the ode, probably follows from this: the poverty of the novel's formal conventions would seem to be the price it must pay for its realism.

But the absence of formal conventions in the novel is unimportant compared to its rejection of traditional plots. Plot, of course, is not a simple matter, and the degree of its originality or otherwise is never easy to determine; nevertheless a broad and necessarily summary comparison between the novel and previous literary forms reveals an important difference: Defoe and Richardson are the first great writers in our literature who did not take their plots from mythology, history, legend or previous literature. In this they differ from Chaucer, Spenser, Shakespeare and Milton, for instance, who, like the writers of Greece and Rome, habitually used traditional plots; and who did so, in the last analysis, because they accepted the general premise of their times that, since Nature is essentially complete and unchanging, its records, whether scriptural, legendary or historical, constitute a definitive repertoire of human experience.

This point of view continued to be expressed until the nineteenth century; the opponents of Balzac, for example, used it to deride his preoccupation with contemporary and, in their view, ephemeral reality. But at the same time, from the Renaissance onwards, there was a growing tendency for individual experience to replace collective tradition as the ultimate arbiter of reality; and this transition would seem to constitute an important part of the general cultural background of the rise of the novel.

It is significant that the trend in favour of originality found its first powerful expression in England, and in the eighteenth century; the very word 'original' took on its modern meaning at this time, by a semantic reversal which is a parallel to the change in the meaning of 'realism'. We have seen that, from the mediaeval belief in the reality of universals, 'realism' had come to denote a belief in the individual apprehension of reality through the senses: similarly the term 'original' which in the Middle Ages had meant 'having existed from the first' came to mean 'underived, independent, first-hand'; and by the time that Edward Young in his epoch-making *Conjectures on Original Composition* (1759) hailed Richardson as 'a genius as well moral as original',[4] the word could be used as a term of praise meaning 'novel or fresh in character or style'.

The novel's use of non-traditional plots is an early and probably independent manifestation of this emphasis. When Defoe, for example, began to write fiction he took little notice of the dominant critical theory of the day, which still inclined towards the use of traditional plots; instead, he merely allowed his narrative order to flow spontaneously from his own sense of what his protagonists might plausibly do next. In so doing Defoe initiated an important new tendency in fiction: his total subordination of the plot to the pattern of the autobiographical memoir is as defiant an assertion of the primacy of individual experience in the novel as Descartes's *cogito ergo sum* was in philosophy.

After Defoe, Richardson and Fielding in their very different ways continued what was to become the novel's usual practice, the use of non-traditional plots, either wholly invented or based in part on a contemporary incident. It cannot be claimed that either of them completely achieved that interpenetration of plot, character and emergent moral theme which is found in the highest examples of the art of the novel. But it must be remembered that the task was not an easy one, particularly at a time when the established literary outlet for the creative imagination lay in eliciting an individual pattern and a contemporary significance from a plot that was not itself novel.

(b)
Much else besides the plot had to be changed in the tradition of fiction before the novel could embody the individual apprehension of reality as freely as the method of Descartes and Locke allowed their thought to spring from the immediate facts of consciousness. To begin with, the actors in the plot and the scene of their actions had to be placed in a new literary perspective: the plot had to be acted out by particular people in particular circumstances, rather than, as had been common in the past, by general human types against a background primarily determined by the appropriate literary convention.

This literary change was analogous to the rejection of universals and the emphasis on particulars which characterises philosophic realism. Aristotle might have agreed with Locke's primary assumption, that it was the senses which 'at first let in particular ideas, and furnish the empty cabinet' of the mind.[5] But he would have gone on to insist that the scrutiny of particular cases was of little value in itself; the proper intellectual task of man was to rally against the meaningless flux of sensation, and achieve a knowledge of the universals which alone constituted the ultimate and immutable reality.[6] It is this generalising emphasis which gives most Western thought until the seventeenth century a strong enough family resemblance to outweigh all its other multifarious differences: similarly when in 1713 Berkeley's Philonous affirmed that 'it is an universally received maxim, that *everything which exists is particular*',[7] he was stating the opposite modern tendency which in turn gives modern thought since Descartes a certain unity of outlook and method.

Here, again, both the new trends in philosophy and the related formal characteristics of the novel were contrary to the dominant literary outlook. For the critical tradition in the early eighteeth century was still governed by the strong classical preference for the general and universal: the proper object of literature remained *quod semper quod ubique ab omnibus creditum est*. This preference was particularly pronounced in the neo-Platonist tendency, which had always been strong in the romance, and which was becoming of increasing importance in literary criticism and aesthetics generally. Shaftesbury, for instance, in his *Essay on the Freedom of Wit and Humour* (1709), expressed the distaste of this school of thought for particularity in literature and art very emphatically: 'The variety of Nature is such, as to distinguish every thing she forms, by a *peculiar* original character; which, if strictly observed, will make the subject appear unlike to anything extant in the world besides. But this effect the good poet and painter seek industriously to prevent. They hate *minuteness,* and are afraid of *singularity.*'[8] He continued: 'The mere Face-Painter, indeed, has little in common with the Poet; but, like the mere Historian, copies what he sees, and minutely traces every feature, and odd mark'; and concluded confidently that "Tis otherwise with men of invention and design.'

Despite Shaftesbury's engaging finality, however, a contrary aesthetic tendency in favour of particularity soon began to assert itself, largely as a result of the application to literary problems of the psychological approach of Hobbes and Locke. Lord Kames was perhaps the most forthright early spokesman of this tendency. In his *Elements of Criticism* (1762) he declared that 'abstract or general terms have no good effect in any composition for amusement; because it is only of particular objects that images can be formed';[9] and Kames went on to claim that, contrary to general opinion, Shakespeare's appeal lay in the fact that 'every article in his descriptions is particular, as in nature'.

In this matter, as in that of originality, Defoe and Richardson established the characteristic literary directions of the novel form long before it could count on any support from critical theory. Not all will agree with Kames that 'every article' in Shakespeare's descriptions is particular; but particularity of description has always been considered typical of the narrative manner of *Robinson Crusoe* and *Pamela*. Richardson's first biographer, indeed, Mrs Barbauld, described his genius in terms of an analogy which has continually figured in the controversy between neo-classical generality and realistic particularity. Sir Joshua Reynolds, for example, expressed his neo-classical orthodoxy by preferring the 'great and general ideas' of Italian painting to the 'literal

Humanist Readings

truth and . . . minute exactness in the detail of nature modified by accident' of the Dutch school;[10] whereas the French Realists, it will be remembered, had followed the *'vérité humaine'* of Rembrandt, rather than the *'idéalité poétique'* of the classical school. Mrs Barbauld accurately indicated Richardson's position in this conflict when she wrote that he had 'the accuracy of finish of a Dutch painter . . . content to produce effects by the patient labour of minuteness'.[11] Both he and Defoe, in fact, were heedless of Shaftesbury's scorn, and like Rembrandt were content to be 'mere face-painters and historians'.

The concept of realistic particularity in literature is itself somewhat too general to be capable of concrete demonstration: for such demonstration to be possible the relationship of realistic particularity to some specific aspects of narrative technique must first be established. Two such aspects suggest themselves as of especial importance in the novel – characterisation, and presentation of background: the novel is surely distinguished from other genres and from previous forms of fiction by the amount of attention it habitually accords both to the individualisation of its characters and to the detailed presentation of their environment.

Notes

1. See BERNARD WEINBERG, *French Realism: The Critical Reaction 1830–1870* (London, 1937), p. 114.

2. See R. I. AARON, *The Theory of Universals* (Oxford, 1952), pp. 18–41.

3. See S. Z. HASAN, *Realism* (Cambridge, 1928), Chs 1 and 2.

4. *Works* (1773), V, 125; see also MAX SCHELER, *Versuche zu einer Soziologie des Wissens* (München and Leipzig, 1924), pp. 104ff.; ELIZABETH L. MANN, 'The Problem of Originality in English Literary Criticism, 1750–1800', *PQ*, XVIII (1939), 97–118.

5. *Essay Concerning Human Understanding* (1690), Bk I, Ch. 2, sect. xv.

6. See *Posterior Analytics*, Bk I, Ch. 24; Bk II, Ch. 19.

7. First *Dialogue between Hylas and Philonous*, 1713 (Berkeley, *Works*, ed. Luce and Jessop (London, 1949), II, 192).

8. Pt IV, sect. 3.

9. 1763 edn, III, 198–9.

10. *Idler*, No. 79 (1759). See also SCOTT ELLEDGE, 'The Background and Development in English Criticism of the Theories of Generality and Particularity', *PMLA*, LX (1945), 161–74.

11. *Correspondence of Samuel Richardson*, 1804, I, CXXXVII. For similar comments by contemporary French readers, see JOSEPH TEXTE, *Jean-Jacques Rousseau and the Cosmopolitan Spirit in Literature* (London, 1899), pp. 174–5.

Part Three

Modern Readings

Marxist

The two essays representative of Marxist readings of realism were published some thirty years apart: Georg (György) Lukács' piece on Balzac's *Lost Illusions* (*Illusions perdues*, 1837) originally appeared in the late 1930s but was translated into English only in 1950 (trans. Edith Bone, London: Hillway Press). Pierre Macherey's essay on Balzac's *The Peasants* (*Les Paysans*, 1844) came out in 1966 in his collection *Pour une théorie de la production littéraire*, translated in 1978 by Geoffrey Wall as *A Theory of Literary Production* (London: Routledge & Kegan Paul).

Lukács is a classic Marxist, who holds that literature can be properly understood only within the larger framework of the society that has shaped it. He therefore applies to it the reflection model, which assumes that the text is a direct reflection of a social reality, and which is particularly apt to the realist novel with its self-proclaimed mimetic intent. Lukács envisages *Lost Illusions* as giving a terrifyingly accurate picture of the workings of the capitalist system and its effect on all who live under it. He dwells on the impact of rising capitalism and the consequent **commodification** of all goods, including literature.

Macherey's approach differs significantly from Lukács' in that he has developed an alternative model of the relationship between social reality and the literary work – one that places major emphasis on the concept of production. He sees literature as a form of productive labour, in which raw materials are turned into an end-product. In his discussion of *Les Paysans* he shows how the text was produced out of the combination of an encounter with the prevailing social reality and the author's ideology. But, he argues, the novel is not merely an expression of Balzac's ideology and the reflection of its social background; it is rather a fictional production of both these elements. As a result, it is necessarily 'disparate', i.e. contradictory and incomplete, and of special interest for the tensions it embodies.

11   Georg Lukács on Balzac's *Lost Illusions**

Balzac wrote this novel in the fullness of his maturity as a writer; with it he created a new type of novel which was destined to influence decisively the literary development of the nineteenth century. This new type of novel was the novel of disillusionment, which shows how the conception of life of those living in a *bourgeois* society – a conception which although false, is yet necessarily what it is – is shattered by the brute forces of capitalism.

It was not, of course, in the works of Balzac that the shipwreck of illusions made its first appearance in the modern novel.

The first great novel, Cervantes' *Don Quixote*, is also a story of lost illusions. But in *Don Quixote* it is the nascent *bourgeois* world which destroys the still lingering feudal illusions; in Balzac's novel it is the conceptions of mankind, human society, art, etc., necessarily engendered by *bourgeois* development itself – i.e. the highest ideological products of the revolutionary development of the *bourgeoisie* – which are shown to be empty illusions when measured by the standards set by the realities of capitalist economy.

The eighteenth-century novel also dealt with the destruction of certain illusions, but these illusions were feudal survivals still lingering in the sphere of thoughts and emotions; or else certain groundless, pedestrian conceptions imperfectly anchored in reality were dispelled by another more complete conception of the same reality viewed from the same angle.

But it is in this novel of Balzac that the bitter laughter of derision at the highest ideological products of *bourgeois* development itself is heard for the first time – it is here that we see for the first time, shown in its totality, the tragic self-dissolution of *bourgeois* ideals by their own economic basis, by the forces of capitalism. Diderot's immortal masterpiece *The Nephew of Rameau* is the only work that can be regarded as the ideological precursor of this Balzac novel.

---

* Reprinted from 'Balzac: *Lost Illusions*' in *Studies in European Realism*, trans. Edith Bone (London: Hillway, 1950), pp. 47–60, 63–4.

Of course Balzac was by no means the only writer of the time who chose this theme. Stendhal's *Scarlet and Black* and Musset's *Confessions of a Child of the Century* even preceded *Lost Illusions* in time. The theme was in the air, not because of some literary fashion but because it was thrown up by social evolution in France, the country that provided the pattern for the political growth of the *bourgeoisie* everywhere. The heroic epochs of the French revolution and the First Empire had awakened, mobilized and developed all the dormant energies of the *bourgeois* class. This heroic epoch gave the best elements of the *bourgeoisie* the opportunity for the immediate translation into reality of their heroic ideals, the opportunity to live and to die heroically in accordance with those ideals. This heroic period came to an end with the fall of Napoleon, the return of the Bourbons and the July revolution. The ideals became superfluous ornaments and frills on the sober reality of everyday life and the path of capitalism, opened up by the revolution and by Napoleon, broadened into a convenient, universally accessible highway of development. The heroic pioneers had to disappear and make way for the humanly inferior exploiters of the new development, the speculators and racketeers.

'*Bourgeois* society in its sober reality had produced its true interpreters and spokesmen in the Says, the Cousins, the Royer-Collards, the Benjamin Constants, the Guizots; its real generals sat at the counting-house desks and their political head was the fat-head Louis XVIII' (Marx).

The drive of ideals, a necessary product of the previous necessarily heroic period, was now no longer wanted; its representatives, the young generation schooled in the traditions of the heroic period, were inevitably doomed to deteriorate.

This inevitable degradation and frustration of the energies born of the revolution and the Napoleonic era was a theme common to all novels of disillusionment of the period, an indictment common to them all of the prosaic scurviness of the Bourbon restoration and the July monarchy. Balzac, although politically a royalist and legitimist, yet saw this character of the restoration with merciless clarity. He writes in *Lost Illusions*:

'Nothing is such a condemnation of the slavery to which the restoration has condemned our youth. The young men who did not know what to do with their strength, have harnessed only to journalism, political conspiracies and the arts, but in strange excesses as well . . . If they worked, they demanded power and pleasure; as artists, they desired treasures, as idlers passionate excitement – but be that as it may, they demanded a place for themselves and politics refused it to them . . .'

It was the tragedy of a whole generation and the recognition of this fact and the portrayal of it is common to Balzac and his contemporaries both great and small; but in spite of this common trait, *Lost Illusions* in its portrayal of the time rises to a solitary height far above any other French literary work of the period. For Balzac did not content himself with the recognition and description of this tragic or tragi-comic social situation. He saw farther and delved deeper.

He saw that the end of the heroic period of French *bourgeois* evolution was at the same time the beginning of the rapid development of French capitalism. In almost every one of his novels Balzac depicts this capitalist development, and the transformation of traditional handicrafts into modern capitalist production; he shows how stormily accumulating money-capital usuriously exploits town and countryside and how the old social formations and ideologies must yield before its triumphant onslaught.

Lost Illusions is a tragi-comic epic showing how, within this general process, the spirit of man is drawn into the orbit of capitalism. The theme of the novel is the transformation of literature (and with it of every ideology) into a commodity and this complete 'capitalization' of every sphere of intellectual, literary and artistic activity fits the general tragedy of the post-Napoleonic generation into a much more profoundly conceived social pattern than can be found in the writings even of Stendhal, Balzac's greatest contemporary.

The transformation of literature into a commodity is painted by Balzac in great detail. From the writer's ideas, emotions and convictions to the paper on which he writes them down, everything is turned into a commodity that can be bought and sold. Nor is Balzac content merely to register in general terms the ideological consequences of the rule of capitalism – he uncovers every stage in the concrete process of 'capitalization' in every sphere (the periodical press, the theatre, the publishing business, etc.) together with all the factors governing the process.

'What is fame?' asks Dauriat, the publisher, and answers himself: 'Twelve thousand francs' worth of newspaper articles and three thousand francs' worth of dinners. . . .' Then he expounds: 'I haven't the slightest intention of risking two thousand francs on a book merely in order to make the same amount by it. I speculate in literature; I publish forty volumes in an edition of ten thousand copies each. – My power and the newspaper articles which I get published thus, bring me in business to the value of three hundred thousand francs, instead of a measly two thousand. A manuscript which I buy for a hundred thousand francs is cheaper than the manuscript of an unknown author which I can get for a mere 600 francs.'

The writers think as the publishers do.

'Do you really believe what you write?' Vernon asks sarcastically. 'But surely we are word-merchants and are talking shop . . . The articles that the public reads today and has forgotten by tomorrow have no other meaning for us save that we get paid for them.'

With all this, the writers and journalists are exploited, their talent has become a commodity, an object of profiteering by the capitalist speculators who deal in literature. They are exploited but they are also prostitutes; their ambition is to become exploiters themselves or at least overseers over other exploited colleagues. Before Lucien de Rubempré turns journalist, his colleague and mentor Lousteau explains the situation to him in these terms:

'Mark this, my boy: in literature the secret of success is not work, but the exploitation of the work done by others. The newspaper-owners are the building contractors and we are the bricklayers. The more mediocre a man is, the sooner he will reach his goal, for he will at need be willing to swallow a frog, and do anything else to flatter the passions of the little literary sultans. Today you are still severe and have a conscience, but to-morrow your conscience will bow to the ground before those who can tear success from your grasp and those who could give you life by a single word and yet refuse to speak that word, for believe me, a fashionable author is haughtier and harsher towards the new generation than the most leech-like of publishers. Where the publisher sees only a loss of money, the fashionable author fears a rival; the publisher merely rejects the beginner, the fashionable author annihilates him.'

This breadth of the theme – the capitalization of literature, embracing everything from the manufacturing of paper to the lyrical sensibility of a poet, determines the artistic form of the composition in this as in all other works of Balzac. The friendship between David Séchard and Lucien de Rubempré, the shattered illusions of their enthusiastic youth and their mutually complementary contrasting characters are the elements that provide the general outline of the story. Balzac's genius manifests itself even in this basic lay-out of the composition. The objective tensions inherent in the theme are expressed through the human passions and individual aspirations of the characters: David Séchard, the inventor who discovers a cheaper method of making paper but is swindled by the capitalists, and Lucien de Rubempré, the poet who carries the purest and most delicate lyrical poems to the capitalist market of Paris. On the other hand, the contrast between the two characters demonstrates the extremely different ways in which men can react to the abominations accompanying the transition to capitalism. David Séchard is a puritan stoic while Lucien de Rubempré incarnates perfectly the sensual love of pleasure and the rootless, over-refined epicureanism of the post-revolutionary generation.

Balzac's composition is never pedantic; unlike his later successors he never affects a dry 'scientific' attitude. In his writings the unfolding of material problems is always indissolubly bound up with the consequences arising from the personal passions of his characters. This method of composition – although it seems to take the individual alone for its starting-point – contains a deeper understanding of social interconnections and implications, a more correct evaluation of the trends of social development than does the pedantic, 'scientific' method of the later realists.

In *Lost Illusions* Balzac focuses his story on Lucien de Rubempré's fate and with it the transformation of literature into a commodity; the capitalization of the material basis of literature, the capitalist exploitation of technical progress is only an episodic final chord. This method of composition, which apparently reverses the logical and objective connection between the material basis and the **superstructure**, is extremely skilful both from the artistic point of view and from the angle of social criticism. It is artistically skilful because the rich diversity of Lucien's changing destinies, unfolded before our eyes in the course of his struggle for fame, provides a much more colourful, lively and complete picture than the pettily infamous intrigues of the provincial capitalists out to swindle David Séchard. It is skilful from the point of view of social criticism because Lucien's fate involves in its entirety the question of the destruction of culture by capitalism. Séchard, in resigning himself to his fate, quite correctly feels that what is really essential is that his invention should be put to good use; the fact that he has been swindled is merely his personal bad luck. But Lucien's catastrophe represents at the same time the capitalist debasement and prostitution of literature itself.

The contrast between the two principal characters illustrates most vividly the two main types of personal reaction to the transformation of ideology into a commodity. Séchard's reaction is to resign himself to the inevitable.

Resignation plays a very important part in the *bourgeois* literature of the nineteenth century. The aged Goethe was one of the first to strike this note of resignation. It was the symptom of a new period in the evolution of the *bourgeoisie*. Balzac in his utopian novels follows in Goethe's footsteps: only those who have given up or who must give up their personal happiness can pursue social, non-selfish aims. Séchard's resignation is, of course, of a somewhat different nature. He gives up the struggle, abandons the pursuit of any aim and wants only to live for his personal happiness in peace and seclusion. Those who wish to remain pure must withdraw from all capitalist business – it is in this, not ironical, not in the least Voltairean sense that David Séchard withdraws to 'cultivate his own garden'.

Lucien for his part plunges into life in Paris; he is determined to win through and establish the rights and power of 'pure poetry'. This struggle makes him one of those post-Napoleonic young men who either perished with polluted souls during the restoration or adapted themselves to the filth of an age turned unheroic and in it carved a career for themselves, like Julien Sorel, Rastignac, de Marsay, Blondet and others of the same kidney. Lucien belongs to the latter group but occupies an entirely independent position in this company. With admirable daring and sensitivity Balzac created a new, specifically *bourgeois* type of poet: the poet as an Aeolian harp sounding to the veering winds and tempests of society, the poet as a rootless, aimlessly drifting, over-sensitive bundle of nerves, – a type of poet as yet very rare in this period, but most characteristic for the subsequent evolution of *bourgeois* poetry from Verlaine to Rilke. This type is diametrically opposed to what Balzac himself wanted the poet to be; he portrayed his ideal poet in the person of Daniel D'Arthez, a character in this novel who is intended for a self-portrait.

The characterization of Lucien is not only true to type, it also provides the opportunity for unfolding all the contradictions engendered by the penetration of capitalism into literature. The intrinsic contradiction between Lucien's talent and his human weakness and rootlessness makes him a plaything of the political and literary trends exploited by the capitalists. It is this mixture of instability and ambition, the combination of a hankering for a pure and honourable life with a boundless but erratic ambition, which makes possible the brilliant rise of Lucien, his rapid prostitution and his final ignominious disaster. Balzac never serves up his heroes with a sauce of morality; he shows the objective dialectic of their rise or fall, always motivating both by the total sum of their own natures and the mutual interaction of this their nature with the total sum of objective circumstances, never by any isolated value-judgment of their 'good' and 'bad' qualities.

Rastignac, the climber, is no worse than Lucien, but in him a different mixture of talent and demoralization is at work, which enables him adroitly to turn to his own advantage the same reality on which Lucien, for all his naive Machiavellianism, is shipwrecked both materially and morally.

Balzac's sour remark in *Melmoth Reconciled* that men are either cashiers or embezzlers, i.e. either honest fools or clever rogues, is proved true in endless variety in this tragi-comic epic of the capitalization of the spirit.

Thus the ultimate integrating principle of this novel is the social process itself and its real subject is the advance and victory of capitalism. Lucien's personal catastrophe is the typical fate of the poet and of true poetic talent in the world of fully developed capitalism.

Nevertheless Balzac's composition is not abstractly objective and this novel is not a novel with a theme, not a novel relating, in the manner of the later novelists, to one sphere of society alone, although Balzac by a most subtle weaving of his story introduces every feature of the capitalization of literature and brings onto the scene none but these features of capitalism. But here as in all other works of Balzac the general social fabric is never directly shown on the surface. His characters are never mere lay figures expressing certain aspects of the social reality he wants to present. The aggregate of social determinants is expressed in an uneven, intricate, confused and contradictory pattern, in a labyrinth of personal passions and chance happenings. The characters and situations are always determined by the totality of the socially decisive forces, but never simply and never directly. For this reason this so completely universal novel is at the same time the story of one particular individual, an individual different from all others. Lucien de Rubempré, on the stage, seems to react independently to the internal and external forces which hamper his rise and which help or hinder him as a result of apparently fortuitous personal circumstances or passions, but which, whatever form they take, always spring from the same social environment which determines his aspirations and ambition.

This unity of the multifarious is a feature peculiar to Balzac; it is the poetic form in which he expresses his conception of the working of social forces. Unlike many other great novelists he does not resort to any machinery such as, for instance, the tower in *Wilhelm Meister's Apprenticeship*; every cog in the mechanism of a Balzacian plot is a complete, living human being with specific personal interests, passions, tragedies and comedies. The bond which links each character with the whole of the story is provided by some element in the make-up of the character itself, always in full accordance with the tendencies inherent to it. As this link always develops organically out of the interests, passions etc. of the character, it appears necessary and vital. But it is the broader inner urges and compulsions of the characters themselves which give them fulness of life and render them non-mechanical, no mere components of the plot. Such a conception of the characters necessarily causes them to burst out of the story. Broad and spacious as Balzac's plots are, the stage is crowded by so many actors living such richly varied lives that only a few of them can be fully developed within one story.

This seems a deficiency of Balzac's method of composition; in reality it is what gives his novels their full-blooded vitality and it is also what made the cyclic form a necessity for him. His remarkable and nevertheless typical characters cannot unfold their personality fully within a single novel, but only certain features of it and that only episodically; they protrude beyond the framework of one novel and demand another, the plot and theme of which permit them to occupy the centre of the stage and develop to the full all their qualities and possibilities. The characters who remain in the background in *Lost Illusions*, Blondet, Rastignac, Nathan, Michel Chrestien, play leading parts in other novels. The cyclical interdependence of Balzac's novels derives from his urge to develop every one of his characters to the full and hence is never dry and pedantic as cyclic novels of other, even very

good writers, so often are. For the several parts of the cycle are never
determined by circumstances external to the characters, i.e. by
chronological or objective limits.

The general is thus always concrete and real because it is based on a
profound understanding of what is typical in each of the characters
figuring in it – an understanding so deep that the particular is not
eclipsed but on the contrary emphasized and concretized by the typical,
and on the other hand the relationship between the individual and the
social setting of which it is the product and in which – or against which –
it acts, is always clearly discernible, however intricate this relationship
may be. The Balzac characters, complete within themselves, live and act
within a concrete, complexly stratified social reality and it is always the
totality of the social process that is linked with the totality of the
character. The power of Balzac's imagination manifests itself in his ability
to select and manipulate his characters in such a way that the centre of
the stage is always occupied by the figure whose personal, individual
qualities are the most suitable for the demonstration, as extensively as
possible and in transparent connection with the whole, of some
important single aspect of the social process. The several parts of a
Balzacian cycle have their own independent life because each of them
deals with individual destinies. But these individual destinies are always
a radiation of the socially typical, of the socially universal, which can be
separated from the individual only by an analysis *a posteriori*. In the
novels themselves the individual and the general are inseparably united,
like a fire with the heat it radiates. Thus, in *Lost Illusions* the development
of Lucien's character is inseparably bound up with the capitalist
penetration of literature.

Such a method of composition demands an extremely broad basis for
characterization and plot. Breadth is also required to exclude the element
of chance from that accidental intertwinement of persons and events
which Balzac, like every other great epic poet, uses with such sovereign
superiority. Only a great wealth of multiple interconnections affords
sufficient elbow-room in which chance can become artistically productive
and ultimately lose its fortuitous character . . .

The poetic presentation of necessity by Balzac rests on his profound
grasp of the line of development concretely incarnated in the theme in
hand. By means of a broad and deep conception of his characters, a
broad and deep portrayal of society and of the subtle and multiple
interconnections between his characters and the social basis and setting
of their actions, Balzac creates a wide space within which hundreds of
accidents may intersect each other and yet in their aggregate produce
fatal necessities.

The true necessity in *Lost Illusions* is that Lucien must perish in Paris.
Every step, every phrase in the rise and decline of his fortunes provide

ever more profound social and psychological links in this chain of necessity. The novel is so conceived that every incident is a step towards the same end, although each single happening, while helping to reveal the underlying necessity, is in itself accidental. The uncovering of such deep-seated social necessities is always effected by means of some action, by the forceful concentration of events all moving towards the catastrophe. The extensive and sometimes most circumstantial descriptions of a town, a dwelling or an inn are never mere descriptions; by means of them Balzac creates again and again the wide and varied space required for the explosion of the catastrophe. The catastrophe itself is mostly sudden, but its suddenness is only apparent, for the traits brightly illuminated by the catastrophe are the same traits we have long been able to observe, even though at a much lower intensity.

It is most characteristic of Balzac's methods that in *Lost Illusions* two great turning-points in the story occur within a few days or even within a few hours of each other. A few days suffice for Lucien de Rubempré and Louise Bargeton to discover of each other that they are both provincials – a discovery that causes each of them to turn from the other. The catastrophe occurs during an evening spent together at the theatre. Even more sudden is Lucien's journalistic success. One afternoon, in despair, he reads his poem to the journalist Lousteau; Lousteau invites him to his office, introduces him to his publisher, takes him to the theatre; Lucien writes his first review as a dramatic critic and awakes next morning to find himself a famous journalist. The truth of such catastrophes is of a social nature; it lies in the truth of the social categories which in the final count determine such sudden turns of fortune. The catastrophe produces a concentration of essential determinants and prevents the intrusion of inessential details.

The problem of the essential and inessential is another aspect of the problem of chance. From the point of view of the writer every quality of every human being is an accident and every object merely a piece of stage property, until their decisive interconnections are expressed in poetic form, by means of some action. Hence there is no contradiction between the broad foundations on which Balzac's novels are built up and their pointed, explosive action which moves from catastrophe to catastrophe. On the contrary, the Balzacian plots require just such broad foundations, because their intricacy and tension, while revealing ever new traits in each character, never introduce anything radically new, but merely give explicit expression in action to things already implicitly contained in the broad foundation. Hence Balzac's characters never possess any traits which are in this sense accidental. For the characters have not a single quality, not even a single external attribute which does not acquire a decisive significance at some point in the plot. Precisely for this reason Balzac's descriptions never create a setting in the sense in which the word was later used in positivist sociology and it is for the same reason that for instance Balzac's very detailed descriptions of people's houses never appear as mere stage settings.

Consider, for instance, the part played in Lucien's first disaster in Paris by his four suits of clothes. Two of these he has brought with him from Angoulême and even the better of the two proves quite impossible during the very first walk Lucien takes in Paris. His first Paris-made suit also turns out to be an armour with too many chinks in the first battle with Parisian society which he has to fight in Madame d'Espard's box at the Opera. The second Parisian suit is delivered too late to play a part in this first phase of the story and is put away in a cupboard during the ascetic, poetic period – to emerge again later for a short time in connection with the journalistic episode. All other objects described by Balzac play a similar dramatic part and embody similar essential factors.

Balzac builds his plots on broader foundations than any other author before or after him, but nevertheless there is nothing in them not germane to the story. The many-sided influence of multifariously determined factors in them is in perfect conformity with the structure of objective reality whose wealth we can never adequately grasp and reflect with our ever all too abstract, all too rigid, all too direct, all too unilateral thinking.

Balzac's many-sided, many-tiered world approaches reality much more closely than any other method of presentation.

But the more closely the Balzacian method approaches objective reality, the more it diverges from the accustomed, the average, the direct and immediate manner of reflecting this objective reality. Balzac's method transcends the narrow, habitual, accepted limits of this immediacy and because it thus runs counter to the comfortable, familiar, usual way of looking at things, it is regarded by many as 'exaggerated' or 'cumbersome'. It is the wide sweep, the greatness itself of Balzac's realism which forms the sharpest contrast to the habits of thought and the experience of an age which is to an increasing degree turning away from objective reality and is content to regard either immediate experience, or experience inflated into a myth as the utmost that we can grasp of reality.

But it is, of course, not only in the breadth, depth and multifariousness of his reproduction of reality that Balzac transcends the immediate. He goes beyond the boundaries of average reality in his mode of expression as well. D'Arthez (who is meant for a portrait of Balzac himself) says in this novel: 'And what is art? Nothing more than concentrated nature. But this concentration is never formal; on the contrary, it is the greatest possible intensification of the content, the social and human essence of a situation.'

Balzac is one of the wittiest writers who ever lived. But his wit is not confined to brilliant and striking formulations; it consists rather in his ability strikingly to present some essential point at the maximum tension of its inner contradictions. At the outset of his career as a journalist, Lucien de Rubempré must write an unfavourable review of Nathan's novel which he greatly admires. A few days later he has to write a second article refuting his own unfavourable review. Lucien, the novice journalist, is at first completely at a loss when faced with such a task. But first Lousteau and then Blondet enlighten him. In both cases Balzac gives us a brilliant discourse, perfect in its reasoning. Lucien is amazed and dismayed by Lousteau's arguments. 'But what you are saying now,' he exclaims, 'is perfectly correct and reasonable.' 'Well, could you tear Nathan's book to pieces, if it were not?' asks Lousteau. Many writers after Balzac have described the unprincipled nature of journalism and shown how men wrote articles against their own convictions and better knowledge; but only Balzac penetrated to the very core of the journalistic sophism when he made his journalists playfully and brilliantly marshal the arguments for and against any issue according to the requirements of those who paid them and turn the ability to do this into a trade in which they are highly skilled, quite without relation to their own convictions.

On this level of expression the Balzacian 'stock-exchange of the spirit' is revealed as a profound tragi-comedy of the spirit of the *bourgeois* class. Later realist writers described the already completed capitalist corruption of bourgeois ethics; but Balzac paints its earlier stage, its primitive accumulation in all the sombre splendour of its atrocity. In *Lost Illusions* the fact that the spirit has become a commodity to be bought and sold is not yet accepted as a matter of course and the spirit is not yet reduced to the dreary greyness of a machine-made article. The spirit turns into a commodity here before our very eyes; it is something just happening, a new event loaded with dramatic tension. Lousteau and Blondet were yesterday what Lucien turns into in the course of the novel: writers who have been forced to allow their gifts and convictions to become a commodity. It is the cream of the post-war *intelligentsia* which is here driven to take the best of their thoughts and feelings to market, offering for sale the finest, if belated flowering of the ideas and emotions produced by the *bourgeois intellectuals* since the days of the Renaissance. And this late flowering is not merely an aftermath of epigones. Balzac endows his characters with an agility, scope and depth of mind, with a freedom from all provincial narrowmindedness, such as had never before been seen in France in this form, even though its dialectic is constantly twisted into a sophistic toying with the contradictions of existence. It is because this fine flowering of the spirit is at the same time a swamp of self-prostitution, corruption and depravity that the tragi-comedy enacted before us in this novel achieves a depth never before attained in *bourgeois* literature . . . .

In *Lost Illusions* Balzac created a new type of novel of disillusionment, but his novel far outgrew the forms which this type of novel took later in the nineteenth century. The difference between the latter and the former, which makes this novel and Balzac's whole *oeuvre* unique in the literature of the world, is a historical difference. Balzac depicted the original accumulation of capital in the ideological sphere, while his successors, even Flaubert, the greatest of them, already accepted as an accomplished fact that all human values were included in the commodity structure of capitalism. In Balzac we see the tumultuous tragedy of birth; his successors give us the lifeless fact of consummation and lyrically or ironically mourn the dead. Balzac depicts the last great struggle against the capitalist degradation of man, while his successors paint an already degraded capitalist world. Romanticism – which for Balzac was only one feature of his total conception, a feature which he overcame and developed further – was not overcome by his successors, but lyrically and ironically transmuted into reality which it overgrew, blanketing the great motive forces of evolution and providing only elegiac or ironical moods and impressions instead of an active and objective presentation of things in themselves. The militant participation in the great human struggle for liberation slackens into mourning over the slavery that capitalism has brought on mankind and the militant anger at this degradation dies down to an impotently arrogant passive irony. Thus Balzac not only created the novel of disillusionment but also exhausted the highest possibilities of this type of novel. His successors who continued in his footsteps moved on a downward slope, however great their literary achievements may have been. Their artistic decline was socially and historically unavoidable.

12 Pierre Macherey on Balzac's *Les Paysans**

The novelistic project as conceived by Balzac is not simple but divided, announced simultaneously along several divergent lines. Everything comes about as though Balzac, in making a book, had wanted to say several things at once: as we shall see, he effectively managed to *write* several, not necessarily those which he had intended. The important thing is to know how the work undergoes the test of this diversity: does the dislocation between the several different types of utterance succeed in unmaking the book? Is it not, on the contrary, *made* from their contrast?

We know from the 1842 preface to *La Comédie humaine* (*The Human Comedy*, uniform edition, trans. K. P. Wormeley, London, The Athenaeum Press, from which all Balzac quotations in this chapter are taken) that the book is supposed to conform to several different models. In a first gesture, the examples of Buffon's natural history and Walter Scott's historical novels are proposed together. The former gives the author his subject (the representation of the social species); the latter indicates the means of its realisation (the sequence of novels). Thus we have a form adapted to a content, and a theoretical juncture between literature (the novel) and reality (men as precisely differentiated by their mutual social relations). In fact, things do not work so simply, and this first opposition is false. Reality, modelled on the form of natural history as the author undertakes to represent it, is not an independent reality, but a reality already elaborated by means of an analogy which is formulated with very little regard for objectivity:

> There is but one animal. The creator works on a single model for every organised being. 'The Animal' is elementary and takes its external form, or, to be more accurate, the differences in its form, from the

---

* Reprinted from 'Balzac's *Les Paysans*: A Disparate Text' in *A Theory of Literary Production*, trans. Geoffrey Wall (London and Boston: Routledge & Kegan Paul, 1978), pp. 258–98.

environment in which it is obliged to develop. Zoological species are the result of these differences . . .

I, for my part, convinced of this scheme of nature long before the discussion to which it has given rise, perceived that in this respect society resembled nature. For does not society modify man, according to the conditions in which he lives and acts, into men as manifold as the species within zoology.

(Preface to *La Comédie humaine*)

The transformist novel is not a scientific novel: the myth of science gives only an image of objective reality, and thus lends a form to the writer's general project. The symmetry proposed between science and the novel is obviously false: it serves to justify, by means of whatever theory, a pre-existing anthropological project ('I must paint man'); it does not establish an authentically new content, but provides the means of realising an already given subject – by analogy with the natural sciences to represent human variety. The choice of a scientific model does not introduce science into the novel by adapting objectivity and fiction. The choice merely proposes a novelistic *process* which is allied to what certain formalists have called 'characterisation', which will here be called the process of *differentiation*: to paint man the differences between the various 'species' must be represented; as we shall see, this image borrowed from natural history serves to overturn the traditional technique of the novel by suggesting the use of new techniques to the novelist. Science is not Balzac's path to new realities; rather, it supplies a style, in the most general sense of the word. But this new instrument implies that the novel has been penetrated by a *doctrine*, an unscientific doctrine which will eventually be inverted: the process of variation is used to portray a certain conception of *man*.

In the second instance, there is a new form of duality which is even more characteristic; Balzac claims to create a new genre, half-way between political ideology and literature. In innumerable texts he defines himself first as a political thinker and only afterwards as a novelist. Paraphrasing Rousseau, he writes in the dedication to *Les Paysans* (*The Peasants*) 'I study the movement of my epoch, *and* I publish this work'; the construction of the sentence reveals an effort to join together two different undertakings which were independent from the beginning. The scheme of the ethical novel is transposed into that of the novel of manners. The production of the literary work is subordinated to a 'study', which may use the novel in which to formulate its results, but goes largely beyond the novel in its scope. Balzac calls himself a historian of manners rather than a novelist: guided by a great historical thought, he only thought of giving this a literary form after the event: as we know, the actual order of events was a precise inversion of this account. If we

111

are to credit the author's declared intentions, it seems to be the political content which is most important, which gives the work both unity and originality. To read correctly, according to these instructions, is to ascend from the provisional form to the basic content, to hear the lesson which is uttered on the edges of the story. For the writer can only be a novelist and a historian if he is also an ideologue: a master and a judge.

> The law of the writer, by virtue of which he is a writer, and which I do not hesitate to say makes him the equal, or perhaps the superior of the statesman, is his judgment, whatever it may be, on human affairs, and his absolute devotion to certain principles . . . 'A writer ought to have settled opinions on morals and politics; he should regard himself as a tutor of men; for men need no masters to teach them to doubt,' says Bonald. I took these noble words as my guide long ago; they are the written law of the monarchical writer just as much as that of the democratic writer.

(Preface to La Comédie humaine)

After Buffon and Scott, Bonald determines the third model which will shape the work. It is not enough to have a knowledge of men, as the analogy with the natural sciences might have led one to believe; they have to be instructed, inculcated with the principles which are supposed to guide the work of the novelist. Engels, who knew Balzac's work well, was to say that the writer asks questions but does not answer them. According to Balzac, however, the writer must ask questions in order to be able to answer them. Perhaps, in fact, these two propositions are compatible: the one defines the novelistic *project*, while the other defines its real *product*; Balzac compels himself to 'give answers' though perhaps he does something entirely different. However, it is altogether remarkable to find announced in the preface to the *Comédie humaine* a *universal* law, one which applies not only to Balzac but to the monarchist writer as well as to the democratic writer. It is a matter of an objective necessity rather than a novel constraint: it is not a question of forcibly inserting ideology into literature, any more than was the case with science. All literary works are determined by their relation to an ideology. A good novelist without an ideology is inconceivable: the excellence of the novelist lies not in his ideology but in the fact that he confronts *an* ideological utterance with *a* fictional utterance. According to Balzac himself, then, it appears that ideology does not have a distinct independent form in relation to the work: it realises a *literary* function at its own autonomous level; without ideology there could be no fictional lesson, and probably no novel either.

In relation to the novel, ideology does not play the same role as science: it does not offer the global image of a style which can be copied,

but produces specific utterances which can be inserted into the tissue of
the novel; meanwhile, in their different ways, both are internalised,
taken up in the work of the writer, for which they are not distant models
but immediate transformable material. The relation between the novel
and ideology, no more than the relation between the novel and science,
as it appears explicitly in Balzac's project, is not a real relation between
independently existing terms: it is a matter of a double analogical
implication which defines the very movement of the novelistic
undertaking. Ideology is to be used (and thus modified), science is to be
imitated; the novelist draws on them only to serve his own ends. We will
not be asking, in an aside: Which science does Balzac borrow from? What
is his ideology? Each time, in a different form, we are asking the same
question: What kind of novel did he want to write: To put it simply, the
study of Balzac's doctrine ought to contribute to a definition of the
novelist rather than the propagandist. Balzac's 'thought' is of interest
only as an element of literary production: caught up in a text whose
importance is not to be measured by its ideological quality. We should
forswear this negative and reductive reading which, claiming to eliminate
an inessential and deceptive surface, goes directly to the depth of the
work, doubly destroying it by decomposing it and extracting that which
gives it value. If Balzac's 'thought' had a meaning in itself, the work
would simply be a translation of the thought, simply a reading and a
commentary on the thought, lacking any objective necessity. Indeed, any
such thought runs the risk of a superficial originality: it is essentially
borrowed, and, in so far as it has an independent existence, it does not
define the enterprise of literary production. The understanding of the
work does not involve unmaking it and studying separately the elements
of which it is composed. At this point we meet with a formidable
problem of method: these elements are not to be isolated, but neither
must they be confused, otherwise the real complexity of the work is lost.
In writing a novel, Balzac undertakes to say *two things at once* which
cannot be taken for each other: on the one hand, he must tell the truth,
he must know and he must display this knowledge; on the other hand,
he must select and propagate a decorous fiction (*vérité de convenance*), that
Monarchy and Catholicism alone can ensure the future of French society.
These two intentions could be co-extensive: the statements of principle
relying on the analysis of fact (objective description of a situation and a
nature), the principles eliciting the meaning from the facts. In fact, there
is nothing of the sort: there are two different movements which are
opposed rather than complementary, mutually conflicting rather than
converging. The author wants to *know* and to *judge*: in the work, two
types of utterance correspond to these two projects, utterances dislocated
in their relation because the one expresses the lucid and the other the
confused. A knowledge of the Balzacian novel must begin from a grasp

of the manner in which these two utterances are *fused* together. Balzac's work is the site of a contrast which is its defining principle; the text is not simple and unified, it is uneven, disparate.

If Balzac has indeed written two things at once, and if the novel is the product of this encounter, to read one of his novels is to read twice, to read two books which are neither separate nor mingled but united. The text offers not one but several meanings. This possibility of a double reading is most clearly announced in the dedication to *Les Paysans*:

> The object of this particular study – startling in its truth so long as society makes philanthropy a principle instead of regarding it as an accident – is to bring to sight the leading characters of a class too long unheeded by the pens of writers who seek novelty as their chief object. Perhaps this forgetfulness is only prudent in these days when the people are heirs of all the sycophants of royalty. We make criminals poetic, we commiserate with hanged men, we have all but deified the proletariat. Sects have arisen, and cry by every pen, 'Rise, working men!' just as formerly they cried, 'arise arise!' to the third estate. None of these Erostrates, however, have dared to face the country solitudes and study the unceasing conspiracy of those whom we term the weak against those others who fancy themselves strong, that of the peasant against the proprietor. It is necessary to enlighten not only the legislator of today but him of tomorrow. In the midst of the present democratic ferment into which so many of our writers blindly rush it becomes an urgent duty to exhibit the peasant who renders Law inapplicable, and who has made the ownership of land to be a thing that is, and that is not. You are now to behold that indefatigable mole, that rodent which undermines and disintegrates the soil, parcels it out and devours an acre into a hundred fragments – ever spurred on to his banquet by the lower middle-classes who make him at once their auxiliary and their prey. This essentially unsocial element, created by the Revolution, will some day absorb the middle classes, just as the middle classes have destroyed the nobility. Lifted above the law by its own insignificance, this Robespierre with one head and twenty million arms is at work perpetually; crouching in country districts, entrenched in the municipal councils, under arms in the national guard in every canton in France, – one result of the year 1830, which failed to remember that Napoleon preferred the chances of defeat to the danger of arming the masses.

To the careful reader, this text offers precisely two meanings. There is a simple and unequivocal intention, and yet through its formulation it appears – though untainted with ambiguity – *other than it is*; rather than being uttered, it is displayed, indicated from a distance, and thus stripped of any immediate presence given up to its *remoteness*. What is actually at issue here – the communication of an 'appalling truth'?: doubly appalling, first because it is unconscious and secret; second because, with regard to the political choice advertised here by Balzac, it announces the advent of a *danger*. Accordingly, a double rupture has to be brought about by the novel: at the level of knowledge, and at the level of judgment. In a single movement (but is it really one?) the author intends to inform and to disquiet. The ideological proposition is the most apparent; but it is easy to reveal by its side, as the condition of its realisation, the utterance of the fact which contests it. Balzac writes *against* the people: it is impossible to be unaware of this decision, to pay no attention to it by assimilating the author of *Les Paysans* to the 'democratic' writers, Victor Hugo and George Sand, precisely those with whom he does not want to be associated. This decision in principle, which in itself does not directly affect the writer's work (it is not enough to be against the people or with them in order to write), receives its real meaning when, to support his denunciation, it imposes the preliminary or the correlative of an analysis. If one is going to speak against the people, effectively, one must speak *of* the people: they must be seen, given form, *allowed to speak*. Like eulogy, condemnation is not in itself enough: the ideological claim inevitably requires a presentation and a disclosure; then the argumentation turns into style. In proportion to its double meaning, this text makes possible a double reading: the reductive reading attends only to the explicit; a different reading will try to extricate the conditions which make its utterance possible. Without separating the utterance from the project, without making them independent of each other, this reading will see them in their relative autonomy, which is also their contrast. In showing a workers' rising, or how it is prevented, though he does not summon them to rise, Balzac is nearer to Marx than was Victor Hugo for example: for does he not say, even if it is in the opposite direction and with different means, the *same thing*?

Thus it must not be thought that ideology, metamorphosed into art, becomes insignificant and effaces itself as ideology: no more than we can isolate doctrine and judge it for itself, aside, should we privilege the art of the writer, and invoke this art to veil that which gives it substance and meaning. Balzac's novels exist because they are rooted in this double project. We should not be trying to evade this duplicity, but to explain it.

In relation to *Les Paysans* we will ask ourselves the question: What is writing a novel? The first answer, given by Balzac himself, is that it is to solve the great question of the hour. 'But what will emerge from this ever more passionate debate, between the rich and the poor? This study is written solely to elucidate this terrible social question.'

Notice that two questions are being asked together, a question of fact and a question of power: the novel has to *show* the rich matched against the poor, and also to protect the rich from the poor, to ensure the junction of (natural) history and (political) ideology. In fact, in a paradox which is in some degree the source of the work, the motive of its writing, *the rich are weak: they need protection*. The question is accordingly an *enigma and a scandal*. Why are the rich so weak? This can be understood as a harmony of two notes. We observe the initial junction of the judgment of fact and the judgment of value: the novel undertakes an inspired ideological vindication, and also an exact knowledge; this initial paradox must be explained and subdued.

The scandal is affirmed, acknowledged from the beginning: thus it cannot establish a true progression. The novel moves forward by exploring the enigma: since the ideological purpose is already an answer, passing itself off as a question, the endeavour to know should resolve a real difficulty; this image of *resolution* affords the possibility of constructing the novel. The rich are weak: thus there is another rich class, hidden, stronger than the former. Thus the novel is elaborated in two periods: the first shows the confrontation of the rich and the poor in its most extreme (and scandalous) form: represented by the encounter between the cottage and the castle.

> Have you now taken in all the many details of this hovel, planted about five hundred feet away from the pretty gate of Les Aigues? Do you see it crouching there, like a beggar beside a palace? Well, its roof covered with velvet mosses, its clacking hens, its grunting pig, its straying heifer, all its rural graces have a horrible meaning.
>
> (*Les Paysans*, Vol. I, Ch. 3)

We are dealing with a special secret: the cottage ('this fatal cottage' built on the ruins of the castle) is a tavern, which is to say, by definition, an unsavoury place. It is foretold that behind the poetic pastoral façade there is a chance of finding something 'horrible' and unexpected. This insignificant secret is the allegory of the great secret which supplies the subject of the work.

Across the great gap which separates the two powers, their debate seems hollow, insoluble and artificial; and from this situation, which on its own terms seems to be a false situation, there gradually emerges a *boundless anxiety* which lends a secretly dramatic tone to the first chapters of the novel. By means of this contrast, the question is exhibited in all its acuteness. In the second period, much more extensively, we are progressively given the missing link, which explains everything: the bourgeois community, the 'mediocracy', presented in its fissured complexity: eager for the same prize, they are temporary allies but they are not united. Then the tone changes, and throughout the description of the mediocrity of this intermediate world (which is not the *demi-monde*) Balzac recovers a certain victorious gaiety. The infinite untenable gap which separates the extremes of the cottage and the castle, the poor and the rich, is now *filled*: here is to be played out the decisive event, of which the episodes of the plot are merely an *effect*.

> From the peasant sphere this drama will now raise itself to the high region of the middle classes of Soulanges and of La-Ville-aux-Fayes, curious figures whose appearance in the narrative, far from arresting its development, will accelerate it, like the villages engulfed in an avalanche which make its passage the more swift.
>
> (*Ibid.*, Vol. I, Ch. 13)

This progression is gratifying, in so far as it satisfies a curiosity, but it is also disquieting, it justifies a galloping indignation: the narrative, as expected, moves in two opposite directions.

This first, very rudimentary analysis shows that, like so many other novels by Balzac, *Les Paysans* is a prophetic meditation on the events of 1830 (the action is set in 1823): it deals with the period in which the bourgeoisie appears on the surface of history to take charge in its own name, to take history as its private property. This accession, this arousal, has to be not only evoked but *reproduced* by the whole of the novel, furnishing an equivalent rather than an image. At this point the historical purpose is accompanied by a properly novelistic exigency: to display the *thing* as it is (the triumph of the bourgeoisie) it is not enough to show it, since, precisely, it is not there (on the one hand it is hidden; and on the other hand, in the presence of reality itself, the novel would lose its *raison d'être*): by appropriate means a substitute must be supplied. Accordingly, behind the historical project and the ideological project, or rather in between them, assuring their connection and their separation, there emerges, in its specificity, a literary project which no longer consists in knowing or judging. It is a matter of *writing a book which shall be like a world*. This new problem – it is a problem, since the means of realising this intention must be found – is the real origin of the novel.

Two complementary solutions are adopted together: the one is external to this particular novel, the other organises it internally. The novel is initially situated in a network of books which replaces the complexity of real relations by which a world is effectively constituted. Located within the totality of a corpus, within a complex system of relationships, the novel is, in its very letter, allusion, repetition and resumption of an object which now begins to resemble an inexhaustible world. Conceived according to this principle, the work is a combination of elements which together have a substance and a complexity analogous to that of reality. The imaginary universe is not a reflection of the real universe: it constitutes a system of reality; whence we realise how inevitably remote is the project of writing a novel from that of telling the truth: it is not enough 'to study poverty from the life', it must still be communicated by the elaboration of an imaginary object. The technique of 'reappearances', of the recurring character, corresponds to this wish to *situate* the novel in relation to the external. But we must not narrow our definition of this technique to the mere fact that the same characters pass through different plots; it is important that these characters (as well as places and situations) are also playing an *analogical* role, that they are always, explicitly or implicitly, one term in a comparison. Because they are defined by their relations to one another, they manifest their unity within a unique world whose existence they accordingly assure: 'This miller, a Sarcus-Taupin, was the Nucingen of the valley.' Thus the totality of the work is like a vast ground upon which each individual element appears. This is why, to read a Balzac novel adequately, you must read two at once – any two if necessary. In this way one discovers the necessary redoubling of meaning which takes the place of an absent reality. The work itself is vast enough for each of its moments to suggest a multiplicity of possible relations and itineraries. The order of the work tends to produce this illusion of diversity: these dimensions have to be such that no memory can grasp the work in its entirety. This is why Balzac worked so much, at such speed. Michel Butor has demonstrated in *Répertoire I* that an essential component of the *Comédie humaine* is this possibility which it offers of being read in more than one direction, of being conscientiously and thoroughly explored or rearranged in a different sequence on each occasion. It thus has a bulk which is more than the mere sum of its parts. For a knowledge of Balzac the writer, all beginnings are valid, in the knowledge that they are only ever one beginning among others. . . .

The first chapter, accordingly, gives the narrative a true point of departure (and not simply a beginning): it establishes a novelistic perspective, both particular and complex. Far from being limited and static, this perspective is the origin of a movement because of the internal imbalance which moves it; it implies the transition to a new perspective. Thus the character of Blondet (and he plays a relatively secondary role in the plot) determines the construction of the narrative: here the novelistic element precedes and defines the reality of which it has to produce the illusion. Significantly, this same Blondet has the task of bringing the novel to its conclusion.

The novelistic system attains an effect of reality, not by means of descriptions (that is to say, direct imitations of reality, pure visions), but by means of contrasts and discords. The function of Balzac's descriptions, one which has hardly been grasped, is always to *produce a difference*. But to recognise this it is obviously not enough to duplicate these descriptions, making them the *object* of a description, projecting on to them what one imagines is there. Literary analysis is commonly stuck in an *ideology of description*, finding everywhere texts that describe or texts to be described.

We can now understand how it will be possible to pass from the point of view of Blondet to that of Fourchon, the initiator of the peasant world, and then, by a *swerve*, from the chateau to the cottage. This new point of view will obviously be communicated in a different way: one cannot produce a letter from Fourchon. (Not that he is unable to write, since he has been a schoolmaster, but to whom could he write? In the system Fourchon's special place is marked by the fact that he has no answering Nathan.) But note that Fourchon, in relation to the rural world, is in a situation analogous to that of Blondet in relation to the world of property: he is not entirely at home (a failed farmer, fallen from his class, he is a close companion of the peasants but he remains at the edges of their universe); thus another sliding will be possible, moving the story to another level. Just as Blondet is not altogether an owner, because he has nothing, but above all because he writes, so Fourchon is not altogether a peasant, because he is a spokesman. But also, just as the works of the journalist or the writer do not belong entirely to him – this theme is generally developed in *Les Illusions perdues* (*Lost Illusions*) – so Fourchon's words *escape* from their owner, and finish by representing something entirely different from the social realm to which he directly belongs.

> Let it be the law of public necessity or the tyranny of the old lords, it is all the same; we are condemned to dig the soil for ever. There, where we are born, there we dig it, that earth! and spade it, and manure it, and delve in it, for you who are born rich just as we are born poor. The masses will always be what they are, and stay what they are. The number of us who manage to rise is nothing like the number of you who topple down! We know that well enough though we have no education! We let you alone, and you must let us alone. If not, and things get worse, you will have to feed us in your prisons, where we'd be much better off than in our homes. You want to remain our masters, and we shall always be enemies, as much as we were thirty years ago. You have everything, we have nothing; you can't expect we should ever be friends.
>
> (*Les Paysans*, Vol. I, Ch. 5)

Listening to this astonishing speech one may well ask why Balzac has been taken for a realistic writer in the narrow sense. In fact, all the possibile improbabilities seem to be gathered on this page. Improbability of situation: although this theme is mentioned in the title of the chapter ('The Enemies Face Each Other') it is rather unlikely that such a direct confrontation should bring together the heroes of the contradiction, the rich and the poor; this encounter is essentially unreal, largely symbolic. Improbability of tone: in spite of the rags of peasant idiom in which the speech is clothed, a sort of emphasis raises it and carries it beyond its immediately representative character; by a formal augmentation, the expression is adapted to an unusual situation. Improbability of content: 'Nailed by the law of necessity' – to depict the limits of his condition, this untypical peasant has access to a borrowed knowledge; it remains to be seen whether these limits are real limits or the limits of a form of knowledge (particular or general). In short, the clarity and extremity with which the conflict is presented reveals a transposition which belongs to the novelistic rather than the real.

We are even more surprised to hear this speech when we remember that we have already heard it in analogous (at least convergent) form from the abbé Brossette, a character from an entirely different realm. It is important to note, in passing, that this same Brossette will appear, transformed, in another sphere: he will be the worldly confessor of Beatrix.

> And thus it was that the abbé Brossette, after studying the morals of his parishioners, made this pregnant remark to his bishop:
> 'Monseigneur, when I observe the stress that the peasantry lay on their poverty, I know how they fear to lose that excuse for their immorality.'
> (*Ibid.*, Vol. I, Ch. 2)

> 'Madame la Comtesse,' said the abbé, 'in this district we have none but voluntary paupers. Monsieur le comte does all he can; but we have to do with a class of persons who are without religion and who have but one idea, that of living at your expense.'
> (*Ibid.*, Vol. I, Ch. 5)

Formulated differently, taken in an opposite sense, the same idea appears: for Brossette as for Fourchon, the peasant is marked by his condition to the point of being imprisoned in it. And thus his struggle against the rich is not spontaneous, episodic and individual, but is inevitably determined by a class conflict. This idea essential to the development of the novel (it supplies its title) is presented at least *twice*: it derives its meaning from the difference which the duplication establishes. What appears to Fourchon as a law is for the priest the fact of deliberate sinfulness, a subjective system of theft and debauchery. Whether fatality or perversity, the situation is thus presented, partially in the discourse of the two privileged observers, as a form of knowledge. This is not an expression of the author's beliefs. In opposition to Brossette, Balzac thinks that the system of poverty is objective and does not depend on the individual will (which is why charity to individuals is denounced in this novel as futile); but in opposition to Fourchon, Balzac does not believe that it is a destiny. The world of the poor is not eternally fixed; on the contrary, it *evolves* historically (this gives weight to the threat against the bourgeoisie; soon the poor will lay the blame directly on you), and it can be *modified* (this is the meaning of the great social novels: *Le Médecin de campagne*, and *Le Curé de village* (*The Village Priest*)). . . .

To summarise: the institution of a fictional reality is accomplished by the complex arrangement of differential elements. The wish to know the social world and to present a substitute for it is realised in the production of a diversity.

'Reread this kaleidoscopic work, here you will find that no two garments, no two heads are the same' – thus the 1835 preface (signed Félix Darvin).

It might be thought that this is merely a question of a trick (*procédé*); of a neutral technique, serving only to realise, to translate an intention already worked out. As we shall see, this is not so. The process constitutes the intention itself; it is, in fact, open to so many variations that it seems impossible to conceive of it as a purely material instrument. Whether it is the instrument of two very different intentions, or whether it can only be used in the vicinity of many different intentions, or whether it can only be used in the vicinity of a different opposing intention, it appears to be caught up in the movement of the novel as one of its constitutive elements, perhaps even as its real subject.

Indeed, the work thus constituted in its systematic unity seems to be coherent and full, finished. To such an extent that one might ask: Why this unity rather than another? For the work to have consistency, it is not enough for it to be a system: the system itself must be determined, must not be simply any system. This is why it is not enough to analyse the mechanism of the novel in order to understand, or rather, to explore it: we must see how this mechanism actually functions, whether it is utilised directly, naturally, or whether it does not undergo a characteristic modification whereby it becomes the *object of the novel*.

Once in operation, the system has a life of its own, and produces an unexpected effect. The instrument which, in theory, enables us to make distinctions (to know and to display reality) will in fact serve to confuse (to judge). This is because one means can be adapted to several different incompatible uses: as though it possessed a power of its own, a power to produce a meaning or meanings, that multiplicity of meanings which constitutes it.

We must now return to the ideological project, temporarily forgotten. The narrative as conceived by Balzac must, we remember, realise two requirements at once. It must take the place of two narratives at once. By means of the narrative we can see and we can judge: each of these attitudes implies a different partition of reality. The problem faced by the writer is thus how to reconcile, how to connect and adapt these two shapes? Balzac's solution is disconcertingly simple: it is enough to superimpose them, to compel one means to serve the production of its opposing meaning, reconciling confusion and clarity in the coincidence of meanings.

Thus, to take an immediate and elementary example, if there is a description it must, in principle and from the first, be distinct; but it must also corroborate an accusation. Thus the man of the people, not as a general idea but as a real plea in the novel, is, as already announced in the preface to *Les Paysans*, the *savage*. This metaphor obviously implies the idea of distance; the peasant is not a man like any other.

> 'What can be the ideas, the morals, the habits of such a being? What is he thinking of?' thought Blondet, seized with curiosity. 'Is he my fellow-creature? We have nothing in common but shape, and even that!'
>
> (*Les Paysans*, Vol. I, Ch. 2)

The image will recur endlessly. It is introduced by Blondet:

> 'Here's one of Cooper's redskins,' thought Blondet; 'one needn't go to America to study savages.'
>
> (*Ibid.*)

> 'Well, well!' cried Blondet, laughing, 'so here we are, like Cooper's heroes in the forests of America, in the midst of traps and savages.'
>
> (*Ibid.*, Vol. I, Ch. 5)

and it is taken up again by the abbé Brossette (whose place in the novelistic system is symmetrical with that occupied by Blondet):

> By the nature of their social functions, the peasants live a purely material life which approximates to that of the savages, and their constant union with nature tends to foster it.
>
> (*Ibid.*, Vol. I, Ch. 3)

> My bishop sent me here as if on a mission to savages; but, as I had the honour of telling him, the savages of France cannot be reached. They make it a law unto themselves not to listen to us; whereas the church does get some hold on the savages of America.
>
> (*Ibid.*, Vol. I, Ch. 5)

Used differently in each particular case, the image is not only representative of a particular point of view. It is used anonymously, from that point of view, outside the flow of the narrative which is that of the author:

> The savage, and the peasant who is much like a savage, seldom speak unless to deceive an enemy.
>
> (*Ibid.*, Vol. I, Ch. 6)

It even shapes the narrative at its most anecdotal:

> This piercing scream echoed through the woods like a savage war-cry.
>
> (*Ibid.*, Vol. I, Ch. 10)

In its multiple uses, the image finally acquires, to some extent, an autonomous value. It characterises the peasant by demonstrating his original relationship to nature; but in this case it is allegorical, that is to say, inadequate. The peasant is not a true savage; the nature which he inhabits is unnatural – diversified and permeated by the different modes of appropriation. It presupposes the existence of a society. But the comparison has an exotic value, above all in its remote displaced character: it does not correspond exactly to a reality which it represents by distortion. The artificiality becomes clearer when we find it being used very differently, applied by Mme Soudry to Rigou:

> The tall, stiff usurer always had an imposing effect upon Madame Soudry's company, who instinctively recognised in his nature the cruelty of the tiger with steel claws, the craft of a savage.
>
> (*Ibid.*, Vol. II, Ch. 2)

Clearly, now, the comparison with the savage signifies a profound *misunderstanding*: by its incoherence, this is what Balzac's text itself is saying. To see a savage within the peasant, as do Blondet or Brossette, is not to see the peasant entirely as he is: the image is significant principally because of the gap which paradoxically links it to its model.

Les Paysans is a novel in the style of Fenimore Cooper, because it describes the same 'primitive' violence. The landscapes of Morvan, 'countryside', are not pastoral; they show the image (even before the appearance of the inhabitants) of a disquieting virgin nature, the very same which is supposedly inhabited by the American Indians.

But if there are savages, and if the peasant is indeed a savage, there is nowhere in a savage state: every place shown in the *Comédie humaine* is the setting in front of which a social relationship is enacted. Thus we see a very primitive discord between the place and its occupant, which will be the focus of novelistic curiosity. This importance of the *place*, which is the first object of the analysis of manners, ought to be remembered: the conception of the relation between man and the surrounding nature is a specifically literary means – not a datum but the product of the work of the writer. But this instrument has a double value: it shapes the novel and determines its content. That the forests of Morvan should be described in the same terms as the forests of America, and this with an explicit reference to the writer who popularised this setting, is initially an artifice of writing: the same artifice which will, for example, make Rigou a 'Heliogabalus', a 'Louis XV without a throne', the 'Tiberius of the Avonne valley', the 'Lucullus of Blangy', a 'village Sardanapolis'; but that the 'man of the woods' should be, because of this metaphor, the same here and there, is a historical, critical and polemical thesis which, using the same means, produces a meaning radically opposed to that which the system (as it has been analysed) produced. Far from a distinction, it seems, it is now a question of a mingling and a confusion. As we shall see, this coexistence of two kinds of statement is typical of the work of Balzac the writer: it is this which, in the juncture (*rencontre*) which it establishes between a knowledge which is distinct and an ideology which is confused, makes the work literary (and not, as Balzac sometimes says, historical or political). This is why, from a theoretical point of view, nothing prevents our making a special study of the *form of the work*: we are certain to find implied there the reality principle which fills it.

The form which organises the fictional debate – a real historical debate, and an artificial debate (because it derives from a technique of literary composition) – also endows this debate with content: a study of the process of writing is inadequate in so far as it inevitably encounters the object of history itself.

Balzac resolves the technical problem posed by this *double game*, but by emphasising and giving new life to a traditional form, the fictional *type*, which has already been discussed. Let us say, rather, that he *encounters* the solution to this problem, because this time it does not depend on the conscious control of a technical means: he encounters it in the ordeal of that change of meaning which unforeseen functions confer on a system of representation.

The choice of typical objects (characters, places, situations, periods . . .) is an initial response to the necessity of describing: it makes possible an identification of reality as such, a representation of each element of a situation. It would be easy to show how in *Les Paysans* the diversity of the characters, which has an indistinctly psychological and sociological function, catches precisely, because it involves discrimination, the complexity of the bourgeois world, its demultiplication into different spheres, spheres temporarily and precariously in relation. This difference and mobility of 'characters' makes it possible to show all aspects of the bourgeoisie in its complex reality. By means of the 'type', ever more accurate identifications of social categories can be made. But the use of fictional types eventually produces a very different effect: the initially constituted reality is now judged according to a theory of society. Thus the literary instrument receives its true meaning, not from the necessity of reflecting reality itself, but from its place in the novelistic system, conceived as the best vantage point on this reality.

If the novel involves the use of 'types', this is because these types have between them relations other than real (the real relations between types are determined by the real existence of the social groups of which they give a fictional image), relations determined by their very nature as types, ideal relations: in which case the function of the type will be to confuse rather than to clarify.

It is this double nature of the fictional object which gives reality and even matter to Balzac's project, which makes this project into a work. The two meanings are each affirmed in turn, and there is an endless sliding from one to the other.

This can be more easily explained by means of an example. We know of the importance of place in the development of a novel: It must be shown that this typical function is ambiguous. The opening of *Les Petits Bourgeois* provides an excellent example of the first conception of the fictional object: a long description of *things* (a house, furniture) in the form of an exploration (so characteristic of the Balzac exposition) exhibiting what *Un Début dans la vie* called 'the social material of an epoch': all the details of the house serve to show how the *petite bourgeoisie* is determined in relation to the bourgeoisie, both by it and against it. This very complex relation is *constituted* by the articulation of the novelistic description: the typically 'petit-bourgeois' furniture is positioned in front of 'bourgeois' walls, which it both conceals and reveals; it is this material occultation which gives an image of reality. All of Balzac's descriptions obey such norms; thus, in *Les Paysans*, three of the important locations are characterised by a system of oppositions:

> We ask those who really know France, if these houses – those of Rigou, Soudry and Gaubertin – are not a perfect presentation of the village, the little town, and the seat of a sub-prefecture?
>
> (*Les Paysans*, Vol. II, Ch. 4)

Each of these locations is typical of a specific social unit, in which the relations between the social groups are formed in a singular way: the three important forms of the bourgeois coalition in the provinces are thus changed into novelistic objects. It is extraordinary that Balzac is never satisfied with the truth of the realised type, that he refuses to accept it as definitive. From one novel to another the type undergoes a variation: if

Soudry's house represents perfectly *the* small town, and Gaubertin's the departmental capital, the provincial village is just as much Saumur as it is Issoudun, just as much Angoulême as it is Bayeux, or equally those imaginary places in *Les Paysans*. This variation is not dictated by anecdotal requirements (for example, an attention to the picturesque), a mere geographical colouring appropriate to the setting: it answers the desire to *fill* this frame by diversification. Only Paris has the right to be unique, because it is multiplicity itself: but the small town, if it is to retain its identity, requires the description of other small towns, which are finally so many aspects of it; the total conception of the *Comédie humaine* resolves this problem of interminable description. Contrary to any initial beliefs, the type is all the more representative in that it partakes of several specimens, unique and original.

But, as we have said, the function of the type is interrupted, becomes ambiguous, when it is related to other types, not in a real relationship of difference, but in a relation of analogy obviously fantastic. With regard to the same example, this is what happens when Balzac says that the provincial town is Paris at a slower pace, as he does in *Les Illusions perdues*. In the same way, in *Les Petits Bourgeois*, in contradiction with the initial precision of the décor, the bourgeois salon is later presented as a reduction of the Faubourg Saint-Germain. These comparisons between types no longer simply diverse, but really opposed, are not made in passing: they are on the contrary one of the constants of Balzac's style. The type loses its function of reality to become a troubled image: it is no longer representative in the strict sense of the word, but the term of a systematic identity.

In order to understand this sliding, the system which determines the organisation of the narrative must be constructed in its entirety. With Balzac, the novel takes the *scene* for its general frame – a scene which is neither a unity of place nor a unity of time, but a fictional element, defined by the light of a theory of society, independently of the differential method which elsewhere sufficed to describe it. We meet again with a feature of the Balzac novel which has already been described, though now it has a different meaning: an essentially *unbalanced* construction. The rhythm of the narrative is broken, the succession of episodes is abrupt and discontinuous. This answers to a demand for progression which defined the nature of the scene. *La Rabouilleuse* (*The Fisherwoman*) offers a good example of these formal ruptures: after a static and very extended account of life in Issoudun, which forms a complete narrative unit, the sudden entry of Philippe Bridau into the village, on the initiative of Desroches, is related. Nothing enabled us to foresee this event: abruptly the narrative takes on a new dimension, is played out at an entirely different level. Always the novel is shaped by the same structure: very long, isolated elements of description are brutally cut short by an unexpected event, an event in relation to which the description seems insufficient, and thereby arises the need for a new description; thus a progression is established within a demonstrative system. The event is the appearance of an individual, previously described in a portrait. The narrative model, the scene, is the infinitely varied and renewed encounter of a situation and a portrait, from which emerges a dynamic individuality, what Balzac calls 'moral power': in the wake of this encounter the situation is changed and a new narrative element impels the scene.

This extremely simple narrative organisation depends on a systematic representation of the plot: the plot is derived from the impact of a 'moral force' on a real situation, which produces displacements and readjustments. The 'moral world' is always confronted with the real world, but is always autonomously determined. The situation and the individual 'force' are reciprocal though never mingled. Thus we see that the important theme of the work is that of *success* and of *depravity*. This theme is both 'moral' and 'social': through this theme we shall discover that articulation which is the characteristic object of the scene. There is depravity whenever the gap between the force and the situation is such that their confrontation is indecisive. This is what happens to Maxence Gilet, as it is described at the end of *La Rabouilleuse*:

> Thus perished one of those men destined to do great things, had they remained in their proper sphere; a man who was nature's favourite child, for she gave him courage, composure and the political acumen of a Cesare Borgia. But education had not endowed him with that nobility of thought and conduct without which nothing is possible in any career.
>
> (*La Rabouilleuse*, Ch. I)

Education is obviously the only feature linking the 'situation' and the 'force': and this is why all Balzac's novels will deal with either an education or a decline.

Un Début dans la vie is the supreme example of the novel of adaptation; *Les Illusions perdues* that of a novel of maladaptation:

> We can expect anything from Lucien, good as well as evil.
>
> (Arthez' letter)

> Ah! his is a nature which is splendid only in its setting, only in its sphere, its climate.
>
> (David Séchard)

The encounter can culminate in a reconciliation or can produce aberrant results which deform the situation (see *La Rabouilleuse*) or the individual (Rubempré): in which case the initial force expands in the form of a vice.

> The superimposition of the character of Rastignac, who triumphs, on that of Lucien, who fails, is simply a large-scale representation of a capital fact of our epoch: the ambition which succeeds, the ambition which is thwarted, the ambition of the first steps in life.
>
> (David Séchard, preface to the first edition)

'A capital fact of our epoch': with this fact, the analysis of manners takes fictional form. Adaptation and maladaptation are *generalities*, typical elements which persist whatever the variety of the situations.

This is all therefore both very coherent and very simple, so that the coherence is not that which has previously been identified. Every man carries with him a 'moral world': the question is whether, placed in contact with one or several situations, this world will succeed in realising itself, and in what direction; in fact, a moral world can develop in contradictory directions:

> All the laws of nature have a double action, each in an opposite direction.
>
> (*Les Illusions perdues*)

The ideal programme of the *Comédie humaine* consists in realising all the possible encounters between moral forces and real situations, and in representing all the forms of 'moral' adaptation.

We find the 'theory' of this adaptation in its simplest form in *Les Illusions perdues*:

> The organisation of modern society, infinitely more complicated in its machinery than in the ancient world, has produced a subdivision in man's faculties. Previously eminent men, compelled to be universal, appeared in small numbers like torches in the midst of the ancient nations. More recently, though the faculties may have specialised, excellence was achieved in a wide sphere. Thus a man of supreme cunning, as Louis XI was considered to be, could apply his skill to everything; but nowadays the accomplishment has subdivided itself. For example, there are as many tricks as there are professions. A clever diplomat may well be deceived in some provincial matter by a lowly attorney or by a peasant. The craftiest journalist may find that he is a complete simpleton in commercial matters,

– and a great novelist may not succeed in business. The problem of adaptation is posed when a kind of technical division establishes a diversity, this time within the moral world. To hold up the edifice of the scene a new kind of type now becomes necessary: the moral type.

All these speculations, which are of an ideological nature, could be explained by reference to a tradition (Swedenborg, St Martin, the philosophical novel). It seems more significant to interpret them in relation to a problematic of literary forms. The scene, the composition of the narrative (situation–explosion), the type, are not initially ideas about the world and man, but fictional objects, which Balzac has chosen or established less because they may have seemed to him to be true or real than because they were the vehicles, *par excellence,* of the fiction. Thus we see that it is the problem of literature itself which is posed by the articulation of two conceptions of the type (the real type, the moral type).

With Balzac, as the preface informs us, the novel ceases to represent individual relations, encounters in the anecdotal sense of the word. These relations are only objects for the new novel because they are capable of extension: the individual has a place in the novel only because he is the term in a series. But Balzac's entire work is built upon a double characterisation of this extension. The individual exists in relation to a situation, but this situation is only apparently simple: in fact, it results from an intersection, which produces a coincidence between the real milieu, the real setting (represented by means of diversity: Balzac's first system), and the moral world (represented by means of confusion: Balzac's second system). The fictional element is doubly representative because of this double inscription. Individual encounters, which form the very substance of the plot, are significant because the individual is himself the product of an encounter (he is doubly determined).

The 'moral type' is a literary means equal in status to the 'real type': in fact, in the development of fictional discourse, they are even usually confused; the same type can be both moral and real. The difference emerges when the question of the relations between the two different types is posed. Two connections are in fact possible: a relation of difference and opposition which expresses a real relation; an ideal unity which evokes an absolute universality. We have already given sufficient examples of this first type of connection. For its part, the moral universe is a Leibnizian world, where 'it is always and everywhere the same, almost to perfection': concierges in this world are like duchesses, priests or like all the other kinds of celibate; the rich and the poor can no longer be distinguished.

The wit of a peasant or labourer is very Attic; it consists in speaking out his mind and giving it a grotesque expression. We find the same thing in a drawing-room. Delicacy of wit takes the place of picturesque vulgarity, and that is really all the difference.

(Les Paysans, Vol. I, Ch. 4)

Ornamental language in all its generality is characteristic, typical: in this case differences are secondary. Comparing and uniting, literature in this case takes no notice of real relations, real limits, and discovers everywhere the confused identity which joins man to man, *beyond* social differences: a single individual relates to a real series and to a moral series (Mme Soudry is typical of the small provincial town, but she is also typical of certain aspects of human nature).

Is not this a picture of life as it is at all stages of what we agree to call society? Change the style, and you will find that nothing more and nothing less is said in the gilded salons of Paris.

(Ibid., Vol. I, Ch. 2)

Le Curé de Tours (*The Vicar of Tours*) gives an example of this new lesson which has insinuated itself into the novel: a lesson via identification, and no longer by differentiation.

This history is commonplace: it would suffice to enlarge slightly the narrow circle within which these characters will act in order to find the coefficient reason for happenings in even the highest levels of society.

The scene itself is typical, since it is that element of literature, both the most simple and the most determinate, in which are reflected all the varieties of the moral world. The scene, lacking in doors or windows on to the diversity of the real world, carries in itself the infinity of the moral universe:

Perhaps the crudity of this portrait will be criticised, the brightness of the character of the fisherwoman deemed to have been borrowed from that truth which the painter ought to leave in shadow. Oh, well! this scene, endlessly repeated, with appalling variants, is, in its rough form and its horrible veracity, the very type of those which all women play out, at whatever rung of the social ladder they may find themselves, whenever any kind of interest has diverted them from the path of obedience and they have seized power. As with great politicians, in their eyes, all means are justified by the end. Between Flore Brazier and the duchess, between the duchess and the richest citizen, between the citizen and the most lavishly kept woman, there are no differences other than those due to the education they have had and the circles in which they have lived,

– and it does not seem that these differences are really important.

However, whilst it is thus formulating, in the confusion of the universal, the 'coefficient reasons', the scene establishes the combination of a world analogous to the real world, and the same instruments assist in the realisation of these contradictory and complementary operations: distinction and confusion. Everywhere in *Le Curé de Tours*, the types which had been used for an ideal demultiplication also serve to clarify real relations by showing a play of conflicts and alliances. At the beginning, the abbé Birotteau, and with him the Listomere clan, represents the old aristocracy in a provincial town; Troubert, on the other hand, with the friends of Mlle Gamard, is the advance troop of the bourgeoisie. The novel progresses only because these terminations seem retrospectively precarious and temporary. Behind Troubert, the Congregation is seen in profile; Birotteau, progressively deprived of his 'traditional resources', finally has recourse to the services of a liberal lawyer. Thus a historical contradiction explodes, the very contradiction which made 1830: it shows the decomposition of the old ruling class under the Restoration, and the help which, if it is to survive, it must seek from the bourgeoisie, who are revealed as the true leaders of reaction. Mlle Gamard is one of the terms of this subtle and precise historical analysis, but she is also 'one of those typical old maids'. The type serves to describe, but it also serves to interpret and to judge, within the framework of a false universality.

The disproportion between the real world and the moral world is simultaneously produced and reduced by the work: outside the work this disproportion has no status, no existence; yet this gap establishes it only after the event through a kind of reversal of the fictional machine; it is a question of a second effect, not a product of chance but determined and constitutive of the work. This enables us better to understand the place of ideology in a *literary work*: it is unimportant whether the author is the partisan of an ideology which is by definition external to the enterprise of writing; what is important is that the operation of a fictional system ultimately produces an ideological effect (confusion). Thus ideology is part of the system, not independent of it. Following the model of other analyses one could say that this ideological surge denotes the presence of a gap, a defect in the work, a complexity which makes it *meaningful*. Balzac's work is the best example of this obligation which every writer discovers, that in order to say one thing he must also say several others at the same time. The constitution of Balzac's narrative is open to two explanations: this narrative tends to realise simultaneously two forms of generalisation. Must we choose between the two explanations, must we say that the one is more profound than the other, must we then emphasise this explanation? It seems that we ought rather to preserve the play of this double explanation which establishes simultaneously two

meanings and the gap between them. Balzac is not more of an artist than
he is a politician: he is both together, one against the other, one with the
other. Separately, the artistic reading and the political reading are false
readings: it is their inevitable companionship which must be
remembered.

One could, in a very general way, distinguish two types of utterance in
the Balzacian narrative: certain utterances are directly linked to the
functioning of the fictional system; other utterances are 'detachable' –
they seem to have been taken as they are from ideology and inserted into
the texture of the novel (and could probably return just as easily to their
place of origin). If, in many cases, they are not distinguishable, they are
indissociable: the novel is made from their contrast. The literary text does
not constitute a homogeneous whole: it does not inhabit a single place
prepared in advance to receive it. However, these detachable utterances
are not detached utterances: they are in the work not as real utterances,
but as fictional objects; in the work they are the term of a designation, of
a demonstration; in spite of appearances their status is not directly
ideological; the mode of their presence is that of a *presentation* which
hollows them, exhibits a fundamental disparity in them. Thus, they are
not in the text as intruders, but as *effects*: they have meaning only by that
metamorphosis which makes of them elements among others in the
process of fictional production.

In his course upon fictional subjectivity (given at the Ecole normale
supérieure in 1965–6; the relevant section has been published in *Cahiers
marxistes-léninistes* of October 1966), A. Badiou has clearly posed the
problem of the relations between ideological utterances and properly
fictional utterances. He has shown that in the novel one cannot isolate
ideological utterances and consider them as independent realities, as
enclaves: ideology is so caught in the tissue of the work that it there takes
on a new status, its immediate nature is transformed. One could say, to
take up a vocabulary already familiar: from the illusion that it was, it
becomes fictive.

We now understand why to forget political ideology in Balzac's work
(to pretend that it does not exist, to excuse or condemn it) is to
misunderstand it as a literary work. To read the *Comédie humaine*
indignantly is to reduce it to its ideological process, to see it as no more
than the work of a historian or a journalist. To dissociate something
derived from pure art as though the rest were unimportant is to be
unaware of its necessary complexity.

Structuralist

Although structuralism was at its height in the 1960s and 1870s, its origins, as explained in the Introduction (see pp. 9–10), lie in Russian Formalism and the Prague School of almost fifty years earlier. The linguistic analyses of Ferdinand de Saussure and Roman Jakobson provided models of the structuralist approach to literary critics.

The first example of structuralism is by Roland Barthes, one of the leading French exponents of this school who wrote extensively on both structuralist theory and practice. His famous essay 'The Reality Effect' was first published in 1968 in the journal *Communications* **11** (pp. 84–9), and appeared in English in *French Literary Theory Today* (ed. Tzvetan Todorov, trans. R. Carter, Cambridge and New York: Cambridge University Press, 1982). The phrase 'reality effect' has become naturalised into critical language; several other authors in this volume (Macherey, Lodge, Miller) use it. The short, penetrating essay asserts that realism is essentially a verbal 'effect', derived not from any direct reference to an extraneous order of reality, but from descriptive details, 'fillers, padding', superfluous to the action itself but coalescing cumulatively to give readers the impression of the real. Using a semiotic method, Barthes examines aspects of Flaubert's story *Un Coeur simple (A Simple Heart)* and *Madame Bovary* to make his points. He argues, for instance, that the description of Rouen in *Madame Bovary* is governed by 'the tyrannical constraints of what must be called aesthetic plausibility' rather than by close attention to the actual model. He concludes that the new (i.e., structuralist) verisimilitude (*'vraisemblance'*) differs from the old mimetic view insofar as its intention is to create a direct encounter between the object and the sign, omitting reference to any extraneous reality. However, in so doing it tends to undermine the validity of the sign, and with it the formerly accepted aesthetics of representation.

Compared with Barthes, the British critic and novelist David Lodge is considerably less radical. His piece, an extract from his book *Working with Structuralism* (London: Routledge & Kegan Paul, 1981), is concerned primarily to test the usefulness of structuralism in enriching our readings. Thus Lodge opens with a critical survey of various structuralist methods in narratology, asking to what extent they help readers to a better understanding of the texts. He goes on to give a positive answer to his question by illustrating how a practical application of a structuralist mode of analysis throws new light on to Ernest Hemingway's brief tale 'Cat in the Rain', which is reprinted at the end of Lodge's interpretation but should be read before his discussion of it.

13 Roland Barthes on the Reality Effect in Descriptions*

When Flaubert, describing the room occupied by Madame Aubain, Félicité's mistress, tell us that 'on an old piano, under a barometer, there was a pyramid of boxes and cartons',[1] or when Michelet, describing the death of Charlotte Corday and reporting that in prison, before the arrival of the executioner, she was visited by an artist who painted her portrait, gives us the detail that 'after an hour and a half, someone knocked softly at a little door behind her',[2] these authors, like so many others, produce *notations* (data, descriptive details) which structural analysis, occupied as it is with separating out and systematising the main articulations of narrative, ordinarily, and up to the present, has left out, either by excluding from its inventory (by simply failing to mention them) all those details which are 'superfluous' (as far as structure is concerned), or else by treating these same details (as the present author has himself attempted to do)[3] as fillers, padding (catalyses), assigned indirect functional value in that, cumulatively, they constitute an indication of characterisation or atmosphere, and so can finally be salvaged as part of the structure.

It would seem, however, that if we want the analysis to be truly exhaustive (and what would any method be worth which did not account for the whole of its object, in the present case, the entire surface of the narrative fabric), to try to encompass the ultimate detail, the indivisible unit, the fleeting transition, in order to assign these a place in the structure, we will inevitably be confronted with *notations* which no function (not even the most indirect) will allow us to justify: these details are scandalous (from the point of view of structure), or, even more disturbingly, they seem to be allied with a kind of narrative *luxury*, profligate to the extent of throwing up 'useless' details and increasing the cost of narrative information. So, although it may be possible just to regard the detail of the piano as a sign of the bourgeois status of its owner, and that of the boxes as a sign of disorder and something like a

---

* Reprinted from 'The reality effect' in *French Literary Theory Today*, ed. Tzvetan Todorov, trans. R. Carter (New York: Cambridge University Press, 1982), pp. 11–17.

reverse or fall in status, appropriately evocative of the Aubain household, there seems to be no such end in view to justify the reference to the barometer, an object which is neither incongruous nor significant, and which, therefore, at first sight, seems not to belong to the domain of the *notable*. In Michelet's sentence, also, it is difficult to account structurally for all the details: the only thing that is indispensable to the account is the statement that the executioner came after the painter. How long the sitting lasted, and the size and location of the door, are useless (but the theme of the door, and death's soft knocking, have indisputable symbolic value). Even if they are not plentiful, 'useless details' thus seem inevitable: any narrative, at least any Western narrative of the ordinary sort, has some.

Insignificant *notation* (taking 'insignificant' in the strong sense – apparently detached from the semiotic structure of the narrative)[4] – is related to description, even if the object seems to be denoted by a single word (in reality, the pure word does not exist: Flaubert's barometer is not cited as an isolated unit, it is situated, placed in a **syntagm** that is both referential and syntactic). This underlines the enigmatic character of any description, of which something must be said. The general structure of the narrative, at least as this has been analysed at one time or another up to the present, appears essentialy predictive; to be extremely schematic, ignoring the numerous digressions, delays, changes of direction, or surprises which the narrative conventions add to this schema, it can be said that, at each juncture of the narrative syntagm, someone says to the hero (or to the reader, it does not matter which): if you act in this way, if you choose this alternative, then this is what will happen (the *reported* nature of these predictions does not alter their practical effect). Description is quite different: it has no predictive aspect; it is 'analogical', its structure being purely additive, and not incorporating that circuit of choices and alternatives which makes a narration look like a vast traffic control centre, provided with referential (and not merely discursive) temporality. This is an opposition which has its importance for anthropology: when, influenced by the work of von Frisch, some imagined that bees might have a language, it had to be recognised that, while these animals might have a predictive system of dances, used in food-gathering, they possess nothing resembling a *description*.[5] Description thus appears to be a characteristic of so-called higher languages, in that seemingly paradoxically, it is not justified by any purpose of action or communication. The singularity of the description (or of the 'useless detail') in the narrative fabric, its isolatedness, brings up a question of primary importance for the structural analysis of narrative. This question is the following: is everything in the narrative meaningful, significant? And if not, if there exist insignificant stretches, what is, so to speak, the ultimate significance of this insignificance?

It should first be recalled that Western culture, in one of its major currents, has certainly not left description without a meaning, but has in fact assigned to it an end perfectly well recognised by the institution of literature. This current is rhetoric, and the end is 'beauty': description has long had an aesthetic function. Very early in antiquity, to the two explicitly functional genres of oratory – legal and political discourse – was added a third, epideictic discourse, the set speech whose goal was to excite the admiration of the audience (and not to persuade it); and this genre, whatever the rituals governing its use – whether praise of a hero or an obituary – contained the seeds of the notion of an aesthetic purpose in language. In Alexandrian neo-rhetoric of the second century AD there was an infatuation for the *ekphrasis*, a polished piece, and detachable (thus having its own purpose, independent of any general function), whose object was to describe places, times, people or works of art; and this tradition was maintained down through the Middle Ages. As Curtius[6] has emphasised, throughout this period description was not constrained by any desire for realism; truth, or even verisimilitude, was of little moment – nobody was bothered when lions or olive trees were placed in a northern landscape. The only constraints that mattered were descriptive ones; plausibility was not referential, but overtly discursive; it was the rules of the discourse genre which laid down the law.

Moving ahead to Flaubert, we see that the aesthetic intention of description is still very strong. In *Madame Bovary*, the description of Rouen (a real referent if there ever was one) is subjected to the tyrannical constraints of what must be called aesthetic plausibility, as is attested by the corrections made in this passage in the course of six successive versions.[7] We note first of all that the corrections are in no way due to closer attention to the model: Rouen, as perceived by Flaubert, stays the same, or more exactly, if it changes a little from one version to the next, this is only because it was necessary to tighten up an image or avoid a phonetic redundancy condemned by the rules of *le beau style*, or else to create the appropriate environment for some happy but quite contingent expressive find.[8] Next we see that the descriptive fabric, which at first glance seems to assign great importance (by its length and attention to detail) to the object *Rouen*, is really no more than a kind of background or setting meant to receive the jewels of a few precious metaphors, the neutral matter enveloping the precious symbolic ingredients, as if, in Rouen, all that was important was the rhetorical figures available for describing what one sees, as if Rouen was only notable via its substitutions ('the masts like a forest of needles, the islands like great immobile black fish, the clouds like aerial waves silently breaking against a cliff'). Lastly, one sees that the entire description *is constructed* so as to associate Rouen with a painting: it is a painted scene taken on by language. ('Thus, seen from above, the entire landscape looked as motionless as a painting'). The writer fulfils here the definition given by Plato of the artist: a maker in the third degree, since he imitates what is already the simulation of an essence.[9] So although the description of Rouen is perfectly 'irrelevant' to the narrative structure of *Madame Bovary* (it can be attached to no functional sequence, nor to any signified (*signifié*) of characterisation, atmosphere, or information), it is in no way shocking, being justified, if not by the logic of the work, at least by the laws of literature; it has a meaning, but that meaning is given by its conformity, not to the object of description, but to the cultural rules governing representation.

Nevertheless, the aesthetic intention of Flaubertian description is totally interwoven with the imperatives of 'realism', as if exactitude of reference, superior or indifferent to all other functions, of itself commanded and justified description of the referent, or, in the case of a description reduced to a single word, its denotation. Here aesthetic constraints are impregnated – at least as an alibi – with referential constraints: it is probable that, if one had arrived at Rouen by stagecoach, the view one would have had descending the hill road which leads to the city would not have been 'objectively' different from the panorama described by Flaubert. This mixing, this interweaving of constraints, has two advantages: on the one hand the aesthetic function, by conferring a meaning on the set piece, is a safeguard against a downward spiral into endless detail. For, when discourse is no longer guided and limited by the structural imperatives of the story (functions and signals), there is nothing to tell the writer why he should stop descriptive details at one point rather than another: if it was not subject to aesthetic or rhetorical choice, any 'seeing' would be inexhaustible by discourse; there would always be some corner, some detail, some nuance of location or colour to add. On the other hand, by stating the referent to be real, and by pretending to follow it slavishly, realistic description avoids being seduced into fantasising (a precaution which was believed necessary for the 'objectivity' of the account). Classical rhetoric had in a sense institutionalised the fantasy under the name of a particular figure, hypotyposis, whose function was to 'place things before the hearer's eyes', not in a neutral manner, merely reporting, but by giving to the scene all the radiance of desire (this was a division of vividly illumined discourse, with prismatic outlines: the *illustris oratio*). Having proclaimed its renunciation of the constraints of the rhetorical code, realism had to find a new reason to describe.

What the irreducible residues of functional analysis have in common is that they denote what is commonly called 'concrete reality' (casual movements, transitory attitudes, insignificant objects, redundant words). Unvarnished 'representation' of 'reality', a naked account of 'what is' (or was), thus looks like a resistance to meaning, a resistance which confirms the great mythical opposition between the true-to-life (the living) and the intelligible. It suffices to recall that for the ideology of our time, obsessive reference to the 'concrete' (in what is grandiloquently asked of the sciences of man, of literature, of behaviour) is always brandished as a weapon against meaning, as if there were some indisputable law that what is truly alive could not signify – and vice versa. The resistance of 'reality' (in its written form, of course) to structure is quite limited in fictional narrative, which by definition is constructed on a model which has, on the whole, no other constraints than those of intelligibility. But this same 'reality' becomes the essential reference in historical narrative, which is supposed to report 'what really happened'. What does it matter that a detail has no function in the account as long as it denotes 'what took place'? 'Concrete reality' becomes a sufficient justification for what is said. History (historical discourse: *historia rerum gestarum*) is in fact the model for those narratives which accept, as a filling for the gaps in their functions, *notations* which are structurally superfluous. It is logical, therefore, that realism in literature should have been, give or take a few decades, contemporaneous with the reign of 'objective' history, to which should be added the present-day development of techniques, activities, and institutions based on an endless need to authenticate the 'real': photography (direct evidence of 'what was there'), reportage, exhibitions of ancient objects (the success of the Tutankhamun show is a sufficient indication), tours to monuments and historical sites. All this demonstrates that the 'real' is assumed not to need any independent justification, that it is powerful enough to negate any notion of 'function', that it can be expressed without there being any need for it to be integrated into a structure, and that the *having-been-there* of things is a sufficient reason for speaking of them.

Since antiquity, the 'real' and history have gone together (seemingly truthful), but this helped to oppose it to the **'vraisemblable'** that is, to the very nature of narrative (imitation or 'poetry'). The whole of classical culture was for centuries nourished by the idea that there could be no contamination of the 'vraisemblable' by the real. At first because what is 'vraisemblable' is never other than the thinkable: it is entirely subject to (public) opinion. Nicole said: 'One must not view things as they are in themselves, nor as he who speaks or writes knows them to be, but only in relation to what the reader or the hearer knows of them'.[10] Then because it was thought that what is 'vraisemblable' is general and not particular, as is history (hence the tendency, in classical texts, to functionalise every detail, to produce strong structures and, it would seem, to leave no notation which is justified only by its conformity of 'reality'). Finally because, with the 'vraisemblable', the opposite is never impossible, since description is founded on majority, but not unanimous, opinion. The motto implicitly prefacing all classical discourse (obeying the ancients 'vraisemblance') is: *Esto* (Let there be, suppose . . .). The kind of 'real', fragmented, interstitial descriptive *notation* we are dealing with here does not appeal to this implicit introduction, and it takes its place in the structural fabric with no hint of such a hypothetical qualification. Just for that reason, there is a break between the old 'vraisemblance' and modern realism; but for that reason also, a new 'vraisemblance' is born, which is precisely what is called 'realism' (taking this term to refer to any discourse which accepts statements whose only justification is their referent).

Semiotically, the 'concrete detail' is constituted by the *direct* collusion of a referent and a signifier; the signified is expelled from the sign, and along with it, of course, there is eliminated the possibility of developing a *form of the signified*, that is, the narrative structure itself. (Realist literature is, to be sure, narrative, but that is because its realism is only fragmentary, erratic, restricted to 'details', and because the most realistic narrative imaginable unfolds in an unrealistic manner.) This is what might be called the *referential illusion*.[11] The truth behind this illusion is this: eliminated from the realist utterance as a signified of denotation, the 'real' slips back in as a signified of connotation; for at the very moment when these details are supposed to denote reality directly, all that they do, tacitly, is signify it. Flaubert's barometer, Michelet's little door, say, in the last analysis, only this: we are the real. It is the category of the 'real', and not its various contents, which is being signified; in other words, the very absence of the signified, to the advantage of the referent, standing alone, becomes the true signifier of realism. An *'effet de réel'*, (a reality effect) is produced, which is the basis of that unavowed 'vraisemblance' which forms the aesthetic of all the standard works of modernity.

This new 'vraisemblance' is very different from the old, for it is neither a respect for the 'laws of the genre', nor even a disguise for them, but arises rather from an intention to alter the tripartite nature of the sign so as to make the descriptive notation a pure encounter between the object and its expression. The disintegration of the sign – which seems in fact to be the major concern of modernism – is indeed present in the realist enterprise, but in a somewhat regressive manner, since it is accomplished in the name of referential plenitude, while on the contrary the goal today is to empty the sign and to push back its object to infinity to the point of calling into question, in radical fashion, the age-old aesthetic of 'representation'.

Notes

1. G. FLAUBERT, *Un Coeur simple* in *Trois Contes* (Paris: Charpentier-Fasquelle, 1893), p. 4.

2. J. MICHELET, *Histoire de France, La Révolution*, Vol. V (Lausanne: Editions Rencontre, 1967), p. 292.

3. Introduction à l'analyse structurale des récits', *Communications* 8 (Nov. 1966), pp. 2–27.

4. In this brief survey, we give no examples of 'insignificant' *notation*, since the insignificant can be illustrated only within the framework of a very large structure; when cited, a *notation* is neither significant nor insignificant: it requires a previously analysed context.

5. F. BRESSON, 'La Signification', in *Problèmes de psycho-linguistique* (Paris: PUF, 1963).

6. E.R. CURTIUS, *La Littérature européenne et le Moyen Age latin* (Paris: PUF, 1956), Ch. 10.

7. The six successive versions of this description are given by A. Albalat in *Le Travail du style* (Paris: A. Colin, 1903), pp. 72ff.

8. The mechanism is well noted by Valéry, in *Littérature*, when he comments on a line of Baudelaire's: 'The servant with the big heart . . .' ('This line *came* to Baudelaire . . . And Baudelaire continued. He buried the cook in a lawn, which goes against the custom, but goes with the rhyme . . .').

9. PLATO, *Republic*, X: 599.

10. Cited by R. BRAY in *Formation de la doctrine classique* (Paris: Nizet, 1963), p. 208.

11. The illusion is clearly illustrated by the programme which Thiers established for the historian: 'To be simply true, to be as things themselves are, to be nothing more than them, to be nothing other than by them, like them, as much as them' (cited by C. Jullian, *Historiens français du XIXe siècle* (Paris: Hachette, n.d.), p. lxiii).

14 David Lodge on Hemingway's 'Cat in the Rain'*

I

It is a commonplace that the systematic study of narrative was founded by Aristotle, and scarcely an exaggeration to say that little of significance was added to those foundations until the twentieth century. Narrative theory in the intervening period was mainly directed (or misdirected) at deducing from Aristotle's penetrating analysis of the system of Greek tragedy a set of prescriptive rules for the writing of epic. The rise of the novel as a distinctive and eventually dominant literary form finally exposed the poverty of neoclassical narrative theory, without for a long time generating anything much more satisfactory. The realistic novel set peculiar problems for any formalist criticism because it worked by disguising or denying its own conventionality. It therefore invited – and received – criticism which was interpretative and evaluative rather than analytical. It was not until the late nineteenth and early twentieth centuries that something like a poetics of fiction began to evolve from the self-conscious experiments of novelists themselves, and was elaborated by literary critics. At about the same time, developments in linguistics, folklore and anthropology stimulated a more broad-ranging study of narrative, beyond the boundaries of modern literary fiction. For a long time these investigations were pursued on parallel tracks which seldom converged. In the last couple of decades, however, the Anglo-American tradition of formalist criticism, essentially empirical and text-based, theoretically rather underpowered but hermeneutically productive, has encountered the more systematic, abstract, theoretically rigorous and 'scientific' tradition of European structuralist criticism. The result has been a minor 'knowledge explosion' in the field of narrative theory and poetics of fiction.

---

* Reprinted from 'Analysis and Interpretation of the Realist Text: Ernest Hemingway's "Cat in the Rain"' in *Working with Structuralism* (London: Routledge and Kegan Paul, 1981), pp. 17–36, 197–8.

The question I wish to raise in this essay is whether progress in theory and methodology means progress in the critical reading of texts. Is it possible, or useful, to bring the whole battery of modern formalism and structuralism to bear upon a single text, and what is gained by so doing? Does it enrich our reading by uncovering depths and nuances of meaning we might not otherwise have brought to consciousness, help us to solve problems of interpretation and to correct misreadings? Or does it merely encourage a pointless and self-indulgent academicism, by which the same information is shuffled from one set of categories to another, from one jargon to another, without any real advance in appreciation or understanding? The analysis offered here of a short story by Ernest Hemingway is intended to support a positive answer to the first set of questions, a negative answer to the second set. But first it may be useful to remind ourselves of the range and variety of theories, methodologies and 'approaches' now available to the critic of fiction. I would group them into three categories, according to the 'depth' at which they address themselves to narrative structure.

1 *Narratology and Narrative Grammar* – i.e. the effort to discover the *langue* of narrative, the underlying system of rules and possibilities of which any narrative *parole* (text) is the realisation. With a few arguable expections – e.g. Northrop Frye's *Anatomy of Criticism* (1957) and Frank Kermode's *The Sense of an Ending* (1966) – this enterprise has been almost exclusively dominated by European scholars – **Propp**, **Bremond**, **Greimas**, **Lévi-Strauss**, Todorov and Barthes, among others. Crucial to this tradition of inquiry are the ideas of function and transformation. In the theory of Greimas, for instance, all narrative consists essentially of the transfer of an object or value from one 'actant' to another. An actant performs a certain function in the story which may be classified as Subject or Object, **Sender** or **Receiver**, Helper or Opponent, and is involved in doing things which may be classified as performative (tests, struggles, etc.), contractual (establishment and breaking of contracts) and disjunctional (departure and returns). These functions are not simply identifiable from the surface structure of a narrative text: for instance, several characters may perform the function of one actant, or one character may combine the functions of two actants. All concepts are **semantically** defined by a binary relationship with their opposites (e.g. Life/Death) or negatives (e.g. Life/Non-Life) yielding the basic semiotic model A:B :: $-$A:$-$B (e.g. Life:Death :: Non-Life:Non-Death), so that all narrative can be seen as the transformation into actants and actions of a thematic four-term homology.[1]

It is often said that this kind of approach is more rewarding when applied to narratives of a traditional, formulaic and orally transmitted type, rather than sophisticated literary narratives; and the exponents of narratology themselves frequently remind us that their aim is not the explication of texts but the uncovering of the system that allows narrative texts to be generated and competent readers to make sense of them. Narratology does, however, bring to the attention of the literary critic factors involved in reading narrative that are important, but in a sense so obvious that they tend to be overlooked. Roland Barthes has very fruitfully applied to the analysis of literary fictions the idea, derived from structuralist narratology, that narrative is divisible into sequences that open or close possibilities for the characters, and thus for the reader. The interest of these openings and closures may be either retrospective, contributing to the solution of some enigma proposed earlier in the text (the hermeneutic code), or prospective, making the audience wonder what will happen next (the proairetic code).[2] Curiosity and suspense are therefore the two basic 'affects' aroused by narrative, exemplified in a very pure form by the classic detective story and the thriller, respectively, as Tzvetan Todorov observes.[3] A story of any sophistication will also, as Kermode points out in *The Sense of an Ending*, make use of what Aristotle called peripeteia, or reversal, when a possibility is closed in a way that is unexpected and yet plausible and instructive. The reversal tends to produce an effect of irony, especially if it is anticipated by the audience.

Two problems arise in applying this kind of approach to realistic fiction. If we segment a text into its smallest units of information, how do we identify those which are functional on the basic narrative level, and what do we do with those units (the majority) which are not? Roland Barthes suggests one solution in his 'Introduction to the Structural Analysis of Narratives' where, drawing his illustrations mainly from Ian Fleming's *Goldfinger*, he classifies the narrative units as either *nuclei* or *catalysers*. Nuclei open or close alternatives that are of direct consequence for the subsequent development of the narrative and cannot be deleted without altering the story. Catalysers are merely consecutive units which expand the nuclei or fill up the space between them. They can be deleted without altering the narrative, though not, in the case of realistic narrative, without altering its meaning and effect, since segments which connect not, or not only, with segments at the same level, but with some more generalised concept such as the psychological makeup of the characters, or the atmosphere of the story, function as *indices*, or (if merely factual) *informants*. Jonathan Culler has suggested that our ability to distinguish nuclei from catalysers intuitively and to rank them in order of importance is a typical manifestation of reader-competence, verified by the fact that different readers will tend to summarise the plot of a given story in the same way. The intuitive recognition or ranking of nuclei is 'governed by readers' desire to reach an ultimate summary in which plot as a whole is grasped in a satisfying form'.[4] In short, the structural coherence of narratives is inseparable from their meaning, and reading them is inseparable from forming hypotheses about their overall meaning.

2 *Poetics of Fiction* Under this head I include all attempts to describe and
classify techniques of fictional representation. The great breakthrough in
this field in the modern era was undoubtedly the Russian Formalists'
distinction between *fabula* and *sjuzet*: on the one hand, the story in its most
neutral, objective, chronological form – the story as it might have been
enacted in real time and space, a seamless continuum of innumerable
contiguous events; and on the other hand, the actual text in which this
story is imitated, with all its inevitable (but motivated) gaps, elisions,
emphases and distortions. Work along these lines in Europe, culminating
in Gérard Genette's 'Discours du récit' (1972), established two principal
areas in which *sjuzet* significantly modifies *fabula*: time, and what is
generally called 'point of view' in Anglo-American criticism – though
Genette correctly distinguishes here between 'perspective' (who sees the
action) and 'voice' (who speaks the narration of it). He also distinguishes
most suggestively three different categories in the temporal organisation
(or deformation) of the *fabula* by the *sjuzet*: order, duration and frequence.
The first of these concerns the relation between the order of events in the
fabula, which is always chronological, and the order of events in the *sjuzet*,
which, of course, need not be. The second category concerns the relation
between the putative duration of events in the *fabula* and the time taken to
narrate them (and therefore to read the narration) in the *sjuzet*, which may
be longer, or shorter, or approximately the same. The third category
concerns the relationship between the number of times an event occurs in
the *fabula* and the number of times it is narrated in the *sjuzet*. There are
four possibilities: telling once what happened once, telling *n* times what
happened *n* times, telling *n* times what happened once, and telling once
what happened *n* times.[5]

The choices made by the narrative artist at this level are in a sense
prior to, or 'deeper' than his stylistic choices in composing the surface
structure of the text, though they place important constraints upon what
he can achieve in the surface structure. They are also of manifest
importance in the realistic novel which, compared to other, earlier
narrative forms, is characterised by a carefully discriminated, pseudo-
historical treatment of temporality, and a remarkable depth and flexibility
in its presentation of consciousness.

A good deal of Anglo-American critical theorising about the novel,
from Percy Lubbock's *The Craft of Fiction* (1921) to Wayne Booth's *The
Rhetoric of Fiction* (1961), was implicitly, if unconsciously, based on the
same distinction between *fabula* and *sjuzet*, between 'story' and 'way of
telling it'. The cross-fertilisation of the two critical traditions has
produced much interesting and illuminating work, analysing and
classifying novelistic techniques and covering such matters as tense,
person, speech and indirect speech in fictional narrative; and we are
now, it seems to me, within sight of a truly comprehensive taxonomy of

fictional form at this level. Two recent books which have made particularly valuable contributions in this respect are Seymour Chatman's *Story and Discourse: Narrative Structure in Fiction and Film* (1978) and the more narrowly focused *Transparent Minds: Narrative Modes for Presenting Consciousness in Fiction* by Dorrit Cohn (1978).

3 *Rhetorical Analysis*   By this I mean analysing the surface structure of narrative texts to show how the linguistic mediation of a story determines its meaning and effect. This is a kind of criticism in which Anglo-American tradition is comparatively strong, because of the close-reading techniques developed by the New Criticism. Mark Shorer's essays 'Technique as Discovery' (1948) and 'Fiction and the Analogical Matrix' (1949)[6] are classic statements of this approach. The stylistics that developed out of Romance Philology, represented at its best by Spitzer and Auerbach,[7] also belongs in this category. When I wrote my first book of criticism, *Language of Fiction* (1966), this seemed the best route by which to achieve a formalist critique of the realistic novel.

The underlying aim of this criticism was to demonstrate that what looked like redundant or random detail in realistic fiction was in fact functional, contributing to a pattern of motifs with expressive and thematic significance. Much of this criticism was therefore concerned with tracing symbolism and keywords in the verbal texture of novels. Though very few of the New Critics were aware of the work of Roman Jakobson, he provided a theoretical justification for this kind of criticism in his famous definition of literariness, or the poetic function of language, as 'the projection of the principle of equivalence from the axis of selection to the axis of combination'.[8] What the New Critics called 'spatial form'[9] was precisely a pattern of paradigmatic equivalences concealed in the narrative syntagm. Furthermore, as I tried to show in my book *The Modes of Modern Writing* (1977), in his distinction between metaphor and metonymy,[10] Jakobson provided a key to understanding how the realistic novel contrives to build up a pattern of equivalences without violating its illusion of life.

Metaphor and metonymy (or **synecdoche**) are both figures of equivalance,[11] but generated by different processes, metaphor according to similarity between things otherwise different, metonymy according to contiguity or association between part and whole, cause and effect, thing and attribute, etc. Thus, if I transform the literal sentence 'Ships sail the sea' into 'Keels plough the deep', *plough* is equivalent to 'sail' because of the similarity between the movement of a plough through the earth and a ship through the sea, but *keel* is equivalent to 'ship' because it is part of a ship (synecdoche) and *deep* is equivalent to 'sea' because it is an attribute of the sea (metonymy). In fact, metonymy is a non-logical (and therefore foregrounded or rhetorical) condensation achieved by transformations of kernel sentences by deletion (*the keels of the ships* condensed to *keels* rather than *ships*, *deep sea* to *deep* rather than *sea*). Metonymy thus plays with the combination axis of language as metaphor plays with the selection axis of language, and together they epitomise the two ways by which any discourse connects one topic with another: either because they are similar or because they are contiguous. Jakobson's distinction thus allows the analyst to move freely between deep structure and surface structure.

Realistic fiction is dominantly metonymic: it connects actions that are contiguous in time and space and connected by cause and effect, but since it cannot describe exhaustively, the narrative *sjuzet* is always in a metonymic (or synecdochic) relation to the *fabula*. The narrative text necessarily selects certain details and suppresses or deletes others. The selected details are thus foregrounded by being selected, and their recurrence and interrelation with each other in the narrative text becomes aesthetically significant (what the Prague School calls systematic internal foregrounding). Furthermore, these details may carry connotations, building up a still denser pattern of equivalences, especially (though not exclusively) when they are described in figurative language, using the verbal tropes of metonymy or metaphor. This is usually (and rather loosely) called 'symbolism' in Anglo-American criticism. Barthes calls it connotation, the process by which one signifier acts as the signifier of another signified not actually named. Jakobson's distinction enables us to distinguish four different ways in which it operates in literary texts, two of which are especially characteristic of realistic fiction:

A Metonymic Signified I metonymically evokes Signified II (e.g. the hearth fire in *Jane Eyre*, an invariably selected detail in any description of domestic interiors, signifying 'inhabited room', also symbolises comfort, intimacy, security, etc., cause evoking effect).
B Metonymic Signified I metaphorically evokes Signified II (e.g. mud and fog at the beginning of *Bleak House*, signifying 'inclement weather', also symbolise the obfuscation and degradation of goodness and justice by the Law, because of the similarity between the effects of the elements and those of the institution).
C Metaphoric Signified I metonymically evokes Signified II (e.g. the description of the night in Llaregyb, by Dylan Thomas's *Under Milk Wood*, as 'bible-black', symbolises the Protestant chapel-going religious culture of the community; part, or attribute, standing for the whole).
D Metaphoric Signified I metaphorically evokes Signified II (e.g. in the opening lines of Yeats's poem, 'The Second Coming' –

> Turning and turning in the widening gyre
> The falcon cannot hear the falconer

where the metaphor *gyre* applied to the spiralling movement of the falcon also symbolises the cyclical movement of history).

Realistic fiction relies principally upon symbolism of types A and B, in which the primary signified is introduced into the discourse according to the metonymic principle of spatial or temporal contiguity with what has come before.

II

No choice of a text for illustrative purposes is innocent, and no analysis of a single text could possibly provide universally valid answers to the questions posed at the beginning of this essay. These questions will not be settled until we have a significant corpus of synthetic or pluralistic readings of narrative texts of various types. Two distinguished achievements of this kind come to mind: Barthes's *S/Z* and Christine Brooke-Rose's study of *The Turn of the Screw*.[12] The following discussion of Hemingway's short story 'Cat in the Rain' (1925)* follows the model of the latter in taking the problem of interpretation as its starting-point, but it is necessarily much more modest in scope and scale than either. Two considerations prompted the choice of this story, apart from its convenient brevity. (1) A staff seminar on it in my own department at Birmingham revealed that it presents certain problems of interpretation, though without being quite so heavily encrusted with the deposits of previous readings and misreadings as *The Turn of the Screw*. (2) It is both realistic and modern, cutting across that historicist and tendentious distinction between the *lisible* and the *scriptible* which I personally find one of the less helpful features of the work of Barthes and his disciples.[13] The implied notion of *vraisemblance* on which Hemingway's story depends, the assumed relationship between the text and reality, is essentially continuous with that of classic bourgeois realism, yet in the experience of readers it has proved ambiguous, polyvalent and resistant to interpretative closure.

This is what Carlos Baker, in the standard critical work on Hemingway, had to say about 'Cat in the Rain' (he discusses it in the context of a group of stories about men–women relationships):

> 'Cat in the Rain', another story taken in part from the woman's point of view, presents a corner of the female world in which the male is only tangentially involved. It was written at Rapallo in May, 1923. From the window of a hotel room where her husband is reading and she is fidgeting, a young wife sees a cat outside in the rain. When she

---

* Reprinted at the end of this essay, pp. 157–61.

goes to get it, the animal (which somehow stands in her mind for comfortable bourgeois domesticity) has disappeared. This fact is very close to tragic because of the cat's association in her mind with many other things she longs for: long hair she can do in a knot at the back of her neck; a candle-lighted dining table where her own silver gleams; the season of spring and nice weather; and of course, some new clothes. But when she puts these wishes into words, her husband mildly advises her to shut up and find something to read. 'Anyway,' says the young wife, 'I want a cat. I want a cat. I want a cat now. If I can't have long hair or any fun, I can have a cat.' The poor girl is the referee in a face-off between the actual and the possible. The actual is made of rain, boredom, a preoccupied husband, and irrational yearnings. The possible is made of silver, spring, fun, a new coiffure, and new dresses. Between the actual and the possible, stands the cat. It is finally sent up to her by the kindly old inn-keeper, whose sympathetic deference is greater than that of the young husband.[14]

There are several things to quibble with in this account of the story. Most important perhaps is Baker's assumption that the cat sent up by the hotel-keeper at the end is the same as the one that the wife saw from her window. This assumption is consistent with Baker's sympathy with the wife as a character, implied by his reference to her as 'the poor girl' and his description of the disappearance of the cat as 'very close to tragic'. The appearance of the maid with a cat is the main reversal, in Aristotelian terms, in the narrative. If it is indeed the cat she went to look for, then the reversal is a happy one for her, and confirms her sense that the hotel-keeper appreciated her as a woman more than her husband. In Greimas's terms, the wife is the subject of the story and the cat the object. The hotel-keeper and the maid enact the role of helper and George is the opponent. The story is disjunctive (departure and return) and concerns the transfer of the cat to the wife.

The description of the tortoise-shell cat as 'big', however, suggests that it is not the one to which the wife referred by the diminutive term 'kitty', and which she envisaged stroking on her lap. We might infer that the padrone, trying to humour a client, sends up the first cat he can lay hands on, which is in fact quite inappropriate to the wife's needs. This would make the reversal an ironic one at the wife's expense, emphasising the social and cultural abyss that separates her from the padrone, and revealing her quasi-erotic response to his professional attentiveness as a delusion.

I shall return to this question of the ambiguity of the ending. One more point about Baker's commentary on the story: he says that the cat 'somehow stands in [the wife's] mind for comfortable bourgeois domesticity', and speak of its 'association in her mind with many other things she longs for'. In other words, he interprets the cat as a metonymic symbol of type A above. Indeed he sees the whole story as turning on the opposition between two groups of metonymies. 'The actual is made of rain, boredom, a preoccupied husband, and irrational yearnings. The possible is made of silver, spring fun, a new coiffure, and new clothes.'

John V. Hagopian gives a very different reading of this story. It is, he says, about 'a crisis in the marriage . . . involving the lack of fertility, which is symbolically foreshadowed by the public garden (fertility) dominated by the war monument (death)' in the first paragraph. These again are metonymic symbols of type A, effect connoting cause; but Hagopian's reading of the story hinges on the identification of the cat as a symbol of a wanted child, and of the man in the rubber cape (lines 52–3) as a symbol of contraception – symbolism of type B, in which a metonymic signified evokes a second signified metaphorically, i.e. by virtue of similarity.

> As [the wife] looks out into the wet empty square, she sees a man in a rubber cape crossing to the café in the rain . . . The rubber cape is a protection from rain, and rain is a fundamental necessity for fertility and fertility is precisely what is lacking in the American wife's marriage. An even more precise interpretation is possible but perhaps not necessary here.[15]

What Hagopian is presumably hinting at is that 'rubber' is an American colloquialism for contraceptive sheath, and that the wife notices the man in the rubber cape because of the subconscious association – a piece of classic Freudian 'symbolism'. It is an ingenious interpretation and all the more persuasive because there seems to be no very obvious reason for introducing the man in the cape into the story – he is not an actant in the narrative but an item of the descriptive background, and his appearance does not tell us anything about the weather or the square that we do not know already. Admittedly, the cape does signify, by contrast, the wife's lack of protection from the rain, thus emphasising the padrone's thoughtfulness in sending the maid with the umbrella. But if we accept Hagopian's reading then the umbrella itself, opening with almost comical opportuneness and effortlessness behind her, becomes a symbol of how the wife's way of life comes between her and a vital, fertile relationship with reality. Her later demands for new clothes, a new hairstyle, a candle-lit dining-table are, according to Hagopian, expressions of a desire that never reaches full consciousness, for 'motherhood, a home with a family, an end of the strictly companionate marriage with George'. And

the cat, he says, is by this stage in the story 'an obvious symbol for a
child.'

Unlike Baker, Hagopian sees the final reversal in the story as ironic:

> The girl's symbolic wish is grotesquely fulfilled in painfully realistic
> terms. It is George, not the padrone, by whom the wife wants to be
> fulfilled, but the padrone has sent up the maid with a big tortoise-shell
> cat, a huge creature that swings down against her body. It is not clear
> whether this is exactly the same cat as the one the wife had seen from
> the window – probably not; in any case, it will most certainly not do.
> The girl is willing to settle for a child-surrogate, but the big tortoise-
> shell cat obviously cannot serve that purpose.[16]

The reason why this story is capable of provoking these two very
different interpretations might be expressed as follows: although it is a
well-formed narrative, with a clearly defined beginning, middle and end,
the primary action is not the primary vehicle of meaning. This can be
demonstrated by testing upon the story Jonathan Culler's hypothesis that
competent readers will tend to agree on what is and is not essential to
the plot of a narrative text. Before the seminar at Birmingham University,
participants were invited to summarise the action of the story in not
more than thirty words of continuous prose.[17] All the contributors
mentioned the wife, the cat, the rain, and the hotel manager; most
mentioned the nationality of the wife and her failure to find the cat under
the table; about half mentioned the husband, located the story in Italy,
and made a distinction between the two cats. None mentioned the maid,
or the bickering between husband and wife.

These omissions are particularly interesting. The non-appearance of
the maid is easily explained: on the narrative level her function is
indistinguishable from that of the manager – both are 'helpers' and the
narrative would not be significantly altered *qua* narrative if the maid were
deleted from the story and her actions performed by the manager
himself. She does contribute to the symmetry of the story both
numerically and sexually: it begins by pairing husband and wife, then
pairs wife and manager, then wife and maid, then (in the wife's
thoughts) maid and manager, then wife and manager again, then wife
and husband again, and ends by pairing husband and maid. But this
seems to be a purely formal set of equivalences with no significance in
the hermeneutic or proairetic codes (such as would obtain if, for instance,
there were some intrigue linking the husband with the maid and the
manager, the kind of plotting characteristic of the *lisible* text). The main
function of the maid in the story is to emphasise the status of the wife as
a client and expatriate, and thus to act as a warning or corrective against

the wife's tendency to attribute to the padrone a deeply personal interest in herself.

Both Baker and Hagopian agree that the rift between husband and wife is what the story is essentially about, even if they disagree about the precise cause. That none of the synopses should make any allusion to the bickering between the couple is striking evidence that the meaning of the story does not inhere in its basic action. In trying to preserve what is essential to that action in a very condensed summary – the quest for the cat, the failure of the quest, the reversal – one has to discard what seems most important in the story as read – the relationship between husband and wife. Adopting Barthes's terminology in 'The Structural Analysis of Narratives', there are only four nuclei in the story, opening possibilities which might be closed in different ways: will the wife or the husband go to fetch the cat? will the wife get the cat? will she get wet? who is at the door? There is perhaps another possibility tacitly opened around line 115, and closed, negatively, at line 131: namely, that George will put down his book and make love to his wife. All the rest of the story consists of catalysers that are indexical or informational, and since most of the information is given more than once, these too become indexical of mood and atmosphere (for instance, we are told more than once that it is raining). One might indeed describe the story generically as indexical: we infer its meaning indexically from its non-narrative components rather than hermeneutically or teleologically from its action. Another way of putting it would be to invoke Seymour Chatman's distinction between the resolved plot and the revealed plot:

> In the traditional narrative of resolution, there is a sense of problem solving . . . of a kind of ratiocinative or emotional teleology. . . . 'What will happen?' is the basic question. In the modern plot of revelation, however, the emphasis is elsewhere, the function of the discourse is not to answer that question or even to pose it. . . . It is not that events are resolved (happily or tragically) but rather that a state of affairs is revealed.[18]

Chatman offers *Pride and Prejudice* and *Mrs Dalloway* as examples of each kind of plot. 'Cat in the Rain' seems to share characteristics of both: it is, one might say, a plot of revelation (the relationship between husband and wife) disguised as a plot of resolution (the quest for the cat). The ambiguity of the ending is therefore crucial. By refusing to resolve the issue of whether the wife gets the cat she wants, the implied author indicates that this is not the point of the story.

There are several reasons why this ending is ambiguous. One, obviously, is that the story ends where it does, for if it continued for another line or two, or moment or two, it would become apparent from the wife's response whether the cat was the one she had seen from the window, whether she is pleased or disconcerted by its being brought to her, and so on. In other words, the *sjuzet* tantalisingly stops just short of that point in the *fabula* where we should, with our readerly desire for certainty, wish it to. In other respects there is nothing especially striking about the story's treatment of time, though we may admire the smooth transition in the first paragraph from summary of a state of affairs obtaining over a period of days or weeks to the state of affairs obtaining on a particular afternoon, and the subtle condensation of durational time in the final scene between husband and wife, marked by changes in the light outside the window. The order of events is strictly chronological (characteristic, Chatman observes, of the resolved plot). As regards what Genette calls frequency, the story tends towards reiteration rather than summary, telling *n* times what happened *n* times or *n* times what happened once rather than telling once what happened *n* times. This is important because it reinforces the definition of the characters according to a very limited repertoire of gestures. Thus the wife is frequently described as looking out of the window, the husband as reading, the manager as bowing (and the weather as raining).

The story of the quest for the cat involves four characters, and in theory could be narrated from four points of view, each quite distinct and different in import. The story we have is written from the point of view of the American couple rather than that of the Italian hotel staff, and from the wife's point of view rather than the husband's. We must distinguish here between what Genette calls voice and perspective. The story is narrated throughout by an authorial voice which refers to the characters in the third person and uses the past tense. This is the standard mode of authorial narration and by convention the narrator is authoritative, reliable and, within the fictional world of the discourse, omniscient. The authorial voice in this story, however, renounces the privilege of authorial omniscience in two ways, firstly by abstaining from any comment or judgment or explanation of motive regarding the behaviour of the characters, and secondly by restricting itself to the perspective of only two of the characters, and for part of the story to the perspective of only one. By this I mean that the narrator describes nothing that is not seen by either husband or wife or both. Yet it is not quite true to say that the narrator has no independent angle of vision: he has. As in a film, we sometimes see the wife from the husband's angle, and the husband sometimes from the wife's angle, but much of the time we see them both from some independent, impersonal angle.

The first paragraph adopts the common perspective of the American couple, making no distinction between them. With the first sentence of the second paragraph, 'The American wife stood at the window looking out', the narrative adopts her perspective but without totally identifying

with it. Note the difference between '*her* husband' in line 30, which
closely identifies the narration with her perspective, and 'the husband' in
line 33, 'the wife' in line 36, which subtly reasserts the independence of
the authorial voice. From this point onwards, however, for the next fifty
lines the narration identifies itself closely with the wife's perspective,
following her out of the room and downstairs into the lobby, and
reporting what she thinks as well as what she sees. The anaphoric
sequence of sentences beginning 'She liked' (lines 45–50) affect us as
being a transcription rather than a description of her thoughts because
they could be transposed into monologue (first person/present tense)
without any illogicality or stylistic awkwardness. Sentences in free
indirect speech, 'The cat would be round to the right. Perhaps she could
go along under the eaves' (54–5) and 'Of course, the hotel-keeper had
sent her' (59), mark the maximum degree of identification of the
narration with the wife's point of view. When she returns to the room
the narration separates itself from her again. There is a lot of direct
speech from now on, no report of the wife's thoughts, and occasionally
the narration seems to adopt the husband's perspective alone, e.g.
'George looked up and saw the back of her neck, clipped close like a
boy's (109–10) and – very importantly:

> Someone knocked on the door.
> 'Avanti,' George said. He looked up from his book.
> In the doorway stood the maid. She held a big tortoise-shell cat . . .
> $$(142–4)$$

We can now fully understand why the ending of the story is so
ambiguous: it is primarily because the narration adopts the husband's
perspective at this crucial point. Since he did not rise from the bed to
look out of the window at the cat sheltering from the rain, he has no way
of knowing whether the cat brought by the maid is the same one – hence
the non-committal indefinite article, 'a big tortoise-shell cat'. If however,
the wife's perspective had been adopted at this point and the text had
read,

> 'Avanti,' the wife said. She turned round from the window.
> In the doorway stood the maid. She held a big tortoise-shell cat . . .

then it would be clear that this was not the cat the wife had wanted to
bring in from the rain (in which case the definite article would be used).
It is significant that in the title of the story, there is no article before 'Cat',
thus giving no support to either interpretation of the ending.

Carlos Baker's assumption that the tortoise-shell cat[19] and the cat in the
rain are one and the same is therefore unwarranted. Hagopian's reading

of the ending as ironic is preferable but his assumption that the wife's desire for the cat is caused by childlessness is also unwarranted. Here, it seems to me, the structuralist notion of language as a system of differences and of meaning as the product of structural oppositions can genuinely help to settle a point of interpretation. Hagopian's interpretation of the man in the rubber cape as a symbol of contraception depends in part on the association of rain with fertility. Now rain *can* symbolise fertility – when defined by opposition to drought. In this story, however (and incidentally, throughout Hemingway's work), it is opposed to 'good weather' and symbolises the loss of pleasure and joy, the onset of discomfort and ennui. Hagopian's comments on the disappearance of the painters, 'The rain, ironically, inhibits creativity,'[20] is a strained attempt to reconcile his reading with the text: there is no irony here unless we accept his equation, rain = fertility.

The cat as a child-surrogate is certainly a possible interpretation in the sense that it is a recognised cultural stereotype, but again Hagopian tries to enlist in its support textual evidence that is, if anything, negative. He comments on the description of the wife's sensations as she passes the hotel-keeper for the second time: '"very small and tight inside . . . really important . . . of supreme importance" all phrases that might appropriately be used to describe a woman who is pregnant'.[21] But not, surely, to describe a woman who merely *wants* to be pregnant. Indeed, if we must have a gynaecological reading of the story it is much more plausible to suppose that the wife's whimsical craving for the cat, and for other things like new clothes and long hair, is the result of her *being* pregnant. There is, in fact, some extratextual support for this hypothesis. In his biography of Hemingway, Carlos Baker states quite baldly that 'Cat in the Rain' was about Hemingway, his wife Hadley and the manager and chambermaid at the Hotel Splendide in Rapallo, where the story was written in 1923. He also states, without making any connection between the two items, that the Hemingways had left the chilly thaw of Switzerland and gone to Rapallo because Hadley had announced that she was pregnant.[22]

At about the same time, Hemingway was evolving 'a new theory that you could omit anything if you knew what you omitted, and the omitted part would strengthen the story and make people feel something more than they understood'.[23] This is, I think, a very illuminating description by Hemingway of his application of the metonymic mode of classic realism to modernist literary purposes. Metonymy, as I said earlier, is a device of non-logical deletion. Hemingway's word is 'omission'. By omitting the kind of motivation that classic realistic fiction provided, he generated a symbolist polyvalency in his deceptively simple stories, making his readers 'feel more than they understood'. It would be a mistake, therefore, to look for a single clue, whether pregnancy or barrenness, to the meaning of 'Cat in the Rain'. That the wife's (and, for that matter, the husband's) behaviour is equally intelligible on either assumption is one more confirmation of the story's indeterminacy.

Hemingway's stories are remarkable for achieving a symbolist resonance without the use of rhetorical figures and tropes. Not only does 'Cat in the Rain' contain no metaphors and similes – it contains no metonymies and synecdoches either. The story is 'metonymic' in the structural sense defined above: its minimal semantic units are selected from a single context, a continuum of temporal and spatial contiguities, and all foregrounded simply by being selected, repeated and related to each other oppositionally. Consider, for example, the opening paragraph, which establishes the story's setting in diction that is apparently severely denotative, with no metaphors or metonymies, similes or synecdoches, no elegant variation or pathetic fallacies, yet is nevertheless highly charged with connotative meaning.

There were only two Americans stopping at the hotel. Americans opposed to other nationalities: index of cultural isolation.

They did not know any of the people they passed on the stairs on their way to and from their room. Index of social isolation and mutual dependence – vulnerability to breakdown in relationship.

Their room was on the second floor facing the sea. Culture faces nature.

It also faced the public garden and the war monument. Culture paired with nature (public : garden) and opposed to nature (monument : garden). Pleasure (garden) opposed to pain (war).

There were big palms and green benches in the public garden. Culture and nature integrated. Benches same colour as vegetation.

In the good weather there was always an artist with his easel. Artists liked the way the palms grew and the bright colors of the hotels facing the gardens and the sea. Culture and nature happily fused. Image of euphoria.

Italians came from a long way off to look up at the war monument. Euphoria qualified. War monument attracts the living but commemorates the dead. Looking associated with absence (of the dead). 'Italian' opposed to 'American'.

It was made of bronze and glistened in the rain. Inert mineral (bronze) opposed to organic vegetable (palm). Rain opposed to good weather. Euphoria recedes.

It was raining. Rain dripped from the palm trees. Euphoria recedes further. Weather uninviting.

Water stood in pools on the gravel paths. Image of stagnation.

The sea broke in a long line in the rain and slipped back down the beach to come up and break again in a long line in the rain. Excess of wetness. Monotony. Ennui.

The motor cars were gone from the square by the war monument. Across the square in the doorway of the café a waiter stood looking out at the square. Images of absence, loss, ennui.[24]

The first paragraph, then, without containing a single narrative nucleus, establishes the thematic core of the story through oppositions between nature and culture, joy and ennui. Joy is associated with a harmonious union of culture and nature, ennui is the result of some dissociation or discontinuity between culture and nature. The wife, looking out of the window at a scene made joyless by the rain, sees a cat with whose discomfort she emotionally identifies. Her husband, though offering to fetch it, implies his indifference to her emotional needs by not actually moving. The husband is reading, a 'cultural' use of the eyes. The wife is looking, a 'natural' use of the eyes. Her looking, through the window, expresses a need for communion. His reading of a book is a substitute for communion, and a classic remedy for ennui. It is worth noticing that he is reading on the bed – a place made for sleeping and making love; and the perversity of his behaviour is symbolised by the fact that he is lying on the bed the wrong way round. As the story continues, the contrast between looking and reading, both activities expressing the loss or failure of love, becomes more insistent. Denied the kitty, a 'natural' object (opposed to book) which she could have petted as a substitute of being petted, the wife looks in the mirror, pining for a more natural feminine self. Then she looks out of the window again, while her husband, who has not shifted his position (his immobility opposed to the padrone's punctilious bowing), reads on and impatiently recommends her to 'get something to read'. One could summarise this story in the style of Greimas, as follows: loving is to quarrelling as stroking a cat is to reading a book, a narrative transformation of the opposition between joy and ennui, thus:

Loving (Joy):Quarrelling (Ennui) :: stroking a cat (Non-joy, a giving but not receiving of pleasure):reading a book (Non-ennui).

Such a summary has this to recommend it, that it brings together the overt action of the story (the quest for the cat) with its implicit subject (the relationship between husband and wife). Whether it, and the preceding comments, enhance our understanding and appreciation of Hemingway's story, I leave others to judge.

'Cat in the Rain'

There were only two Americans stopping at the hotel. They did not know any of the people they passed on the stairs on their way to and from their room. Their room was on the second

floor facing the sea. It also faced the public   5
garden and the war monument. There were big
palms and green benches in the public garden.
In the good weather there was always an artist
with his easel. Artists liked the way the palms
grew and the bright colors of the hotels facing   10
the gardens and the sea. Italians came from a
long way off to look up at the war monument.
It was made of bronze and glistened in the rain.
It was raining. The rain dripped from the palm
trees. Water stood in pools on the gravel paths.   15
The sea broke in a long line in the rain and
slipped back down the beach to come up and
break again in a long line in the rain. The motor
cars were gone from the square by the war
monument. Across the square in the doorway   20
of the café a waiter stood looking out at the
empty square.

The American wife stood at the window looking out. Outside right under their window a
cat was crouched under one of the dripping   25
green tables. The cat was trying to make herself
so compact that she would not be dripped on.

'I'm going down and get that kitty,' the
American wife said.

'I'll do it,' her husband offered from the bed.   30

'No, I'll get it. The poor kitty out trying to
keep dry under a table.'

The husband went on reading, lying propped
up with the two pillows at the foot of the bed.

'Don't get wet,' he said.   35

The wife went downstairs and the hotel owner
stood up and bowed to her as she passed the
office. His desk was at the far end of the office.
He was an old man and very tall.

'Il piove,' the wife said. She liked the hotel-   40
keeper.

'Si, si, Signora, brutto tempo. It is very bad
weather.'

He stood behind his desk in the far end of
the dim room. The wife liked him. She liked   45
the deadly serious way he received any complaints. She liked his dignity. She liked the
way he wanted to serve her. She liked the way

he felt about being a hotel-keeper. She liked
his old, heavy face and big hands.   50
    Liking him she opened the door and looked
out. It was raining harder. A man in a rubber
cape was crossing the empty square to the café.
The cat would be around to the right. Perhaps
she could go along under the eaves. As she stood   55
in the doorway an umbrella opened behind her.
It was the maid who looked after their room.
    'You must not get wet,' she smiled, speaking
Italian. Of course, the hotel-keeper had sent her.
    With the maid holding the umbrella over her,   60
she walked along the gravel path until she was
under their window. The table was there,
washed bright green in the rain, but the cat was
gone. She was suddenly disappointed. The
maid looked up at her.   65
    'Ha perduto qualque cosa, Signora?'
    'There was a cat,' said the American girl.
    'A cat?'
    'Si, il gatto.'
    'A cat?' the maid laughed. 'A cat in the   70
rain?'
    'Yes,' she said, 'under the table.' Then, 'Oh,
I wanted it so much. I wanted a kitty.'
    When she talked English the maid's face
tightened.   75
    'Come, Signora,' she said. 'We must get
back inside. You will be wet.'
    'I suppose so,' said the American girl.
    They went back along the gravel path and
passed in the door. The maid stayed outside to   80
close the umbrella. As the American girl passed
the office, the padrone bowed from his desk.
Something felt very small and tight inside the
girl. The padrone made her feel very small and
at the same time really important. She had a   85
momentary feeling of being of supreme importance. She went on up the stairs. She opened
the door of the room. George was on the bed,
reading.
    'Did you get the cat?' he asked, putting the   90
book down.
    'It was gone.'

'Wonder where it went to,' he said, resting
his eyes from reading.

She sat down on the bed.   95

'I wanted it so much,' she said. 'I don't
know why I wanted it so much. I wanted that
poor kitty. It isn't any fun to be a poor kitty
out in the rain.'

George was reading again.   100

She went over and sat in front of the mirror
of the dressing table looking at herself with the
hand glass. She studied her profile, first one
side and then the other. Then she studied the
back of her head and her neck.   105

'Don't you think it would be a good idea
if I let my hair grow out?' she asked, looking
at her profile again.

George looked up and saw the back of her   110
neck, clipped close like a boy's.

'I like it the way it is.'

'I get so tired of it,' she said. 'I get so tired
of looking like a boy.'

George shifted his position in the bed. He
hadn't looked away from her since she started   115
to speak.

'You look pretty darn nice,' he said.

She laid the mirror down on the dresser and
went over to the window and looked out. It   120
was getting dark.

'I want to pull my hair back tight and smooth
and make a big knot at the back that I can feel,'
she said. 'I want to have a kitty to sit on my
lap and purr when I stroke her.'

'Yeah?' George said from the bed.   125

'And I want to eat at a table with my own
silver and I want candles. And I want it to be
spring and I want to brush my hair out in front
of a mirror and I want a kitty and I want some
new clothes.'   130

'Oh, shut up and get something to read,'
George said. He was reading again.

His wife was looking out of the window. It
was quite dark now and still raining in the palm
trees.   135

'Anyway, I want a cat,' she said, 'I want a

cat. I want a cat now. If I can't have long
hair or any fun, I can have a cat.'

George was not listening. He was reading
his book. His wife looked out of the window   140
where the light had come on in the square.

Someone knocked at the door.

'Avanti,' George said. He looked up from
his book.

In the doorway stood the maid. She held a   145
big tortoise-shell cat pressed tight against her
and swung down against her body.

'Excuse me,' she said, 'the padrone asked me
to bring this for the Signora.'

Notes

1. See A.J. GREIMAS, *Sémantique structurale* (Paris, 1966), *Du Sens* (Paris, 1970),
   and *Maupassant: La sémiologie du texte: exercices pratiques* (Paris, 1976). See also
   Ann Jefferson's long review of this last work in *Poetics and Theory of Literature*,
   II (London, 1977), pp. 579–88.

2. ROLAND BARTHES, 'Introduction to the Structural Analysis of Narratives' in
   Image–Music–Text, ed. and trans. Stephen Heath (London, 1977; first
   published 1966), and *S/Z*, trans. Richard Miller (London, 1975; first published
   1970).

3. TZVETAN TODOROV, *The Poetics of Prose*, trans. Richard Howard (London, 1977;
   first published 1971), p. 47.

4. JONATHAN CULLER, 'Defining Narrative Units' in *Style and Structure in
   Literature*, ed. Roger Fowler (Oxford, 1975), p. 139.

5. GÉRARD GENETTE, 'Discours du récit' in *Figures III* (Paris, 1972). An English
   translation of this treatise, entitled *Narrative Discourse*, has been published by
   Basil Blackwell (Oxford, 1979). For the sake of simplicity I have not introduced
   the terms (*récit, discours, histoire, narration*) in which Genette and other
   contemporary French critics have, with bewildering inconsistency, developed
   the Russian Formalists' *fabula/sjuzet* distinction. These terms, and Genette's
   theory of narrative in particular, are very elegantly elucidated in Shlomith
   Rimmon's 'A Comprehensive Theory of Narrative: Genette's *Figures III* and
   the Structuralist Study of Fiction in *Poetics and Theory of Literature*, I (1976), pp.
   32–62.

6. MARK SHORER, 'Technique as Discovery', *Hudson Review*, I (1948), pp. 67–87,
   and 'Fiction and the Analogical Matrix', *Kenyon Review*, XI (1949), pp. 539–60.

7. See LEO SPITZER, *Linguistics and Literary History: Essays in Stylistics* (Princeton,
   NJ, 1948), and Eric Auerbach, *Mimesis* (Princeton, NJ, 1953).

8. ROMAN JAKOBSON, 'Closing Statement: Linguistics and Poetics' in *Style and
   Language*, ed. Thomas A. Sebeok (Cambridge, Mass., 1960), p. 358.

9. JOSEPH FRANK, 'Spatial Form in Modern Literature', *Sewanee Review*, LIII (1945), pp. 221–40, 433–56, 643–53.

10. ROMAN JAKOBSON, 'Two Aspects of Language and Two Types of Linguistic Disturbances' in *Fundamentals of Language* by Jakobson and Morris Halle (The Hague, 1956).

11. This point was blurred in Lodge's discussion of Jakobson's theory in the first edition of *The Modes of Modern Writing*. It is clarified in a Prefatory Note to the second impression of the book (a paperback edition published by Arnold in 1979).

12. CHRISTINE BROOKE-ROSE, 'The Squirm of the True', *Poetics and Theory of Literature*, I (1976), pp. 265–94, 513–46, and II (1977), pp. 517–61.

13. The distinction is made at the beginning of *S/Z*, whose English translator renders these terms as 'readerly' and 'writerly'. The classic realistic novel is 'readerly': it is based on logical and temporal order, it communicates along an uninterrupted chain of sense, we consume it, passively, confident that all the questions it raises will be resolved. The modern text is in contrast 'writerly': it makes us not consumers but producers, because we write ourselves into it, we construct meanings for it as we read, and ideally these meanings are infinitely plural.

14. CARLOS BAKER, *Hemingway: The Writer as Artist* (Princeton, NJ, 1963), pp. 135–6.

15. JOHN V. HAGOPIAN, 'Symmetry in "Cat in the Rain"' in *The Short Stories of Ernest Hemingway: Critical Essays*, ed. Jackson J. Benson (Durham, NC, 1975), p. 231.

16. *Ibid.*, p. 232.

17. Lodge's own effort was as follows: 'Bored young American staying with her husband at Italian hotel fails to rescue a cat seen sheltering from the rain but is provided with a cat by the attentive manager'.

18. SEYMOUR CHATMAN, *Story and Discourse: Narrative Structure in Fiction and Film* (Ithaca, NY, 1978), p. 48.

19. It has been pointed out that tortoise-shell cats are usually female and that since feminine pronouns are applied to the 'kitty' in lines 26–7, this suggests that it and the tortoise-shell cat are one and the same. Lodge is doubtful whether so specialised a piece of knowledge should be allowed to disambiguate the conclusion, and in any case it is not conclusive evidence. It seems clear that if Hemingway had wanted to establish that the two cats were one and the same, he would have described the kitty as 'tortoise-shell'.

20. Hagopian, *op. cit.*, p. 230.

21. *Ibid.*, p. 231.

22. CARLOS BAKER, *Ernest Hemingway* (Harmondsworth, 1972), pp. 159, 161.

23. *Ibid.*, p. 165.

24. The hotel in Rapallo at which the Hemingways stayed in 1923 still stands (now called the Hotel Riviera) and its outlook corresponds closely to the description in the first paragraph of 'Cat in the Rain' – with one interesting difference. The

David Lodge on Hemingway's 'Cat in the Rain'

'war monument' is, in fact, a statue of Christopher Columbus, erected in 1914 by grateful local businessmen who had made their fortunes in America and returned to enjoy their affluence in the homeland. As it is inconceivable that Hemingway should have mistaken the nature of the monument, one may legitimately conclude that he converted it into a war memorial for his own symbolic purposes. These, it should be said, are much more obvious to the reader when the story is read in its original context, the collection of stories and fragments *In Our Time* (1925), many of which are directly concerned with the war, and the experience of pain and death.

Rhetorical

Rhetorical

Rhetorical readings have a venerable history going right back to the theory and practice of rhetoric in classical times, but for a time were overlaid by the materialistic, thematic emphasis of nineteenth-century positivistic scholarship. 'Rhetoric' is at once the most problematic and most pervasive category: problematic in that the idea of style or calculated effect stands at the opposite extreme to realism's espoused truthful or utilitarian form of language and language-use; yet pervasive in that realism, once examined, becomes a very particular form of stylistics. The notion of language as rhetoric is in fact at the heart of every one of the other approaches isolated and examined in this collection, e.g. Barthes, Lodge, Miller, Boumelha, Brooks.

The first example of a rhetorical reading is an extract from a lengthy article by the French structuralist critic Philippe Hamon entitled 'Un discours contraint' ('A Constrained Discourse'), which originally appeared in a special issue of the journal *Poétique* (**16**, 1973) devoted entirely to realist discourse. It has been translated for the first time for inclusion in this volume. The main value of Hamon's article resides in its attempt to discern the dominant features of realist discourse, of which no fewer than fifteen are enumerated (see Introduction, p. 13). The listing is, by Hamon's own admission, 'pell-mell', but the resulting profile of realist writing is a reversal of its older image as a plain and innocent mode. Hamon articulates the internal contradictions of realist discourse (see p. 14) and concludes that it is far more constrained by its own inner laws than it appears to be.

While Hamon ranges far and wide (though almost exclusively in French literature), the British critic and novelist David Lodge focuses on one work in his study of 'The Rhetoric of *Hard Times*', which is the third chapter of his book *The Language of Fiction* (London: Routledge & Kegan Paul; New York: Columbia University Press, 1966). Lodge opens by referring to previous judgements on *Hard Times*, the most notable of which is that by F.R. Leavis in his important book *The Great Tradition* (1948). Lodge points out that although Leavis singled out *Hard Times* for special praise among Dickens' novels, he made no attempt to substantiate this claim. Lodge's stance is more qualified than Leavis'; he sees *Hard Times* as a composite of success and failure, and aims to show how these vicissitudes are dependent on its rhetoric as well as closely related to the negative and positive aspects, respectively, of the argument inherent in the novel. Thus rhetoric functions here in its traditional role as the vehicle of an argument. A rhetorical reading is also particularly apposite to *Hard Times* because its narrating voice is so insistent, public, oratorical, indeed histrionic (cf. Miller's analysis of *Sketches by Boz* in the Postmodern section).

15   Philippe Hamon on the Major Features of Realist Discourse*

We can perhaps begin to make an inventory, pell mell, of a certain number of procedures which would constitute criteria for realist discourse, procedures many of which overlap or reciprocally imply each other and of which none, taken separately, constitutes, strictly speaking, a sufficient condition.

1. Among the procedures guaranteeing overall coherence for a **statement**, we can list the flash-back, the memory, the summary, the childhood traumatism, obsessions, mention of the family, or heredity, or tradition, reference to a cycle, or an ancestor, etc.: the text refers us back to something that has already been said. Conversely, by various procedures such as *prediction*, presentiment, the fixing of a programme, a project, an indication, lucidity, a curse, an order, the establishment of a contract, desire, the taking into consideration of a deficiency, etc., the text allows a preview of what is to come.

The use of heredity or a family history as a figure simultaneously offering a realist mooring point, classification, the recollection of and appeal to information (and we know that present-day geneticists readily conceptualise their discipline in terms borrowed from information theory), a figure, then, for the transference and circulation of a certain genetic *knowledge* (and we will perpetually come up against this problem of the circulation of knowledge), is undoubtedly an important figure of realist discourse in one form or another, and not limited to Zola. It also entails a character destined to reappear often, that of the *doctor*, or the *family friend*, or the *childhood friend* (who knows the pre-history), together with certain typical scenes such as the revelatory psychological *crisis* (an illness, or a crisis of puberty, or alcoholism, or a hereditary disease, etc.), and all the scenes of a family *concord* (meals, anniversaries, various reunions, family councils . . .) or *discord* (the *quarrel*, for example, which allows the author to have characters ready for other encounters, to

---

* Reprinted from 'Un discours contraint' in *Poétique* **16** (1973), pp. 411–45.
Trans. Lilian R. Furst and Seán Hand, 1991.

describe other milieux, etc.). So the family forms a sort of 'motivated', 'transparent' (Saussure) derivational field, wherein the surnames play somewhat the role of a linguistic root or stem conveying a particular piece of information (hereditary facts, etc. – Macquart, Rougon, Thibault, Forsyte, Guermantes) while the first names act as a kind of inflection, offering complementary information (Nana, Pauline, Gervaise . . .), structures, then, functioning as a sort of 'grammar' of characters (form of classification, selective restrictions, predictability of behaviour, etc.). They also form a suitable *locus* for the circulation of knowledge destined for the reader (in the form of tittle-tattle, gossip, curses, avowals, etc.), knowledge that is necessary in order to understand the intrigue, or for the circulation of *objects* (the Inheritance).

2. Another ingredient of readability and narrative coherence is the *psychological motivation* (of the characters), which functions as an *a posteriori* justification of the narrative's functional web, (the logical sequence of 'functions', in Propp's sense of the term), the narrative's 'post hoc ergo propter hoc' form of explanation.

3. Similarly, there is the parallel story: the narrative is set in motion on top of a mega (extra) History that lies just beneath the surface. This History doubles, illuminates and predetermines the narrative, creating in the reader a series of lines that mark out the path of least resistance, foreshadowings, a system of expectations, by referring back implicitly or explicitly (via a quotation, an allusion, etc.) to an already written text that the reader knows. This text can be either sacred or profane (for example the references to the siege of Paris in Maupassant's *Deux Amis*, or the references to *Genesis* in Zola's *La Faute de l'abbé Mouret*, or the furtive appearance of Napoléon III in Zola's *La Débâcle*). But the realist text will doubtless privilege the profane text (History), which it will site as close as possible to its reader. References to *an elsewhere* (exoticism) will therefore be reduced, and the realist hero will not travel far from his environment: History will come to him, rather than his going very far to seek History [*l'Histoire*] or just to look for trouble [*des histoires*]. By systematically coupling itself in this way to a historical and political background, the text constructs itself as foreseeable, and reduces its combinatory 'capacity'; narrative sequences such as 'The two friends laid an ambush and killed Bismarck' or 'The two friends, at the head of their battalion, launched an attack and saved Paris from the Prussian encirclement' become impossible (agrammatical, as it were). Historical and geographical proper names (Rouen, rue de Rivoli, Notre-Dame de Paris, etc.), which refer to stable semantic entities, which, incidentally, do not need so much to be understood as to be recognised as proper names (and here the capital letter is the differential typographical mark), function somewhat like *quotations*, in scholarly discourse: they guarantee mooring points, re-establish the performance (guaranteed by the authors) of the

referential statement by coupling the text with a validated extra-text, allow the economy of a descriptive statement, and guarantee an overall effect of reality which even transcends any decoding of detail, an effect of reality often accentuated in topographical descriptions by the use of the present tense to back up or bear witness (see Georges Blin on Stendhal's use of such phrases, as in: 'The little wood *overlooks* the Cours de la Fidélité at Verrières', or 'Upon leaving Carville, *one finds*. . . .').

4. Another important factor in the text's *readability* (a factor certainly not peculiar to realist discourse) is the systematic motivation of the characters' first names and surnames and the names of places. Several procedures are possible: thus a usurer will be called 'Pinchpenny', a simpleton 'Simplet', a one-eyed person 'The One-Eyed', a paradisical garden the 'Paradou', etc. The discourse of the marvellous also favours this **onomastic** transparency. But realist discourse will play on the connotation of a *social* content (a certain first name or surname will, for example, connote the plebeian state, the aristocracy, trade, etc.) rather than on the denotation of a character or physical trait. Its motivation even can provoke the effect of reality by implicitly referring to contents as diffuse as: banality, simplicity, daily life, average person, prosaic status (Mr, Mrs . . .), etc., hence its privileged position in that strategic spot, the *title*, where it functions as a true indicator of the 'realist' genre (*Moll Flanders, Thérèse Raquin, Madame Bovary, Madame Gervaisais*, etc.). Various explanatory procedures can reinforce this onomastic transparency in the narrative: a search for origins, etymological research, etc. which then lead to the creation of typical figures like the philologist, the guide, the genealogist, the geographer, and to typical scenes such as the baptism, the imposition of a name, a visit to a place, scenes of introduction ('Allow me to introduce you to Mr X who . . .'), scenes which will take place for example in the course of a reunion, a reception, some celebration or ceremony; consequently: the realist character will rarely be *alone*: he will have friends, will meet acquaintances during his walks, will be worldly, will have tact (see the semantic status of narrators in Maupassant's short stories).

5. In its efforts to provide information, the realist text will be able to play fully on semiotic complementarity: the text thus presents itself as overcoded (a feature of mass communication: the receiver who does not have access to code [*a*] will have access to code [*b*]), and can enter into superfluousness by using illustrations (J. Verne and Rieu), photographs (*Nadja*), drawings (*Life of Henri Brulard*), diagrams (the genealogical tree of the Rougon-Macquart appended to *Une Page d'amour*), or even replicate information by internal diagrammatic procedures: *Les Djinns* by Victor Hugo, the Proustian phrase as 'syntactical onomatopoiea' (Leo Spitzer), Flaubert's mimetic phrase, or even, indirectly, by reference to the visual arts in general (painting in Balzac and Stendhal, etc.) or to a specific art work signfied by the text (the paintings described in the discourse of

Raymond Roussel, such as an engraving hanging on the wall of the hero's room, for example, which reiterates or announces his destiny, etc.). Realist discourse could, therefore, be defined as a *paraphrasable* discourse. We have here the **doxa**: 'As for me, I believe only what I see.'

6. Every message presupposes, even in the case of differred (written) communication, an origin. All the P phrases of the message thus presuppose an implicit articulation of the kind: *I, author, say that P . . .* On the other hand, the pedagogical act presupposes the absence of this agency of articulation at the cost of introducing into the act a certain interference, a 'noise', some disquiet (Who is speaking? What does the author mean? Why is he intervening? Why is he modalising his remarks, etc.). On the other hand again, the 'realist' author (like the pedagogue) is in possession of a certain *knowledge* (his *notes*, his acquaintance with an 'object', an 'environment', a 'decor', some portion of the referent), which he regards as exhaustive and which he will distribute (for example) in the form of *descriptions*. Whence the problem to resolve: how to establish indirectly the performance of my descriptive statement, how to give it authority, weight (that of my 'note', my knowledge, my 'witnessing'), how to make my reader believe that what I say is 'true', and that I myself, author, believe in the veracity of what I say (a game that involves hypnotising oneself as well as the other person, as Georges Blin shows clearly in the introduction to his book *Stendhal et les problèmes du roman*)?

The implicit formula: I, author, absent from the articulation guarantee to you, uninformed reader, precise and verifiable information about object x by telling you that ($a . . . b . . . c . . . d . . . e . . . n . . .$) (there follows a description or some information about the object in question) will become: A character, P, an 'expert', present in the statement, participating in the narrative, says that ($a . . . b . . . c . . . d . . . e . . . n . . .$) to another character P, who is uninformed (or not an expert, but also a participant in the narrative).

The guaranteeing source of the information is thus incarnated in the narrative in a character who bears all the signs of scientific respectability: a medical description will be supported and carried by the mouth of a character who is a doctor, aesthetic information by the mouth of a character who is a painter, a description of a church or information about religion through the character of a priest, etc. In *Le Ventre de Paris*, for example, Zola uses a completely episodic character, the painter Claude Lantier, to justify descriptions of the kind: 'light tint of an acquarelle' (dawn), 'winedregs with carmine bruises' (red cabbages), 'the immense working drawing in Indian inkwash on phosphorescent velum' (the market at *Les Halles*). It is thus *knowledge*, an informational 'note', which often pre-exists the construction of the narrative in the novelist's sketches (and this habit of composition, of writing is also a hallmark of realist discourse) which creates the fictive persona: the latter is thus no more than the justification, the *a posteriori* medium for this knowledge, the plausible guarantor of a technical, lexical piece that needs to be 'placed'. He is there to justify a certain phraseology (the priest's Latin, the technical terms of the painter, the aesthete, the doctor, a particular professional slang, etc.) or to authenticate a denomination, the ideal representative of the author's notebook on the scene of the text. At its extreme, reality is no more than a *linguistic mosaic* (there is the priest's Latin, the clichés of the lowly, the wit of the man of the world, the soldier's slang, the child's remark, etc.), every manifestation of an **idiolect** being charged to provoke an effect of reality. Realist discourse is thus characterised by what could be called a *translative hypertrophy*, a process which still assimilates realist discourse to pedagogical discourse (transmitting a certain body of knowledge by basing it on a conventionally recognised authority, that of the *auctores*), and in which the author perpetually delegates his status as addressor. Hence this paradoxical trait of realist discourse, which takes a lot of trouble to conceal the place from which it speaks, as well as its author's pedagogical status and the conditions of its production (the documentation, the notebook, the presuppositions, the technical vocabulary, etc.), but which draws the following cardinal figure:

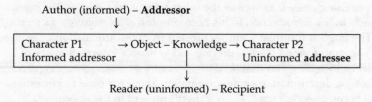

Author (informed) – **Addressor**
↓

Character P1	→ Object – Knowledge → Character P2
Informed addressor	Uninformed **addressee**

↓
Reader (uninformed) – Recipient

generating the typical narrative syntagm (which can exist in a more or less redundant or elliptical form):

conjunction of two characters (the one informed – a potential addressor, the other uninformed – a potential addressee	→ question from the uninformed character to the informed character – position of an articulation's contract	→ acceptance of the contract

→ reply of the informed character (real addressor) → acquisition of knowledge by the uninformed character (real addressee). The articulation's contract is fulfilled.

We will thus find in the roles of addressor of knowledge those characters typical of realist discourse: the engineer (see J. Verne), the expert, the scholar, the native, the doctor (Zola), the maniac, the eccentric, the character on a hobby-horse, the professor, the boss, etc., and in the role of the uninformed questioning addressee: the neophyte, the apprentice, the voyeur, the curious character, the disciple, the autodidact, the spy, the gossip, the intruder, the explorer, the naive person, the traveller, etc. Psychological motivations like curiosity, desire for information, volubility will be invoked to justify these descriptive lexical segments. The translative syntagm can comprise variants:

conjunction of a character P1 (curious, interested, eager to gain information, before a meeting, marking a pause, etc.) and of an object O (broken down into the nomenclature of a technical vocabulary enumerating the parts of the same whole)	→ *gaze* of P1 on O	→ transference of knowledge to P1

or else:

conjunction of a character P1 (technician, expert, worker, artisan, etc.) and of an object O to be described	→ *work* of P1 on O (the layout of the text follows then from the mode of usage, P1 manipulating the parts of O one after the other)	→ transference of information to a spectator character P2 (admiring, neophyte, apprentice, curious, etc.)

From this we get the regressive and plausible chains: a statement [*dire*] will presuppose *wanting to say something* [or *meaning to say something: vouloir dire*] (characters disseminating information, in a talkative, kindly or knowledgeable way, etc.); a *gaze* presupposes *wanting to see* (the character will be a 'snooper', a 'spy', a 'voyeur', etc.), and *being able to see* (the gaze will have to be able to survey a body or transparent air, a window, from the height of a look-out, through a downward view, through natural or artificial light). It is the eternal naturalist *window*, the crystal porthole of the *Nautilus*, etc.

It should be noted finally that the three pretext-functions opening the descriptive sections (the attentive *gaze*, the explanatory and voluble *word*, and the arranged and organised *technical act*, already noted in Homer by Lessing) can be combined: a certain character, for example, will demonstrate a locomotive before an apprentice who will watch him at work and to whom he will comment on the successive details of the pieces being manipulated, naming them one by one. What must be seen is that it is rare for such sequences of the transmission of knowledge to open up an uncertainty for the ensuing narrative, to play a 'disjunctive' role, opening up 'narrative possibilities', or that they can be put into logical relationship with other sequences, which shows that they belong more to the level of *articulation* (an author transmitting a selective piece of information to a reader) than to that of the *statement*, where their functionality is nil; the fabricated object, the decor arranged by the character's *work*, will count for nothing in the future; the *knowledge* that the character acquires of a panorama or an object, through his gaze, will not thereafter determine his actions; the *information* that he gains is forgotten as soon as it is transmitted. We are dealing with a knowledge void of functionality from the narrative point of view (but not from the pedagogical point of view, where the important thing is 'to transmit'). Or, indeed, when it has a role at the level of the *statement*, it is purely a role of cohesion, of plausible filling, like those sequences clearly pinpointed by Propp with the term *liaisons*, whose common object is equally the transmission of information (the uncovering of a secret, news, slanders, confidences, gossip, boasts, complaints, recriminations, perception of a sign, etc.) and the restriction of a certain coherence to the *statement*, a certain smoothness to the narrative. But in no case is it a matter, in the realist text, of an overall and 'essential' (functional) search for *knowledge* (as in fantastic discourse: Who is the Horla? What is happening to me? – see Maupassant's interrogatory titles: *A madman? mad? him? Who knows?* – or as in the detective novel *Who killed Harry?*), or of a search for the power that this knowledge would procure (quest for a secret, or a magic formula, etc.). Realist discourse is simply a discourse *ostentatious with knowledge* (the descriptive note) which it wants to *show* (to the reader) by *circulating* it (in and through a narrative).

In realist discourse there would thus be present and recordable at the level of its narrative structures what could be called an especially dense *topology of knowledge*, the statement being monopolised solely for the benefit of scenes of transference, acquisition, transmission, etc. of this modality, whether these scenes themselves are only textual manifestations of an overall scheme of articulation, the outgrowth of the author's notes, or whether they merely fill the empty spots in the narrative and restore its verisimilitude. This discourse is, therefore, fundamentally phantasmatic, insofar as it indefinitely re-works the same scenario, that of its own production, concealed by the pedagogical presupposition of objectivity, impersonality, and realist discourse could thus be defined as that in which the *semantic structures of the articulation merge to the highest degree with the semantic structures of the statement*. Moreover, in doing this, it shows clearly the confusion on which it is based, the assimilation of *reality* to the *knowledge* one has of the object one is describing; the more one knew it, the more realist one would be, so the realist author is an avid reader of encyclopaedias, always after 'the latest' in scientific knowledge. See Zola and **Dr Lucas**, the impressionists and neo-impressionists and **Chevreul**, etc. Whence the corresponding belief of numerous critics, that this or that modern author would be more 'realistic' than this or that ancient author because the state of knowledge about reality has increased, etc.

7. The realist text is therefore characterised by a marked redundancy and foreseeability of its content. For example, the character presupposes: (*a*) the description of his physical sphere of activity (socio-professional environment); (*b*) the description of the place of his activity (the priest will be described in his church, the butcher in his store, etc.); (*c*) the description of his professional activity itself (the butcher will be described in his store making his sausage; the priest in his church saying mass, etc.); these acts, these pseudo-functions are always reducible to the character's permanent qualification; they merely illustrate it as a social role, and the descriptive segment only declines and displays in the present the potential paradigm of the character's organised professional acts, or the potential paradigm of the parts of a whole, of the objects present in a decor. Typical scenes will come to concretise this, like those frequent scenes of moving in or out of dwelling places, together with a predilection for all the *ritualised* activities of daily life: official banquets, family meals, religious or civil ceremonies, fixed timetables, etc., places or moments where each thing is classified, has its place, plays its role, is ranked, 'articulated' moments or composed and composite places and object-systems like the machine (made up of pieces), the house (likewise composed of 'pieces' – and it is well known that the middle-class house is a particularly saturated and redundant place), the meal (and its 'menu'), the shop (and its labelled and ordered 'articles'), the town (and its 'districts', its 'classified' monuments (and note how, these days, curiously enough, town planners conceive of their discipline in terms of 'readability'), the body (and its 'articulations'), society (and its 'classes'), etc. The most extremely typical scene, where the narrative tale coincides most closely with the linguistic task of denomination, is the scene of the *inventory*: in Zola's *Au Bonheur des dames* a whole chapter is devoted to the store's inventory (made by the employees and all the personnel on a special day when the shop is closed): there is, obviously, no better procedure to review all the objects in it. For realist discourse, an object (or a character) will thus essentially be (*a*) an amalgam of enumerable occurrences (its parts); (*b*) belonging to an endogenous network (such as a piece of furniture is part of a large decor which contains it); (*c*) or exogenous (the enumeration of its procedures of fabrication, its uses, its upkeep). Realist discourse in particular will thus not be able to avoid the description of that typically programmed act, the sexual act (caresses → intermission of the penis → ejaculation → detumescence). As a

technological discourse, it thus recuperates a theme generally excluded (work, the body), and the reticence it provokes therefore becomes understandable: vulgarity, prosaicness, obscenity. According to the formula of R. Barthes (*S/Z*, pp. 82–3), the readable is always only the 'unfolding' (*explanation*: we again find our topology of knowledges) of a name, the deployment of potential paradigms, or the latent 'constellations' (Saussure) of language. The reality effect is thus, quite often, only the reader's euphoric recognition of a certain vocabulary. It is therefore normal to come across, in someone like Zola, at the opening of a series of denominations or of a descriptive 'segment', an extraordinary frequency of verbs such as *to explain* or *to name*: 'Silvère, whom she felt trembling at her side, bent over towards her ear, and named to her the various contingents as they appeared' (*La Fortune des Rougon*); 'The young man, inspired by the desire to convince him, threw himself more into the task, and explained to him the mechanism of the new trade' (*Au Bonheur des dames*); 'Nervously, delighted to have a subject, he gave endless details' . . .' (*ibid.*); 'He explained why, in broken phrases, interrupted by continual parentheses' (*La Terre*); 'He was explaining Plassans to the abbé Faujas' (*La Conquête de Plassans*); 'He explained to him [. . .] he did not spare details' (*Le Ventre de Paris*); 'The roofer explained to her [. . .] indicating the different pieces with his finger' (*L'Assommoir*), etc [. . .] Here are found all the principal traits of all the 'descriptive genres' (Riffaterre): nomination, classification, predication, exaltation (exultation), and these explanations are always at the same time *exploits* (*ex-plicitum*, in the juridical sense of citation, notification and assignation), always assertive nominations, and a comparative citation of reality, accompanied by all the authority of a guaranteeing character (the specialist or the ushering character).

8. On the overall scale of the entire narration, a narrative concretisation (alibi) of the performance of the discourse can also be observed: the author will delegate the whole of his text to a narrator-character, as in most of Maupassant's stories, where a *contract of articulation* (command and acceptance of the type: 'Tell us your story? – All right! Well, here it is', etc.) launches the narration; the same tactic in the epigraph ('The truth, the blunt truth'; 'The novel is a mirror that is walked along a road', etc.) or in the plausible prefaces where a witness intervenes to guarantee the authenticity of the manuscript or the word of a witness (the 'traveller' at the beginning of *Le Rouge et le noir*, the 'we' at the beginning of *Madame Bovary*, etc.). In all these cases, it is a matter of authenticating an act of speaking, of justifying a content by guaranteeing its origin: the editor was the author's *friend* who entrusted the manuscript to him; the narrator tells a story that *happened to him*; the narrator tells an event at which he was present *in his professional capacity*;

the editor, *who has suffered identical passions*, publishes a manuscript whose veracity he guarantees, etc.

This is why the *openings* in realist discourse are so important, for they immediately define a horizon of realist expectation for the reader, and create as quickly as possible an effect of reality and an indication of 'genre': we have already seen the preference for *titles* made up of prosaic proper names; prefaces, epigraphs, chapter titles, the text's opening will try to create what is most lacking in realist discourse, mediatisation via a 'genre'.

9. Realist discourse, like pedagogic discourse, will in general reject reference to the process of articulation, and move instead towards a 'transparent' writing dominated only by the transmission of information. This leads to what could be called a neutralisation or a *detonalisation* of the message, that is to say, to a symmetrical absence of participation by author and reader. To be sure, the author must intervene surreptitiously in an oblique manner, in order to guarantee the credibility of his information; similarly, the reader must participate in the author's referential intention and must in reading recognise a certain number of indicative signs. But this double participation is informative, and must not be emotional. So, on the one hand, realist discourse will present itself as highly *demodalised* and assertive (no quotation marks, italics, emphases or terms of endearment; no verbs, turns of phrase, or adverbs such as: perhaps, probably, somewhat, a sort of, to seem, so to speak, one might say that, a certain, one would think, etc.). These modalisations, let it be noted, are the privileged marks of the discourse of hesitation (fantastic discourse), of ironic discourse (see Stendhal's use of italics), of the discourse of horror or science fiction (the unnamed and the unnameable can be approached only by way of approximation or modalised periphrasis). Avoiding therefore all 'distancing' of this type, realist discourse will present itself as essentially a serious discourse. R. Barthes in *S/Z* makes the *serious* the major characteristic of the readable text; Auerbach likewise. Consequently, this secondary but important problem for the realist author: how to be witty?

On the other hand, the detonalisation of the message leads also to the rejection of any euphoric theme (description of idyllic places, love scenes, touching family scenes, ecstatic passions, tender infant characters, etc.) as of every dysphoric theme (spectacular deaths, murky places, crises of passions, etc.). Such 'storybook' themes can, incidentally, be embodied in the appearance or citation of this or that famous work which implicitly or explicitly will be condemned or derided. Lamartine's *Jocelyn*, which appears on a kitchen table in Zola's *Pot-Bouille, Lucia di Lammermoor* in Rouen in *Madame Bovary*, etc. Realist discourse, since it is unable (at least before the nineteenth century) to place itself in relation to a historically defined and instituted genre, places and defines itself by integrating what it considers to be its 'literary' opposites and by rejecting them; but one sees that this rejection and this intertextual game can lead straight to parody, and thus come to undermine the *seriousness* of the discourse; another crucial problem of compatibility to be resolved by the 'realist' author.

10. This tonal levelling of the text poses another problem for the realist author: that of the *hero*. Here I take this term in its narrow sense of 'principal character', and not in its larger sense of 'character'. We know how Tomashevsky defines it: one's emotional relationship with the hero (sympathy and antipathy) is developed on a moral basis. Positive and negative types are a necessary element in the construction of the fable (. . .). The character who has the most vivid and the most marked emotional colouring is called the hero (in *Théorie de la littérature: textes des formalistes russes*, edited by Tzvetan Todorov, Paris, 1965. p. 265). The hero is thus an important element in a narrative's *readability*, and his identification must leave no doubt for the reader; a whole series of procedures, *qualitative* (for example, the hero has a name, a first name and a surname, moral or psychological qualities validated by the culture, etc.), *quantitative* (it is he who appears most frequently), or *functional* (it is he who is given adjuncts, dissipates the initial lack, and functions as the agent-subject) generally underline his role. Insofar as he 'grids' and organises the narrative's moral space, he mounts it on the cultural extra-text, common to the author and the reader, and thereby constitutes an important factor for reducing ambiguity. Let us note that this process of reducing ambiguity can, in the explicit mode, be signified by a whole series of paraphrases interior to the text, which will come to present elements of the narrative in their functionality and hierarchy of effective values: the traitor will be called *traitor*, the hero *hero*, a test a *victory* or a *defeat*: a typical character, who recurs often, is the 'lucid' or 'frank' character (the one who says: so and so will go far, so and so is a traitor, or a great man, the one who calls a spade a spade, etc.). [. . .] We can therefore say that the readable text is not only **anthropomorphic** (it will reject, for example, allegory, the animation of objects, etc.) but also **anthropocentric**. It is *centred*, not only in the descriptions (the hero's gaze will take charge of them and will organise them with: to the left, to the right, up front, in the distance, above, etc. – phrases used by the looking hero I), but emotionally and ideologically.

[. . .] But if the realist author over-accentuates, differentially, the hero-character, there is great risk of also provoking a 'deflation' of the realist illusion and of reintroducing the 'storybook', the heroic and the marvellous as *genres*. Several procedures are at the author's disposal to level his text, to 'defocalise' it, such as, for example, the procedure which consists of constantly changing the point of view (novels in letter form, etc.), or in not bestowing on one and the same character the functions of the agent and the validated qualities. In this way, in contrast to the marvellous kind of story, the character will not act simultaneously as subject and beneficiary, and the author will make the character an *object*, for example, or a *potential* subject who never accedes to the status of a *real* (and glorified) subject, or a beneficiary of negative values (he will have illnesses, setbacks, false information, etc. – see the 'novel of failure' in the nineteenth century). From this stems the problem that critics pose occasionally: who or what is the hero of Zola's *Pot-Bouille*? But what holds for the hero holds also for the character (in the wide sense: all the *actors*, all the participants, even the very episodic ones) of the realist narrative: a certain qualitative and functional disappearance. As we have seen, the hero is reduced to the role of *opener* of a description (created by the gaze, for example) or of a segment of knowledge (communication of some information, support for an explanatory paraphrase, etc.). [. . .] This can be generalised to apply to all the characters in realist discourse: the author forgets them, they 'forget themselves', they are 'thoughtful', and this is the consequence of the descriptive programme, which makes them vanish behind the note, the descriptive enumeration, or the series of denominations or actions, which they are simply given the job of introducing and guaranteeing. As a result, the discontinuity of their affective or physiological lives, often made up of an alternation of moments of health and illnesses, of euphoric expansions and dysphoric withdrawals, which parallel the character's movements, and the complexity (an open, abounding, discontinuous world) or simplicity (a simple, closed world) of the environment they pass through: Emma Bovary's 'expansion' before the large panorama of Rouen, the 'asphyxiation' of Zola's heroes in enclosed spaces, etc. It is the text, the fullness of the description which often dictates to the character his or her euphoria or unease, success or failure. Here also there are often problems of compatibility (between the *permanence* of action which the readable text demands and this inconsistency and variability of the actors).

11. Realist discourse will also be characterised, for the sake of verisimilitude, by a (utopian) thrust towards **monosemesis** in the terms and unities manipulated by the narrative. This works on several levels, and has the aim of reducing the ambiguity of the text. Hence the refusal to play on words (other than those put into the mouth of a character *categorically* designated as *witty*), or to confuse the literal with the metaphorical; hence the predilection for that very specific semiotic system represented by numbers (ordinal and cardinal) and by technical vocabularies that are morphologically 'transparent'; like every type of discourse, realist discourse can undoubtedly be characterised by the discourses that it mimics, in this case *scholarly* discourse, scientific discourse (numbers, symbols, diagrams), technological discourse (directed sequences of programmed actions), and historical discourse

(proper names, citations); hence the frequent references to 'the knowledgeable observer' or to *the historian* as typical guarantors (in Balzac, for example). This mimicry of scientific discourse is often visible in the *titles* or *subtitles* of works (history, chronicle, physiology, morphology, etc.), which strive, once again, to hide the poetic nature of the discourse (where the only persistent categories are the readable and the unreadable – or the writerly, to follow Barthes) in order to become integrated into discourses where the pertinent categories are those of the felicitous or the infelicitous (instructions for use, cooking recipes), of the true and the false, the reproducible and the non-reproducible, the verifiable and the non-verifiable. Hence texts like Michel Butor's *La Modification*, which mimes 'the operable', the practical statement, the cooking recipe, from which it does not differ formally ('You take a chicken, you cut it up, you brown the pieces, etc'), or certain texts of the naturalist 'experimental novel' (novel = experiment). This mirage of reproducibility and of verifiability can become manifest in the text itself though the *repetition* of certain of the characters' actions (which will serve to 'prove' some character or psychological trait), through the *lucidity* of certain characters (who, like the scientist, can 'predict' certain developments, etc.). Here we find the fundamental characteristic of social realisms, which is precisely their wish to be *operable*, to provoke action by presenting models that are simultaneously technological, moral and political (by describing for example the action of 'positive heroes'), thereby effacing as much as possible the distinction between the semantics of a statement and the semantics of an articulation (maxims, ritual, history, etc.).

12. At the level of the characters, realist discourse, always in search of transparency and the circulation of knowledge, will strive to reduce the imbalance that exists between the *being* and the *appearance* of objects or characters, the former being revealed by the latter (a multiplication of signs or symptoms, different physiognomies, etc.), or else the latter existing without the former, at which point things and objects exist only through their appearance (an 'impressionist' tendency, architectural *trompe-l'oeil*, etc.). It will therefore avoid things or characters which exist without appearing (invisible beings, mysterious beings, occult forces, hidden treasures), as well as things and characters whose being does not coincide with their appearance: false characters, sexually ambiguous characters, hypocrites, homosexuals, castratos, characters endowed with ubiquity: this will also exclude scenes of recognition, brutal revelations of psychological traits, etc. In logical terms, it could be postulated that the realist text will avoid the neutral (neither . . . nor . . .) or complex (and . . . and . . .) poles of logical schemata, terms much used, by contrast, by fantastic discourse, and privilege instead a dialogue based on opposites and contradictions. Lévi-Strauss explicitly recognises in certain character

types (tricksters, Cinderella . . .) an 'ambiguous and equivocal'
personality because they are incarnations of 'dualities' or 'mediations'.
Insofar as they pose problems of *readability*, they would be excluded from
realist discourse; or else this discourse, in order to integrate them, must
develop a system of explanatory paraphrase, or a compensatory system
of parallel information – for example by confronting them with a *lucid*
character type or a *reader of signs and symptoms* who sees through them, or
by developing intrigues which gradually eliminate them [. . .] It should
be noted that, when a 'mixedness' is invoked, it is often not in order to
introduce an ambiguity or to create a 'deceptive' narrative, but to bring in
intermediary places or characters, whose function is to circulate
information or characters from place to place, or to reconcile antagonistic
salons or rival groups: their mixedness then serves only to make these
movements seem plausible, and so justify a multiplicity of *introductions,*
bits of gossip, descriptions, guaranteeing that the review we get is an
exhaustive one (two quotations taken from Balzac's *La Vieille Fille*: 'These
two other salons communicated via some characters mixed in with the
house of Cormon, and vice versa'; 'This mixed salon, where the minor
aristocracy with fixed appointments, the clergy or the magistrature, met
each other, exercises a great influence'). The topology of knowledge and
the topography of the world overlap. Inevitably we will find again our
doctor character, a mobile being *par excellence* (an expert, who infiltrates
every home and is received in every salon), or his vulgar double (who
acquires knowledge little by little), the picaro, driven away from every
house.

As a corollary, we can predict the appearance of characters who are
'simple' (*Un Coeur simple*), 'not complicated', voluble, boastful, parvenus,
etc. Hence this privileged figure of the *glass house*: 'This house was of
glass, like all houses in the provinces' (Balzac, *La Vieille Fille*); 'He
dreamed of embracing his mistresses in glass houses' (Zola, *Les Mystères*
de Marseille), about a parvenu); 'Through mirrors so large and so clear
that they seemed (. . .) put there in order to display to the outside the
interior splendour' (Zola, *La Curée* – about the large house of the parvenu
Saccard). The realist author is haunted by the myth of **Asmodeus**, the
desire to lift the roofs, to see through, 'to undress', etc. Let us recall that
it is the habit of certain 'realist' painters (such as David) first to paint
their figures *nude*, before afterwards painting them, in the final picture,
dressed, and to work in their studios with an *écorché*. Here again it is a
matter of knowing before painting. Metaphors to do with 'alcoves', or
'working behind the scenes' (Zola), or the social 'mechanism' which
needs to be shown, or the 'wheels' that have to be described, or the
'springs' that need to be revealed will naturally crop up, together with a
certain interest in describing social and economic mechanisms (the sub-
structure of *work*) and in revealing unconscious mechanisms (the sub-

structure of the *body*). As Gaston Bachelard puts it in *La Formation de l'esprit scientifique*: 'realism is essentially a reference to an intimacy, and the psychology of intimacy a reference to reality'.

There are thus two complementary (contradictory?) tendencies in realist discourse: the first, which would be called *horizontal* (to unfurl lexical and technological paradigms, to make an inventory of the lexical fields proposed by language), referring back to a 'lexical competence' common to the author and the reader, leading to an aesthetics of discontinuity and of non-narrativity; the second, *vertical* (to decipher, to seek out and read the signs of the intimate, 'true' and deep being), leading to an aesthetics of unity, reintroducing the narrative as a quest for knowledge, and reinstating a pedagogical type of relationship (the author transmits information to an 'uninformed' reader).

13. The realist text is a text 'in a hurry', characterised by what might be called its *accelerated semanticisation*, by a maximum foreshortening of the journey and the distance between the functional kernels of the narration. If every narrative can in fact be summarily defined as a dialectic of complementary logical categories, an authorised dialectic that simultaneously controls the preservation of meaning and its transformation, the author can in principle play on the textual disjunction of these complementary categories by placing the maximum distance between:

question and answer

position of appearance – position of being

position of potentiality – actualisation of potentiality

indeterminate – determinate

position of a programme – realisation of the programme

order – acceptance

departure – return

cause – effect

naming of an object or person – description of the object or person

lack – dissipation of the lack, etc.

This serves to introduce into the narrative 'traps', 'slow-downs', distortions, waits, etc. Realist discourse will reject this: the appearance of a new character, manifested by the appearance of a proper name, i.e. of an 'asemanteme', will immediately be followed by the information to which it will refer in the rest of the text: biography, physical or psychological description, characteristic act, programme of action; the outline will be followed by its realisation; the appearance of a blacksmith by the description of the smithy and the blacksmith at work; etc. Hence a certain flattening of the text in its haste to fulfil the horizons of expectation created by the appearance of every new indeterminacy. It could thus be said that realist discourse has a horror of the informational gap, and that it will in general reject dilatory procedures: nothing more alien to realist discourse than any intrigue that involves 'suspense' or 'deceptiveness', any structural layout 'in parts', 'in strands', etc. or any 'elliptical' structure that would skip a necessary step in the logical overall cohesion of the discourse.

14. On a more general semantic level, one wonders whether the necessity of keeping in view both terms of each logical opposition does not create a special (and very elementary) narrative system of a manic-depressive kind: alternating highs and lows, a failure after a victory, a birth after a death, a rise to riches after a fall into poverty, etc. which, incidentally, gives a glimpse of a voluntary ethics of stasis (eternal return to the status quo, 'objective' balance between good and evil; – see the end of Zola's *Pot-Bouille*: 'Then Octave felt a strange sense of beginning again (. . .) today repeated yesterday, there was neither any stopping or ending', etc.). Hence the absence of a 'nexus', an often amorphous intrigue, chapter or narrative endings in the 'minor' key, without strong accentuation, without paroxysms, an intrigue strung together (rather than organised) by the elementary procedure of *conjunction* (encounters, reunions, meetings, receptions, arrivals, meals) or of *disjunction* (quarrels, separations, departures) of characters and/or places.

15. In the realist programme the world is describable, open to denomination. In this respect it is the opposite to fantastic discourse (the unnameable, the indescribable, the monster . . .); it is also characterised by its will to exhaustiveness (fantastic discourse is often partial and parsimonious) and reality is then envisaged as a complex, abounding, discontinuous, 'rich' and numberable and nameable field, which has to be inventoried. We have already seen the consequences of this presupposition for the *characters*. Foreseeably, taking into consideration the discrete and the discontinuous in this way will easily translate into an aesthetics of discontinuity and juxtapostion: impressionist **parataxes**, an accumulation of adjectives and relative propositions, Flaubertian paragraphs, composition by 'pictures', by 'slices of life', by 'scenes', by descriptions, by 'details'. It is well known that very many authors make maniacal reference to detail, to the 'little true fact', to anecdotes or trivial news items, articles or press cuttings. We have already recorded (see number 7 above) realist discourse's predilection for 'articulated' times and spaces, cut up in advance by custom, ritual or lexicology. Hence the synecdochic fragmentation, and the frequent impression of a 'mosaic' that one experiences in the face of a realist text. But if realist discourse multiplies the descriptions, description is certainly not unique to realist discourse. We have tried elsewhere to classify several major types of descriptive systems, and to address problems that can perhaps be reformulated here with greater precision:

(*a*) Does description occupy privileged *places* in realist discourse, different, for example, from the places it can occupy in fantastic discourse? This is the problem of its distribution (**aleatory** or not) and of its function (specific or not). Insofar as the realist text is a text 'in a hurry', and wants to be readable, description will probably tend to assume in it the role of facilitating readability, of *enframing* the actual narrative statement, thus guaranteeing the statement a logical, often **syllogistic** concatenation. Through this distribution realist discourse again comes close to the properly technological statement, which is also generally enframed between two descriptions: 'You take a chicken, young and plump (there follows a brief description of an adequate chicken) → you cut it up → you brown it → you make a sauce → you salt it (a programmed series of narrative statements) → you obtain (there follows the final description, often with a photograph, of the finished dish ready to serve)'. Let us risk the following syntax/narrative homology, which would define a cell typical of the readable-realist narrative (imperfect: simple past: description: narration: cause: consequence):

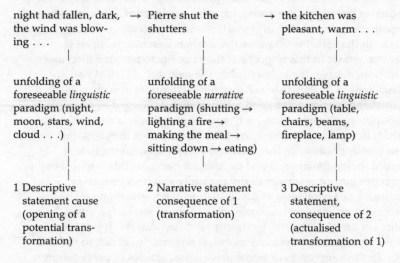

night had fallen, dark, the wind was blowing . . .	→	Pierre shut the shutters	→	the kitchen was pleasant, warm . . .
unfolding of a foreseeable *linguistic* paradigm (night, moon, stars, wind, cloud . . .)		unfolding of a foreseeable *narrative* paradigm (shutting → lighting a fire → making the meal → sitting down → eating)		unfolding of a foreseeable *linguistic* paradigm (table, chairs, beams, fireplace, lamp)
1 Descriptive statement cause (opening of a potential transformation)		2 Narrative statement consequence of 1 (transformation)		3 Descriptive statement, consequence of 2 (actualised transformation of 1)

(*b*) Does realist description carry specific demarcational *signs* at its beginning and at its end? We have noted a recurrent thematics of 'emptiness' (the gaze, the open window, the open door, the lamp being lit, the ascent to a high place, etc.) which *frames* the description (opening of the window or door → closing of the window or door; ascent → descent; lamp lit → lamp extinguished); the description thus will crown an interval between two pseudo-functions (opening/closing, lifting one's eyes/lowering one's eyes, ascending/descending, etc.) which have no narrative role. Hence this extraordinary concatenation in realist discourse: the narrative statement is framed by related descriptive statements which justify it as a unit of transformation, and the descriptive statement is itself framed by two related (pseudo) narrative statements which give it plausibility.

(c) Does realist description have a specific *internal mode of functioning*? The 'types of unfolding' associated with readability must be closely studied: opening of the description of a generic pivotal term, whose presence is obligatory (the denomination of the whole precedes that of the parts; quite the contrary to the puzzle); stereotypical filters produced from the grid laid down by the five senses or from topographical frames (before, behind . . .); **anagrammatisation** of the pivotal term throughout the description; paraphrasing of the unreadable terms by readable terms; systematic usage of certain figures designed to reduplicate the information conveyed, like comparisons in which the two elements are chosen to underscore the **isotopism** of the description by their contiguity (for example in the famous description of Rouen in *Madame Bovary*, where Flaubert compares the *islands* to *fish*), etc. Recognition, as a preliminary to the *description* acting as a general semiotic unity, as a stereotypical matrix governing the play of the signifiers, will certainly facilitate the definition of a specifically realist description, beside other sub-types (fantastic description . . .) which govern otherwise, according to other strategies, the semantic circulation within the 'compartments' of the descriptive system.

(d) Does realist description maintain a specific semantic relationship to the rest of the statement? Insofar as the author's realist presuppositions enclose the latter in a series of confrontations: *subject/world, referent/sign, signifier/signified, character/environment*, etc., this also imposes on him an obligatory thematics: not only *window*, or *eye* (movement from subject to world), *explanation* (movement from sign to referent) and *motivation* (movement from signifier to signified), but also *need* (directed movement: character → environment) and its symmetrical companion, *influence* (directed movement: environment → character). The description will thus often be only the presentation of a *collective agent*, often endowed either with the active status of *object* (object of a 'need', or a 'desire', or an 'appetite', etc.), or else of *addressor* – that is to say with the same active status as the pedagogical subject of the articulation: such and such a decor, such and such an environment, such and such an object will transmit to the character a certain number of values, will propose a programme of action, will advise him, will 'whisper in his ear', will influence him, will 'remind' him of something, etc. In this our topology of knowledge will certainly be found again, imposing here on the author, for better or for worse, a 'sociological' vision (influence of environment, etc.) as well as, curiously, two adjacent meanings of the word *motivation*: the customary meaning in the first case (such and such a character is *motivated* by such and such a need to possess, to transform or to consume the world), in the second case the symbolical-semiotic sense (such and such a description, for example the topos of the **locus amoenus**, serves as a 'motivated' signifier for a character in a euphoric situation). Hence the circularity and the redundancy of this discourse, the world inspiring in the character desires which find their incarnation in the objects of the world, and the object reduplicating the character's 'psychology'.

To conclude rapidly: from the open and quite heterogeneous general set of criteria articulated above, it will be difficult to construct a special *type* of realist discourse. The conditions of exhaustiveness and of simplicity have obviously not been fulfilled and the chosen criteria are probably neither necessary nor sufficient. The examples chosen, as will have been noticed, have hardly departed from the realist *school* of the nineteenth century, which means that the ambiguity mentioned at the outset has not been removed. What mattered here was to reopen a dossier that had been closed by a certain form of terrorism springing from semiotic textuality, rather than to bring definitive new revelations. Moreover, to establish a unity (such and such a type of sequence, such and such a typical character, etc.) does not allow us to prejudge its functionality, since the latter can be defined only by taking into consideration the textual context in which it is embedded. On the other hand, it must be remembered that a statement is never *homogeneous*, that it is a product of a *constructed* theoretical type, and that it would therefore be vain to seek out an exemplary occurrence. In the last resort, it is perhaps through these specific contradictions that realist discourse could best be characterised, contradictions between the opening presuppositions (utopia of language as nomenclature, of the transparent message, etc.) and the ignorance of the constraints innate to the text and its writing. We have, in the course of this consideration, identified some of them:

use of technical terms (monosemic vocabulary)	BUT	problem of their readability
immediate information (narrative 'in a hurry')	BUT	perpetual delays in the narrative from the multiplication of descriptive parentheses
authorial knowledge	BUT	the character's knowledge to be made plausible
multiplication of characters so as to introduce and guarantee segments of knowledge (biographies, descriptions, information)	BUT	psychological 'fragmentation', 'forgetting' of the character who no longer has any narrative role, disappearance of the hero

redundancy, foreseeability, semantic saturation, readability, **anaphoras**	BUT	how to place the extraneous 'detail' which provokes 'the effect of reality'
style as an element of cohesion or 'continuity' (Flaubert), as the author's *know how*	BUT	the text as a linguistic 'mosaic' of jargon, technical slang, idioms, effacing of the author's style
linguistic knowledge (the description unfolds the stereotypical and expected paradigm of the lexical series); this knowledge is common to reader and author	BUT	'ontological' knowledge to unveil the world's real and inner *being*); this knowledge is not common to author and reader and defines a pedagogical relationship
discontinuity of flow and of denomination	BUT	loss of overall coherence claimed by the pedagogical presupposition, etc.

It is up to the author to resolve these contradictions in his own way by developing adequate *compensatory systems*: the various kinds of *knowledge* circulating must be 'put in phase'; the character of the technician will 'explain' the meaning of this or that unreadable technical term, the mobile character and the circularity of the comparisons will compensate for the synecdochic discontinuity, the childhood friend will 'unveil' the mystery of a life story, etc. In these ways one feels the pressures exerted on realist discourse, a discourse more constrained than it appears.

16 David Lodge on Dickens' *Hard Times**

'It is the least read of all the novels and probably also the least enjoyed by those who read it,' said Humphrey House of *Hard Times* in *The Dickens World* (1941).[1] The first part of this statement, at least, has probably not been true since *The Great Tradition* was published (1948). Of *Hard Times*, it will be remembered, Dr Leavis said, '. . . of all Dickens' works, it is the one that has all the strength of his genius, together with a strength no other of them can show – that of a completely serious work of art'.[2]

There are of course two propositions here: one, that *Hard Times* is a complete and satisfactory work of art; and two, that this novel is the crown of Dickens' achievement. The latter proposition has had the greater notoriety, yet it is essentially an aside which Leavis does not attempt to argue through. The first proposition is far more susceptible of fruitful criticial discussion, and as John Holloway's recent article, '*Hard Times*, a History and a Criticism',[3] is the most interesting expression of dissent it has provoked, I shall take the article as a starting point.

Holloway's case can be summarized as follows: that the Utilitarian philosophy Dickens claims to be representing in the novel is a crude travesty of the reality, shallowly conceived as a mere blind faith in statistics; that it is opposed by an equally shallow plea for 'play' and 'fancy', represented by the Slearies 'not as vital horsemen but as plain entertainers'; that Dickens' attitude to Trade Unions and labour problems is unenlightened; that, in short, the novel as a whole is the product of a mind not prophetic and profound, but bourgeois and philistine. There is considerable force in all these arguments, and in some respects they merely consolidate points previously made by Humphrey House and Raymond Williams.[4] There are two interconnected grounds for caution in accepting Holloway's arguments, however: they are extensively documented with external evidence – such as contemporary Utilitarian

---

* Reprinted from 'The Rhetoric of *Hard Times*' in *The Language of Fiction* (London: Routledge & Kegan Paul and New York: Columbia University Press, 1966), pp. 144–63.

works and Dickens' journalism; and they tend towards an assessment of the novel itself even lower than Holloway wishes to reach. Thus he is compelled to make a divorce between the achievements of the novel and Dickens' manifest intentions:

> The passages in *Hard Times* where Dickens is most freely himself, are not those where he is most engaged with his moral fable or intent (if we think, mistakenly that he is at all) on what Dr Leavis has called 'the confrontation of Utilitarianism by life'.[5]

While agreeing that 'life' (with the special resonances Dr Leavis gives to that word) is far too grand a term for the values which Dickens opposes to the world of Gradgrind and Bounderby, I suggest that Dickens' achievements in the novel can no more be separated from his polemical intention than can his failures.

On every page *Hard Times* manifests its identity as a polemical work, a critique of mid-Victorian industrial society dominated by materialism, acquisitiveness, and ruthlessly competitive capitalist economics. To Dickens, at the time of writing *Hard Times,* these things were represented most articulately, persuasively (and therefore dangerously) by the Utilitarians. It is easy to abstract the argument behind the novel, and to demonstrate its logical and practical weaknesses. The argument has two stages: (1) that the dominant philosophy of Utilitarianism, particularly as it expresses itself in education, results in a damaging impoverishment of the moral and emotional life of the individual; and (2) that this leads in turn to social and economic injustice, since individuals thus conditioned are incapable of dealing with the human problems created by industrialism. On the level of plot (1) is expounded in terms of the Nemesis which punishes Gradgrind through his children and (2) is expounded in terms of Stephen Blackpool's sufferings. That Dickens makes a connection between the two propositions and the two areas of the plot is made clear in the scene where Blackpool confronts Bounderby and Harthouse, and is challenged to offer a solution for the 'muddle' he is always complaining about. Stephen expresses himself negatively. He repudiates the employers' exploitation of their power ('the strong hand will never do't'); their reliance on *laissez faire* ('lettin alone will never do't'); withdrawal from social contact with the working classes ('not drawin nigh to fok, wi' kindness and patience an' cheery ways . . . will never do't'); and, 'most o' 'aw', their mental habit of regarding the workers as soulless units in the economic machine while inconsistently accusing them of ingratitude if they protest:

> 'Most o' aw, rating 'em as so much Power, and reg'lating 'em as if they was figures in a soom, or machines; wi'out loves and likens, wi'out

memories and inclinations, wi'out souls to weary and souls to hope –
when aw goes quiet draggin' wi' 'em as if they'd nowt o' th'kind, and
when aw goes onquiet, reproachin' 'em for their want o' sitch humanly
feelins in their dealins wi' yo – this will never do't, Sir, till God's work
is onmade.'

(II, v)

It is clear that Dickens is speaking through Stephen here, and what the
speech amounts to in positive terms is a plea for generosity, charity,
imaginative understanding of the spiritual and emotional needs of
humanity.

While these values have an obvious relevance to the field of personal
relations (the Gradgrind–Bounderby circle) they are less viable as a basis
for reform of the body politic, because there are no sanctions to ensure
their application. They are not – apart from Louisa's abortive attempt to
help Stephen – shown in action in the novel vertically through the class
structure: Stephen's martyr-like death bears witness to this. Yet Dickens
could only offer a disembodied and vaguely defined benevolence as a
cure for the ills of Coketown because he had rejected all the alternatives.
In his hostile portrait of Gradgrind, Dickens repudiated not only the
narrowest kind of Utilitarian rationalism, but also, as House and others
have pointed out, the processes by which most of the great Victorian
reforms were carried out – statistical enquiry, commissions, reports,
acted on by Parliamentary legislation.[6] In his hostile portrait of
Slackbridge, and his account of Stephen's ostracism because of his refusal
to join the Trade Union, Dickens repudiated the workers' claim to secure
justice by collective bargaining. Dickens is, then, opposed to any change
in the political and economic structure of society, and places his hopes
for amelioration in a change of heart, mind, and soul in those who
possess power, who will then disseminate the fruits of this change over
the lower echelons of society. Dickens' ideal State would be one of
'benevolent and genial anarchy'.[7]

This is an insecure basis from which to launch a critique of society, and
its insecurity becomes all the more obvious when we look outside *Hard
Times* to Dickens' journalism of the same period, and find him enthusing
over the wonders of Victorian manufacture[8] and expressing surprised
admiration for the Preston cotton-workers' conduct of their strike in
1854.[9]

And yet, when all this has been said, and the contradictions,
limitations, and flaws in Dickens' argument extrapolated, *Hard Times*
remains a novel of considerable polemical effectiveness. The measure of
this effectiveness, it seems to me, can only be accounted for in terms of

Dickens' rhetoric. This approach should recommend itself to the author of *The Victorian Sage*, a study which shows how many key Victorian writers, disarmed of logic by their opponents, resorted to non-logical methods of persuasion in order to communicate their ideas. In the criticism of fiction we have learned, notably from Wayne Booth, to use 'rhetoric' as a term for all the techniques by which a novelist seeks to persuade us of the validity of his vision of experience, a vision which cannot usually be formulated in abstract terms. But in a novel like *Hard Times*, which can be called a *roman à thèse*, rhetoric functions very nearly in its traditional rôle as the vehicle of an argument.

There is another reason why rhetoric seems a particularly useful term in discussing Dickens' work. Not only is the 'author's voice' always insistent in his novels, but it is characteristically a public-speaking voice, an oratorical or histrionic voice; and it is not difficult to see a connection between this feature of his prose and his fondness for speech-making and public reading of his works.

I shall try to show that *Hard Times* succeeds where its rhetoric succeeds and fails where its rhetoric fails; and that success and failure correspond fairly closely to the negative and positive aspects, respectively, of the argument inherent in the novel.

The very first chapter of *Hard Times* affords an excellent illustration of Dickens' rhetoric, and it is short enough to be quoted and analysed in its entirety.

HARD TIMES

BOOK THE FIRST. SOWING

CHAPTER I

THE ONE THING NEEDFUL

'Now, what I want is, Facts. Teach these boys and girls nothing but Facts. Facts alone are wanted in life. Plant nothing else, and root out everything else. You can only form the minds of reasoning animals upon Facts: nothing else will ever be of any service to them. This is the principle on which I bring up my own children, and this is the principle on which I bring up these children. Stick to Facts, Sir!'

The scene was a plain, bare, monotonous vault of a schoolroom, and the speaker's square forefinger emphasised his observations by underscoring every sentence with a line on the schoolmaster's sleeve. The emphasis was helped by the speaker's square wall of a forehead, which had his eyebrows for its base, while his eyes found commodious cellarage in two dark caves, overshadowed by the wall. The emphasis was helped by the speaker's mouth, which was wide, thin, and hard set. The emphasis was helped by the speaker's voice, which was inflexible, dry, and dictatorial. The emphasis was helped by the speaker's hair, which bristled on the skirts of his bald head, a plantation of firs to keep the wind from its shining surface, all covered with knobs, like the crust of a plum pie, as if the head had scarcely warehouse-room for the hard facts stored inside. The speaker's obstinate carriage, a square coat, square legs, square shoulders – nay, his very neckcloth, trained to take him by the throat with an unaccommodating grasp, like a stubborn fact, as it was – all helped the emphasis.

'In this life, we want nothing but Facts, Sir; nothing but Facts!'

The speaker, and the schoolmaster, and the third grown person present, all backed a little, and swept with their eyes the inclined plane of little vessels then and there arranged in order, ready to have imperial gallons of facts poured into them until they were full to the brim.

This chapter communicates, in a remarkably compact way, both a description and a judgment of a concept of education. This concept is defined in a speech, and then evaluated – not in its own terms, but in terms of the speaker's appearance and the setting. Dickens, of course, always relies heavily on the popular, perhaps primitive, assumption that there is a correspondence between a person's appearance and his character; and as Gradgrind is a governor of the school, its design may legitimately function as a metaphor for his character. Dickens also had a fondness for fancifully appropriate names, but – perhaps in order to stress the representativeness of Gradgrind's views – he does not reveal the name in this first chapter.[10]

Because of the brevity of the chapter, we are all the more susceptible to the effect of its highly rhetorical patterning, particularly the manipulation of certain repeated words, notably *fact*, *square*, and *emphasis*. The kind of education depicted here is chiefly characterized by an obsession with facts. The word occurs five times in the opening speech of the first paragraph, and it is twice repeated towards the end of the second, descriptive paragraph to prepare for the reintroduction of Gradgrind speaking – ' "we want nothing but Facts, sir – nothing but Facts" '; and it occurs for the tenth and last time towards the end of the last paragraph. In Gradgrind's speeches the word is capitalized, to signify his almost religious devotion to Facts.

Gradgrind's concept of education is further characterized in ways we can group into three categories, though of course they are closely connected:

(1) It is authoritarian, fanatical and bullying in its application.
(2) It is rigid, abstract and barren in quality.
(3) It is materialistic and commercial in its orientation.

The first category is conveyed by the structure of the second paragraph, which is dominated by 'emphasis'. This paragraph comprises six sentences. In the first sentence we are told how the 'speaker's square forefinger emphasized his observations'. The next four, central sentences are each introduced, with cumulative force, by the clause 'The emphasis was helped', and this formula, translated from the passive to the active voice, makes a fittingly 'emphatic' conclusion to the paragraph in the sixth sentence: 'all helped the emphasis'. This rhetorical pattern has a dual function. In one way it reflects or imitates Gradgrind's own bullying, over-emphatic rhetoric, of which we have an example in the first paragraph; but in another way it helps to *condemn* Gradgrind, since it 'emphasizes' the narrator's own pejorative catalogue of details of the speaker's person and immediate environment. The narrator's rhetoric is, as it must be, far more skilful and persuasive than Gradgrind's.

The qualities in category (2) are conveyed in a number of geometrical or quasi-geometrical terms, *wide, line, thin, base, surface, inclined plane* and, particularly, *square* which recurs five times; and in words suggestive of barren regularity, *plain, bare, monotonous, arranged in order, inflexible*. Such words are particularly forceful when applied to human beings – whether Gradgrind or the children. The metamorphosis of the human into the non-human is, as we shall find confirmed later, one of Dickens' main devices for conveying his alarm at the way Victorian society was moving.

Category (3), the orientation towards the world of commerce, is perhaps less obvious than the other categories, but it is unmistakably present in some of the boldest tropes of the chapter: *commodious cellarage, warehouse-room, plantation, vessels, imperial gallons*.

The authoritarian ring of *'imperial'* leads us back from category (3) to category (1), just as *'under-scoring* every sentence with a *line'* leads us from (1) to (2). There is a web of connecting strands between the qualities I have tried to categorize: it is part of the rhetorical strategy of the chapter that all the qualities it evokes are equally applicable to Gradgrind's character, person, ideas, his school and the children (in so far as he has shaped them in his own image).

Metaphors of growth and cultivation are of course commonplace in discussion of education, and we should not overlook the ironic invocation of such metaphors, with a deliberately religious, prophetic implication (reinforced by the Biblical echo of the chapter heading, 'The One Thing Needful'[11]) in the title of the Book, 'SOWING', later to be followed by Book the Second, 'REAPING', and Book the Third, 'GARNERING'. These metaphors are given a further twist in Gradgrind's recommendation to 'Plant nothing else and root out everything else' (except facts).

If there is a flaw in this chapter it is the simile of the plum pie, which has pleasant, genial associations alien to the character of Gradgrind, to whose head it is, quite superfluously, applied. Taken as a whole, however, this is a remarkably effective and densely woven beginning of the novel.

The technique of the first chapter of *Hard Times* could not be described as 'subtle'. But subtle effects are often lost in a first chapter, where the reader is coping with the problem of 'learning the author's language'. Perhaps with some awareness of this fact, sharpened by his sense of addressing a vast, popular audience, Dickens begins many of his novels by nailing the reader's attention with a display of sheer rhetorical power, relying particularly on elaborate repetition. One thinks, for instance, of the fog at the beginning of *Bleak House* or the sun and shadow in the first chapter of *Little Dorrit*. In these novels the rhetoric works to establish a symbolic atmosphere; in *Hard Times*, to establish a thematic Idea – the despotism of Fact. But this abstraction – Fact – is invested with a remarkable solidity through the figurative dimension of the language.

The gross effect of the chapter is simply stated, but analysis reveals that it is achieved by means of a complex verbal activity that is far from simple. Whether it represents fairly any actual educational theory or practice in mid-nineteenth-century England is really beside the point. It aims to convince us of the *possibility* of children being taught in such a way, and to make us recoil from the imagined possibility. The chapter succeeds or fails as rhetoric; and I think it succeeds.

Dickens begins as he means to continue. Later in the novel we find Gradgrind's house, which, like the school-room, is a function of himself, described in precisely the same terms of fact and rigid measurement, partly geometrical and partly commerical.

A very regular feature on the face of the country, Stone Lodge was. Not the least disguise toned down or shaded off that uncompromising fact in the landscape. A great square house, with a heavy portico darkening the principal windows, as its master's heavy brows over-shadowed his eyes. A calculated, cast up, balanced and proved house. Six windows on this side of the door, six on that side; a total of twelve in this wing, a total of twelve in the other wing; four and twenty carried over to the back wings. A lawn and garden and an infant avenue, all ruled straight like a botanical account-book.

(I, iii)

It has been observed[12] that Dickens individualizes his characters by making them use peculiar locutions and constructions in their speech, a technique which was particularly appropriate to serial publication in which the reader's memory required to be frequently jogged. This technique extends beyond the idiosyncratic speech of characters, to the language in which they are described. A key-word, or group of key-words, is insistently used when the character is first introduced, not only to identify him but also to evaluate him, and is invoked at various strategic points in the subsequent action. Dickens' remarkable metaphorical inventiveness ensures that continuity and rhetorical emphasis are not obtained at the expense of monotony. The application of the key-words of the first chapter to Mr Gradgrind's house gives the same delight as the development of a metaphysical conceit. The observation that Mrs Gradgrind, 'whenever she showed a symptom of coming to life, was invariably stunned by some weighty piece of fact tumbling on her' (I, iv), affords a kind of verbal equivalent of knock-about comedy, based on a combination of expectancy (we know the word will recur) and surprise (we are not prepared for the particular formulation).

Bounderby offers another illustration of Dickens' use of key-words in characterisation. He is first introduced as 'a big, loud man, with a stare, and a metallic laugh' (I, iv). The metallic quality is shortly afterwards defined as 'that brassy speaking-trumpet of a voice of his' (*ibid*). His house has a front door with 'BOUNDERBY (in letters very like himself) upon a brazen plate, and a round brazen door-handle underneath it, like a brazen full stop' (I, xi). Bounderby's bank 'was another red brick house, with black outside shutters, green inside blinds, a black street door up two white steps, a brazen door-plate, and a brazen door-handle full-stop' (II, i). The buildings Bounderby inhabits take their character from him, as Gradgrind's do from him. But here the emphasis is on the brass embellishments which, by the use of the word *brazen* (rather than *brass* used adjectivally) epitomize several facets of his character: his hardness, vanity, crude enjoyment of wealth, and, most important of all, the fact that he is a brazen liar. (We do not know for certain that he is a liar until the end of the novel; the 'brazen' fittings reinforce other hints which prepare us for the revelation.)

The failures of characterization in *Hard Times* are generally failures in using rhetorical strategies which Dickens elsewhere employs very successfully. The portrait of Slackbridge, the trade union demagogue, for instance, seeks to exploit a relationship between character and appearance in a way which is familiar in Dickens and well exemplified in the first chapter; but it does so crudely and clumsily:

> Judging him by Nature's evidence, he was above the mass in very little but the stage on which he stood. In many respects he was essentially below them. He was not so honest, he was not so manly, he was not so good-humoured; he substituted cunning for their simplicity, and passion for their safe solid sense. An ill-made, high shouldered man, with lowering brows, and his features crushed into an habitually sour

expression, he contrasted most unfavourably, even in his mongrel dress, with the great body of his hearers in their plain working clothes.

(II, iv)

Apart from the vividness of 'crushed', the description of Slackbridge is carelessly vague, and we miss the metaphorical inventiveness that characterizes Dickens' best descriptions of people. But the main error of the passage is the ordering of its material. The rhetorical strategy announced by the opening sentence is that Slackbridge's character is to be read in his appearance. But in fact the character is read *before* we are given the appearance. It is as if Dickens has so little confidence in his own imaginative evidence that he must inform us, over-explicitly, what conclusions we are to draw, before we come to the evidence. We know from external sources that Dickens was in a confused state of mind about the trade union movement at the time of writing *Hard Times*,[13] and we can rarely expect to receive a balanced account of organized labour from any middle-class Victorian novelist. However, the failure of understanding here reveals itself in the first place as a failure of expression; the portrait of Gradgrind, on the other hand, though it probably derives from an equivalent misunderstanding of Utilitarianism, succeeds.

Another, more significant failure of Dickens' rhetoric is to be observed in the treatment of Tom Gradgrind. In this connection, I must register my disagreement with John Holloway's opinion that 'the gradual degeneration of Tom . . . is barely (as in fact it is treated) related to Dickens' major problems in the book, though it is one of its best things'.[14] It is gradual (though not very extensively treated) up to the beginning of Book II, by which point we have gathered that Tom, so far from drawing strength of character from his repressive and rationalist upbringing, is turning into a selfish young man prepared to exploit others for his own advantage. He is still a long way, however, from the depravity that allows him to connive at the seduction of his own sister and to implicate an innocent man (Stephen Blackpool) in his own crime. This moral gap is rather clumsily bridged by Dickens in the second chapter of Book II, where he suddenly introduces a key-word for Tom: 'whelp'.

The Bounderbys are entertaining James Harthouse to dinner. Louisa does not respond to Harthouse's attempts to flirt, but when Tom comes in, late, 'She changed . . . and broke into a beaming smile. . . .'

'Ay ay?' thought the visitor. 'This whelp is the only creature she cares for. So, so!'

The whelp was presented, and took his chair. The appellation was not flattering, but not unmerited.

(II, ii)

The chapter ends very shortly afterwards, but Dickens contrives to use the word 'whelp' three more times, and the title of the following chapter (II, iii), in which Tom betrays Louisa's situation to Harthouse, is entitled 'The Whelp'.

'Whelp' is a cliché, and it will be noticed that the word is first used by Harthouse, and then adopted by the novelist in his authorial capacity. When a novelist does this, it is usually with ironical intent, suggesting some inadequacy in the speaker's habits of thought.[15] Dickens plays on Gradgrind's 'facts' to this effect. But in the case of Harthouse's 'whelp' he has taken a moral cliché from a character who is morally unreliable, and invested it with his own authority as narrator. This gives away the fact that Tom is being forced into a new rôle halfway through the book. For Tom's degeneration *should* be related to the major problems with which Dickens is concerned in *Hard Times*. According to the overall pattern of the novel, Tom and Louisa are to act as indices of the failure of Mr Gradgrind's philosophy of education, and should thus never be allowed to stray outside the area of our pity, since they are both victims rather than free agents. But Tom's actions do take him beyond our pity, and diminish the interest of his character.

Perhaps Dickens was misled by feeling the need to inject a strong crime-interest into his story, of which Tom was a handy vehicle; or perhaps he lost his head over the preservation of Louisa's purity (the somewhat hysterical conclusion to Chapter iii, Book II, 'The Whelp', seems to suggest this). Whatever the explanation, 'the whelp', unlike those key-words which organize and concentrate the represented character of individuals and places, acts merely as a slogan designed to generate in the reader such a contempt for Tom that he will not enquire too closely into the pattern of his moral development – a pattern that will not, in fact, bear very close scrutiny.

In the conduct of his central argument, Dickens explicitly calls our attention to a 'key-note'. The first occasion on which he does so is when introducing the description of Coketown, in Chapter v of Book I, entitled 'The Key-note':

COKETOWN, to which Messrs. Bounderby and Gradgrind now walked, was a triumph of fact; it had no greater taint of fancy in it than Mrs Gradgrind herself. Let us strike the key-note, Coketown, before pursuing our tune.

It was a town of red brick, or of brick that would have been red if the smoke and ashes had allowed it; but as matters stood it was a town of unnatural red and black like the painted face of a savage. It was a town of machinery and tall chimneys, out of which interminable serpents of smoke trailed themselves for ever and ever, and never got uncoiled. It had a black canal in it, and a river that ran purple with ill-smelling dye, and vast piles of building full of windows where there was a rattling and a trembling all day long, and where the piston of the steam engine worked monotonously up and down like the head of an elephant in a state of melancholy madness. It contained several large streets all very like one another, and many more small streets still more like one another, inhabited by people equally like one another, who all went in and out at the same hours, with the same sound upon the same pavements, to do the same work, and to whom every day was the same as yesterday and tomorrow, and every year the counterpart of the last and the next.

Dorothy Van Ghent has commented on the effects Dickens gains by investing the inanimate with animation and vice versa. 'The animation of inanimate objects suggests both the quaint gaiety of a forbidden life, and an aggressiveness that has got out of control. . . . The animate is treated as if it is a thing. It is as if the life absorbed by things had been drained out of people who have become incapable of their humanity.'[16] The description of Coketown illustrates this process. The buildings and machinery of Coketown are invested with a sinister life of their own, the life of savages, serpents, and elephants (the serpent and elephant images are reiterated at least five times in the novel).[17] The people of Coketown, on the other hand, take their character from the architecture of the town non-metaphorically conceived – 'large streets all very like one another, and many small streets still more like one another'. They are reduced to indistinguishable units caught up in a mindless, monotonous, mechanical process, superbly represented in the droning repetition of sound and syntax in the last sentence of the passage quoted.

In the rest of this chapter Dickens goes on to say that, despite the efficiency of the town, it was afflicted by *malaise*, social and moral: drunkenness, idleness, irreligion. 'Is it possible,' he asks, 'that there was an analogy between the case of the Coketown populace and the little Gradgrinds?' He goes on to suggest that in both 'there was fancy in them demanding to be brought into healthy existence instead of struggling on in convulsions'.

The antithesis of 'fact and fancy' introduces the chapter (see the quotation above). It has been previously introduced in the school-room chapters, where Cissy Jupe's words, 'I would fancy – ', are rudely interrupted by the government official:

'Ay, ay, ay! But you mustn't fancy,' cried the gentleman, quite elated by coming so happily to his point. 'That's it! You are never to fancy. . . . You are to be in all things regulated and governed . . . by fact. . . . You must discard the word Fancy altogether.'

(I. ii)

A very similar interruption establishes the same antithesis in slightly different terms in Chapter viii, Book I, 'Never Wonder', where Dickens again proposes to strike the key-note:

LET us strike the key-note again, before pursuing the tune. When she was half a dozen years younger, Louisa had been overheard to begin a conversation with her brother one day, by saying 'Tom, I wonder' – upon which Mr Gradgrind, who was the person overhearing, stepped forth into the light, and said, 'Louisa, never wonder!'

Herein lay the spring of the mechanical art and mystery of educating the reason without stooping to the cultivation of the sentiments and affections. Never wonder. By means of addition, substraction, multiplication and division, settle everything somehow, and never wonder. Bring to me, says M'Choakumchild, yonder baby just able to walk, and I will engage that it shall never wonder.

The antithesis between fact and fancy (or wonder), is, then, the dominant key-note of *Hard Times*. It relates the public world of the novel to the private world, the *malaise* of the Gradgrind–Bounderby circle to the *malaise* of Coketown as a social community; and it draws together the two stages of the central argument of the book; the relationship between education in the broad sense and social health. In this respect Dickens is not so very far removed from the position of the Romantic critics of industrialist society. Compare Shelley:

We have more moral, political and historical wisdom than we know how to reduce into practice; we have more scientific and economical knowledge than can be accommodated to the just distribution of the produce which it multiplies. The poetry, in these systems of thought, is concealed by the accumulations of facts and calculating processes. . . . We want the creative faculty to imagine that which we know. . . . To what but a cultivation of the mechanical arts in a degree disproportioned to the presence of the creative faculty, which is the basis of all knowledge, is to be attributed the abuses of all invention for abridging and combining labour, to the exasperation of the inequality of mankind? From what other cause has it arisen that the discoveries which should have lightened, have added a weight to the curse of

Adam? Poetry, and the principle of Self, of which money is the visible incarnation, are the God and Mammon of the world.[18]

There is a real community of feeling between Shelley and Dickens here: one might almost think that *Hard Times* takes its cue for the criticism of 'the accumulation of facts', 'calculating processes', and 'the principle of Self' from the *Defence*. But whereas Shelley opposes to these things poetry, imagination, the creative faculty, Dickens can only offer Fancy, wonder, sentiments – though he does so with the same seriousness and the same intentions as Shelley, as a panacea for the ills of modern society. It is tempting to relate the inadequacy of Dickens' concept of Fancy[19] to the discussions familiar to Romantic criticism of Fancy and Imagination. But it is on the rhetorical level that the inadequacy of Dickens' concept manifests itself. In the first 'key-note' chapter, the authorial voice inquires, with heavy irony, whether we are to be told 'at this time of day'

> that one of the foremost elements in the existence of the Coketown working-people had been for scores of years deliberately set at nought? That there was any Fancy in them demanding to be brought into healthy existence instead of struggling on in convulsions? That, exactly in the ratio as they worked long and monotonously, the craving grew within them for some physical relief – some relaxation, encouraging good humour and good spirits, and giving them a vent – some recognised holiday, though it were but for an honest dance to a stirring band of music – some occasional light pie in which even M'Choakumchild had no finger – which craving must and would be satisfied aright, or must and would inevitably go wrong, until the laws of the Creation were repealed?
>
> (I, v)

The rhetorical questions here impede and confuse the argument. The parallelism of 'which craving must and would be satisfied aright, or must and would inevitably go wrong' is tired and mechanical. A mathematical image is enlisted in arguing *against* the mathematical, calculating faculty: it is precisely Dickens' case in the novel as a whole that the 'laws of Creation' are not accountable in terms of 'ratios'. The vagueness of '*some* relaxation', '*some* recognized holiday' is by no means clarified by the unexciting offer of an 'honest dance' or a 'light pie' as specific palliatives for the people of Coketown.

Dickens is struggling to assert, here, the existence of universal need in humanity, a need which arises from quite a different side of man's nature from that which is occupied with the mechanical processes of industrialism, a need which must be satisfied, a need distantly related to that need for poetry which Shelley asserts. But whereas Shelley's 'poetry' is a faculty which involves and enhances and transforms the total activity of man – 'We must imagine that which we know' – Dickens' Fancy is merely a temporary escape from what is accepted as inevitably unpleasant. It is 'relief', 'a vent', 'a holiday'. To be cruel, one might say that Dickens offers the oppressed workers of Coketown bread and circuses: bread in the metaphorical 'light pie' and circuses in the 'honest dance' – and, of course, in Mr Sleary's circus.

The realm of Fancy is most vividly evoked by the rhetoric of *Hard Times* in what might be called the 'fairy-tale' element of the novel.[20] Many of the characters and events are derived from the staple ingredients of the fairy-tale, and this derivation is clearly revealed in the language.

Louisa and Tom first figure as the brother and sister who often appear in fairy-tales as waifs, exiles, victims of circumstance, hedged about with dangers (the Babes in the Woods, etc.). As they sit by the fire of their room, 'Their shadows were defined upon the wall, but those of the high presses in the room were all blended together on the wall and on the ceiling, as if the brother and sister were overhung by a dark cavern' (I, viii). In their childhood their father wears the aspect of an 'Ogre':

Not that they knew, by name or nature, anything about an Ogre. Fact forbid! I only use the word to express a monster in a lecturing castle, with Heaven knows how many heads manipulated into one, taking childhood captive, and dragging it into gloomy statistical dens by the hair.

(I, iii)

Later, Louisa becomes the enchanted princess with a heart of ice, while Tom takes on the rôle of the knave. Harthouse is the demon king, popping up suddenly in the action with mischievous intent, in a cloud of (cigar) smoke:

James Harthouse continued to lounge in the same place and attitude, smoking his cigar in his own easy way, and looking pleasantly at the whelp, as if he knew himself to be a kind of agreeable demon who had only to hover over him, and he must give up his whole soul if required.

(II, iii)

Cissy tells Mrs Gradgrind that she used to read to her father 'About the fairies, sir, and the dwarf, and the hunchback, and the genies' (I, vii); and the circus folk in *Hard Times* are comparable to the chorus of benevolent, comic, grotesque, half-supernatural creatures who inhabit the world of romance and fairy-tale. They are persistently associated with legend and myth – Pegasus (I, v), Cupid (*ibid*), Jack the Giant Killer (III, vii), etc. Mr Bounderby's mother, Mrs Pegler, 'the mysterious old woman' (III, v), is the crone who figures in many fairy-tales and who brings about a surprising turn in the action. Mr Bounderby refers to her as 'an old woman who seems to have been flying into the town on a broomstick now and then' (II, viii). But the proper witch of the story, and Dickens' most effective adaptation of a stock-figure from fairy-tale, is Mrs Sparsit. 'Mrs Sparsit considered herself, in some sort, the Bank Fairy', we are told, but the townspeople 'regarded her as the Bank Dragon, keeping watch over the treasures of the mine'. Her heavy eyebrows and hooked nose are exploited for vivid effects of cruelty:

> Mr Bounderby sat looking at her, as, with the points of a stiff, sharp pair of scissors, she picked out holes for some inscrutable purpose, in a piece of cambric. An operation which, taken in connexion with the bushy eyebrows and the Roman nose, suggested with some liveliness the idea of a hawk engaged upon the eyes of a tough little bird.
>
> (I, xvi)

She flatters Bounderby to his face, but secretly insults his portrait. She wills Louisa into Harthouse's clutches, figuring Louisa's progress as the descent of a 'Giant's Staircase', on which she keeps anxious watch (II, x). The boldest treatment of Mrs Sparsit as a witch occurs in the scene where she steals through the grounds of Mr Gradgrind's country house, hoping to catch Louisa and Harthouse together.

> She thought of the wood and stole towards it, heedless of long grass and briers: of worms, snails, and slugs, and all the creeping things that be. With her dark eyes and her hook nose warily in advance of her, Mrs Sparsit softly crushed her way through the thick undergrowth, so intent upon her object that she would probably have done no less, if the wood had been a wood of adders.
>   Hark!
>   The smaller birds might have tumbled out of their nests, fascinated by the glittering of Mrs Sparsit's eyes in the gloom . . .
>
> (II, xi)

When a thunderstorm bursts immediately afterwards, Mrs Sparsit's appearance becomes still more grotesque:

> It rained now, in a sheet of water. Mrs Sparsit's white stockings were of many colours, green predominating; prickly things were in her

shoes; caterpillars slung themselves, in hammocks of their own
making, from various parts of her dress; rills ran from her bonnet, and
her Roman nose.

(II, xi)

Traditionally, witches are antipathetic to water. It is appropriate,
therefore, that the frustration of Mrs Sparsit's spite, when she loses track
of Louisa, is associated with her ludicrous, rain-soaked appearance (see
the conclusion to II, xi).

We may add to these examples of the invocation of fairy-tale, the
repeated description of the factories illuminated at night as 'fairy palaces'
(I, x; I, xi; II, i, *et passim*), and Mr Bounderby's often expressed conviction
that his men 'expect to be set up in a coach and six, and to be fed on
turtle soup and venison and fed with a gold spoon' (I, xi; I, vi; II, i, *et
passim*). These phrases contrast ironically with the actual drab
environment and existence of the Coketown people.

It is, indeed, as an *ironic* rhetorical device that the fairy-tale element
operates most successfully. On one level it is possible to read the novel
as an ironic fairy-tale, in which the enchanted princess is released from
her spell but does not find a Prince Charming, in which the honest,
persecuted servant (Stephen) is vindicated but not rewarded, and in
which the traditional romantic belief in blood and breeding, confirmed by
a discovery, is replaced by the exposure of Bounderby's inverted
snobbery.

In other respects, however, the fairy-tale element sets up unresolved
tensions in the novel. It encourages a morally-simplified non-social, and
non-historical view of human life and conduct, whereas Dickens'
undertaking in *Hard Times* makes quite opposite demands. Mr Sleary's
ruse for releasing Tom from the custody of Bitzer, for instance (III, viii),
is acceptable on the level of fairy-tale motivation: he returns Mr
Gradgrind's earlier good deed (the adoption of Cissy) and scores off an
unsympathetic character (Bitzer). But the act is essentially lawless, and
conflicts with Dickens' appeals elsewhere in the novel for justice and
social responsibility. As long as the circus folk represent a kind of life
that is anarchic, seedy, socially disreputable, but cheerful and humane,
they are acceptable and enjoyable. But when they are offered as agents or
spokesmen of social and moral amelioration, we reject them. The art they
practise is Fancy in its tawdriest form, solemnly defended by Mr Sleary
in terms we recognize as the justification of today's mass entertainers:

'People mutht be amuthed. They can't be alwayth a learning, nor yet
they can't be alwayth a working, they an't made for it. You *mutht* have
uth, Thquire.

(III, viii)

Cissy is meant to represent a channel through which the values of the circus folk are conveyed to the social order. But her one positive act, the dismissal of Harthouse (III, ii), depends for its credibility on a simple faith in the superiority of a good fairy over a demon king.

In other words, where Dickens invokes the world of fairy-tale ironically, to dramatize the drabness, greed, spite and injustice which characterize a society dominated by materialism, it is a highly effective rhetorical device; but where he relies on the simplifications of the fairy-tale to suggest means of redemption, we remain unconvinced.

If Dickens' notion of Fancy was attached mainly to fairy-tale and nursery rhyme (cf. the allusions to the cow with the crumpled horn and Peter Piper in I, iii), his own art is very much one of Fancy in the Coleridgean sense: 'Fancy has no other counters to play with, but fixities and definites. The Fancy is indeed no other than a mode of Memory emancipated from the order of time and space. . . .'[21] This seems an appropriate description of Dickens' method in, for instance, the first chapter of *Hard Times*, or in the description of Coketown, or in the treatment of Mrs Sparsit as a witch. To appreciate this, is to feel that Coleridge was wrong to depreciate Fancy as a literary mode; but it is also to understand why Dickens' greatest achievement as a novelist is his depiction of a disordered universe in which the organic and the mechanical have exchanged places, rather than in his attempts to trace moral and emotional processes within the individual psyche.

In *Hard Times*, Dickens expounds a diagnosis of the ills of modern industrial society for which no institutions can supply a cure: society, represented by a group of characters, must therefore change itself, learning from a group outside the social order – the circus. But Dickens' characters are incapable of change: the language in which they are embodied fixes them in their 'given' condition. They can only die (like Stephen Blackpool) or be broken (like Mr Bounderby). Mr Gradgrind may lose his 'squareness', but he is left a shadow: he cannot become a Michelin Man, all circles and spheres. Louisa when her heart has been melted is a far less convincing character than Louisa with a heart of ice. (This can be quickly seen by comparing the scene of her interview with Gradgrind to discuss Bounderby's proposal (I, xv), rightly singled out for praise by Leavis, with the parallel scene at the end of the book where she returns to her father to reproach him for her upbringing, and where she is given the most embarrassing lines in the novel to speak (II, xii). Dickens falters in his handling of the character of Tom Gradgrind precisely because he uses a device for fixing character (*whelp*) to express a process of change.

If *Hard Times* is a polemical novel that is only partially persuasive, it is because Dickens' rhetoric is only partially adequate to the tasks he set himself.

Notes

1. HUMPHREY HOUSE, *The Dickens World* (Oxford Paperback edn, 1960), p. 203.

2. F.R. LEAVIS, *The Great Tradition* (Penguin edn, 1962), p. 249.

3. JOHN HOLLOWAY, 'Hard Times, a History and a Criticism', *Dickens and the Twentieth Century*, ed. John Gross and Gabriel Pearson (1962), pp. 159–74. Since Lodge wrote this chapter David Hirsch has published another dissenting opinion, 'Hard Times and F.R. Leavis', *Criticism*, IV (Winter 1964), pp. 1–16 – an effective but rather negative contribution to the debate.

4. See House, *op. cit.*, pp. 103–11, and RAYMOND WILLIAMS, *Culture and Society 1780–1950* (Penguin edn, 1961), pp. 104–8.

5. Holloway, *op. cit.*, p. 174.

6. E.g.: 'He [Mr Gradgrind] then returned with promptitude to the national cinder-heap, and resumed his sifting for the odds and ends he wanted, and his throwing of the dust into the eyes of other people who wanted other odds and ends – in fact, resumed his parliamentary duties' (II, xi)

7. 'From one point of view Buckle's book can be seen as an attempt to erect the doctrine of *laissez-faire* into a philosophy of history, and to defend civilized society as a state of benevolent and genial anarchy.' House, *op cit.*, pp. 173–4, commenting on H.T. Buckle's *History of Civilization* (1857–61), quoted with approval by Dickens in 1869.

8. See House, *op, cit.*, pp. 166.

9. See note 13 below.

10. MARY MCCARTHY has suggested '(Characters in Fiction', *The Partisan Review Anthology*, 1962, pp. 260–1) that an anonymous 'he' at the beginning of a novel usually moves the reader to sympathetic identification. That the effect is quite the reverse in this example shows that the effect of any narrative strategy is determined finally by the narrator's langauge.

11. Chapter ii of Book I is called 'Murdering the Innocents'.

12. RANDOLPH QUIRK, 'Some Observations on the Language of Dickens', *Review of English Literature*, II (1961), pp. 20–1.

13. House (*op. cit.*, pp. 206–8) says that Dickens deliberately went to Preston to observe the cotton strike there early in 1854, in order to gather material for *Hard Times*, and notes that his report in *Household Words* ('On Strike', II Feb. 1854) shows a somewhat surprised respect for the orderly and efficient conduct of the strikers. K.J. Fielding, in his *Charles Dickens: A Critical Introduction* (1958) argues (pp. 134–5) that 'the conditions described in *Hard Times* are much closer to the engineering strike of 1852 than to the dispute at Preston' and quotes a contemporary letter of Dickens:

> As to the Engineers . . . I believe the difficulty in the way of compromise,

> from the very beginning, is not so much with the masters as with the men. Honorable, generous and free-spirited themselves, they have fallen into an unlucky way of trusting their affairs to contentious men, who work them up into a state of conglomeration and irritation, and are the greatest pests that their own employers can encounter upon earth.

This is certainly the attitude Dickens adopts in *Hard Times*. But on a more fundamental level he also distrusted the trade unions as a threat to the liberty of the individual. He weakens his own case, however, by making Stephen refuse to join the union because of a mysterious and apparently meaningless promise he has made to Rachel (II, vi). See Raymond Williams (*op. cit.*, pp. 99–119) for a discussing of the distrust of organised labour by Victorian novelists who sympathised with the oppressed working classes.

14. Holloway, *op. cit.*, p. 171.

15. Compare E.M. Forster, a master of this device, in *A Room with a View* (George Emerson has been indiscreet enough to mention in company that his father is taking a bath):

> 'Oh dear!' breathed the little old lady, and shuddered as if all the winds of heaven had entered the apartment. 'Gentlemen sometimes do not realise – ' Her voice faded away. But Miss Bartlett seemed to understand, and a conversation developed in which gentlemen who did not realise played a principal part.' (I, I)

Much later in the novel, Lucy, engaged to another, is desperately fighting off the advances of George. 'What does a girl do when she comes across a cad?' she asks Miss Bartlett.

> 'I always said he was a cad, dear. Give me credit for that at all events. From the very first moment – when he said his father was having a bath.' . . . She moved feebly to the window, and tried to detect the cad's white flannels among the laurels. (II, 16)

16. DOROTHY VAN GHENT, 'The Dickens World: A View from Todgers's', *The Dickens Critics*, ed. George H. Ford and Lauriat Lane Jr (Ithaca, 1961), p. 214.

17. Chapters I, xi; I, xii; II, i; III, v.

18. *Peacock's Four Ages of Poetry, Shelley's Defence of Poetry, Browning's Essay on Shelley*, ed. H.F.B. Brett-Smith (Oxford, 1921), p. 52.

19. Dickens' commitment to 'Fancy' is not restricted to *Hard Times*, as P.A.W. Collins shows in his very thorough study of Dickens' use of the word: 'Queen Mab's Chariot among the Steam Engines: Dickens and Fancy', *English Studies*, XLII (1961), pp. 78–90.

20. The author's attention was first directed to this (apart from the characterization of Mrs Sparsit) by a Birmingham undergraduate, Miss Margaret Thomas. He adds that possibly it had been observed before, but that he had not been able to find it in Dickens criticism.

21. COLERIDGE, *Biographia Literaria*, Ch. XIII.

Reader-oriented

Reader-oriented criticism has developed significantly as a concomitant of structuralism and of rhetorical approaches, both of which envisage readers as active participants in the construction of the text. It assumes a variety of guises, including the subjective, in which readers' personal, affective responses are explored, the **phenomenological**, which focuses on the processes whereby readers 'objectify' the text, and the aesthetic, which asks how the text produces its effect on readers.

Both the pieces reprinted here underscore the play and interplay between text and readers. Wolfgang Iser's 'The Play of the Text' was originally published in *The Language of the Unsayable* (ed. S. Budick and W. Iser, Columbia University Press, 1989). Iser's aim is to re-examine the relationship between author, text and readers. He regards it as a performative one in which authors play various games with readers, for which the text is the playground. The nature of these games is discussed in the Introduction (see p. 15). All of them are forms of staging, ways of crossing the boundaries between the real world and the realm of the fiction. In delineating the games, Iser suggests how that staging and its consequent transformations are accomplished.

The crossing of boundaries is a central topic, too, in Kendall L. Walton's 'Appreciating Fiction: Suspending Disbelief or Pretending Belief?' which first appeared in the journal *Dispositio* (5, 1980). For Walton the crucial step is readers' willingness not merely to suspend disbelief but positively to pretend belief. His approach is essentially aesthetic: he conceives the world of the fiction as adjacent to that of reality, and as producing its own fictional truths, to which readers are persuaded to subscribe through their capacity to enter believingly into the created realm.

17   Wolfgang Iser on the Play of the Text*

It is reasonable to presuppose that author, text, and reader are closely interconnected in a relationship that is to be conceived as an ongoing process that produces something that had not existed before. This view of the text is in direct conflict with the traditional notion of representation, insofar as mimesis entails reference to a pregiven 'reality' that is meant to be represented. In the Aristotelian sense, the function of representation is twofold: to render the constitutive forms of nature perceivable; and to complete what nature has left incomplete. In either case mimesis, though of paramount importance, cannot be confined to mere imitation of what is, since the processes of elucidation and of completion both require a performative activity if apparent absences are to be moved into presence. Since the advent of the modern world there is a clearly discernible tendency toward privileging the performative aspect of the author–text–reader relationship, whereby the pregiven is no longer viewed as an object of representation but rather as material from which something new is fashioned. The new product, however, is not predetermined by the features, functions, and structures of the material referred to and encapsulated in the text.

There are historic reasons for this shift in focus. Closed systems, such as the cosmos of Greek thought or of the medieval world picture, gave priority to representation as mimesis because of their overriding concern that whatever existed – even if it eluded perception – should be translated into something tangible. When the closed system, however, is punctured and replaced by open-endedness, the mimetic component of representation declines and the performative one comes to the fore. The process then no longer entails reaching behind appearances in order to grasp an intelligible world in the Platonic sense, but turns into a 'way of world-making.' If what the text brings about were to be equated with world-making, the question would arise whether one could continue to

---

* Reprinted from 'The Play of the Text' in *Languages of the Unsayable*, ed. S. Budick and W. Iser (New York: Columbia University Press, 1989), pp. 325–39.

speak of 'representation' at all. The concept could be retained only if the 'ways of world-making' themselves became the referential object for representation. In this case, the performative component would have to be conceived as the pregiven of the performative act. Irrespective of whether this might or might not be considered tautological, the fact remains that it would lead to a host of problems that are not within the scope of this essay. There is, however, one inference that is highly relevant to my discussion: what has been called the 'end of representation'[1] may, in the final analysis, be less a description of the historical state of the arts than the articulation of misgivings relating to the ability of representation as a concept to capture what actually happens in art or literature.

This is not to deny that the author–text–reader relationship contains a vast number of extratextual elements that undergo processing, but these are only material components of what happens in the text and are not represented by it one to one. It therefore seems fair to say that representation in the sense in which we have come to understand it cannot embrace the performative operation of the text as a form of happening. Indeed, it is striking to note that there are hardly any clear-cut theories of representation that actually set out the workings necessary to bring about mimesis.

Among the rare exceptions is Gombrich's idea of representation: he broke up the received notion into clearly distinguishable phases of a process, starting out from the interaction between painter and inherited schemata, followed by the correction of the latter in the painting, and eventually by the deciphering activity of the beholder, whose reading of the corrected schemata brings the object of representation to fruition.[2]

The following essay is an attempt to raise play above representation as an umbrella concept to cover all of the ongoing operations of the textual process. It has two heuristic advantages: 1. Play does not have to concern itself with what it might stand for. 2. Play does not have to picture anything outside itself. It allows author–text–reader to be conceived as a dynamic interrelationship that moves toward a final result.

Authors play games with readers,[3] and the text is the playground. The text itself is the outcome of an intentional act whereby an author refers to and intervenes in an existing world, but though the act is intentional, it aims at something that is not yet accessible to consciousness. Thus the text is made up of a world that is yet to be identified and is adumbrated in such a way as to invite picturing and eventual interpretation by the reader. This double operation of imagining and interpreting engages the reader in the task of visualising the many possible shapes of the identifiable world, so that inevitably the world repeated in the text begins to undergo changes. For no matter which new shapes the reader brings to life, they are all certain to encroach on – and hence to change – the referential world contained in the text. Now, since the latter is fictional, it automatically invokes a convention-governed contract between author and reader indicating that the textual world is to be viewed, not as reality, but as if it were reality. And so whatever is repeated in the text is not meant to denote the world, but merely a world enacted. This may well repeat an identifiable reality, but it contains one all-important difference: what happens within it is relieved of the consequences inherent in the real world referred to. Hence, in disclosing itself fictionality signalises that everything is only to be taken as if it were what it seems to be, to be taken – in other words – as play.

The world repeated in the text is obviously different from the one it refers to, if only because, as a repetition, it must differ from its extratextual existence, and this holds equally true of all types of discourse, textual or otherwise, since no rendering can be that which it renders. There are therefore various levels of difference that occur simultaneously in the text:

1. Extratextually:
   a. Between the author and the world in which he or she intervenes.
   b. Between the text and an extratextual world as well as between the text and other texts.
2. Intratextually:
   a. Between the items selected from extratextual systems.
   b. Between semantic enclosures built up in the text.
3. Between text and reader:
   a. Between the reader's natural attitudes (now bracketed off) and those he or she is called upon to assume.
   b. Between what is denoted by the world repeated in the text, and what this denotation – now serving as a guiding analogue – is meant to adumbrate.

The levels of difference are quite distinct, but all of them constitute the basic blank of the text which sets the game in motion.

The movement is one of play in three different respects:

1. On each level distinguishable positions are confronted with one another.

2. The confrontation triggers a to-and-fro movement which is basic to play, and the ensuing difference has to be eradicated in order to achieve a result.

3. The continual movement between the positions reveals their many different aspects, and as one encroaches on the other, so the various positions themselves are eventually transformed. Every one of these differences opens up space for play, and hence for transformation, which even at this early stage of my argument would appear to discredit the traditional notion of representation.

Games head toward results, and when the differences are either bridged or even removed, play comes to an end. The result of the textual game, however, must be highly reductive, since the moves of the game split positions up into multifarious aspects. If we take the result of the textual game to be meaning, then this can only arise out of arresting the play movement which, more often than not, will entail decision making. But any decision will eclipse countless aspects brought to view by the constantly shifting, constantly interacting, and hence kaleidoscopically iterating positions of the game, so that the game itself runs counter to its being brought to an end.

Thus the duality of play comes to the fore. It is directed toward winning something, thereby ending itself at the same time as it removes difference. But it also refutes any such removal of difference, and outstrips its achievements in order to reestablish its own freedom as an ever-decentering movement. In short, it upholds the difference it seeks to eradicate.

These mutually exclusive features inscribe themselves into one another and so turn the meaning of the text into something of a 'supplement.' The multiplicity of differences that give rise to play and also result from it can never be totally removed but may in fact increase with attempts at eradication. Consequently, the 'supplement' arises not only out of the winning of the game (i.e. establishing meaning) but also, and at the same time, out of freeplay – not least because freeplay itself would remain ungraspable if it did not have some form of manifestation. If the 'supplement' is the product of these two countervailing features, we may draw two conclusions: 1. The 'supplement' as the meaning of the text is generated through play, and so there is no meaning prior to play. 2. The generation of the 'supplement' through play allows for different reenactments by different readers in the act of reception – even to the extent that it can be played either as achieving victory (establishing meaning) or as maintaining freeplay (keeping meaning open-ended).

This duality of play – removing and maintaining difference – defies further conceptualisation. It cannot be reduced phenomenologically by tracing it back to an underlying cause. Even such one-sided play theories as that of Huizinga assert that play precedes all of its possible explanations.[4] Therefore, the play of the text can only be assessed in terms of its possibilities, by way of the strategies of playing and the games actually played in the text.

As a playground between author and reader, the literary text can be described on three different levels: structural, functional, and interpretive. A structural description will aim to map out the playground, a functional one will try to explain the goal, and an interpretive one will ask why we play and why we need to play. An answer to this last question can only be interpretive, since play is apparently built into our anthropological makeup and may indeed help us to grasp what we are.

We must now look in more detail at the three different levels. First, that of structure. The focus here is on countermovement as the basic feature of play. The operational mode of the countermovement converts the text from a mimetic to a performative act. It manifests itself by creating what we might call the play spaces of the text which, it must be remembered, both repeats and encapsulates extratextual worlds whose return is indicative of a difference. In **Gregory Bateson**'s words, it is 'a difference which makes a difference'[5] – for a great many differences arise out of the initial one between the components of the text. The difference, as we have seen, triggers the to-and-fro movement, which opens up play spaces between the positions it separates.

The smallest play space is produced by the split signifier, which is stripped of its designating function so that it may be used figuratively, thanks to the text's fictional indication that what is said is only to be taken as *if* it meant what it said. The signifier therefore denotes something, but at the same time negates its denotative use without abandoning what it has designated in the first instance. If the signifier means something and simultaneously indicates that it does not mean that something, it functions as an analogue for figuring something else which it helps to adumbrate. If what is denoted is transformed into an analogue both triggering and shaping a picturing activity, then something absent is endowed with presence, though that which is absent cannot be identical to the analogue that facilitated its conceivability. Thus the split signifier – which is simultaneously denotative and figurative – invokes something that is not a pregiven for the text, but is generated by the text, which enables the reader to endow it with a tangible shape.

Thus the play movement turns the split signifier into a matrix for double meaning, which manifests itself in the analogue as the mutual interpenetration of the denotative and figurative functions. In terms of the text, the analogue is a 'supplement'; in terms of the recipient, it is the guideline enabling him to conceive what the text adumbrates. But the moment this becomes conceivable the recipient will try to ascribe significance to the 'supplement,' and whenever this happens, the text is translated into the dispositional terms of the individual reader, who ends the play of the split signifier by blocking it off with a meaning. If the meaning of a text, however, is not inherent but is ascribed and only achieved through play movement, then meaning is a metastatement about statements, or even a metacommunication about what is supposed to be communicated (i.e. experience by means of the text).

Another basic play space in the text is opened up by the schema. A schema, so **Piaget** maintains in his play theory, is the outcome of our constant endeavor to adapt to the world we are in.[6] In this respect it is not dissimilar to imitation, since it is motivated by the desire to overcome the difference that marks our relation to the world. First and foremost, it is perception that has to work out these schemata of adaptation.

Once these schemata have been formed, the first vital step is for them to be internalised, so that they may function subconsciously. This means that they tend to become ritualised in one way or another, and when this happens, they become separable from the very objects that initially gave rise to their formation. The conventions of art are nothing but sets of such schemata, which lend themselves very easily to new uses, especially when they have been separated from the world of objects.

Instead of facilitating adaptation to the physical world, the schemata may be used to pattern things that are otherwise ungraspable or that we want to bring within reach on our own conditions. Just as schemata enable us to adapt ourselves to objects, so too do they allow us to assimilate objects into our own disposition. When this reversal occurs, it opens up the play space. The schema is dissociated from its accommodating function and, in becoming subservient to the assimilative function, permits whatever is withheld from us to be staged as both present and manageable. This process is immediately evident in child's play. The play movement takes place when the schema ceases to function as a form of accommodation, and instead of taking its shape from the object to be imitated, now imposes a shape on that which is absent. In other words, the schema of accommodation copies the object, whereas the schema of assimilation shapes the object in accordance with the needs of the individual. Play therefore begins when assimilation displaces accommodation in the use of schemata, and when the schema is turned into a projection in order to incorporate the world in a book and to chart it according to human conditions.

A striking feature of the assimilative use of schemata is that they become subject to disfigurement. This highlights the switch in their function, and also the difference in their application. It is a duality inherent in all textual schemata, where the original function of the schema is backgrounded, though retaining its shape, and now instead of imitating something it serves to represent the unrepresentable.

In this respect, the inverted schema bears a close resemblance to the split signifier. Both form basic play spaces of the text, and set the game in motion. And in both cases, a basic function is transformed into a medium for something else: with the signifier the denotative function becomes the medium for figuration, and with the schema, the accommodating function becomes the medium for shaping the featureless. The original functions, however, are never totally suspended, and so there is a continual oscillation between denotation and figuration, and between accommodation and assimilation. This oscillation, or to-and-fro movement, is basic to play, and it permits the coexistence of the mutually exclusive. It also turns the text into a generative matrix for the production of something new. It forces the reader to play the games of the text, and to finish playing by coming up with what he or she considers to be its meaning. In the final analysis, oscillation is a patterning of freeplay – which may be a feature of nature or even of human nature, but is not one of the text. Oscillation, however, can also restrain freeplay. This is evident when we see how the strategies of the text restructure the manner in which the respective duality of the split signifier and the inverted schema is played out.

There are four main strategies, each of which allows for a different type of game. They are *agon, alea, mimicry*, and *ilinx*. The mixture of Greek and Latin terms may be jarring, but the expressions have become standard terms in game theory since Caillois,[7] although he himself did not relate them to texts as verbal structures.

Let me first explain the terms and the types of games they cover, in order to ascertain the patterns of gaming that they organise:

1. *Agon* is a fight or contest, and is a common pattern of play when the text centers on conflicting norms and values. The contest involves a decision to be made by the reader in relation to these opposing values, which are in collision with one another.

2. *Alea* is a pattern of play based on chance and the unforeseeable. Its basic thrust is defamiliarisation, which it achieves through storing and telescoping different texts, thus outstripping what their respective, identifiable segments were meant to mean. By overturning familiar semantics, it reaches out into the hitherto inconceivable and frustrates the reader's convention-governed expectations.

3. *Mimicry* is a play pattern designed to generate illusion. Whatever is denoted by the signifier or foreshadowed by the schemata should be taken as if it were what it says. There are two different reasons for this: a) the more perfect the illusion, the more real will seem the world it depicts; b) if the illusion, however, is punctured and so revealed as what it is, the world it depicts turns into a looking glass enabling the referential world outside the text to be observed.

4. *Ilinx* is a play pattern in which the various positions are subverted, undercut, canceled, or even carnivalised as they are played off against one another. It aims at bringing out the rear view of the positions yoked together in the game.

Although these play strategies allow for different games to be played, more often than not they link up as mixed modes. For instance, if *ilinx* plays against or is combined with *agon*, there may be two possible types of game: *ilinx* gains the upper hand, in which case the contest between norms and values becomes illusory, or *agon* dominates, and then the contest becomes more differentiated. These strategies can even be inverted, playing against their own underlying intentions. For example, *agon* appears to be directed toward winning the game, but in postmodern literature it is frequently used to play a losing game. This may entail all conflicts of norms and values being deliberately marked as things of the past, thus exposing the closed nature of the systems that gave them their function and validity. It may also show that all forms of meaning are nothing but defense mechanisms designed to achieve closure in a world where open-endedness reigns.

These four strategies of play can be combined in a vast number of ways, and whenever they are combined, each of them takes on a particular role. All roles – as we have to remind ourselves – are characterised by an intrinsic doubleness: they represent something they aim to project, and yet simultaneously they lack total control over the intended achievement, so that there is always an element in role playing that eludes the grasp of the player.[8] This applies equally to the play patterns outlined above when they become roles, and so the game to be played may either enhance or restrict the degree of uncontrollability.

Now, no matter what type of game ensues from indulging in the doubleness of role playing, it is always governed by one of two different sets of rules. In game theory these are called *conservative* and *dissipative* rules.[9] With regard to the text, they may be called *regulative* (which function according to stabilised conventions), and *aleatory* (which set free whatever has been restrained by the conventions). Aleatory rules apply to what cannot be controlled by the role in question, whereas regulatory rules organise what the role represents in terms of hierarchical, causal, subservient, or supportive relationships. Aleatory rules unleash what regulative rules have tied up, and thus they allow for freeplay within an otherwise restricted game.

Let me now summarise my structural description so far: the split signifier and the inverted schemata open up the play space of the text. The resultant to-and-fro movement is patterned by four basic strategies of play: *agon, alea, mimicry,* and *ilinx*. These in turn may undergo innumerable combinations, thereby turning into roles. Roles are double faced, with representation inevitably shading off into uncontrollable adumbrations. The games ensuing from roles may be acted out in accordance with regulative rules, which make the game basically conservative, or aleatory rules, which make it basically innovative.

All of these structural features provide a framework for the game. They mark off both the limits and the free areas of play, and so represent the preconditions for 'supplements' – in the form of meaning – as well as for the playful undoing of these 'supplements.' Thus there is a countervailing movement in which play strives for a result and freeplay breaks up any result achieved.

The structural features, however, assume significance only in relation to the function meant to be performed by the play of the text. Since play strives for something but also undoes what it achieves, it continually acts out difference. Difference, in turn, can be manifested only through play, because only play can make conceivable the absent otherness which lies on the reverse side of all positions. Thus the play of the text is neither winning nor losing, but is a process of transforming positions, thereby giving dynamic presence to the absence and otherness of difference. Consequently, what the text achieves is not something pregiven, but a transformation of the pregiven material that it encapsulates. If the text highlights transformation, it is bound to have a play structure, otherwise transformation would have to be subsumed under a cognitive framework, thus obliterating its very nature. Should the notion of representation be retained at all, one would have to say that the text 'represents' play, insofar as it spells out the individual process of transformation as it is happening in the text.

This process of transformation is common to the literary text, and it unfolds through all the various interconnected phases that we have outlined so far – from split signifier through inverted schemata, and strategic roles of *agon, alea, mimicry,* and *ilinx,* to the mutual interference of regulative and aleatory rules. Although I have separated these phases for analytical purposes, they in fact overlap and interlink, but through them we may observe transformation in slow motion, as it were, thereby rendering this otherwise intangible process perceivable.

Transformation, however, comes to full fruition through the recipient's imaginative participation in the games played, for it is only a means to an end, and not an end in itself. The more the reader is drawn into the proceedings by playing the games of the text, the more he or she is also played by the text. And so new features of play emerge – it assigns certain roles to the reader, and in order to do this, it must clearly have the potential presence of the recipient as one of its component parts. The play of the text is therefore a performance for an assumed audience, and as such it is not just a game as played in ordinary life, but it is actually a staged play enacted for the reader, who is given a role enabling him or her to act out the scenario presented.

The staged play of the text does not, then, unfold as a pageant which the reader merely watches, but *is* both an ongoing event and a happening for the reader, causing his or her direct involvement in the proceedings and indeed in the staging. For the play of the text can be acted out individually by each reader, who by playing it in his or her own way produces an individual 'supplement' considered to be the meaning of the text. The meaning is a 'supplement' because it arrests the ongoing process of transformation, and is additional to the text without ever being authenticated by it.

In this respect something important is to be revealed by the textual play. As a means of transformation, play does not only undercut the position presented in the text; it also undercuts the status of that which transformation has moved from absence into presence, i.e. the 'supplement' that the reader has added onto the text. But the undercutting, even if it may seem negative, in fact is highly productive, because it brings about transformation and generates 'supplements.' Hence this operation is driven by negativity, which is basically an enabling structure. Negativity is therefore far from negative in its effects, for it lures absence into presence, but by continually subverting that presence, turns it into a carrier for absence of which we would otherwise not know anything. Through these constant shifts, the play of the text uses negativity in a manner that epitomises the interrelation between absence and presence. And herein lies the uniqueness of play – it produces, and at the same time allows the process of production to be observed. The reader is therefore caught up in ineluctable doubleness: he or she is involved in an illusion, and is simultaneously aware that it is an illusion. It is through this incessant hovering between the closed and punctured illusion that the transformation effected by the play of the text makes itself felt to the reader.

Transformation, in turn, appears to head toward some aim that must be realised by the reader, and so the play of the text can be ended in various ways: one is in terms of semantics. In this case what is paramount is our need for understanding and our urge to appropriate the experiences given to us. This might even indicate a defense mechanism operating within ourselves, as the search for meaning may be our means of warding off the unfamiliar.

Another way in which we may play the text is by obtaining experience. Then we open ourselves up to the unfamiliar, and are prepared to let our own values be influenced or even changed by it.

A third mode of play is that of pleasure. We then give precedence to the enjoyment derived from an unusual exercise of our faculties which enables us to become present to ourselves. Each of these options represents a tendency according to which the play of the text can be acted out.

I now come to the final point: what is play, and why do we play? Any answer to this fundamental question can only be in the nature of tentative interpretation. In phylogenetic terms, play in the animal kingdom begins when the space of the habitat expands. Initially it appears to be an activity for its own sake, exploring the bounds of the possible, in view of the fact that everything is now possible. But we may also see it as a would-be action, or a trial run that trains the animal to cope with the unforeseeable that is to come. The more the animal's territory expands, the more important and sometimes the more elaborate play becomes as a means of preparing for survival.

In ontogenetic terms, there is a distinction to be observed in child's play between perception and meaning. When a child rides a hobbyhorse, i.e. a riding stick, he is engaged in a mental action that is quite distinct from what he actually perceives. He does not, of course, perceive a real horse, and so the play consists in splitting the object (horse) and the meaning of that object in the real world. Its play is therefore an action in which a defamiliarised meaning is acted out in a real situation.

What these two instances of playing have in common is a form of staging. But in neither case is the staging carried out for its own sake. In the animal kingdom, it serves to anticipate and prepare for future actions; in child's play, it permits real limitations to be overstepped. Staging, then, is basically a means of crossing boundaries, and this holds equally true for the play of the text, which stages transformation and at the same time reveals how the staging is done. This duality arises largely from the fact that transformation here has no pragmatic outcome: it does not change one thing into another. It is, rather, a purpose that can be properly fulfilled only if its own procedural workings are exhibited.

What is the nature of this purpose? Transformation is an access road to the inaccessible, but staged transformation does not only make available the unavailable. Its achievement is perhaps even more gratifying. It allows us to have things both ways, by making that which is inaccessible both present and absent. Presence comes about by means of the staged transformation, and absence by means of the fact that the staged transformation is only play. Hence every presented absence is qualified by the caveat that it is only staged in the form of make-believe, through which we can conceive what would otherwise elude our grasp. Herein lies the extraordinary achievement of play, for it appears to satisfy both epistemological and anthropological needs. Epistemologically speaking, it imbues presence with adumbrated absence by denying any authenticity to the possible results of play. Anthropologically speaking, it allows us to conceive that which is withheld from us. Interestingly enough, the epistemological and anthropoligical perspectives do not conflict, even though they may appear to run counter to each other. If there were a clash, it would undo the play, but as there is not, the cognitive irreconcilability in fact reveals something of our own human makeup. By allowing us to have absence as presence, play turns out to be a means whereby we may extend ourselves. This extension is a basic and ever-fascinating feature of literature, and the question inevitably arises as to why we need it. The answer to that question could be the starting point for a literary anthropology.

Notes

1. See MICHEL FOUCAULT, *The Order of Things: An Archaeology of the Human Sciences* (London: Tavistock, 1970), pp. 217–49, and JACQUES DERRIDA, *Writing and Difference*, trans Alan Bass (London: Routledge & Kegan Paul, 1978); especially the essay on 'Artaud'. For a detailed exploration of that issue see GABRIELE SCHWAB, *Samuel Becketts Endspiel mit der Subjektivität: Entwurf einer Psychoästhetik des modernen Theaters* (Stuttgart: J. B. Metzler, 1981), pp. 14–34.

2. E. H. GOMBRICH, *Art and Illusion: A Study in the Psychology of Pictorial Representation* (London: Phaidon Press, 1962), especially pp. 154–244.

3. PETER HUTCHINSON, *Games Authors Play* (London: Methuen, 1983), provides a catalogue of the various games played in literary texts.

4. JOHAN HUIZINGA, *Homo Ludens: Vom Ursprung der Kultur im Spiel* (Hamburg: Rowohlt, 1956), pp. 9–14.

5. GREGORY BATESON, *Steps to an Ecology of the Mind* (San Francisco: Chandler, 1972), p. 315.

6. JEAN PIAGET, *Nachahmung, Spiel und Traum (Gesammelte Werke 5)*, trans Leo Montada (Stuttgart: Ernst Klett, 1975), pp. 178–216.

7. ROGER CAILLOIS, *Man, Play, and Games*, trans Meyer Barash (New York: Free Press of Glencoe, 1961), p. viii.

8. IRVING GOFFMAN, *The Presentation of Self in Everyday Life* (Garden City, New York: Doubleday, 1959), pp. 8f, 141–66.

9. MANFRED EIGEN and RUTHHILD WINKLER, *Das Spiel: Naturgesetze steuern den Zufall* (Munich: R. Piper, 1985), pp. 87–121.

18   Kendall L. Walton on Pretending Belief[1]*

Human beings make up stories and tell them to each other. They also listen, entranced, to stories which they know are made up.

This is astonishing! Why should we be interested in the exploits of Superman, for example, if there is no Superman? How can we care what happens to Desdemona or to Willy Loman if we know – as we do – that since there are no such people *nothing* can happen to them?

Astonishing though it is, the telling and hearing of stories does not very often astonish us. This is partly because it is so common. Fiction is such a familiar feature of our lives that we almost don't even notice it, let alone wonder about it. And those of us who do notice it often deny what is most astonishing about it: that appreciators of fiction are interested in, fascinated by, people and events they *know* to be non-existent. We *suspend our disbelief*, it is said. Appreciating fiction is supposed to involve believing, at least temporarily, that Superman or Desdemona or Willy Loman really exists.

> [W]hile we read a novel, we are insane-bonkers. We believe in the existence of people who aren't there, we hear their voices, we watch the battle of Borodino with them. . . . Sanity returns (in most cases) when the book is closed.[2]

Sometimes sanity does not return. Some theorists think that appreciators' beliefs at least in the existence of Superman and Desdemona and Willy Loman are true; they continue to believe in such characters even when they are theorising rather than reading or listening to stories.[3] Of course theorists do not suppose that Superman and Desdemona are *actual* people like you and me: they are rather fictional characters. We might describe the difference by saying that Superman and Desdemona belong to 'fictional worlds' whereas you and I belong to the 'real world.' But it is

---

* Reprinted from 'Appreciating Fiction: Suspending Disbelief or Pretending Belief?' in *Dispositio* **5** (1983), pp. 1–18.

easy to think that *there are* fictional worlds and that the contents of
fictional worlds exist just as surely as do the contents of the real world. If
someone asks whether or not there is such a character as Desdemona,
the appropriate answer, it would seem, is that there is indeed such a
character.

I claim that appreciators of fiction do not believe in the existence of
fictional characters. Appreciation involves playing games of make-
believe, and as part of these games appreciators *pretend* to believe in
characters. These games are seductive, and theorists as well as
appreciators are easily lured into them. An enigmatic saying of R. D.
Laing nicely sums up the situation.

> They are playing a game. They are playing at not playing a game. If I
> show them I see they are, I shall break the rules and they will punish
> me. I must play their game, of not seeing I see the game.[4]

I too will play along with the game for awhile. But eventually we must
step outside it in order to see it more clearly. To play the game is to
pretend that it is not a game, and it is crucial to realise that it is one.
Doing so will force us to face squarely the astonishing fact of fiction. And
it will put us in a position to begin explaining what fiction is all about –
why it is important, why people take it seriously, why they do not
simply dismiss it as 'mere fiction.'

I

I will pretend for now that the universe contains fictional characters, and
that they live in 'fictional worlds.' Let us begin by asking what relations
can hold between the real world and fictional worlds. Can real people
interact with fictional characters?

We are likely to feel that fictional worlds are insulated or isolated, in
some peculiar way, from the real world, that there is a logical or
metaphysical barrier between them. That, indeed, is why we call them
different 'worlds.' From our position in the real world we cannot rescue
Robinson Crusoe from his island or send flowers to Tom Sawyer's
relatives grieving at his funeral. A Frankenstein monster may threaten
with destruction any character who has the misfortune of sharing its
world, but we in the real world are perfectly safe from it.

The barrier between worlds is not air tight. It does not prevent us from
knowing a great deal about what happens in fictional worlds. And we
respond to what we know about fictional worlds in many of the ways
that we respond to what we know about the real world – or at least it
seems that we do. When we learn that Tom Sawyer and Becky are lost in
a cave we worry about whether they will find their way out. We

sympathise with the plight of Willy Loman. We are terrified of the Frankenstein monster.

Nevertheless, interaction of a more physical sort between worlds seems out of the question. We cannot rescue Robinson Crusoe from his island no matter how deep our concern for him; indeed we cannot even try to. Our 'fear' of the Frankenstein monster is a peculiarly unfounded one, since we are certain to survive even if the monster ravishes the entire world!

But this needs a closer look. Is physical interaction across worlds really impossible? Consider the classic story of Henry, a backwoods villager watching a theatrical performance, who leaps to the stage to save the heroine from the clutches of the villain and a horrible death. Of course Henry is mistaken if he thinks he can save the *actress*; she is not in danger. But the character she portrays is in danger and does need saving. Can Henry help *her*, despite the fact that he does not live in her world?

Suppose that if the performance proceeded according to plan, the villain would tie the heroine to railroad tracks and a passing train would do her in. This is to be portrayed as follows: There are two parallel two-by-fours on the stage floor representing the railroad tracks. The actor playing the villain places the actress playing the heroine on the two-by-fours and passes a rope around her body. The curtains close, and the passing of a train is indicated by appropriate sound effects. Now, if Henry rushes to the stage and removes the actress from the two-by-fours before the stagehand responsible for sound effects brings the train through, hasn't he saved the heroine? He has prevented the performers from portraying the heroine's death. And since what happens in the fictional world is just what is portrayed as happening, it seems that Henry has prevented the heroine's death.

It is not necessary that Henry be naive about the play, that he think it is the real world actress who is in danger. Suppose he knows perfectly well that what he is watching is a play, and that only a fictional woman is in danger. But suppose he feels so strongly that such an innocent and beautiful damsel ought to be spared, even in fiction, that he intervenes in her behalf. He may simply pull the plug on the sound effects equipment, thereby diverting the train and saving the heroine.

The principle of this example can be generalized. What happens in the fictional world of a given work depends on the nature of the work. Tom Sawyer attends his own funeral because of the fact that certain combinations of words occur in the novel, *The Adventures of Tom Sawyer*. It is the arrangement of paint on canvas that determines what happens in the fictional world of a painting. This apparently opens the way for almost unlimited intervention in fictional worlds. Since real world novels, plays, paintings, and so forth are what determine what happens in fictional worlds, we can affect fictional worlds to whatever extent the nature of novels, plays, and paintings is within our power. We can destroy an evil picture-man, not with a dagger, perhaps, but with a paint brush – by painting a dagger through him and an expiring look on his face. Or we can bribe or bully the painter to do the picture-man in for us. Painters, authors, and other artists are veritable gods *vis-à-vis* fictional worlds. The isolation of fictional worlds from the real world seems to have vanished.

There is an air of trickery about all this. If it is so easy to save characters in distress, why don't we do so more often? One possible answer is that jumping on the stage or otherwise interfering with the performance is *inappropriate*, a violation of the conventions of the theater. But there are no conventions prohibiting authors, playwrights, and painters from sparing their characters. And anyway, would we let mere conventions deter us from saving a life?

Perhaps we feel that fictional lives do not matter in the way that real ones do. But it seems that we do, sometimes, care very much about fictional characters. We are distressed at the plight of Tom and Becky in the cave; we hope fervently that the hero will arrive in time to rescue the hapless heroine. And we may pass moral judgment on a character who is in a position to help but does not – even while we ourselves sit glued dumbly to our seats!

Is our concern for the heroine a sham? If we really do blame the villain for doing awful things to the heroine, shouldn't we blame even more the author who put him up to it? Why not get at the root cause of the evil? But we may have nothing but praise for the author, even when we purport to bemoan the calamities he allows to befall his characters. Moreover, it is not hard to find reasons for secretly wishing the heroine ill. Watching fictional suffering can be thrilling, instructive, cathartic. And we may think that if the heroine does not suffer the work will be insipid, a namby-pamby, everyone-lives-happily-ever-after affair.[5] We appreciate and admire tragedies, and we hope that the work turns out to be a tragedy, despite the fact that this means disaster for the heroine. We are willing to sacrifice her for the sake of our aesthetic experience. (Compare a person watching a bullfight whose selfish desire to be entertained overcomes his natural compassion for the bull.)

But do we ever suffer even the slightest pangs of conscience for allowing our desire for a valuable aesthetic experience to interfere with our concern for a character in distress? It hardly seems that we *consider* intervening in behalf of the heroine but fail to act when our selfish urges get the best of us; we do not think of intervention as a live alternative. This is no ordinary instance of mixed motives, of conflicting desires or interests.

Perhaps our motives are not mixed. Perhaps we have no concern whatever for heroines in distress, and this is why we rarely try to rescue them. But then what are we to make of the feelings which unquestionably we often do have when we experience tragic works, and which we readily describe as feelings of concern or pity for characters, or worry about what might happen to them?

II

Much of the trouble stems from confusion about the nature of fiction. How are we to construe fictional statements such as:

> An innocent damsel fell into the clutches of a wicked villain [said with reference to the theatrical event].
> Robinson Crusoe survived a shipwreck.

A ready suggestion is that they are elliptical for:

> In the play, an innocent damsel fell into the clutches of a wicked villain.
> In the novel, Robinson Crusoe survived a shipwreck.

'In the novel' must not be construed as indicating in what manner, or 'where,' it is true that Crusoe survived. 'In the novel Crusoe survived,' properly construed, does not imply that it is true in any manner at all that Crusoe survived. My view is that this statement characterizes the proposition that Crusoe survived, not as being true, but as having a different attribute, that of being 'fictional.' To make this clear I will substitute 'It is fictional that Crusoe survived' for 'In the novel Crusoe survived.' Similarly, I will say that it is fictional that an innocent damsel fell into the clutches of an evil villain.

Which propositions are fictional depends on the nature of novels, pictures, films, and theatrical events. The words which occur in *Robinson Crusoe* are what make it fictional that Crusoe survived a shipwreck. It is fictional that an innocent damsel fell into the clutches of an evil villain because of what happens on stage during the performance of the play.

Does Henry save the heroine when he leaps to the stage upsetting the performance just before her fate is sealed? There are two separate questions here: Is it *true* that Henry saves the heroine? and, Is it *fictional* that he saves her?

It is not true, for the heroine does not exist, and non-existent people cannot be saved. Nor is it fictional that Henry saves the heroine. When he pulls the plug on the sound effects, for example, it is not fictional that he exists, and it cannot be fictional that one does any saving unless it is fictional that one exists. There is no understanding (in traditional theater) whereby Henry's action counts as his fictionally saving the heroine. His behavior is understood not as part of the theatrical event, but as an intrusion on it.

What *is* true is that Henry makes it fictional that the heroine survives. He arranges things in such a way that this fictional truth is generated. Doing this is not *saving* the heroine, neither really nor fictionally. Henry brings it about that fictionally the heroine survives, but he does not save her, nor is it fictional that he saves her.

This bears out our original feeling that fictional worlds are somehow insulated from the real world. What happens in fictional worlds, what fictionally is the case, can indeed be affected by what happens in the real world. But one person can *save* another only if they 'live in the same world.' *Cross-world* saving is ruled out, and for similar reasons so is cross-world killing, congratulating, handshaking, and so forth.

But we must be careful how this isolation is described. It *can* be fictional that a real person such as Henry saves a heroine, or destroys a villain, or congratulates a hero. For real people can 'exist in fictional worlds'; it can be true of Henry, or of any actual person, that fictionally he exists. Julius Caesar belongs to the fictional world of Shakespeare's play, as well as to the real world. Suppose that Henry is not just a spectator of the play but also a character in it; suppose that one of the actors portrays him. Obviously, then, it might be fictional that Henry saves the heroine – depending, of course, on what the actor portraying him does on the stage. It might be fictional that Henry rides heroically to the rescue just in the nick of time. It is also possible that Henry should do the acting himself, that he should play himself. In that case whether it is fictional that Henry saves the heroine will depend on what Henry in his role as an actor does.

This might appear to constitute a major breach in the barrier between worlds. But the appearance is deceiving. When it is fictional that Henry saves the heroine the interaction between him and the heroine occurs entirely 'within the fictional world.' This is not a case of interaction *between* worlds. It happens that Henry, besides existing in the fictional world and in that world saving the heroine, exists also in the real world. But he does not reach over *from* the real world to the fictional one to save the heroine; he does not need to since he belongs to the fictional world too. Saving can take place only within a single world. Cross-world saving, properly so-called, remains excluded.

III

The notion of an unbridgeable gulf separating fictional worlds from the real world is thus neatly vindicated. But this vindication may seem too neat, too easy. For if the gulf is as unbridgeable as I have made out it may be hard to explain the apparent fact that *psychological* interaction between worlds is possible, and indeed common, the apparent fact that real people fear Frankenstein monsters, pity Willy Loman, admire

Superman, and so on. We feel a psychological bond to fictions, an intimacy with them, of a kind which normally we feel only toward things we take to be actual.

But is it really true that we have psychological attitudes toward fictions? Some of the most plausible examples of this are cases in which spectators of horror movies are said to be afraid of fictional horrors. Let us consider in some detail a case of this kind.

Charles is watching a horror movie about a terrible green slime. He cringes in his seat as the slime oozes slowly but relentlessly over the earth obliterating everything in its path. Soon a greasy head emerges from the undulating mass, two beady eyes roll around, and fix on the camera. The slime, picking up speed, oozes on a new course toward the viewers. Charles emits a shriek and clutches desperately at his chair.

Afterwards, still shaken, Charles confesses that he was 'terrified' of the slime. *Was* he terrified of it?

The non-existence of the slime does not prevent Charles from fearing it. One may fear a ghost or a burglar even if there is none. But a person who fears a non-existent burglar believes that there is one, or at least that there might be one. He believes that he is in danger, that there is a possibility of his being harmed by a burglar. It is conceivable, of course, that Charles should believe himself to be endangered by the slime. He might take the film to be a live documentary, a news flash. If he does, naturally he is afraid. And the object of his fear is, in fact, merely fictional. But the situation I have in mind is one in which Charles is an ordinary sophisticated movie-goer who is not deceived in this straightforward way. Charles knows perfectly well that the slime is not real and that he is in no danger.

Is he afraid even so? He says that he is. And he is in a state which is undeniably similar in important respects to that of a person who is frightened of a pending real world disaster. His muscles are tensed, he clutches his chair, his pulse quickens, his adrenalin flows. Let us call this physiological/psychological state 'quasi-fear.' Our question is whether this state qualifies as one of *actual* fear.

Charles' state is crucially different from that of a person with ordinary fear. The fact that Charles is fully aware that the slime is fictional is, I believe, good reason to deny that what he feels is fear. It seems a principle of common sense, one which ought not to be abandoned if there is any reasonable alternative, that fear[6] must involve a belief that one is in danger. Charles does not believe that he is in danger, so he is not afraid.

Charles might try to convince us that he was afraid by shuddering and declaring dramatically that he was *'really terrified.'* This emphasises the intensity of his experience. But the issue is not whether he had an intense experience. Rather it is whether his experience, however intense, was one of fear of the slime.

Some defenders of the claim that Charles is afraid of the slime might argue that he *does* believe that the slime is real and is a real threat to him. There are, to be sure, strong reasons for allowing that Charles realizes that the slime is only fictional and poses no danger. If he didn't we should expect him to flee the theater, call the police, warn his family. But perhaps it is *also* true that Charles believes, in some way or 'on some level,' that the slime is real and really threatens him. It has been said that in cases like this one 'suspends one's disbelief,' or that 'part' of a person believes something which another part of him disbelieves, or that one finds oneself (almost?) believing something which he nevertheless knows to be false.

One possibility is that Charles *half* believes that there is a real danger, and that he is, literally, at least half afraid.[7] To half believe something is to be not quite sure that it is true, but also not sure that it is not true. If a child is told that his house is haunted, but is uncertain whether the remark is meant seriously or in jest, he may half believe that it is haunted. If he does he will be half afraid of the ghosts which may or may not inhabit it.

But Charles has *no* doubts about whether he is in the presence of an actual slime. If he half believed, and were half afraid, we would expect him to have *some* inclination to act on his fear in the normal ways. Even a hesitant belief, a mere suspicion, that the slime is real would induce any normal person seriously to consider calling the police and warning his family. Charles gives no thought whatever to such courses of action. He is not *uncertain* whether the slime is real; he is perfectly sure that it is not.

Moreover, the fear symptoms which Charles does exhibit are not symptoms of a mere suspicion that the slime is real and a queasy feeling of half fear. His heart pounds violently, he gasps for breath, he grasps the chair until his knuckles are white. This is not the behavior of a man who realizes basically that he is safe but suffers flickers of doubt. If it indicates fear at all, it indicates acute and overwhelming terror.

To compromise on this issue, to say that Charles half believes he is in danger and is half afraid, is not a reasonable alternative.

One who claims that Charles believes he is in danger might argue, not that this is a hesitant or weak or half belief, but rather that it is a belief of a special kind – a 'gut' feeling, as opposed to an 'intellectual' one. Compare a person who hates flying. In one sense he realizes that airplanes are (relatively) safe. He says that they are, and can quote statistics to prove it. Nevertheless, he avoids traveling by air as much as possible. He is brilliant at devising excuses. And if he must board a plane he becomes nervous and upset. I grant that this person believes, at a 'gut' level, that flying is dangerous, despite his 'intellectual' belief to the contrary. I grant also that he is really afraid of flying.

But Charles is different. The air traveler performs *deliberate* actions which one would expect of someone who thinks flying is dangerous, or at least he is strongly inclined to perform such actions. If he does not actually decide against traveling by air he has a strong inclination to do so. And once aboard the airplane he must fight a temptation to get off. But Charles does not have even an inclination to leave the theater or call the police. The only signs that he might really believe he is endangered are his more or less automatic, non-deliberate, reactions: his pulse rate, his sweaty palms, his knotted stomach.

Deliberate actions are done for reasons; they are done because of what the agent wants and what he thinks will bring about what he wants. There is a presumption that such actions are reasonable in light of the agent's beliefs and desires (however unreasonable the beliefs and desires may be). So we postulate beliefs and/or desires which will make sense of them. People also have reasons for doing things which they are inclined to do but which, for other reasons, they refrain from doing. If the air traveler thinks that flying is dangerous, then, assuming that he wants to live, his actions or tendencies thereto are reasonable. Otherwise, they probably are not. So we legitimately infer that, at least on a 'gut' level, he does believe that flying is dangerous.

But we don't have to make the same kind of sense of Charles' automatic responses. One doesn't have reasons for things one doesn't *do*, like sweating, increasing one's pulse rate, knotting one's stomach (involuntarily), etc. So there is no need to attribute beliefs to Charles which will render these responses reasonable.

Thus, we can justifiably infer the air passenger's ('gut') belief in the danger of flying from his deliberate behavior and/or inclinations, and yet refuse to infer that Charles thinks he is in danger from his automatic responses.

Someone might reply to this argument that at moments of special crisis during the movie, when the slime first spots Charles, for example, Charles 'loses hold of reality' and, momentarily, takes the slime to be real and really fears it. These moments are too short for Charles to think about doing anything; hence (one might claim) we should not be surprised that his belief and fear are not accompanied by the normal inclinations to act.

I find this move unconvincing. In the first place, Charles' quasi-fear responses are not merely momentary; he may have his heart in his throat throughout most of the movie, yet without experiencing the slightest inclination to flee or call the police. These long term responses, and Charles' propensity to describe them afterwards in terms of 'fear,' need to be understood even if it is allowed that there are moments of real fear interspersed among them. Moreover, however tempting the momentary-fear idea might be, comparable views of other psychological states are much less appealing. When we say that someone 'pitied' Willy Loman or 'admired' Superman, it is unlikely that we have in mind special moments during his experience of the work at which he forgot, momentarily, that he was dealing with fiction, and felt momentary flashes of actual pity or admiration. The person's 'sense of reality' may well have been robust and healthy throughout his experience of the work, uninterrupted by anything like the special moments of crisis Charles experiences during the horror movie. Furthermore, it may be appropriate to say that a person 'pities' Willy or 'admires' Superman even when he is not watching the play or reading the cartoon. So the momentary-*fear* theory, even if it were plausible, would not be much help in illuminating cases in which we apparently have other psychological attitudes toward fictions.

Although Charles is not really afraid of the fictional slime depicted in the movie, the movie might nevertheless produce real fear in him. It might cause him to be afraid of something else. If Charles is a child, the movie may make him wonder whether there might not be real slimes or other exotic horrors *like* the one depicted in the movie, even if he fully realizes that the movie-slime itself is not real. Charles may well fear these suspected actual dangers; he might have nightmares about them for days afterwards. *Jaws* caused a lot of people to fear sharks which they thought might really exist. But whether they were afraid of the fictional sharks in the movie is another question.

If Charles is an older movie-goer with a heart condition, he may be afraid of the movie itself. Perhaps he knows that any excitement could trigger a heart attack, and fears that the movie will cause excitement, e.g., by depicting the slime as being especially aggressive or threatening. This is real fear. But it is fear of the depiction of the slime, not fear of the slime which is depicted.

IV

Compare Charles and a child playing an ordinary game of make-believe with his father. The father, pretending to be a ferocious monster, cunningly stalks the child and, at a crucial moment, lunges viciously at him. The child flees, screaming. The scream is more or less involuntary, and so is the flight. But the child giggles and unhesitatingly comes back for more. He is perfectly aware that his father is only 'playing,' that the whole thing is 'just a game,' and that only fictionally is there a vicious monster after him. He is not really afraid.

The child obviously belongs to the fictional world of the game of make-believe. It is fictional that the monster lunges, not into thin air, but at the child. Fictionally the child is in grave and mortal danger. And when the child screams and runs, fictionally he knows he is in danger and is afraid. The game is a sort of theatrical event in which the father is an actor portraying a monster and the child is an actor playing himself.

I propose to regard Charles similarly. When the slime raises its head, spies the camera and oozes toward it, it is fictional that Charles is threatened. And when as a result Charles gasps and grips his chair, fictionally he is afraid. Charles is playing a game of make-believe in which he uses the images on the screen as props. He too is an actor impersonating himself.

Charles differs in certain important respects from an ordinary on-stage, self-portraying actor. One difference has to do with what makes it fictional that Charles is afraid. Fictional truths about Charles are generated at least partly by what he thinks and feels, not just how he acts. It is partly the fact that Charles is in a state of quasi-fear, the fact that he feels his heart pounding, his muscles tensed, etc., which makes it fictional that he is afraid. It would be inappropriate to describe him as 'afraid' if he were not in some such state.

Charles' quasi-fear is not responsible, by itself, for the fact that fictionally it is the *slime* which he fears, nor even, I think, for the fact that fictionally he is afraid rather than angry or excited or merely upset. Here Charles' (actual) beliefs come into play. Charles believes, in fact he knows, that fictionally the green slime is bearing down on him and he is in danger of being destroyed by it. His quasi-fear results from this belief. What makes it fictional that Charles is afraid rather than angry or excited or upset is the fact that his quasi-fear is caused by the belief that fictionally he is in danger. And his belief that fictionally it is the slime which endangers him is what makes it fictional that the slime is the object of his fear. In short, my suggestion is this: the fact that Charles is quasi-afraid as a result of realizing that fictionally the slime threatens him makes it fictional that he is afraid of the slime.

An on-stage actor, by contrast, generates fictional truths solely by his acting, by his behavior. Whether it is fictional that the character portrayed is afraid or not depends just on what the actor says and does and how he contorts his face, regardless of what he actually thinks or feels. It makes no difference whether his actual emotional state is anything like one of fear. This is just as true when the actor is playing himself as it is when he is portraying some other character. Of course, the actor may find that putting himself into a certain frame of mind makes it easier to act in the appropriate ways. But still, it is how he acts, not his state of mind, that determines whether fictionally he is afraid.

It is entirely reasonable that our conventions for theater should work this way. Audiences cannot be expected to have a clear idea of an actor's personal thoughts and feelings while he is performing. If fictional truths depended on actors' private thoughts and feelings, it would be unreasonably difficult for spectators to ascertain what is going on in the fictional world. It is not surprising that the fictional truths for which actors on stage are responsible are understood to be generated by just what is visible from the galleries.

But Charles is not performing for an audience. It is not his job to get across to anyone else what fictionally is true of himself. So there is no reason why his actual state of mind should not have a role in generating fictional truths about himself.

It is not clear in the monster game what makes it fictional that the child is afraid of a monster. The child *might* be performing for the benefit of an audience; he might be *showing* someone (an onlooker, or just his father) that fictionally he is afraid. If so, perhaps we should regard his observable behavior as responsible for the fact that fictionally he is afraid.

But let us suppose that the child is participating in the game solely for his own amusement, with no thought of an audience. In this case the child himself, at least, almost certainly understands his fictional fear to depend on his mental state rather than (just) his behavior. In fact, let us suppose that the child is an undemonstrative sort who does not scream or run or betray his 'fear' in any other especially overt way. His participation in the game is purely passive. Nevertheless the child does experience quasi-fear when fictionally the monster attacks him, and he still would describe himself as being 'afraid.' Certainly it is (partly) his quasi-fear which generates the fictional truth he expresses when he says that he is 'afraid.'

My proposal is to construe Charles on the model of this undemonstrative child. Charles may, of course, exhibit his 'fear' in certain observable ways. But his observable behavior is not meant to show anyone else that fictionally he is afraid. It is likely to go unnoticed by others, and even Charles himself may be unaware of it. No one, least of all Charles, regards his observable behavior as generating the truth that fictionally he is afraid.

V

I have argued that Charles belongs to a fictional world, that it is fictional that the slime threatens him and that he is afraid of it. But Charles is not a character in the movie, as the slime is; it is not the fictional world of the movie that he belongs to. Charles plays a game of make-believe with the images on the screen. And the world of his game needs to be distinguished from the world of the movie itself. The world of the game includes fictional truths generated by the screen images, but it includes also fictional truths generated by Charles and his relation to the images, among them fictional truths about Charles himself.

Fictional truths generated by the movie alone are publicly recognized.

But probably only Charles is much interested in those generated by his interactions with the movie. His game of make-believe is a more or less personal one.

Dolls provide a good analogy here. Anyone who sees a doll of a certain sort will recognize that it generates the truth that fictionally there is a blonde baby girl. The doll, regarded simply as a sculpture to be observed from a distance, generates fictional truths such as this. But a child playing with the doll is playing a more personal game of make-believe, one in which she herself is a self-portraying actor and the doll serves as a prop. What she does with the doll generates fictional truths, e.g. the truth that fictionally she is dressing the baby for a trip to town. Similarly, Charles uses the screen images as props in a personal game of make-believe in which he himself is a character. He plays his own game with the images. The screen images, of course, do not lend themselves to being 'dressed' or manipulated in all of the ways that dolls do, and this limits the extent of Charles' participation in the game. But the relations and interactions between Charles and the images do generate a number of important fictional truths: that fictionally Charles notices the slime and stares apprehensively at it, that fictionally it turns toward him and attacks, and that fictionally he is scared out of his wits.

I have portrayed Charles so far as participating rather automatically in his game of make-believe. But he might easily slip into participating deliberately.[8] The naturalness of his doing so gives added support to my claim that Charles does recognize a fictional world which he and the slime share, even when his participation is not deliberate.

Suppose that during the movie Charles exclaims, deliberately, to a companion or to himself, 'Yikes, here it comes! Watch out!' How are we to understand this verbal action? Certainly Charles is not seriously asserting that a slime is coming and warning himself or his companion of it. Presumably he is asserting that it is fictional that a slime is coming. But the indexical, 'here,' carries an implicit reference to the speaker. So Charles' exclamation shows that he takes it to be fictional that the slime is headed toward him; it shows that he regards himself as coexisting with the slime in a fictional world.

But this does not take us to the bottom of the matter. 'Yikes!' and 'Watch out!' are not assertions, and so not assertions of what fictionally is the case. Moreover, if in saying, 'Here it comes,' Charles were merely making an assertion about what fictionally is the case, he could well have made this explicit and exclaimed instead, 'Fictionally the slime is coming!' Or 'The slime is coming, in the fictional world!' But these variants lack the flavor of the original. Charles' exclamatory tone is absurdly out of place when the fictional status of the danger is made explicit. Compare how ridiculous it would be for an actor playing Horatio in a performance of *Hamlet* to exclaim, when the ghost appears, 'Look my lord, it comes, in the world of play!'

The comparison is apt. For Charles is doing just what actors do, *pretending* to make an assertion. He is pretending to assert (seriously) that the slime is headed his way. In my terms, Charles understands his utterance of 'Here it comes!' to generate the truth that fictionally he asserts that the slime is coming. He is playing along with the fiction of the movie, incorporating it into a game of make-believe of his own. This explains what is wrong with 'Here it comes, in the fictional world!' Saying *that* is simply not (normally) how one would pretend to assert that a slime is (really) coming. The rest of Charles' verbal behavior is now easily understandable as well. In saying 'Yikes!' and 'Watch out!' he is pretending to express amazement or terror and pretending to issue a warning; fictionally he is doing these things.[9]

We have now arrived at the solution to a pair of puzzles.

Why is it that in everyday conversation we regularly omit phrases like, 'In the fictional world,' and 'In the novel,' whereas we rarely omit other intentional operators such as 'It is believed that,' 'Jones wishes that,' 'Jones denies that'? Why do we so naturally say just 'Tom and Becky were lost in a cave' rather than 'In the novel Tom and Becky were lost in cave,' whereas it would be almost unheard of to shorten 'Jones wishes that a golden mountain would appear on the horizon' to simply 'A golden mountain will appear on the horizon'?

The explanation lies in our habit of playing along with fictions, of fictionally asserting, pretending to assert, what we know to be only fictionally the case. We must not be too quick to assume that an utterance of a sentence, *p*, is merely an ellipsis for, fictionally *p* (or for, In the novel *p*). This assumption is wrong if the speaker fictionally is asserting that *p*, rather than asserting that fictionally *p*. Charles' frantic, 'Yikes, here it comes!' is an obvious case in point. A case which is only slightly less obvious is that of a person reading *Tom Sawyer* who remarks, gravely and with an expression of deep concern, that Tom and Becky are lost in a cave.

I do not suggest that the omission of 'In the novel' is *never* a mere ellipsis. 'Tom and Becky were lost in a cave' uttered by a critic analyzing the novel could easily have been expanded to 'In the novel Tom and Becky were lost in a cave' without altering the character of the remark. The critic probably is not pretending to assert that Tom and Becky were (actually) lost in a cave. But our habit of dropping fictional operators persists even in sober criticism, and it testifies to the ease with which we can be induced to play along, deliberately, with a work of fiction.

In German the indicative mood is used ordinarily only when the speaker is committed to the truth of the sentence or clause in question. But fictional statements constitute a striking exception to this generalization; the indicative is used in fictional statements even though the speaker is *not* committed to the truth of the sentence or clause. (One says, for example, '*Robinson Crusoe hat einen Schiffbruch überlebt,*' which is indicative, even though one is not claiming that there actually was a Robinson Crusoe who survived a shipwreck.) The speaker is pretending to express his commitment to the truth of the relevant sentence or clause. So naturally he uses the mood of assertion; he speaks as though he is not pretending.

The treatment of Charles' 'fear of the slime' I have just outlined can serve as a model for understanding other psychological attitudes ostensibly directed toward fictional things. When it is said that a reader or spectator pities Willy Loman, or worries about Tom and Becky, or detests Iago, or envies Superman, what is said is probably not literally true (assuming that the person realizes that he is dealing with a work of fiction). It is plausible that psychological attitudes such as pity, worry about, hate, and envy, are such that one cannot have them without believing that the object of the attitude exists, just as one cannot fear something without believing that it threatens him. But the reader or spectator is actually in a distinctive psychological (emotional?) state, even if it is not one of pity or worry or hate or envy. And his being in that state is a result of his awareness of certain fictional truths: that fictionally Willy is an innocent victim of cruel circumstances, that fictionally Iago deceived Othello about Desdemona, that fictionally Superman can do almost anything. The fact that the person's psychological state is as it is and is caused by such beliefs makes it fictional that he pities Willy, worries about Tom and Becky, hates Iago, or envies Superman.

VI

We have here a particularly intimate relation between the real world and fictional ones. Insofar as fictional truths are generated by a spectator's or reader's state of mind he is no mere 'external observer' of the fictional world. Ascertaining what fictionally is true of himself is to a large extent a matter of introspection (or of whatever sort of 'privileged access' one has to his own beliefs and sensations). In fact, when Charles watches the horror movie introspection is involved in ascertaining not merely that fictionally he is afraid of the slime, but also fictional truths about the nature and progress of his fear. If it is fictional that his fear is overwhelming, or that it is only momentary, this is so because his quasi-fear sensations are overwhelming, or are only momentary. Fictionally his fear grows more or less intense, or becomes almost unbearable, or finally subsides, etc., as his quasi-fear feelings change in these ways. So it is by attention to the nature of his own actual experience that Charles is aware of fictional truths about the nature of his fear. He follows the progress of his fictional fear by introspection, much as who is literally afraid follows the progress of his actual fear.

Charles' case contrasts strikingly with others in which an actual person belongs to a fictional world. Consider a performance of William Luce's play about Emily Dickenson, *The Belle of Amherst*, in which Julie Harris plays Emily Dickenson. Suppose that Emily Dickenson herself, with the help of a time machine or a fortuitous reincarnation, is in the audience. In order to discover fictional truths about herself, including what fictionally she thinks and feels, Dickenson must observe Julie Harris' actions, much as any spectator must. It is as though she is watching another person, despite the fact that that 'person,' the character, is herself. Dickenson has no special intimacy with fictional truths about her own mental state. The situation is basically the same if Dickenson should replace Julie Harris and act the part herself. She still must judge from her external behavior, from what spectators could observe, whether or not it is fictional that she is afraid or worried or whatever – and she might easily be mistaken about how she looks to spectators. It is still as though she considers herself 'from the outside,' from the perspective of another person.

This is not true of Charles. It is not as though Charles is confronting another person, a fictional version of himself, but rather as though he himself (actually) fears the slime. Fictional facts about his fear, especially the fact that fictionally it is *his*, are portrayed to Charles in an extraordinarily realistic manner. He feels himself to be part of the fictional world, to be intimately involved with the slime – and with whatever other constituents of the fictional world are, fictionally, objects of his feelings or attitudes.

We see, now, how fictional worlds can seem to us to be almost as 'real' as the real one is, even though we know perfectly well that they are not. We have begun to understand what happens when we get emotionally 'involved' in a novel or play or film, when we are 'caught up in the story.'

The theory I have presented is designed to capture intuitions lying behind the traditional ideas that the normal or desired attitude toward fiction involves a *'suspension of disbelief,'* or a *'decrease of distance.'* These phrases are unfortunate. They suggest that people do not (completely) disbelieve what they read in novels and see on the stage or screen, that, for example, we somehow accept it as fact that a boy named 'Huckleberry Finn' floated down the Mississippi River, at least while we are engrossed in the novel. The normal reader does not accept this as fact, nor should he.

On my theory we accomplish the 'decrease of distance' not by promoting fictions to our level but by descending to theirs. (More accurately, we *extend* ourselves to their level, since we do not stop actually existing when it becomes fictional that we exist.) Fictionally we do believe that Huck Finn floated down the Mississippi; we know that he did. And fictionally we have various feelings or attitudes about him and his adventures. Rather than somehow fooling ourselves into thinking fictions are real, we become fictional. So we end up 'on the same level' with fictions. And our presence there is accomplished in the extraordinarily realistic manner that I described. This enables us to comprehend our sense of closeness to fictions, without attributing to ourselves patently false beliefs.

We are now in a position to expect progress on the fundamental question of why and how fiction is important. Why don't we dismiss novels, plays, films, and the like as 'mere fiction' and hence unworthy of serious attention?

Much has been said about the value and importance of dreams, fantasy, and children's games of make-believe.[10] It has been suggested, variously, that such activities serve to clarify one's feelings, help one to work out conflicts, provide an outlet for the expression of repressed or socially unacceptable feelings, prepare one emotionally for possible future crises by providing 'practice' in facing imaginary ones. It is natural to presume that our experience of representational works of art is valuable for similar reasons. But this presumption is plausible only if something like the theory I have presented is correct.

It is my impression that people are usually, perhaps always, characters in their own dreams and daydreams. We dream and fantasize about ourselves. Sometimes one's role in his dream world or fantasy world is limited to that of observing other goings-on. But to have even this role *is* to belong to the fictional world. (We must distinguish between being, in one's dream, an observer of certain events, and merely 'observing,' having, a dream about those events.) Children are nearly always characters in their games of make-believe. To play dolls or school, hobby horses or mud pies, is to be an actor portraying oneself.

I suggest that much of the value of dreaming, fantasizing, and making-believe depends crucially on one's thinking of oneself as belonging to a fictional world. It is chiefly by fictionally facing certain situations, by fictionally engaging in certain activities and having or expressing certain feelings, that a dreamer, fantasizer, or game player comes to terms with his actual feelings – that he discovers them, learns to accept them, purges himself of them, or whatever exactly it is that he does.

If so, people can be expected to derive similar benefits from novels, plays, and films only if it is fictional that they themselves exist and participate (at least as observers) in the events portrayed in the works.

I find encouragement for these speculations in the deliberate use of role-playing in educational simulation games, and as a therapeutic technique in certain kinds of psychotherapy (e.g., Gestalt therapy). A therapist may ask his patient to pretend that his mother is present, or that some inanimate object is his mother, and to 'talk to her.' He may then be asked to 'be' the mother, and to say how he feels (when he 'is' the mother), how he acts, what he looks like, etc. I will not venture an explanation of how such therapeutic techniques are effective, nor of why simulation games work. But whatever the explanation is, it will, I suspect, go a long way toward explaining why we are as interested in works of fiction as we are. The important place that novels, plays, and films have in our lives appears mysterious only on the supposition that we merely stand outside fictional worlds and look in, pressing our noses against an inviolable barrier. Once our presence within fictional worlds is recognized, suitable explanations seem within reach.

VII

A more immediate benefit of my theory is its capacity to handle puzzles. I conclude with the resolution of two more.

Consider a playgoer who finds happy endings assinine or dull, and hopes that the play he is watching will end tragically. He 'wants the heroine to suffer a cruel fate,' for only if she does, he thinks, will the play be worth watching. But at the same time, he is caught up in the story and 'pities, sympathizes with the heroine'; he 'wants her to escape.' It is obvious that these two apparent desires may perfectly well coexist. Are we to say that the spectator is *torn* between opposite interests, that he wants the heroine to survive and also wants her not to? This does not ring true. Both of the playgoer's 'conflicting desires' may be wholehearted. He may hope unreservedly that the work will end with disaster for the heroine, and he may, with equal singlemindedness, 'want her to escape such an undeserved fate.' Moreover, he may be entirely aware of both 'desires,' and yet feel no particular conflict between them.

My theory provides a neat explanation. It is merely fictional that the spectator sympathizes with the heroine and wants her to escape. And he really wants it to be fictional that she suffers a cruel end. He does not have conflicting desires. Nor, for that matter, is it fictional that he does.

The second puzzle concerns why it is that works last as well as they do, how they can survive multiple readings or viewings without losing their effectiveness.[11]

Suspense of one kind or another is an important ingredient in our experience of most works: Will Jack, of *Jack and the Beanstalk*, succeed in ripping off the giant without being caught? Will Tom and Becky find their way out of the cave? Will Hamlet ever get around to avenging the murder of his father? What is in store for Julius Caesar on the Ides of March? Will Godot come?

But how can there be suspense if we already know how things will turn out? Why, for example, should Tom and Becky's plight concern or even interest a reader who knows already, from reading the novel previously, that eventually they will escape from the cave? One might have supposed that once we have experienced a work often enough to learn thoroughly the relevant features of the plot it would lose its capacity to create suspense, and that future readings or viewings would lack the excitement of the first one. But this frequently is not what happens. *Some* works, to be sure, fade quickly from exposure, and familiarity does alter our experience in certain ways. But the power of many works is remarkably permanent, and the nature of their effectiveness remarkably consistent.[12] In particular, suspense may remain a crucial element in our response to a work almost no matter how familiar we are with it. One may 'worry' just as intensely about Tom and Becky while rereading *Tom Sawyer*, despite one's knowledge of the outcome, as a person reading it for the first time would. A child listening to *Jack and the Beanstalk* for the umpteenth time, long after she has had it memorized word for word, is likely to feel much the same excitement when the giant discovers Jack and goes after him, the same gripping suspense, that she felt when she first heard the story. Children, far from being bored by familiar stories, often beg to hear the same ones over and over again.

None of this is surprising in light of my theory. The child hearing *Jack and the Beanstalk* knows that fictionally Jack will escape, but *fictionally* she does *not* know that he will – until the reading of the passage describing his escape. She is engaged in her own game of make-believe during the reading, a game in which fictionally she learns for the first time about Jack and the giant as she hears about them.[13] It is the fact that fictionally she is uncertain, not any actual uncertainty, that is responsible for the excitement and suspense that she feels. The point of hearing the story is not, or not merely, to learn about Jack's confrontation with the giant, but to play a game of make-believe. One cannot learn, each time one hears the story, what fictionally Jack and the giant do, unless one always forgets in between times. But one can and does participate each time in a game of make-believe. The point of hearing *Jack and the Beanstalk* is to have the experience of being such that fictionally one realizes with trepidation the danger Jack faces, waits breathlessly to see whether the giant will awake, feels sudden terror when he does awake, and finally learns with admiration and relief how Jack chops down the beanstalk killing the giant.

Why play the same game over and over? In the first place, the game may not be exactly the same each time, even if the readings are the same. On one occasion it may be fictional that the child is paralyzed by fear for Jack, overwhelmed by the gravity of the situation, and emotionally

236

drained when Jack finally bests the giant. On another occasion, it may be
fictional that the child is not very seriously concerned about Jack's safety
and that her dominant feelings are admiration for Jack's exploits, the
thrill of adventure, and a sense of exhilaration at the final outcome. But
even if the game is much the same from reading to reading, one's
emotional needs may require the therapy of several or many repetitions.

Notes

1. Portions of this lecture are taken from Walton's 'How Remote Are Fictional
   Worlds from the Real World?' *Journal of Aesthetics and Art Criticism*, Vol.
   XXXVII, No. 1 (Fall 1978), and from his 'Fearing Fictions', *Journal of Philosophy*,
   Vol. LXXV, No. 1 (January 1978). Reprinted by permission of *Journal of
   Aesthetics and Art Criticism*, and *Journal of Philosophy*. The author's work on the
   topic of this lecture was supported partially by fellowships from the American
   Council of Learned Societies and the National Endowment for the
   Humanities. Acknowledgements were made to John G. Bennett, Holly S.
   Goldman, Robert Howell, Brian Loar and others for helpful discussions.

2. URSULA LE GUIN, *The Left Hand of Darkness*, Introduction (New York: Grosset &
   Dunlap, 1969).

3. See, for example, ROBERT HOWELL, 'Fictional Objects: How They Are and How
   They Aren't', *Poetics*, Vol. VIII (1979); TERRENCE PARSONS, 'The Methodology
   of Nonexistence', *Journal of Philosophy*, Vol. LXXVI, No. 11 (November 1979);
   PETER VAN INWAGEN, 'Creatures of Fiction', *American Philosophical Quarterly*,
   Vol. XIV, No. 4 (October 1977).

4. *Knots* (New York: Vintage Books, 1970), p. 1.

5. 'Some people – and I am one of them – hate happy ends. We feel cheated.
   Harm is the norm. Doom should not jam. The avalanche stopping in its tracks
   a few feet above the cowering village behaves not only unnaturally but
   unethically', Vladimir Nabokov, *Pnin*.

6. By 'fear' Walton means fear for oneself. Obviously one can be afraid for
   someone else without believing that one is in danger himself. One must
   believe that the person for whom one fears is in danger.

7. According to Coleridge all 'stage presentations are to produce a sort of
   temporary half-faith', *Selected Poetry and Prose*, ed. Elizabeth Schneider (New
   York: Holt, Rinehart & Winston, 1951), p. 396.

8. Colorado State University once awarded Sherlock Holmes an honorary degree
   for contributions to 'the art of sleuthing'.

9. When Charles says, 'Yikes, watch out! Here it comes!', he is behaving
   deliberately as one who is really afraid would. In this respect he is like the
   person discussed earlier who is afraid of flying. But Charles' deliberate action,
   unlike those of the fearful flyer, is that of deliberately *pretending* to be afraid,
   and so does not support a claim that he really is afraid.

Modern Readings: Reader-oriented

10. A good source concerning make-believe games is Jerome L. Singer *et al.*, *The Child's World of Make-Believe* (New York: Academic Press, 1973).

11. David Lewis pointed out to the author the relevance of his theory to this puzzle.

12. 'I've seen it [*West Side Story*] about five thousand times maybe. And I *always* end up in tears', Leonard Bernstein, CBS interview, 24 January 1979 (quotation approximate).

13. It is probably fictional that someone (the narrator), whose word the child can trust, is giving her a serious report about a confrontation between a boy named 'Jack' and a giant. Cf. Walton's 'Points of View in Narrative and Depictive Representation', *Nous*, X, 1 (March 1976), pp. 49–61.

Psychoanalytic

The two examples of psychoanalytic readings, both by American critics, illustrate differing ways of applying psychoanalytic theories to literary texts. Leo Bersani and Peter Brooks are alike in devolving primarily from Freud, although they emphasise diverse aspects of his ideas, and they do so in disparate ways.

Bersani's 'Realism and the Fear of Desire' forms the second chapter of *A Future for Astyanax: Character and Desire in Literature* (Boston: Little, Brown & Co., 1976). Bersani uses the concept of desire, which he derives from Barthes, as the central principle to examine the relationship between character and identity in a variety of figures in realist narratives. Desire is the factor that fragments realism's presentation of a character as being part of a cohesive and fundamentally intelligible structure. As a result, the presentation of desire in realism is problematic: since desire is a threat to the form of realism, realism admits heroes of desire only in order to 'expel' them. In his discussions of George Eliot's *Middlemarch* (1872) and Balzac's *Peau de chagrin* (1831), as well as of other European and American realist novels, Bersani treats fictive figures as though they were actual people in their psychological needs and fears.

The second piece, 'Repetition, Repression, and Return: The Plotting of *Great Expectations*', is the fifth chapter of Peter Brooks' *Reading for the Plot* (New York: Viking, 1984). In contrast to Bersani, Brooks concentrates on a single work, and specifically on the progression of its plot, showing how the text as a whole is governed by the same drives to repetition, repression, return, deviance and postponement as the behaviour of individuals. In effect, Brooks psychoanalyses the deportment of a plot, revealing the underlying laws that determine its movement.

19 Leo Bersani on Realism and the Fear of Desire*

I want to look at some of the ways in which the nineteenth-century novel has trained us to be compulsive pursuers of significant design in fiction. Whereas twentieth-century writers, especially since Joyce, tend to parody the great myths of Western culture, or to make those myths 'de-signify,' the realistic novelist seems spontaneously to make patterns of meaning from the most isolated and disparate details. The *tour de force* of realistic novelists from Jane Austen to the later Henry James is to combine a superficially loose, even sprawling narrative form with an extraordinary tightness of meaning. The degree of looseness varies, but in writers as different as Jane Austen, Balzac, Dickens and James, we find a shared commitment to the portentous detail. The most casual word, the most trifling gesture, the most tangential episode all submit easily to the discipline of being *revealing* words, gestures and episodes.

Behavior in realistic fiction is continuously expressive of character. Apparently random incidents neatly carry messages about personality; and the world is thus at least structurally congenial to character, in the sense that it is constantly proposing to our intelligence objects and events which contain human desires, which give to them an intelligible form. The realistic novelist can wander, linger and digress as much as he likes; he will absorb any material – as the Balzacian digression supremely illustrates – into a commanding structure of significance. Furthermore, because the realistic novel generally remains faithful to chronological time, the very sequence of events becomes an ordering principle. Even Proust, while he seems to be announcing in *Combray* a nonchronological narrative organized according to the discontinuous resurrections of the past in Marcel's involuntary memories, follows a conventional time sequence from Marcel's childhood to middle age. It's true that certain stretches of Marcel's life are skipped, and it's also true that the linear narrative of *A la Recherche du temps perdu* is complicated by the fact that

---

* Reprinted from 'Realism and the Fear of Desire' in *A Future for Astyanax* (Boston: Little, Brown & Company, 1969), pp. 51–88.

the future of each moment is present in the account being given of it. The Proustian future is not only a time we move toward as we read; it is also the narrator's voice at each point of his return to the past. Nonetheless, given the theoretical statements in the work and the importance of subjective time in any accurate rendering of a man's life, it's striking that the linear sequences of *A la Recherche* remain so clear, and that we almost never have any doubts about what happened when in Marcel's life.

The conservative nature of the Proustian novel in this respect can best be appreciated if we compare it to Robbe-Grillet's *La Jalousie*. The real subversion of chronological time in Robbe-Grillet's novel is accomplished by the simple but radical device of eliminating any temporal reference for the telling of the story. The coherence which chronological time gives to traditional fiction should be measured against the temporally chaotic repetitiousness of *La Jalousie*, in which there is no controlling narrative voice at all to place in time the novel's various pictures. Robbe-Grillet's fictional episodes locate jealousy in space, but they tell us nothing about the historical development of jealousy. Nothing could be more different from the Proustian narrator's scrupulous tracing of different stages in, for example, his jealousy of Albertine. If there is temporal progression at all in *La Jalousie*, it can be discussed entirely in terms of esthetic strategy. We can never know when the various incidents took place (and therefore the question itself is an absurd one for criticism of the work), but we can follow the narrator's manipulation of our own developing sense of how jealousy has infected the entire universe of the novel.

Finally, time in realistic fiction is not merely chronological; it is shaped by a prior imagination of beginnings and ends.[1] Dates are enormously important in realistic fiction, and the first paragraphs of countless nineteenth-century novels give us the exact year when their stories begin. The specified year not only serves the illusion of historical authenticity; it also allows us the luxury of assigning precise beginnings to experience, and of thereby making experience more accessible to our appetite for sense-making distinctions and categories. Conclusions are of course just as important in this enterprise of adding sharper sense to life. Realistic novels tend to end with marriages or deaths, and marriage at the end of *Pride and Prejudice* and *Little Dorrit* is as significant and conclusive a *dénouement* to the novel's drama as is Ahab's death in *Moby-Dick* or Milly Theale's death in *The Wings of the Dove*.

Marriage has more than a purely formal importance in traditional fiction. In *The Theory of the Novel*, Georg Lukács emphasized the differences between the marriages which end novels and those which end neoclassical comedies. The sculptural form of comedy requires 'a purely symbolic ceremony' (similar to the hero's death at the end of tragedy) which emphasizes, in an atemporal way, the contours and limits of the form itself. We might add that the marriages announced in the last acts of *L'Ecole des femmes* and *L'Avare* are essentially insignificant; a proper conjugal match simply strikes a note of bland harmony by which we recognize that the dramatist has finished his work. Marriages in the novel, on the other hand, complete the novel's sense. The happy marriage is as significant as the unhappy one, and while there may be more to say about the latter, the former is equally rich in psychological and moral implications. In Molière, the obstacles to the good lovers' marriages are simply pushed aside by happy strokes of fate. The young people's union is not the result of any growth of moral consciousness: *they* have generally been in love from the very start, and Arnolphe and Harpagon are just as foolish at the end of *L'Ecole des femmes* and *L'Avare* as they were at the beginning. But the happy marriages of Elizabeth and Darcy, of Little Dorrit and Arthur Clennam, and of Dorothea and Will Ladislaw are the just consequences and rewards of just perceptions of character. They are the reliable signs of the hero's and the heroine's matured consciousness, as well as an indication of what constitutes a 'natural' social order in all these novels. And we should make no mistake about the creaky plot machinery sometimes necessary to bring these marriages about – or, more generally, to settle the moral issues of the novel in the 'right' way. Molière proclaims the insignificance of his happy endings (which never really qualify the pessimism of his major plays) by the frivolous ingenuities of plot which make them possible. But in realistic fiction, the unexpected revelation of the surprising coincidence, far from being merely formal conveniences, seem almost to signify an awesome complicity of the most distant or unrelated corners of reality with the requirements of the novel's main psychological and moral structures. Reality is coerced into providing the suitable conclusion to a continuously meaningful chain of events.

The exertion toward significant form in realistic fiction serves the cause of significant, coherently structured character. The revealing incident makes personality intelligible; real beginnings and definitive endings provide a temporal frame in which individuals don't merely exist, but move purposefully from one stage of being to another. Personality is as rigorously structured in the realistic novel as it is in Racinian tragedy. Indeed, in a literary form remarkable for its variety and its concreteness, it's perhaps even more remarkable to find that tendency to allegorize the self which can be seen in Racine. Desire in realistic fiction is generally conceived of either as a ruling passion (Goriot's paternal love, Silas Marner's miserliness, Milly Theale's dovelike mildness), or in terms of that inner chemistry described by Sartre in which mental processes are depicted as syntheses of abstract faculties (in the same way that Phèdre is a certain 'solution' of guilt and sexual passion, Swann's jealousy of Odette alternates with and neutralizes his tenderness for Odette). The richly detailed textures of characterization in realistic fiction seldom

subvert the coherent wholeness of personality – or if they do, criticism
has to deal with what we call an 'interesting' esthetic failure.
Psychological complexity is tolerated as long as it doesn't threaten an
ideology of the self as a fundamentally intelligible structure unaffected by
a history of fragmented, discontinuous desires.

The persistence (or rather the resurgence) of this ideology in nineteenth-
century literature is a curious chapter in the political history of art.
Classical French literature is a conservative social force not merely
because its pessimism about human nature would discourage any
hopeful view of what might be accomplished by changes in social
conditions, but also because it helps to reinforce the hierarchical structure
of seventeenth-century French society. Racinian tragedy is full of chaotic
passions, but as far as ideologies of the self are concerned, the implied
existential chaos is perhaps less important than the Racinian image of a
permanently ordered self. Passion disrupts his characters' lives, but it
also orders their personalities. Thanks to a dominant enslaving passion,
all behavior in Racine can be 'placed' in relation to a fixed psychological
center. Words and gestures can always be referred to that passion; they
can, in other words, be reliably interpreted. The literary myth of a rigidly
ordered self contributes to a pervasive cultural ideology of the self which
serves the established social order. Personality is shown to have the
coherent, hierarchical wholeness suitable to a social system of sharply
distinct ranks. A rigid social hierarchy reproduces, in political structures,
the form of the self, and it is as if Racinian tragedy were certifying the
psychological realism of such hierarchical political structures. True,
classical psychology vindicates authoritarian rule partly by its dismal
view of a human nature in dire need of discipline. From a purely structural
point of view, it also vindicates authoritarianism by its images of a self
whose very irrationality is part of its coherence – a coherence which
lends itself ideally to psychological and social classifications (and control).
    Neoclassical literature and realistic fiction belong to a single
community of cultural assumptions about personality. This statement
obviously involves a huge – and, in a sense, outrageous – historical
jump. Artistic forms develop and thrive in particular social contexts, and
the span of time I'm referring to includes, especially in France, great
social upheavals. Even within the nineteenth century, the differences
between English society in 1813 and England in 1872 should perhaps
discourage us from speaking, as I did a few pages back, as if marriage in
Pride and Prejudice and in *Middlemarch* had the same significance.
Dorothea's aspirations are compromised by her marriage to Will, while
Elizabeth's marriage to Darcy will presumably provide an ideal social
context for her personal worth. In *Pride and Prejudice*, institutionalized
forms can still accommodate individual superiority; *Middlemarch*

documents the *in*adequacy of available social forms to heroic aspirations. In spite of these important differences, there is, I think, a commitment to a *psychological* integrity or intelligibility which has been a constant in Western culture. It is this commitment which we are trying to define here, and it can be distinguished from a more variable historical sense of the relation between social possibility and individual aspiration. Notions about the natural shape of the self create the durable 'field' in which a wide range of historical judgments about the self and society can take place. Finally, however, the field limits the range of this historical variability. And such limitations are not politically neutral. Assumptions about human nature which may seem almost ahistorical (because of the persistence with which a culture has maintained them) nonetheless insure some continuity among all the social arrangements imagined throughout that culture's history. Indeed, the monotonously similar fates, in modern history, of political systems which apparently reflect the most diverse ideologies may be due to a certain politics of the self common to all these ideologies. The potential for change in any new type of social organization depends, ultimately, on ontological assumptions about what the self *is*.

To return to the historical periods from which the examples in this book are being taken, we might say that the availability of Racinian tragedy to psychoanalytic criticism is striking evidence of a continuity in Western thought about the nature of the self. For example, as we saw in the previous chapter, the psychoanalytic interpretations of Racine's theater by Charles Mauron and by Roland Barthes do away with the conscious identities of Racine's characters in order to identify these characters with a variety of roles in unconscious fantasies. But the Racinian self which these readings uncover (Barthes' *homo racianus*) is as highly structured as the one proposed by the traditional academic portraits of Racinian characters. Especially in Mauron, the traditional diagram of conscious passions is replaced by a Freudian diagram of familial sexuality which is equally unreceptive to signs of discontinuous, nonstructurable desires. Neither critical approach, however, violates the Racinian text. Racine himself, a critical vocabulary of conscious passions, and the psychoanalytic reading of unconscious impulses are different versions of a cultural commitment to the notion of structured character. The peculiarity of Freudian analysis is to propose a history of the self's structure which includes, as one of its stages, the solidifying of character structures (which are the post-Oedipal sublimations of pre-Oedipal impulses). Psychoanalysis partially demystifies the notion of such structures by explaining them historically rather than just deducing them from the concept of an ahistorical human nature. But, curiously enough, history is not contingent in Freudian thought, or rather, contingency is restricted to individual variations on permanent structural themes. The stages of human desire described by psychoanalysis happen in time, but this doesn't prevent them from being considered as *necessary* stages. And Freud's recourse to myths in a presumably clinical terminology suggests his wish to avoid arguments about historical conditions and particularities. We no longer have supernatural sanctions for the shape of human character, but biology and psychoanalytic logic can provide those sanctions and vindicate the claim to universal validity for a particular developmental view of the self. . . .

To return to nineteenth-century fiction, it could of course be said that it is precisely by working within a certain field of agreement about the shape of the self that the realistic novelist questions existing orders more seriously than his psychologically playful, even irresponsible eighteenth-century predecessors. The realistic novelist's effort to make us believe in his characters may be the precondition for any challenge to the order of things: Huck Finn, to take a striking example, is socially dangerous to the extent that we do find him believable or 'real.' But it's also true that realistic novelists dramatize the *failure* of all such challenges, and I would suggest that a reluctance to take certain psychological risks with character at least partly explains these novelists' moral and social pessimism. It is not just the nature of nineteenth-century society which defeats the realistic hero. His defeat is also the result of his imprisonment within a psychology which his creator has adopted from the society being contested, a psychology of the coherently structured and significantly expressive self.

The belief in psychic structure and significance is so pervasive in Western culture that it may seem superfluous to assert its influence on a few works of literature. But a confidence in psychological order is an interesting phenomenon in nineteenth-century fiction because social history would seem to have made such a confidence exceedingly difficult to sustain. The realistic novelist is intensely aware of writing in a context of social fragmentation. Jane Austen already sounds the alarm in her second group of novels, and with Dickens and Balzac we have an obsessive concern with chaotically fierce human energies in the jungle of a chaotically 'open' society. On the one hand – and critics have frequently emphasized this – nineteenth-century novelists tend to take a sharply critical view of this society. Even when, as in the case of Balzac, they are fascinated by the mere mass of energies exploding in this social jungle, they also document the dehumanizing brutality of a society in which 'order' is always a mockery of moral orders. Those who have made it in the competitive scramble for power become the standard-bearers of a conservatism concerned with the preserving not of values or traditions, but rather of their acquired power. And, as René Girard has shown, the great nineteenth-century novelists expose a kind of inauthentic community of desire in this society. Social harmony extends no further than the imitation of other people's desires; one needs others to know what is desirable, at the same time that one needs to eliminate others in order to possess the objects which they have designated to the individual's parasitic appetites.

But the critical judgments passed on society in nineteenth-century fiction are qualified by a form which provides this society with a reassuring myth about itself. The realistic novel gives us an image of social fragmentation contained within the order of significant form – and it thereby suggests that the chaotic fragments are somehow socially viable and morally redeemable. The novel makes esthetic sense out of social anarchy. And the society being judged subtly profits from this novelistic order, even though the order includes a great deal of social criticism. A good part of the realistic novelist's imaginative energies – whatever his intentions may be – is devoted to sparing his society the pain of confronting the shallowness of its order and the destructiveness of its appetites. The ordered significances of realistic fiction are presented as immanent to society whereas in fact they are the mythical denial of that society's fragmented nature. In a sense, then, the realistic novelist desperately tries to hold together what he recognizes quite well is falling apart. The looseness or elasticity of novelistic form is a sign of that recognition. The ordering myth of nineteenth-century society can obviously not be given within the narrow formal discipline of classical tragedy. There are too many disparate elements to take into account. The novel welcomes the disparate, it generously gives space to a great variety of experience; but it is essentially an exercise in *containing* the looseness to which it often appears to be casually abandoning itself. And even when novelists seem to become more skeptical about their ability to find a saving form for the disconnected, fragmented lives they represent, they make a last-ditch stand for the redemptive pattern rather than simply abandon the whole pattern-making enterprise.

What alternatives were available to nineteenth-century novelists? To avoid the sort of complicity I'm discussing is an enormously difficult enterprise. It would seem to involve not only a revolution in literary form, but – as a precondition for that – a successful revolt against a culture's most fundamental ways of making sense out of its experience. And surely we should respect the realistic novelist's poignant effort to provide his society with some image of a viable and morally decent order, especially since the work of almost all the most interesting writers of fiction in the nineteenth century amounts to a confession of their failure to find such an order. At the level of visible social organization, the realistic novelist courageously confronts what are after all terrifying images of destructive fragmentation. In the face of these images, the novelist tries and fails to believe in myths of social order. But, once again, I think we have to distinguish between a pessimistic view of moral and social fragmentariness, and a reassuring belief in psychological unity and intelligibility. The latter blinds both the novelist and his society to the psychic discontinuities and incoherence from which all our fragmented experience ultimately derives. A myth about psychic order and structure helps to contain, and to limit, all critiques of disorder. It also makes it practically impossible to begin experimenting with nondestructive versions of fragmented desires. There are models of such experiments in nineteenth-century poetry – in, for example, Wordsworth, Hölderlin, Baudelaire, and as we shall see, Rimbaud. True, the dismissal of psychological order would threaten the character structures without which realistic fiction, unlike lyric poetry, could no longer survive. But, as much nonrealistic fiction since the eighteenth century demonstrates, the psychological resources of fictional prose narratives are by no means exhausted by the realistic novelist's commitment to character structures which depend on the sublimation of desire – and therefore on a negation of both the sensual intensities and the fragmented variety of human desires.

Even without abandoning his character portraits, the realistic novelist might have drawn our attention more willingly to aspects of his own artfulness as an alternative to the sort of intelligibility dramatized in his characters. But in general he is anxious to make us forget his own presence in his work, and he thereby disguises a narrative performance of desiring fantasy which might have contested that organization of desire into coherent personalities which, so to speak, the novelist argues for through his characters. Perhaps only Flaubert is willing to take the risk of drawing our attention to a kind of nonstructurable randomness in his own writing, to give stylistic emphasis to dramatically 'unnecessary' passages, passages which gratuitously supplement the novel's sense. And this narrative waste in Flaubert affects the integrity of the characters whom Flaubert nevertheless takes the trouble to construct – not only their moral integrity (or pretensions), but also their very credibility as full, rounded, coherent personalities of realistic fiction. From *Madame Bovary* to *Bouvard et Pécuchet*, the failure of significance spreads to the characters themselves. Under the pressures of what appears to be a skepticism about the very idea of personality, the Flaubertian character almost ceases to be. Flaubert reacts pessimistically to this potential of self (as a consequence of psychic randomness and self-fragmentation), but his work does suggest the futility, or at least the innocuous nature, of all social criticism which is not included within questions about the nature of the self. The formal and psychological reticence of most realistic fiction makes for a secret complicity between the novelist and his society's illusions about its own order. Realistic fiction serves nineteenth-century society by providing it with strategies for containing (and repressing) its disorder within significantly structured stories about itself.

War and Peace and *Middlemarch* will provide us with two images of this containment. Tolstoy argues in *War and Peace* against all the systematizations by which men try to simplify and make sense of history, but the most positive value in the novel is an institutional simplification of desire. The two most expansive characters in the novel – Pierre and Natasha – presumably realize a Tolstoyan ideal of nature by agreeing to be defined almost exclusively as husband and wife. Lukács spoke of the 'profoundly desperate' state of mind described by Tolstoy in the 'peaceful nursery atmosphere' at the end of *War and Peace*. A love meant to be the victory of nature over the false subtleties of culture is lived, Lukács wrote, as an adaptation to the lowest level of convention. Indeed, as an adequate conclusion to the immense spiritual quest of *War and Peace*, Tolstoy aggressively apotheosizes a slatternly housewife in constant anguish about the state of her babies' diapers. 'Natasha needed a husband. A husband was given her. And her husband gave her a family. And she not only saw no need of any other or better husband but as all her spiritual energies were devoted to serving that husband and family she could not imagine, and found no interest in imagining, how it would be if things were different.' No amount of cant about the great biological community of the family can hide the brutal reductiveness of this passage. Far from being the universalizing of love which is spoken of elsewhere in the novel, Tolstoyan marriage tends to make for an exclusive, self-contained social unit smugly indifferent to the rest of the world. The end of *War and Peace* would propose an authentic image of historic order: not the false intellectual order of historians, but the natural order of the family. But the obvious foundation of the family in nature allows Tolstoy to obscure its social conventionality. The transcendence of culture into nature turns out to be an obedient retreat into a given social form – a retreat which conveniently provides a biological alibi for social conformity.

Middlemarch is a striking example of an ambivalent attitude toward the prospect of establishing significant connections in experience. On the one hand, it is a novel about connecting enterprises which fail. Casaubon's *Key to All Mythologies* is nothing but scattered, unrelated notes. Lydgate has to abandon his medical research into 'the primitive tissue,' the 'common basis' from which he might be able to articulate 'the intimate relations of living structure.' Finally, there is no social medium in which Dorothea's heroism might be adequately enacted, and we are invited to think of her as a modern 'Saint Theresa, foundress of nothing, whose loving heartbeats and sobs after an unattained goodness tremble off and are dispersed among hindrances instead of centring in some long-recognizable deed.' On the other hand, *Middlemarch* is about the power of connections in life – connections between ideals and the social conditions in which they must be tested; between one man's moral choices and the consequences of those choices on other people's lives;

between, as George Eliot put it in a letter, 'character' and 'the medium in which a character moves.' Eliot speaks of her story as her 'particular web'; she is engaged in 'unravelling certain human lots and seeing how they were woven and interwoven.' Now the real connections in *Middlemarch* are ironic commentaries on the ideal connections. The 'embroiled medium' in which George Eliot's characters move is a mockery of the structures they dream of, although Eliot does find some basis for a qualified optimism in the thought that that medium receives and is modified not only by the acts of a Bulstrode, but also by the life of someone like Dorothea. '. . . The growing good of the world is partly dependent on unhistoric acts . . .' and '. . . the effect of [Dorothea's] being on those around her was incalculably diffusive.' We must learn to settle for the 'incalculably diffusive' effect – and, if we do, we will perhaps begin to see innumerable examples of how inextricably involved human lives are with one another.

George Eliot is scarcely happy with the kinds of connections she is able to propose as a substitute for epic life. Nonetheless, like her characters, she does draw some moral comfort from the 'embroiled' and strained relations which are the only connections she can realistically conceive of. She won't abandon the dream of structured significance, even if she has to sustain it by the vague doctrine of individual goodness finally, in some way, affecting the course of history, or by the more desperate move of showing how the very subversion of her protagonists' dreams is itself a proof of the interconnectedness in life. Even modern experience is a significantly structured web, although it is no longer structured for the idealism of a Saint Theresa. Nothing is more terrifying than to have behavior and environment break up into frequently discontinuous, fragmented moves and contexts. Dorothea is jarred 'as with an electric shock' by 'the gigantic broken revelations' of Rome, by the 'vast wreck' of ancient ideals and modern 'forgetfulness and degradation' in the city; 'all her life' the red drapery being hung in Saint Peter's for Christmas (juxtaposed with the 'excited intention' of the figures in the mosaic) will haunt her memory as 'a disease of the retina' spreading itself everywhere.

Finally, George Eliot's very imagination for plot perhaps testifies to a nervous, strained determination to connect the many threads of experience which she has allowed into her work. Of course, literature is always something of an exercise in inventing a dramatic logic for unexpected relations among things. Its nature is to coerce experience into making sense. But each period or genre establishes its own criteria of acceptability for those ingenuities which fit deceptively random lines of action into a single structure. *Oedipus Rex* expresses an unlimited tolerance for coincidence. In a sense, Oedipus's presumption is, precisely, to think that events can ever be safely counted on to remain disconnected; Sophocles' work dramatizes the tragedy of inescapably significant structures. Realistic fiction, on the other hand, prides itself on a more empirical sense of probability. But the *dénouements* in realistic fiction make havoc of the verisimilitudes which the novelist has appeared to be so scrupulously observing. *Middlemarch* ends in structural fireworks; the unexpected link between Bulstrode and Will is a piece of novelistic weaving done with the coarsest, most visible threads. We were perhaps ready to think that Dorothea and Lydgate could be justly reproached for their solipsistic notions of structural harmonies in life. Their moral and scientific idealisms took no account of how those notions might be affected by experiences alien to them. But George Eliot's own indulgence in an ideally unified novelistic structure may make us view with irony *her* irony about her heroes' early views of their relation to the social medium in which they must live. By the end of *Middlemarch*, George Eliot's presence in the novel has become anything but 'incalculably diffusive.' She is making connections which the rest of the novel has trained us to see as naïve, unworkable novelistic connections. The subtle, almost indefinable influence of one life on other lives has been replaced by melodramatic connections of crime and rare coincidence. Thus fiction unexpectedly – and, I think, unintentionally – points to its own status as purely verbal artifice by the ways in which it demonstrates the persistence of significant structures in modern life.

Desire is a threat to the form of realistic fiction. Desire can subvert social order; it can also disrupt novelistic order. The nineteenth-century novel is haunted by the possibility of these subversive moments, and it suppresses them with a brutality both shocking and eminently logical. In formal terms, disruptive desire could be thought of as a disease of disconnectedness in a part of the structure which rejects being defined by its relations to other parts and asserts, as it were, a scandalous affinity with elements alien to the structure. Such desires resist being structured as part of a realistic character portrait. Realistic fiction seems to give an enormous importance to disruptive desires by embodying them in its heroes. Indeed, the most frequent confrontation in the realistic novel is between society and a hero who refuses to accept the definitions which society proposes of his duties and satisfactions. Since these definitions are grounded in an established view of the self, the hero's rebellion is fundamentally against the idea of his own nature implicit in the opportunities being offered to him.

But this centrality of disruptive desire in the novel is very ambiguous. First of all, it is a curious fact that the central figures in many nineteenth-century novels are the vaguest or the most mystifying presences of the works in which they appear. It's not a question of their being psychologically richer – and therefore more difficult to enclose within critical definitions – than other characters. Rather, we could, in many cases, justifiably complain that these heroes and heroines are *less* interesting psychologically than the novelist's other characters, or that they have a kind of density dangerously close to unintelligibility. Many readers have found Milly Theale and Maggie Verver flat, insubstantial heroines; critics have complained that Marcel in *A la Recherche du temps perdu* is insufficiently realized for the amount of moral and esthetic significance he is meant to carry in the novel; Fabrice and Clélia in *La Chartreuse de Parme* are said to be less interesting than Gina and Mosca; the qualities which separate Ahab and Prince Myshkin from the other characters of *Moby-Dick* and *The Idiot* have the ambiguity of intentions for which these novels can provide no clarifying contexts, no field or medium in which they might be distinctly seen. Not only does society in realistic fiction fail to provide occasions for the enactment of exceptional passions; the novelist also indicates in formal terms his own inability (or unwillingness) to imagine these passions in real life. As desire becomes more radically disruptive of established orders, the novel tends to become less realistic, more allegorical: the characters of *Moby-Dick* are frankly emblematic, and Balzac rightly placed the works which dramatize the most extravagant desiring imagination – *La Peau de chagrin*, *La Recherche de l'absolu*, and *Séraphita* – among his 'philosophical novels' and not with the more realistic *Scènes de la vie parisienne* or *Scènes de la vie de province*.

Realistic fiction admits heroes of desire in order to submit them to ceremonies of expulsion. This literary form depends, for its very existence, on the annihilation or, at the very least, the immobilizing containment of anarchic impulses.[2] The hero is an intruder in a world of significantly related structures, of unambiguous beginnings and definitive conclusions. He is alien to the world of realistic fiction – but not because that world is the 'real' world which the novelist objectively shows to be incompatible with quixotic idealisms. That incompatibility is largely an *a priori* choice on the part of the novelist in favor of a particular kind of world which, as I've been suggesting, he severely judges but also (perhaps unintentionally) supports. The technical premises of realistic fiction – the commitment to intelligible, 'full' characters, to historical verisimilitude, to the revealing gesture or episode, to a closed temporal frame – *already* dooms any adventure in the stimulating improbabilities of behavior which would resist being 'placed' and interpreted in a general psychological or formal structure. (It could be said, for example, that the very nature of the novel she appears in determines Isabel's return to Osmond at the end of *The Portrait of a Lady*; her dream of freedom has been defeated by the limited range of possibilities for being free available to the realistic imagination. Isabel *and* James can no longer imagine to what concrete use her desire to be free might be put.) The strange vagueness of certain novelistic heroes and heroines is not so strange at that: in a sense, the realistic novel makes no provision for such figures. It has very little to say about them, although the demonstration of this negative truth frequently generates a sense of the tragedy of limited forms (both social and esthetic) in the novelist, and can therefore constitute a very complex novelistic enterprise. . . .

The terror of desire in nineteenth-century fiction is often dramatized in the heroes themselves. The latter are by no means always the rebellious scapegoats I've just described, and perhaps nothing is more astonishing in the realistic novel than the central position frequently given to characters whose main function seems to be to smother desire, to stifle all movement. I would like to end this general (and partial) survey of nineteenth-century fiction with a study of what we may designate as a heroic stillness in fiction. The immobile hero or heroine is a complex phenomenon. He is occasionally an unambiguous warning about the dangers of desire, but he may also use his stillness as a strategy of retreat from the order which he seems to be defending, and into a realm of being where he will no longer owe anything at all to that order.

The clearest warning I know is sounded by Balzac in *La Peau de chagrin*. The novel obviously violates realistic criteria of probability, but it does provide an exceptionally clear model for the role of desire in Balzac's more realistic work, as well as in much non-Balzacian fiction. The message in *La Peau de chagrin* is simple: desire disintegrates society, the self and the novel. The ass-skein has the magic power to fulfill all Raphaël's desires, but with each desire the talisman shrinks and Raphaël's life grows shorter. Balzac's hero must therefore choose between paying for the immediate satisfaction of all his desires with his life, or prolonging his life by refusing to desire. The novel is skillfully polarized into images of disintegration and images of rigid order. It begins with a nightmare of fragmentation. The antique shop Raphaël wanders into is a chaos of historical reminiscences. 'All the countries of the earth seemed to have brought there some debris from their sciences, a model of their arts.'[3] The fictions of continuous historical time and of coherently organized civilizations are undermined by a mass of unrelated objects from different periods and different places. The spectacle sets off a hallucinated vision in Raphaël, one in which '. . . the universe appeared to him in snatches and in streaks of fire.' Human history is an endless, disconnected poem: 'Forms, colors, thought, everything came back to life; but nothing complete was offered to the soul.' Raphaël's first wish when he takes the ass-skein is for a 'bacchanalian' banquet. His wish is immediately granted, and the banquet begins with an orgy of disconnected conversation among the men during dinner, followed by a sexual orgy with the women brought in by the banker Taillefer. As Raphaël himself points out, he has moved from the spectacle of 'the most poetic ruins of the material world' to 'the debris of all the intellectual treasures which we pillaged' during the banquet, and finally to the courtesans Aquilina and Euphrasie, 'lively and original images of madness.' We of course recognize here the typically rigorous order of a Balzacian narrative scheme. The evidence of fragmentation is somewhat discredited by an obvious concern for thematic continuity. The orgies of disconnectedness are contained within and by a highly structured narrative progress. Nevertheless, the novel does begin with some ominous images of fragmented human energies: the ruins of history in the antique shop, the ruins of thought at the banquet, the sexual anarchy at the orgy.

What are the images of order in the novel? The old antique dealer gives Raphaël the formula to which he owes 'happiness and my longevity': '*Desiring* burns us up and *Having Power* destroys us; but KNOWLEDGE leaves our weak faculties in a perpetual state of calm. Thus desire or will is dead in me, killed by thought . . .' Such distinctions are of doubtful value in Balzac, for whom thought, desire and will are really synonymous. The antique dealer's argument depends on a very theoretical separation of feeling from expression. 'What men call sorrows, loves, ambitions, setbacks, sadness are for me ideas which I can change into reveries; instead of feeling them, I express them, I translate them; instead of letting them devour my life, I dramatize them, I develop them, I enjoy them like novels which I might be reading by means of an inner vision.' The fact that the writing of *La Comédie humaine* virtually devoured Balzac's life would be enough to justify our finding this passage rather glib. Formal unity and stability in Balzac's fiction do seem designed to tame and contain the violently disruptive energies of his style and in his characters, but the frantic pull toward order can hardly be said to end in an unqualified victory for order. The antique dealer's confidence depends on a fantasy of desire as a separate mental organ; but the expression of 'knowledge,' as Balzac well knew, is inevitably an expression of desire, and the novelist *wills* his version of the world on the reader.

But I'm less interested here in questioning the argument than in considering its implications and consequences. The major lesson in Balzac is that desire destroys; the major task is consequently to castrate desire. The antique dealer has apparently saved himself by an esthetic *dédoublement*. He has become the author of his feelings, he has de-energized them by esthetically composing them. The other principal image of amputated desire in *La Peau de chagrin* is provided by Foedora, in whom the fantasy of nondesiring is made more psychologically concrete than in the antique dealer. Foedora certainly has desires, but in order to satisfy them she has killed her sexual desires. She wants social power, and her success depends on her sexual invulnerability. Raphaël undertakes the desperate enterprise of trying to make her love him, but it is he who is almost destroyed by desires he quickly loses control of. There is perhaps a richer sensuality in Balzac's fiction than in that of any other nineteenth-century novelist, and yet he has what almost amounts to a mystique of chastity. Some of the most powerful (and malevolent) creatures in his world have a peculiar sexual purity or, at the very least, an infallible technique for controlling their erotic excitements: Bette, Vautrin, Foedora, Lady Dudley. 'Virginity,' Balzac writes in *La Cousine Bette*, 'like all unnatural phenomena, has special riches, an engrossing majesty. Since he has economized life's forces, the individual virgin's life has a quality of incalculable resistance and duration. His brain has been enriched in the cohesion of faculties held in reserve.' Raphaël's survival depends on his maintaining the virginity of his faculty for desiring. 'To struggle more effectively with the cruel power whose challenge he had accepted, Raphaël had made himself chaste after the manner of Origen, by castrating his imagination.' He is, as it were, the victim of a double castration. There is an obvious enough sexual symbolism in the fact that both the ass-skein and Raphaël's life grow shorter each time he gives in to a desire. But the strategy by which Raphaël tries to save himself from this fate is itself a devirilizing technique, and the nondesiring Raphaël is described as having an 'effeminate grace' and 'hands like those of a pretty woman.'

The fear of desire in Balzac can be discussed as a fear of psychological fragmentation. Desire dynamites the Balzacian view of character – the 'essentialist' psychology which allows Balzac to present characters in terms of a fixed, intelligible, and organizing passion. It threatens, in short, those coherent portraits of personality which are an important part of Balzacian expositions, and which characters' subsequent behavior will mainly illustrate and confirm. Can desires be contained by the ordering strategies of a descriptive narrative? If they cannot, narrative itself risks being fragmented into the mere juxtaposition of images of energy like those which assail Raphaël in the antique shop. The parade of disconnected scenes from human history at the beginning of *La Peau de chagrin* is the rejected alternative to Balzac's usual narrative method. The Balzacian narrator is, precisely, the godlike presence who imposes a kind of providential order on his own fictional histories. And the rigid structure of a Balzac narrative is both menaced and energized by desires which may destroy characters, but which the narrative manages to contain at least formally.

Finally, the containment of desire is a triumph for social stability. 'All excesses are alike,' Raphaël announces in his remarkable dissection of debauchery; war, political power, artistic creation, and mystical ecstasy are 'corruptions' which necessitate 'an exuberant, a prompt dissipation of one's strength.' The poet and the general *spend themselves* with the same extravagance as the *débauché*. And to spend oneself excessively creates debts which can't be paid. Raphaël is incapable of paying himself back the energy he loses in desiring. But hardly less important is the fact that he creates financial debts which also can't be paid. Desire ruins him economically as well as ontologically. Not only do the various kinds of excessive spending resemble one another; all the consequences of such spending are intimately linked. 'A debt is a work of imagination which men don't understand.' The debtor is the poetic victim of a capitalistic society. *La Peau de chagrin* is interestingly suggestive about the connection between a social economy and the imagination of desire. The orgiastic banquet early in the novel is given by the former banker Taillefer. All sorts of 'debauched spending' are inherent to a capitalistic economy. It is an economy dependent on speculation and the accumulation of debts. Indeed, it even glamorizes the speculator: he is the hero of an economy which encourages real debts for the sake of imaginary profits, and which invests its money in the fate of money itself. One can only gamble on the profits of such speculations (*La Peau de chagrin* begins in a gambling casino), but the economy ruthlessly rejects the losing gambler. The gambler and the speculator stake what they have for the sake of what they dream of having, and they are in constant danger of being forced to pay for their imaginative excesses. The effect of a capitalistic economy on the psychology of desire can only be to make desire seem irresistibly lurid: desire is the dangerous condition for enormous gains, a risky willingness to spend which may end in a ruinous obligation to pay.

In his life, Balzac was an inveterate speculator, and the psychology of desire in his work faithfully reflects his reckless financial gamblings. The real fate of speculative desire in capitalistic society thus makes the naturally disruptive nature of desire all the more terrifying. The self must be saved from expenditures of energy imagined to be as ruinous as the capitalist's risky investments. Balzac exposes the melodramatizing effect on desire of a specific economic context by his own vulnerability to that context. Desire in the society of *La Comédie humaine* swings crazily back and forth between catastrophic explosion and a panicky retentiveness. Raphaël's uncontrollable expenditures in *La Peau de chagrin* are balanced by Foedora's dehumanizing capacity for holding back desire. The most successful profiteer – both psychologically and economically – is the hoarder. Foedora, Balzac tells us at the end of the novel, 'is everywhere, she is, if you like, Society.' Her nondesiring egoism profits from the speculative investments of others. She is the prudent saver of desires, and in a sense Balzac's story fully justifies her affective paralysis. And she makes clear what the real basis of order is in Balzacian society. To spend and to desire are to be exploited and finally devoured. The chaos which results from the 'free flow' of desire and of money makes of a personal and social morality of mean economies the only effective formula for survival.

Nothing quite so melodramatic happens in Jane Austen's more authentically realistic novel, *Mansfield Park,* but she too proposes an ethic of stillness. The shift of Jane Austen's sympathies from the lively heroine of *Pride and Prejudice* to the tremblingly still Fanny Price corresponds to her sense of the social dangers of movement. In 1814, English society is on the threshold of major changes. A traditional, stable, rural society is about to be replaced by an industrial, cosmopolitan society; the quiet, morally reflective life of Mansfield Park will be forgotten in the agitated rhythms of life in London. All forms of agitation come in for an extraordinarily severe judgment in *Mansfield Park.* Jane Austen takes a certain risk in passing those judgments: we can easily find the principal 'villains' of her story the most interesting characters in the novel. In one sense, she is scrupulously fair toward Mary and Henry Crawford. They are not merely charming; both brother and sister are capable of certain moral delicacies which Jane Austen carefully underlines. But what dooms the Crawfords morally is the ease with which they move around among various, even contradictory sorts of behavior. Henry renews his flirtation with Maria in London largely because he can't stay still; his moral worthlessness is his inability to *wait* for Fanny to change her mind and agree to marry him. (Fanny, of course, does nothing in the novel but wait for Edmund's sense of the Crawfords to become as morally accurate as hers.) As for Mary, she finally does make Edmund aware of her true nature by seeing nothing intrinsically wrong in her brother's having run away with Maria. 'She saw it only as folly,' Edmund tells Fanny, 'and that folly stamped only by exposure.' The flurry of dramatic events at the end of *Mansfield Park* merely confirms anecdotally a view of the Crawfords' characters which by then we should have independently of any single episode. 'I am not born to sit still and do nothing,' Mary says during the card game of Speculation, and the truth of that remark is enough to condemn her. She is simply the most subtle version of the evils of agitation which we see in much cruder versions in Mrs Norris and in the atmosphere of Fanny's parents' home in Portsmouth.

But what does it mean not to be able to sit still? Why is movement evil in *Mansfield Park*? The home theatricals episode in the novel suggests an answer. The episode is a striking example of something I discussed earlier: the economical use in realistic fiction of significant form. The fact that the Crawfords see nothing wrong in having the theatricals during Sir Thomas's absence is the clearest signal we are given of their moral deficiency. In his introduction to the Penguin edition of the novel, Tony Tanner writes that '. . . Mansfield Park is all but destroyed once "the inclination to act was awakened." For Mansfield Park is a place where you must be true to your best self: the theater is a place where you can explore and experiment with other selves. A person cannot live in both.' And Tanner concludes: '. . . if the self is fluid, there is no limit to what it might do, no knowing how it might behave . . . [Life] may turn into a series of improvisations suggested by the milieu of the moment.' The great threat to Mansfield Park – and to the cultural values it represents – is precisely an improvised self, or the possibility that there is no 'best self' to which one 'must be true.' The very modern Crawfords are ontological floaters. Their liveliness is the style of beings without definition, actively ready to jump from one entertaining performance to the next. Such floating threatens the moral order of *Mansfield Park*, and it threatens a novelistic order in which each episode contributes significantly to coherent portraits of personality. We might say that Mary and Henry (somewhat like Eugenia in James's *The Europeans*) are discredited morally by the mere fact of their psychological indefiniteness.

The profound crisis of being recorded in *Mansfield Park* can be measured by the rigidity necessary to keep things from falling apart. It's as if the slightest agitation of self would be enough to disintegrate the integrity of self. Austen's argument appears to be, as Lionel Trilling has put it, 'that the self may destroy the self by the very energies that define its being, that the self may be preserved by the negation of its own energies.' Fanny Price is rather priggish, but priggishness can be a supreme virtue in a world which anticipates the collapse of its entire structure of values at the slightest movement. Indeed, Fanny is the ideal heroine of this world. She is not merely weak; she almost *is not*. Her years at Mansfield Park have trained her to be 'totally unused to have her pleasure consulted, or to have any thing take place at all in the way she could desire.' Fanny's only activity in the book is to give advice to her younger sister Susan; when she becomes a subscriber to a circulating library in Portsmouth, she is 'amazed at being any thing in *propria persona*, amazed at her own doings in every way; to be a renter, a chuser of books! And to be having any one's improvement in view in her choice!' Never daring to express her own desires (Fanny loves Edmund), Fanny has a kind of negative presence in the novel. She is the moral register of other people's behavior. And it's precisely the qualities we may find disagreeable which best qualify her for the role of moral heroine in the novel. She is a stable, nondesiring center of judgment. Her infallible moral eye preserves an order which even Edmund's behavior occasionally threatens. Edmund's desires lead him to make mistakes (he agrees to participate in the theatricals), while Fanny's asceticism makes her the perfect judge. Nothing is more curious in *Mansfield Park* than this identification of true being – as opposed to the theatrical self-diffusions of the Crawfords – with self-effacement. Non-being is the ultimate prudence in the world of *Mansfield Park*. Fanny is little more than an observant stillness, but because of that she is an excellent judge, and in this deceptively mild novel the structures of self and of society are so dangerously menaced that only the most vigilant judgment and sentencing of others can testify to the continued existence of moral principle. . . .

Thus lack of principle – of a psychological and moral center – is by no means an obstacle to social respectability. Far from creating chaos, the unprincipled, theatrical self lives in harmony with a social order which demands only external conformity. The danger pointed to by *Mansfield Park* is not the disintegration of order in social life; it is rather the survival of mere parodies of social order. Mary Crawford is a threat because she reinforces certain social structures without believing in them. She demonstrates that only cynicism is necessary to accommodate 'floating' desires to social stability. In short, character is not necessary to maintain the structures of community life, and, far from defending a social order on the point of crumbling, Fanny and Edmund are anachronistic survivals of a culture in which external order depended on the careful cultivation of order in personality. Society no longer needs them. To be sure, Fanny's severe stillness wins out over the Crawfords' dangerous liveliness, and Jane Austen piously asserts the renewed vitality of Mansfield Park at the end of her story. But it could also be argued that the novel has demonstrated the obsolescence of Mansfield Park. And in that case, the heroically still insistence on order in the self and in society would be deprived of *any* real context – an extremity which will allow the hero to renounce his mission and make an unexpected leap out of self, society, and the novel itself.

This is exactly what happens in James's *The Wings of the Dove* and *The Golden Bowl*, both of which have interesting analogies with *Mansfield Park*. Disruptive desire in all three novels goes along with the cynical cultivation of social forms. Like Mary Crawford, Kate Croy and Charlotte Stant are immensely adept at giving lively performances of themselves. All three are opposed to silent, nontheatrical heroines; Fanny, Milly and Maggie have no talent for representing the self in the world. And in each case a man hesitates between the flashy, more or less cynically respectable performer and a woman who does little more than wait for him to recognize her spiritual superiority. But in *Mansfield Park* there are demonstrable continuities between Fanny, a certain type of life in society, and also the kind of fiction which Jane Austen is writing. Fanny's judgments give moral significance to the events of *Mansfield Park*. The Crawfords' self-dramatizations have a diffusive effect; by seeing a moral meaning in everything they say or do, Fanny discredits them but also guarantees their suitability as intelligible characters in the novel. She therefore collaborates with Jane Austen's significant form, in which an episode is always a revealing episode, a contribution to the single meaningful structure of the entire work. In James, on the other hand, the resistance to potentially disruptive characters itself disrupts the conditions of realistic fiction. The stillness of Milly Theale and of Maggie

Verver doesn't operate as a magnet which finally draws the errant behavior of Densher and of Amerigo back into an ideal social and novelistic order. Rather, James's heroines draw the two men into a community of passion for which there is no place in the real world, and for which there is no language in realistic fiction.

Under Milly's influence, for example, *The Wings of the Dove* seems to become allegory as the story is being told. Characters lose their identities as 'personalities' and become spiritual alternatives in a struggle between the world of the lioness and the world of the dove for Densher's soul. A realistic conflict between personal loyalties and social opportunities is resolved in a union – between Densher and the spirit of the dead Milly – the nature of which the novel either can't express or is judged unworthy of expressing. Densher will end up living for the letter which Milly sent him before she died, but we are never told what is in the letter. The ultimate justification of his conversion to Milly is thereby saved from the contamination of narrative itself. While she was alive, Milly, unlike Kate, *did* almost nothing. Her effect is most powerful when she is dead, and the nature of her effect is inexpressible. Passivity, absence, and silence in *The Wings of the Dove* are the subterfuges by which James creates an escape from both the literary form of which he was one of the greatest practitioners and the social realities which that form assumes and essentially defends.

In *The Golden Bowl*, the happy marriage which Maggie manages to reconstitute at the end of the story is in fact the experience of a passion to which both marriage and society are irrelevant. In drawing Amerigo back into their marriage (and away from his adulterous relation with Charlotte), Maggie also breaks his ties to his own tradition-laden past and settles him, somewhat ruthlessly, in her own 'improvised "post"' which, James notes, would be marked on a map of social relations only by the geography of 'the fundamental passions.' The conclusion of *The Golden Bowl*, unlike that of *Mansfield Park*, is therefore also a repudiation of the order which it appears to reinstate. Far from asserting the triumph of those social forms and traditions which have been menaced throughout the novel, Maggie's marriage, unlike Fanny Price's, is merely a convenient institutional context for desires which have no place at all on any map of social structures. And since *The Golden Bowl* itself has been an elaborate exercise in structural ingenuities, its ending, once again unlike that of *Mansfield Park*, implicitly dismisses the novelistic mode in which it has been plotted. As we look back on the story, it would seem that Maggie's (and James's) passionate fiction has been sustained by the hope, finally realized in the last lines of *The Golden Bowl*, that the passion can dispense with the fiction. The stillness of Maggie Verver, while it appears to coerce errant desires back into a docile obedience to given structures, also has the opposite effect of surreptitiously providing an 'out' from *all* articulated structures. Without a single flaw in a strategy of 'high decorum,' Maggie's passion nonetheless subverts the decorums of society, of fiction, and of language.

Notes

1. FRANK KERMODE has studied, in *The Sense of an Ending*, the 'paradigms of apocalypse' in Western culture, the 'coherent patterns which, by the provision of an end, make possible a satisfying consonance with the origins and with the middle'.

2. This is true of those great novels which Richard Chase attempted to exonerate from such criticism by calling them romances. These works, as the unfortunate destinies of Huck Finn and Deerslayer show, eventually submit to the pressures that belong to the realistic novel. This point has been eloquently made by Richard Poirier in *A World Elsewhere*.

3. Translations from Balzac are Bersani's.

20 Peter Brooks on the Plot Dynamics of *Great Expectations**

I

. . . . I want in this chapter to discuss in the light of Freud's masterplot a novel that stands firmly within the golden age of plot, one that is centrally, unashamedly, and – at first glance – unsuspiciously concerned with issues of plot and plotting. It is indeed plotting, as an activity, as a dynamic machination, that may provide our best way into the reading of a fully achieved plot. And this activity of plotting may be most readily discernible in a retrospective first-person narrative. When we ask the questions, How do we find significant plots for our lives? How do we make life narratable? we find that the answers are most clearly dramatized in narratives of an autobiographical cast, since these cannot evade an explicit concern with problems of closure, authority, and narratability. As Sartre argued, autobiographical narration must necessarily be 'obituary' – must in any event explicitly show margins outside the narratable, leftover spaces which allow the narrating *I* to objectify and look back at the narrated *I*, and to see the plotted middle as shaped by and as shaping its margins. Hence rather than such novels as *Bleak House* or *Our Mutual Friend*, highly elaborated lengthy arabesques of plot, I choose *Great Expectations*, a more compact example, but one that gives in the highest degree the impression that its central meanings depend on the workings-out of its plot. For in this fictional pseudo-autobiography, Dickens adopts the revealing strategy of taking a 'life' and creating the demarcations of a 'plot' within it. The novel will indeed be concerned with finding a plot and losing it, with the precipitation of the sense of plottedness around its hero, and his eventual 'cure' from plot. The novel images in its structure the kind of structuring operation of reading that plot is.

Great Expectations is exemplary for a discourse on plot in many respects,

---

* Reprinted from 'Repetition, Repression, and Return: The Plotting of *Great Expectations*' in *Reading for the Plot* (New York: Vintage, 1984), pp. 113–42.

not least of all for its beginning. For what the novel chooses to present at its outset is precisely the search for a beginning. As in so many nineteenth-century novels, the hero is an orphan, thus undetermined by any visible inheritance, apparently unauthored. This clears away Julien Sorel's problems with paternity. There may be sociological and sentimental reasons to account for the high incidence of orphans in the nineteenth-century novel, but clearly the parentless protagonist frees an author from struggle with pre-existing authorities, allowing him to create afresh all the determinants of plot within his text. He thus profits from what Gide called the 'lawlessness' of the novel by starting with an undefined, rule-free character and then bringing the law to bear upon him – creating the rules – as the text proceeds. With Pip, Dickens begins as it were with a life that is for the moment precedent to plot, and indeed necessarily in search of plot. Pip when we first see him is himself in search of the 'authority' – the word stands in the second paragraph of the novel – that would define and justify – authorize – the plot of his ensuing life.

The 'authority' to which Pip refers here is that of the tombstone which bears the names of his dead parents, the names that have already been displaced, condensed, and superseded in the first paragraph, where Pip describes how his 'infant tongue' (literally, a speechless tongue: a **catachresis** that points to a moment of emergence, of entry into language) could only make of the name, Philip Pirrip, left to him by the dead parents, the monosyllabic Pip. 'So I called myself Pip, and came to be called Pip.'[1] This originating moment of Pip's narration and his narrative is a self-naming that already subverts whatever authority could be found in the text of the tombstones. The process of reading that text is described by Pip the narrator as 'unreasonable,' in that it interprets the appearance of the lost father and mother from the shape of the letters of their names. The tracing of the name – which he has already distorted in its application to self – involves a misguided attempt to remotivate the graphic symbol, to make it directly mimetic, mimetic specifically of origin. Loss of origin, misreading, and the problematic of identity are bound up here in ways we will further explore later on. The question of reading and writing – of learning to compose and to decipher texts – is persistently thematized in the novel.[2]

The decipherment of the tombstone as confirmation of loss of origin – as unauthorization – is here at the start of the novel the prelude to Pip's *cogito*, the moment in which his consciousness seizes his existence as other, alien, forlorn:

> My first most vivid and broad impression of the identity of things
> seems to me to have been gained on a memorable raw afternoon
> towards evening. At such a time I found out for certain, that this bleak
> place overgrown with nettles was the churchyard; and that Philip

Pirrip, late of this parish, and also Georgiana, wife of the above, were dead and buried; and that Alexander, Bartholomew, Abraham, Tobias, and Roger, infant children of the aforesaid, were also dead and buried; and that the dark flat wilderness beyond the churchyard, intersected with dykes and mounds and gates, with scattered cattle feeding on it, was the marshes; and that the low leaden line beyond was the river; and that the distant savage lair from which the wind was rushing, was the sea; and that the small bundle of shivers growing afraid of it all and beginning to cry, was Pip.

'Hold your noise!' cried a terrible voice . . .

(p. 1).

The repeated verbs of existence – 'was' and 'were' – perform an elementary phenomenology of Pip's world, locating its irreducible objects and leading finally to the individual subject as other, as aware of his existence through the emotion of fear, fear that then appears as the origin of voice, or articulated sound, as Pip begins to cry: a cry that is immediately censored by the command of the convict Magwitch, the father-to-be, the fearful instrusive figure of future authorship who will demand of Pip: 'Give us your name.'

The scenario is richly suggestive of the problem of identity, self-consciousness, naming, and language that will accompany Pip throughout the novel, and points to the original decentering of the subject in regard to himself. For purposes of my study of plot, it is important to note how this beginning establishes Pip as an existence without a plot, at the very moment of occurrence of that event which will prove to be decisive for the plotting of his existence, as he will discover only two-thirds of the way through the novel. Alien, unauthorized, self-named, at the point of entry into the language code and the social systems it implies, Pip will in the first part of the novel be in search of a plot, and the novel will recount the gradual precipitation of a sense of plot around him, the creation of portents of direction and intention.

Schematically, we can identify four lines of plot that begin to crystallize around the young Pip, the Pip of Part I, before the arrival of his 'Expectations':

1. Communion with the convict/criminal deviance.
2. Naterally wicious/bringing up by hand.
3. The dream of Satis House/the fairy tale.
4. The nightmare of Satis House/the witch tale.

These plots, we will see in a moment, are paired as follows: 2/1 = 3/4. That is, there is in each case an 'official' and censoring plot standing over a 'repressed' plot. In terms of Pip's own choices, we could rewrite the formula: 3/4/2/1, to show (in accordance with one of Freud's favorite models) the archaeological layering of strata of repressed material.[3] When the Expectations are announced by Jaggers at the end of Part 1, they will apparently coincide with Pip's choices ('My dream was out; my wild fancy was surpassed by sober reality' [Chapter 18, p. 130]), and will thus appear to take care of the question of plot. But this will be so only on the level of official plots; the Expectations will in fact only mask further the problem of the repressed plots.

I choose the term 'communion' for the first plot because its characteristic symbolic gesture is Pip's pity for the convict as he swallows the food Pip has brought him, a moment of sympathetic identification which focuses a series of suggestive sympathies and identifications with the outlaw: the bread and butter that Pip puts down his leg, which makes him walk like the chained convict; Mrs Joe's belief that he is on his way to the Hulks; Pip's flight from the Christmas dinner table into the arms of a soldier holding out handcuffs, to give a few examples. Pip is concerned to assure 'his' convict that he is not responsible for his recapture, a point he conveys in a mute exchange of glances which the convict understands and which leads him to make a public statement in exoneration of Pip, taking responsibility for stealing the food. This in turn provokes an overt statement of community with the outlaw, which comes from Joe: 'We don't know what you have done, but we wouldn't have you starved to death for it, poor miserable fellow-creatur – Would us, Pip?' (Chapter 5, p. 36).

The fellowship with the convict here stated by Joe will remain with Pip, but in a state of repression, as what he will later call 'that spell of my childhood' (Chapter 16, p. 114) – an unavowable memory. It finds its official, adult, repressive version in the conviction – shared by all the adults in Pip's life, with the exception of the childlike Joe – that children are naturally depraved and need to be corrected, kept in line with the Tickler, brought up by hand lest their natural willfulness assert itself in plots that are deviant, transgressive. Pumblechook and the Hubbles, in their Christmas dinner dialogue, give the theme a choric statement:

> 'Especially,' said Mr Pumblechook, 'be grateful, boy, to them which brought you up by hand.'
> Mrs Hubble shook her head, and contemplating me with a mournful presentiment that I should come to no good, asked, 'Why is it that the young are never grateful?' This moral mystery seemed too much for the company until Mr Hubble tersely solved it by saying, 'Naterally wicious'. Everybody then murmured 'True!' and looked at me in a particularly unpleasant and personal manner.
>
> (Chapter 4, pp. 22–3)

The 'nateral wiciousness' of children legitimates communion with the outlaw, but legitimates it as that which must be repressed, forced into other plots – including, as we shall see, 'binding' Pip as an apprentice.

The dream of Satis House is properly a daydream, in which 'His Majesty, the Ego' pleasures himself with the phantasy of social ascension and gentility. Miss Havisham is made to play the role of Fairy Godmother, her crutch become a magic wand, explicitly evoked twice near the close of Part 1.[4] This plot has adult sanction; its first expression comes from Pumblechook and Mrs Joe when they surmise that Miss Havisham intends to 'do something' for Pip, and Pip comes to believe in it, so that when the 'Expectations' arrive he accepts them as the logical fulfillment of the daydream, of his 'longings.' Yet to identify Satis House with the daydream is to perform a repression of all else that Satis House suggests and represents – all that clusters around the central emblem of the rotting bride cake and its crawling things. The craziness and morbidity of Satis House repose on desire fixated, become fetishistic and sadistic, on a deviated eroticism that has literally shut out the light, stopped the clocks, and made the forward movement of plot impossible. Satis House, as the circular journeys of the wheelchair to the rhythm of the blacksmith's song 'Old Clem' may best suggest, constitutes repetition without variation, pure reproduction, a collapsed metonymy where cause and effect have become identical, the same-as-same. It is significant that when Pip returns from his first visit to Satis House, he responds to the interrogations of Pumblechook and Mrs Joe with an elaborate lie – the story of the coach, the flags, the dogs fighting for 'weal cutlets' from a silver basket – a phantasy that we can read as his response to what he calls a 'smart without a name, that needed counteraction' (Chapter 8, p. 57). All the attempts to read Satis House as a text speaking of gentility and social ascension may be subverted from the outset, in the passage that describes Pip's first impression of Miss Havisham:

It was not in the first few moments that I saw all these things, though I saw more of them in the first moments than might be supposed. But, I saw that everything within my view which ought to be white, had been white long ago, and had lost its lustre, and was faded and yellow. I saw that the bride within the bridal dress had withered like the dress, and like the flowers, and had no brightness left but the brightness of her sunken eyes. I saw that the dress had been put upon the rounded figure of a young woman, and that the figure upon which it now hung loose, had shrunk to skin and bone. Once, I had been taken to see some ghastly waxwork at the Fair, representing I know not what impossible personage lying in state. Once, I had been taken to one of our old marsh churches to see a skeleton in the ashes of a rich dress, that had been dug out of a vault under the church pavement.

Now, waxwork and skeleton seemed to have dark eyes that moved
and looked at me. I should have cried out, if I could.

(Chapter 8, p. 53)

The passage records the formation of a memory trace from a moment of
unmastered horror, itself formed in repetition of moments of past visual
impression, a trace that forces its way through the mind without being
grasped by consciousness and is refused outlet in a cry. Much later in the
novel, Pip – and also Miss Havisham herself – will have to deal with the
return of this repressed.

We have, then, a quadripartite scheme of plots, organized into two
pairs, each with an 'official' plot, or interpretation of plot, standing over
a repressed plot. The scheme may lead us in the first instance to reflect
on the place of repression as one of the large 'orders' of the novel.
Repression plays a dominant role in the theme of education which is so
important to the novel, from Mrs Joe's bringing up by hand, through Mrs
Wopsle's aunt's schoolroom, to Mr Pocket's career as a 'grinder' of dull
blades (while his own children meanwhile are 'tumbling up'). Bringing
up by hand in turn suggests Jaggers's hands, representation of
accusation and the law, which in turn suggest all the instances of
censorship in the name of high authorities evoked from the first scene of
the novel onward: censorship is repression in the name of the Law.[5]
Jaggers's sinister hand-washings point to the omnipresent taint of
Newgate, which echoes the earlier presence of the Hulks, to which Mrs
Joe verbally assigns Pip. Then there is the moment when Pip is 'bound'
as apprentice blacksmith before the magistrates, in a scene of such
repressive appearance that a well-meaning philanthropist is moved to
hand Pip a pamphlet entitled *To Be Read in My Cell*. There is a constant
association of education, repression, the threat of prison, criminality, the
fear of deviance. We might note in passing Dickens's capacity to literalize
the metaphors of education – 'bringing up by hand,' 'grinding' – in a
manner that subverts the order that ought to assure their figural validity.
The particularly sinister version of the *Bildungsroman* presented by *Great
Expectations* derives in some measure from the literalization of metaphors
pertaining to education and upbringing. Societal repression and
censorship are, of course, reinforced by Pip's own, his internalization of
the law and the denial of what he calls the 'old taint' of his association
with the criminal. The whole theme of gentility, as represented by the
Finches of the Grove, for instance, or the punishment of Trabb's boy,
consistently suggests an aggressivity based on denial. One could reflect
here on the splendid name of Pip's superfluous valet: the Avenger.

The way in which the Expectations are instituted, in seeming
realization of the Satis House dream, comprehends 'bringing up by hand'
(the other official plot) in that it includes the disciplines necessary to

gentility: grinding with Mr Pocket, lessons in manners from Herbert, learning to spend one's time and money in appropriate gentlemanly pursuits. There is in this manner a blurring of plot lines, useful to the processes of wish fulfillment in that education and indeed repression itself can be interpreted as agencies necessary to the pursuit of the dream. Realization of the dream permits acceptance of society's interpretations, and in fact requires the abandonment of any effort at personal interpretation: Pip is now enjoined from seeking to know more about the intentions of his donor, disallowed the role of detective which so much animates him in Part 3 of the novel – when the Expectations have proved false – and is already incipiently present in Part 1.

Taking our terminology from the scene where Pip is bound as apprentice, we may consider that education and repression operate in the novel as one form of 'binding': official ways of channeling and tying up the mobile energies of life. It is notable that after he has become apprenticed to Joe, Pip goes through a stage of purely iterative existence – presented in Chapter 14 – where the direction and movement of plot appear to be finished, where all life's 'interest and romance' appear shut out as by a 'thick curtain,' time reduced to repetitive duration. Conversely, when the Expectations have arrived, Miss Havisham is apparently identified as the fairy-tale donor, and the Satis House plot appears securely bound, Pip need only wait for the next stage of the plot to become manifest. Yet it is clear that for the reader neither binding as an apprentice (the first accomplishment of an upbringing by hand) nor the tying up of Satis House as a fairy-tale plot constitutes valid and adequate means of dealing with the disposing of the communion with the convict and the nightmare of Satis House. The energy released in the text by its liminary 'primal scene' – in the graveyard – and by the early visits to Satis House, creating that 'smart without a name,' simply is not and cannot be bound by the bindings of the official, repressive plots. As readers we know that there has been created in the text an intensive level of energy that cannot be discharged through these official plots.

In fact, the text has been working simultaneously to bind these disavowed energies in other ways, ways over which Pip's ego, and the societal superego, have no control, and of which they have no knowledge, through repetitions that, for the reader, prepare an inevitable return of the repressed. Most striking are the periodic fragmentary returns of the convict-communion material: the leg iron used to bludgeon Mrs Joe, guns firing from the Hulks to signal further escapes, and especially the reappearance of Joe's file, the dramatic stage property used by Magwitch's emissary in a 'proceeding in dumb show . . . pointedly addressed at me.' His stirring and tasting his rum and water 'pointedly at' Pip suggests the establishment of an aim (Pip calls his proceeding 'a shot'), a direction, an intention in Pip's life: the first covert announcement of another plot which will come to govern Pip's life, but of course misinterpreted as to its true aim. With the nightmare energies of Satis House, binding may be at work in those repetitive journeys around the rotting bridal cake, suggestive of the reproduction or working through of the traumatic neurotic whose affects remain fixed on the past, on the traumatic moment that never can be mastered. For Miss Havisham herself, these energies can never be plotted to effective discharge; and we will have occasion to doubt whether they are ever fully bound for Pip as well. The compulsive reproductive repetition that characterizes every detail of Satis House lets us perceive how the returns of the convict-communion suggest a more significant working through of an unmastered past, a repetition that can alter the form of the repeated. In both instances – but ultimately with different results – the progressive, educative plots, the plots of repression and social advancement, are threatened by a repetitive process obscurely going on underneath and beyond them. We sense that forward progress will have to recover markings from the beginning through a dialectic of return.

II

In my references to the work of repetition as the binding of energies, I have been implicitly assuming that one can make a transfer from the model of psychic functioning proposed in *Beyond the Pleasure Principle* to the literary text, an assumption that no doubt can never be 'proved' and must essentially find its justification in the illumination it can bring to texts. We saw in Chapter 2 that texts represent themselves as inhabited by energies, which are ultimately images of desire, and correspond to the arousals, expectations, doubts, suspense, reversals, revaluations, disappointments, embarrassments, fulfillments, and even the incoherences animated by reading. If we can accept the idea of a textual energetics, we can see that in any well-plotted novel the energies released and aroused in the text, especially in its early moments, will not be lost: the text is a kind of thermodynamic plenum, obeying the law of the conservation of energy (as well, no doubt, as the law of entropy). Repetition is clearly a major operative principle of the system, shaping energy, giving it perceptible form, form that the text and the reader can work with in the construction of thematic wholes and narrative orders. Repetition conceived as binding, the creation of cohesion – see the French translation of Freud's *Verbindung: liaison*, a word we would commonly use in the description of discourse and argument – may allow us to see how the text and the reader put energy into forms where it can be mastered, both by the logics set in motion by the plot, and by interpretive effort.

Repetition is, of course, a complex phenomenon, and one that has its history of commentary in philosophical as well as psychoanalytic thought. Is repetition sameness or difference? To repeat evidently implies resemblance, yet can we speak of resemblance unless there is difference? Without difference, repetition would be identity, which would not usually appear to be the case, if only because the chronological context of the repeated occurrence differs from that of the 'original' occurrence (the 'original' is thus a concept that repetition puts into question). In this sense, repetition always includes the idea of variation in time, and may ever be potentially a progressive act. As **Kierkegaard** writes near the beginning of *Repetition*, 'Repetition and recollection are the same movement, only in opposite directions; for what is recollected has been, is repeated backwards, whereas repetition properly is repeated forwards.'[6] Freud, as we noted, considers repetition to be a form of recollection, brought into play when conscious mental rememoration has been blocked by repression. Lacan argues that Freud distinguishes between repeating (*wiederholen*) and reproducing (*reproduzieren*): reproduction would be the full reliving, of the original traumatic scene, for instance, that Freud aimed at early in his career, when he still believed in 'catharsis'; whereas repetition always takes place in the realm of the symbolic – in the transference, in language – where the affects and figures of the past are confronted in symbolic form.[7] We can thus perhaps say that for Freud repetition is a symbolic enactment referring back to unconscious determinants, progressive in that it belongs to the forward thrust of desire and is known by way of desire's workings in the signifying chain, but regressive in its points of reference.

We cannot and should not attempt to reduce and resolve the ambiguities of repetition since they are indeed inherent to our experience of repetition, part of what creates its 'uncanny' effect and allows us to think about the intractable problem of temporal form, in our lives and in our fictions. In *Great Expectations*, the repetitions associated with Satis House, particularly as played out by Miss Havisham herself, suggest the reproductive in that they aim to restore in all its detail the traumatic moment – recorded by the clocks stopped at twenty minutes to nine – when erotic wishes were abruptly foreclosed by Compeyson's rupture of faith. On the other hand, the repetitions of the convict material experienced by Pip all imply something to come – something to come that, as we shall see, will take him back, painfully, to the primal scene, yet take him back in the context of difference. Repetition in the text is a return, a calling back or a turning back. And as I suggested earlier, repetitions are thus both returns to and returns of: for instance, returns to origins and returns of the repressed, moving us forward in Pip's journey toward elucidation, disillusion, and maturity by taking us back, as if in obsessive reminder that we cannot really move ahead until we have understood that still enigmatic past, yet ever pushing us forward, since revelation, tied to the past, belongs to the future.

The novelistic middle, which is perhaps the most difficult of Aristotle's 'parts' of a plot to talk about, is in this case notably characterized by the return. Quite literally: it is Pip's repeated returns from London to his home town that constitute the organizing device of the whole of the London period, the time of the Expectations and their aftermath. Pip's returns are always ostensibly undertaken to make reparation to the neglected Joe, an intention never realized; and always implicitly an attempt to discover the intentions of the putative donor in Satis House, to bring her plot to completion. Yet the returns also always bring his regression, in Satis House, to the status of the 'coarse and common boy' (Chapter 29, p. 222) whose social ascension is hallucinatorily denied, his return to the nightmare of unprogressive repetition; and, too, a revival of the repressed convict association, the return of the childhood spell. Each return suggests that Pip's official plots, which seem to speak of progress, ascent, and the satisfaction of desire, are in fact subject to a process of repetition of the yet unmastered past, the true determinant of his life's direction.

The pattern of the return is established in Pip's first journey back from London, in Chapter 28. His decision to visit Joe is quickly thrown into the shade by the presence on the stagecoach of two convicts, one of whom Pip recognizes as the man of the file and the rum and water, Magwitch's emissary. There is a renewed juxtaposition of official, genteel judgment on the convicts, voiced by Herbert Pocket – 'What a vile and degraded spectacle' – and Pip's inward avowal that he feels sympathy for their alienation. On the roof of the coach, seated in front of the convicts, Pip dozes off while pondering whether he ought to restore the two one-pound notes that the convict of the file had passed him so many years before. Upon regaining consciousness, the first two words he hears, continuing his dream thoughts, are 'Two one-pound notes.' There follows the convict's account of his embassy from 'Pip's convict' to the boy who had saved him. Although Pip is certain that the convict cannot recognize him, so changed in age, circumstance, and even name (since Herbert calls him 'Handel'), the dreamlike experience forces a kind of recognition of a forgotten self, refound in fear and pain:

> I could not have said what I was afraid of, for my fear was altogether undefined and vague, but there was great fear upon me. As I walked on to the hotel, I felt that a dread, much exceeding the mere apprehension of a painful or disagreeable recognition, made me tremble. I am confident that it took no distinctness of shape, and that it was the revival for a few minutes of the terror of childhood.
>
> (Chapter 28, p. 217)

The return to origins has led to the return of the repressed, and vice versa. Repetition as return becomes a reproduction and re-enactment of infantile experience: not simply a recall of the primal moment, but a reliving of its pain and terror, suggesting the impossibility of escape from the originating scenarios of childhood, the condemnation forever to replay them.

This first example may stand for the other returns of the novel's middle, which all follow the same pattern, which all double return to with return of and slow Pip's ostensible progress in the world to be subverted by the irradicable presence of the convict-communion and the Satis House nightmare. It is notable that toward the end of the middle – as the novel's dénouement approaches – there is an acceleration in the rhythm of these returns, as if to affirm that all the clues to Pip's future, the forward movement of his plot, in fact lie in the past. Repetition as return speaks as a textual version of the death instinct, plotting the text, beyond the seeming dominance of the pleasure principle, toward its proper end, imaging this end as necessarily a time before the beginning. In the moment of crisis before the climax of the novel's action, Pip is summoned back to the marshes associated with his infancy to face extinction at the hands of Orlick – who has throughout the novel acted the role of Pip's 'bad double,' a hateful and sadistic version of the hero – in a threatened short-circuit of the text, as Pip indicates when he thinks how he will be misunderstood by others if he dies prematurely, without explanation: 'Misremembered after death . . . despised by unborn generations' (Chapter 53, p. 404).[8] Released from this threat, Pip attempts to escape from England, but even this voyage out to another land and another life leads him back: the climax of Magwitch's discovery and recapture are played out in the Thames estuary, where 'it was like my own marsh country, flat and monotonous, and with a dim horizon' (Chapter 54, p. 416). We are back in the horizontal perspectives and muddy tidal flats that are so much a part of our perception of the childhood Pip.

But before speaking further of resolutions, I must say a word about the novel's great 'recognition scene,' the moment at which the latent becomes manifest, the repressed convict plot is forcibly brought to consciousness, a scene that decisively re-enacts both a return of the repressed and a return to the primal moment of childhood. The recognition scene comes in Chapter 39, and it is preceded by two curious paragraphs at the end of Chapter 38 in which Pip as narrator suggests that the pages he has just written, concerning his frustrated courtship of Estella, constitute, on the plane of narration itself, a last binding of that plot in its overt version, as a plot of romance, and that now he must move on to a deeper level of plot – reaching further back – which subsumes as it subverts all the other plots of the novel: 'All the work, near and afar, that tended to the end had been accomplished.' That this long-range plot is presented as analogous to 'the Eastern story' in which a heavy slab of stone is carved out and fitted into the roof in order that it may fall on 'the bed of state in the flush of conquest' seems in coded fashion to suggest punishment for erotic transgression, which we may want to read as return of the nightmare plot of Satis House, forcing its way through the fairy tale, speaking of the perverse, sadistic eroticism that Pip has covered over with his erotic object choice – Estella, who in fact represents the wrong choice of plot and another danger of short-circuit. To anticipate later revelations, we should note that Estella will turn out to be approximately Pip's sister – natural daughter of Magwitch as he is Magwitch's adoptive son – which lends force to the idea that she, like so many Romantic maidens, is marked by the interdict, as well as the seduction, of incest, which, as the perfect androgynous coupling, is precisely the short-circuit of desire.[9]

The scene of Magwitch's return operates for Pip as a painful forcing through of layers of repression, an analogue of analytic work, compelling Pip to recognize that what he calls 'that chance encounter of long ago' is no chance, and cannot be assigned to the buried past but must be repeated, re-enacted, worked through in the present. The scene replays numerous details of their earlier encounter, and the central moment of recognition comes as a re-enactment and revival of the novel's primal scene, played in dumb show, a mute text which the more effectively stages recognition as a process of return to the inescapable past:

> Even yet I could not recall a single feature, but I knew him! If the wind and the rain had driven away the intervening years, had scattered all the intervening objects, had swept us to the churchyard where we first stood face to face on such different levels, I could not have known my convict more distinctly than I knew him now, as he sat in the chair before the fire. No need to take a file from his pocket and show it to me; no need to take the handkerchief from his neck and twist it round his head; no need to hug himself with both his arms, and take a shivering turn across the room, looking back at me for recognition. I knew him before he gave me one of those aids, though, a moment before, I had not been conscious of remotely suspecting his identity.
>
> (Chapter 39, p. 301)

The praeterition on which the passage is constructed – 'no need . . . no need' – marks the gradual retrieval of the past as its involuntary repetition within the present. The repetition takes place – as Magwitch's effective use of indicative signs may suggest – in the mode of the symbolic, offering a persuasive instance of Freud's conception of repetition as a form of recollection brought into action by repression and resistance to its removal. It becomes clear that the necessity for Pip to repeat and work through everything associated with his original communion with Magwitch is a factor of his 'forgetting' this communion: a forgetting that is merely conscious. The reader has undergone a similar process through textual repetition and return, one that in his case has had the function of not permitting him to forget.

The scene of Magwitch's return is an important one for any study of plot since it demonstrates so well how such a novelist as Dickens can make plotting the central vehicle and armature of meaning in the narrative text. All the issues raised in the novel – social, ethical, interpretive – are here simultaneously brought to climax through the peripety of the plot. Exposure of the 'true' plot of Pip's life brings with it instantaneous consequences for all the other 'codes' of the novel, as he recognizes with the statement, 'All the truth of my position came *flashing* on me; and its disappointments, dangers, disgraces, consequences of all kinds' (Chapter 39, p. 303 – my italics). The return of the repressed – the repressed as knowledge of the self's other story, the true history of its misapprehended desire – forces a total revision of the subject's relation to the orders within which it constitutes meaning.

Magwitch poses unanswerable questions, about the origins of Pip's property and the means of his social ascent, which force home to Pip that he has covered over a radical lack of original authority. Like Oedipus – who cannot answer Tiresias's final challenge: who are your parents? – Pip does not know where he stands. The result has been the intrusion of an aberrant, contingent authorship – Magwitch's – in the story of the self. Education and training in gentility turn out to be merely an agency in the repression of the determinative convict plot. Likewise, the daydream/fairy tale of Satis House stands revealed as a repression, or perhaps a 'secondary revision,' of the nightmare. That it should be the criminally deviant, transgressive plot that is shown to have priority over all the others stands within the logic of the model derived from *Beyond the Pleasure Principle*, since it is precisely this plot that most markedly constitutes the detour from inorganic quiescence: the arabesque of the narratable. One could almost derive a narratological law here: the true plot will be the most deviant. We might be tempted to see this deviant arabesque as gratuitous, the figure of 'pure narration.' Yet we are obliged to remotivate it, for the return of the repressed shows that the story Pip would tell about himself has all along been undermined and rewritten by the more complex history of unconscious desire, unavailable to the conscious subject but at work in the text. Pip has in fact misread the plot of his life.

III

The misreading of plots and the question of authority brings us back to the question of reading with which the novel began. Pip's initial attempt

to decipher his parents' appearance and character from the letters traced
on their tombstones has been characterized as 'childish' and
'unreasonable.' Pip's decipherment in fact appears as an attempt to
motivate the arbitrary sign, to interpret signs as if they were mimetic and
thus naturally tied to the object for which they stand. Deriving from the
shape of the letters on the tombstones that his father 'was a square,
stout, dark man, with curly hair,' and that his mother was 'freckled and
sickly,' for all its literal fidelity to the graphic trace, constitutes a
dangerously figural reading, a metaphorical process unaware of itself,
the making of a fiction unaware of its status as fiction making. Pip is here
claiming natural authority for what is in fact conventional, arbitrary,
dependent on interpretation.

The question of texts, reading, and interpretation is, as we earlier
noted, consistently thematized in the novel: in Pip's learning to read
(using that meager text, Mrs Wopsle's aunt's catalogue of prices), and his
attempts to transmit the art of writing to Joe; the expressive dumb shows
between Pip and Joe; messages written on the slate, by Pip to Joe, and
then (in minimum symbolic form) by the aphasic Mrs Joe; the uncanny
text of Estella's visage, always reminding Pip of a repetition of something
else which he cannot identify; Molly's wrists, cross-hatched with
scratches, a text for the judge, and eventually for Pip as detective, to
decipher; Mr Wopsle's declamations of *George Barnwell* and *Richard III*.
The characters appear to be ever on the watch for ways in which to
textualize the world, so that they can give their readings of it: a situation
thematized early in the novel, at the Christmas dinner table, as
Pumblechook and Wopsle criticize the sermon of the day and propose
other 'subjects':

> Mr Pumblechook added, after a short interval of reflection, 'Look at
> Pork alone. There's a subject! If you want a subject, look at Pork!'
> 'True, sir. Many a moral for the young,' returned Mr Wopsle; and I
> knew he was going to lug me in, before he said it, 'might be deduced
> from that text.'
> ('You listen to this,' said my sister to me, in a severe parenthesis.)
> Joe gave me some more gravy.
> 'Swine,' pursued Mr Wopsle, in his deepest voice, and pointing his
> fork at my blushes, as if he were mentioning my christian name,
> 'Swine were the companions of the prodigal. The gluttony of Swine is
> put before us, as an example to the young.'(I thought this pretty well
> in him who had been praising up the pork for being so plump and
> juicy.) 'What is detestable in a pig, is more detestable in a boy.'
> 'Or girl,' suggested Mr Hubble.
> 'Of course, or girl, Mr Hubble,' assented Mr Wopsle, rather irritably,
> 'but there is no girl present.'

'Besides,' said Mr Pumblechook, turning sharp on me, 'think what you've got to be grateful for. If you'd been born a Squeaker – '

'He *was*, if ever a child was,' said my sister, most emphatically.

Joe gave me some more gravy.

'Well, but I mean a four-footed Squeaker,' said Mr Pumblechook. 'If you had been born such, would you have been here now? Not you – '

'Unless in that form,' said Mr Wopsle, nodding towards the dish.

(Chapter 4, p. 23–4)

The scene suggests a mad proliferation of textuality, where literal and figural switch places, where any referent can serve as an interpretant, become the sign of another message, in a wild process of semiosis which seems to be anchored only insofar as all texts eventually speak of Pip himself as an unjustified presence, a presence demanding interpretation.

The novel constantly warns us that texts may have no unambiguous referent and no transcendent signified. Of the many examples one might choose in illustration of the status of texts and their interpretation in the novel, perhaps the most telling is the case of Mr Wopsle. Mr Wopsle, the church clerk, is a frustrated preacher, ever intimating that if the church were to be 'thrown open,' he would really 'give it out.' This hypothetical case never coming to realization, Mr Wopsle is obliged to content himself with the declamation of a number of secular texts, from Shakespeare to Collins's ode. The church indeed remains resolutely closed (we never in fact hear the word of the preacher in the novel, only Mr Wopsle's critique of it), and Mr Wopsle 'has a fall': into play-acting. He undertakes the repetition of fictional texts which lack the authority of that divine word he would like to 'give out.' We next see him playing *Hamlet*, which is of course the text par excellence about usurpation, parricide, lost regal authority, and wrong relations of transmission from generation to generation. Something of the problematic status of textual authority is suggested in Mr Wopsle's rendition of the classic soliloquy:

Whenever that undecided Prince had to ask a question or state a doubt, the public helped him out with it. As for example: on the question whether 'twas nobler in the mind to suffer, some roared yes, and some no, and some inclining to both opinions said 'toss up for it'; and quite a Debating Society arose.

(Chapter 31, p. 240)

From this uncertainty, Mr Wopsle has a further fall, into playing what was known as 'nautical melodrama,' an anonymously authored theater played to a vulgar public in the Surreyside houses. When Pip attends this performance, there occurs a curious mirroring and reversal of the spectacle, where Mr Wopsle himself becomes the spectator, fascinated by the vision, in the audience, of what he calls a 'ghost' from the past – the face of the novel's hidden arch-plotter, Compeyson. The vision leads to a reconstruction of the chase and capture of the convicts, from the early chapters of the novel, a kind of analytic dialogue in the excavation of the past, where Mr Wopsle repeatedly questions: 'You remember?' and Pip replies: 'I remember it very well . . . I see it all before me.' This reconstruction produces an intense visual, hallucinatory reliving of a charged past moment:

> 'And you remember that we came up with the two in a ditch, and that there was a scuffle between them, and that one of them had been severely handled and much mauled about the face, by the other?'
> 'I see it all before me.'
> 'And that the soldiers lighted torches, and put the two in the centre, and that we went on to see the last of them, over the black marshes, with the torchlight shining on their faces – I am particular about that; with the torchlight shining on their faces, when there was an outer ring of dark night all about us?'
>
> (Chapter 47, p. 365)

By an apparently gratuitous free association, from Mr Wopsle's play-acting, as from behind a screen memory, emerges a drama on that 'other stage': the stage of dream, replaying a past moment that the characters have never exorcized, that moment of the buried yet living past which insists on repeating itself in the present.

Mr Wopsle's career as a whole may exemplify a general movement in the novel toward recognition of the lack of authorship and authority in texts: textures of codes without ultimate referent or hierarchy, signs cut loose from their apparent motivation, capable of wandering toward multiple associations and of evoking messages that are entirely other, and that all speak eventually of determinative histories from the past. The original nostalgia for a founding divine word leads to a generalized scene of writing, as if the plotting self could never discover a decisive plot, but merely its own arbitrary role as plotmaker. Yet the arbitrary is itself subject to an unconscious determinant, the reproductive insistence of the past history.

Mr Wopsle's career may stand as a figure for Pip's. Whereas the model of the *Bildungsroman* seems to imply progress, a leading forth, and developmental change, Pip's story – and this may be true of other nineteenth-century educative plots as well – becomes more and more as it nears its end the working through of past history, an attempted return to the origin as the motivation of all the rest, the clue to what must else appear, as Pip puts it to Miss Havisham, a 'blind and thankless' life (Chapter 49, p. 377). The past needs to be incorporated *as past* within the present, mastered through the play of repetition in order for there to be an escape from repetition: in order for there to be difference, change, progress. In the failure ever to recover his own origin, Pip comes to concern himself with the question of Estella's origin, searching for her patronymics where knowledge of his own is ever foreclosed. Estella's story in fact eventually links all the plots of the novel: Satis House, the aspiration to gentility, the convict identity, 'naterally wicious' (the status from which Jaggers rescued her), bringing up by hand, the law. Pip's investigation of her origins as substitute for knowledge of his own has a certain validity in that, we discover, he appeared originally to Magwitch as a substitute for the lost Estella, his great expectations a compensation for the impossibility of hers: a chiasmus of the true situation. Yet when Pip has proved himself to be the successful detective in this quest, when he has uncovered the convergence of lines of plot that previously appeared distinct and indeed proved himself more penetrating even than Jaggers, he discovers the knowledge he has gained to be radically unusable. When he has imparted his knowledge to Jaggers and Wemmick, he reaches a kind of standoff between what he has called his 'poor dreams' and the deep plot he has now exposed. As Jaggers puts it to him, there is no gain to be had from knowledge. We are in the heart of darkness, and the articulation of its meaning must simply be repressed. In this novel full of mysteries and hidden connections, detective work turns out to be both necessary and useless. It can offer no comfort and no true illumination to the detective himself. Like deciphering the letters on the tombstone, it produces no authority for the plot of life.

The novel in fact toward its end appears to record a generalized breakdown of plots: none of the schemes machinated by the characters manages to accomplish its aims. The proof *a contrario* may be the 'oversuccessful' result of Miss Havisham's plot, which has turned Estella into so heartless a creature that she cannot even experience emotional recognition of her benefactress. Miss Havisham's plotting has been a mechanical success but an intentional failure, as her final words, during her delirium following the fire, may suggest:

> Towards midnight she began to wander in her speech, and after that it gradually set in that she said innumerable times in a low solemn voice, 'What have I done?' And then, 'When she first came, I meant to save her from misery like mine.' And then, 'Take the pencil and write under my name, "I forgive her"!' She never changed the order of these three sentences, but she sometimes left out a word in one or other of them; never putting in another word, but always leaving a blank and going on to the next word.
>
> (Chapter 49, p. 381–2)

The cycle of three statements suggests a metonymic movement in search of arrest, a plot that can never find satisfactory resolution, that unresolved must play over its insistent repetitions, until silenced by death. Miss Havisham's deathbed scene transmits a 'wisdom' that is in the deconstructive mode, a warning against plot.

We confront the paradox that in this most highly plotted of novels, where Dickens performs all his thematic demonstrations through the manipulation of plot, we witness an evident subversion and futilization of the very concept of plot. If the chosen plots turn out to be erroneous, unauthorized, self-delusive, the deep plots when brought to light turn out to be criminally tainted, deviant, and thus unusable. Plot as direction and intention in existence appears ultimately to be as evanescent as Magwitch's money, the product of immense labor, deprivation, and planning, which is in the end forfeit to the Crown. Like money in its role as universal modern (capitalist) signifier as described by Roland Barthes in *S/Z*, tied to no referent (such as land), defined only by its exchange value, capable of unlimited metonymic circulation, the expectations of fortune, as both plot and its aim or intention, as vehicle and object of representation, circulate through inflation to devaluation.

The ultimate situation of plot in the novel may suggest an approach to the vexed question of Dickens's two endings to the novel: the one he originally wrote and the revision (substituted at Bulwer Lytton's suggestion) that was in fact printed. I think it is entirely legitimate to prefer the original ending, with its flat tone and refusal of romantic expectation, and find that the revision, with its tentative promise of reunion between Pip and Estella, 'unbinds' energies that we thought had been thoroughly bound and indeed discharged from the text. We may also feel that choice between the two endings is somewhat arbitrary and unimportant in that the decisive moment has already occurred before either of these finales begins. The real ending may take place with Pip's recognition and acceptance of Magwitch after his recapture – this is certainly the ethical dénouement – and his acceptance of a continuing existence without plot, as celibate clerk for Clarrikers. The pages that follow may simply be *obiter dicta*.

If we acknowledge Pip's experience of and with Magwitch to be the central energy of the text, it is significant that the climax of this experience, the moment of crisis and reversal in the attempted escape from England, bears traces of a hallucinatory repetition of the childhood spell – indeed, of that first recapture of Magwitch already repeated in Mr Wopsle's theatrical vision:

> In the same moment, I saw the steersman of the galley lay his hand on the prisoner's shoulder, and saw that both boats were swinging round with the force of the tide, and saw that all hands on board the steamer

were running forward quite frantically. Still in the same moment, I saw
the prisoner start up, lean across his captor, and pull the cloak from
the neck of the shrinking sitter in the galley. Still in the same moment,
I saw that the face disclosed was the face of the other convict of long
ago. Still in the same moment, I saw the face tilt backward with a
white terror on it that I shall never forget, and heard a great cry on
board the steamer and a loud splash in the water, and felt the boat sink
from under me.

(Chapter 54, pp. 421–2)

If this scene marks the beginning of a resolution – which it does in that it
brings the death of the arch-villain Compeyson and the death sentence
for Magwitch, hence the disappearance from the novel of its most
energetic plotters – it is resolution in the register of repetition and
working through, the final effort to master painful material from the
insistent past. Pip emerges from this scene with an acceptance of the
determinative past as both determinative and as *past*, which prepares us
for the final escape *from* plot. It is interesting to note that where the
'dream' plot of Estella is concerned, Pip's stated resolution has none of
the compulsive energetic force of the passage just quoted, but is rather a
conventional romantic fairy-tale ending, a conscious fiction designed, of
course, to console the dying Magwitch, but possibly also a last effort at
self-delusion: 'You had a child once, whom you loved and lost. . . . She
lived and found powerful friends. She is living now. She is a lady and
very beautiful. And I love her!' (Chapter 56, p. 436). If taken as anything
other than a conscious fiction – if taken as part of the 'truth' discovered
by Pip's detections – this version of Pip's experience leads straight to
what is most troubling in Dickens's revised version of the ending: the
suggestion of an unbinding of what has already been bound up and
disposed of, an unbinding that is indeed perceptible in the rather
embarrassed prose with which the revision begins: 'Nevertheless, I knew
while I said these words, that I secretly intended to revisit the site of the
old house that evening alone, for her sake. Yes, even so. For Estella's
sake' (Chapter 59, p. 458). Are we to understand that the experience of
Satis House has never really been mastered? Is its nightmare energy still
present in the text as well? The original end may have an advantage in
denying to Pip's text the possibility of any reflux of energy, any new
aspirations, the undoing of anything already done, the unbinding of
energy that has been bound and led to discharge.

As at the start of the novel we had the impression of a life not yet
subject to plot – a life in search of the sense of plot that would only
gradually begin to precipitate around it – so at the end we have the
impression of a life that has outlived plot, renounced plot, been cured of
it: life that is left over. What follows the recognition of Magwitch is left

over, and any renewal of expectation and plotting – such as a revived romance with Estella – would have to belong to another story. It is with the image of a life bereft of plot, of movement and desire, that the novel most appropriately leaves us. Indeed, we have at the end what could appropriately be called a 'cure' from plot, in Pip's recognition of the general forfeiture of plotting, his renunciation of any attempt to direct his life. Plot comes to resemble a diseased, fevered state of the organism caught in the machinery of a desire which must eventually be renounced. Plot, we come to understand, was a state of abnormality or deviance, suggested thematically by its uneasy position between Newgate and Old Bailey, between criminality and the law. The nineteenth-century novel in general – and especially that highly symptomatic development, the detective story – regularly conceives plot as a condition of deviance and abnormality, the product of cities and social depths, of a world where *récit* is *complot*, where all stories are the result of plotting, and plotting is very much machination. Deviance is the very condition for life to be 'narratable': the state of normality is devoid of interest, energy, and the possibility for narration. In between a beginning prior to plot and an end beyond plot, the middle – the plotted text – has been in a state of *error*: wandering and misinterpretation.

IV

That plot should prove to be deviance and error is fully consonant with Freud's model in *Beyond the Pleasure Principle*, where the narratable life of the organism is seen as detour, a deviance from the quiescence of the inorganic which has been maintained through the dynamic interaction of Eros and the death instinct. What Pip at one point has called his 'ill-regulated aspirations' (Chapter 29, p. 223) is the figure of plot as desire: Eros as the force that binds integers together in ever-larger wholes, totalising, metaphoric, the desire for possesion of the world and for the integration of meaning – whereas, concomitantly, repetition and return have spoken of the death instinct, the drive to return to the quiescence of the inorganic, of the nontextual. Yet the repetitions, which have served to bind the various plots, both prolonging the detour and more effectively preparing the final discharge, have created that delay necessary to incorporate the past within the present and to let us understand end in relation to beginning. Through the erotics of the text, we have inexorably been led to its end, which is precisely quiescence: a time after which is an image of the time before. We have reached the non-narratable. Adducing the argument of 'Remembering, Repeating and Working Through' to that of *Beyond the Pleasure Principle*, we perceive that repetition is a kind of remembering, and thus a way of reorganizing a story whose connective links have been obscured and lost. If repetition speaks of the death instinct, the finding of the right end, then what is being played out in repetition is necessarily the proper vector of the drive toward the end. That is, once you have determined the right plot, plot is over. Plot itself is working-through.

Great Expectations is exemplary in demonstrating both the need for plot and its status as deviance, both the need for narration and the necessity to be cured from it. The deviance and error of plot may necessarily result from the interplay of desire in its history with the narrative insistence on explanatory form: the desire to wrest beginnings and ends from the uninterrupted flow of middles, from temporality itself; the search for that significant closure that would illuminate the sense of an existence, the meaning of life. The desire for meaning is ultimately the reader's, who must mime Pip's acts of reading but do them better. Both using and subverting the systems of meaning discovered or postulated by its hero, *Great Expectations* exposes for its reader the very reading process itself: the way the reader goes about finding meaning in the narrative text, and the limits of that meaning as the limits of narrative.

In terms of the problematic of reading which the novel thematizes from its opening page, we could say that Pip, continuously returning toward origins in order to know the plot whose authority would lead him to the right end but never recovering origins and never finding the authoritative plot, never succeeds in going behind his self-naming to a reading of the missing patronymic. He is ever returned to a rereading of the unauthorized text of his self-given name, Pip. 'Pip' sounded like a beginning, a seed. But, of course, when you reach the end of the name 'Pip,' you can return backward, and it is just the same: a repetitive text without variation or point of fixity, a return that leads to an unarrested shuttling back and forth. The name is in fact a palindrome. In the rereading of the palindrome the novel may offer its final comment on its expectative plot.

What, finally, do we make of the fact that Dickens, master-plotter in the history of the novel, in this most tightly and consistently plotted of his novels seems to expose plot as a kind of necessary error? Dickens's most telling comment on the question may come at the moment of Magwitch's sentencing. The judge gives a legalistic and moralistic version of Magwitch's life story, his violence, his crimes, the passions that made him a 'scourge to society' and led him to escape from deportation, thus calling upon his head the death sentence. The passage continues:

> The sun was striking in at the great windows of the court, through the glittering drops of rain upon the glass, and it made a broad shaft of light between the two-and-thirty [prisoners at the bar] and the Judge, linking both together, and perhaps reminding some among the

audience, how both were passing on, with absolute equality, to the greater Judgment that knoweth all things and cannot err. Rising for a moment, a distinct speck of face in this way of light, the prisoner [Magwitch] said, 'My Lord, I have received my sentence of Death from the Almighty, but I bow to yours,' and sat down again. There was some hushing, and the Judge went on with what he had to say to the rest.

(Chapter 56, p. 434)

The passage is sentimental but also, I think, effective. It juxtaposes human plots – including those of the law – to eternal orders that render human attempts to plot, and to interpret plot, not only futile but ethically unacceptable. The greater Judgment makes human plots mere shadows. There is another end that recuperates passing human time, and its petty chronologies, to the timeless. Yet despite the narrator's affirmations, this other end is not visible, the other orders are not available. As Mr Wopsle's case suggested, the divine word is barred in the world of the novel (it is suggestive that Christmas dinner is interrupted by the command to repair handcuffs). If there is a divine masterplot for human existence, it is radically unknowable.

In the absence or silence of divine masterplots, the organization and interpretation of human plots remains as necessary as it is problematic. Reading the signs of intention in life's actions is the central act of existence, which in turn legitimizes the enterprise of reading for the reader of *Great Expectations* – or perhaps, vice versa, since the reading of plot within the text and as the text are perfectly analogous, mirrors of one another. If there is by the end of the narrative an abandonment of the attempt to read plot, this simply mirrors the fact that the process of narration has come to a close – or, again, vice versa. But that there should be a cure from the reading of plot within the text – before its very end – and the creation of a leftover, suggests a critique of reading itself, which is possibly like the judge's sentence: human interpretation in ignorance of the true vectors of the true text. So it may indeed be: the *savoir* proposed by Balzac's antique dealer is not *in* the text. But if the mastertext is not available, we are condemned to the reading of erroneous plots, granted insight only insofar as we can gain disillusion from them. We are condemned to repetition, rereading, in the knowledge that what we discover will always be that there was nothing to be discovered. Yet the process remains necessary if we are not to be caught perpetually in the 'blind and thankless' existence, in the illusory middle. Like Oedipus, like Pip, we are condemned to reinterpretation of our names. But it is rare that the name coincide so perfectly with a fullness and a negation of identity as in the case of Oedipus. In a post-tragic universe, our situation is more likely to be that of Pip, compelled to reinterpret the meaning of the name he assigned to himself with his infant tongue, the history of an infinitely repeatable palindrome.

Notes

1. CHARLES DICKENS, *Great Expectations* (London: Oxford University Press, 1975), p. 1. References are to this edition, and will hereafter be given in parentheses in the text. Chapter numbers are included to facilitate reference to other editions.

2. On the theme of reading in the novel, see MAX BYRD, ' "Reading" in *Great Expectations*', *PMLA*, **91**, No. 2 (1976), pp. 259–65.

3. On the archaeological model in Freud, see in particular the use he makes of Pompeii in 'Delusions and Dreams in Jensen's *Gradiva*' [*Der Wahn und die Träume in W. Jensens* Gradiva] (1907) in *The Standard Edition of the Complete Psychological Works of Sigmund Freud*, ed. James Strachey (London: Hogarth Press, 1953–74), Vol. 9, pp. 3–95.

4. See *Great Expectations*, Chap. 19, p. 149. Miss Havisham is thus seemingly cast in the role of the 'Donor', who provides the hero with a magical agent, one of the seven *dramatis personae* of the fairy tale identified by Vladimir Propp in *The Morphology of the Folktale*.

5. On the role of the law as one of the formal orders of the novel, see MOSHE RON, 'Autobiographical Narration and Formal Closure in *Great Expectations*', *Hebrew University Studies in Literature*, **5**, No. 1 (1977), pp. 37–66. The importance of criminality in Dickens has, of course, been noted by many critics, including Edmund Wilson in his seminal essay 'Dickens: The Two Scrooges', in *The Wound and the Bow* (Boston: Houghton Mifflin, 1941).

6. SØREN KIERKEGAARD, *Repetition*, trans. Walter Lowrie (Princeton, NJ: Princeton University Press, 1941), pp. 3–4. For other discussions of repetition in literature, see GILLES DELEUZE, *Logique du sens* (Paris: Editions de Minuit, 1969); J. HILLIS MILLER, *Fiction and Repetition* (Cambridge: Harvard University Press, 1982).

7. See FREUD, 'The Dynamics of the Transference' and 'Remembering, Repeating and Working Through', in *Standard Edition*, Vol. 12; JACQUES LACAN, *Le Séminaire, Livre XI: Les Quatre Concepts fondamentaux de la psychoanalyse* (Paris: Editions du Seuil, 1973), pp. 49–50.

8. This scene with Orlick brings to the surface much of the aggressivity latent in the novel, aggressivity that is attributed to Orlick, but may in some sense emanate from Pip himself, as Orlick seems to imply when he repeatedly calls Pip 'wolf' and argues that Pip was really responsible for Orlick's bludgeoning of Mrs Joe. One could make a case for conferring greater interpretive importance on this scene, as is done by Teresa Grant in her excellent essay 'Story *vs.* Discourse: A Dialectical Perspective' (unpublished MS, University of Texas, Austin), which in part takes issue with some of the emphases of an earlier version of the present chapter, published in *New Literary History*, **11**, No. 3 (1980). Yet Brooks is not convinced that Orlick 'works' as a character: his evil

appears so total and gratuitous that he at times appears too easy a device for deflecting our attention from Pip's more hostile impulses.

9. The pattern of the incestuous couple, where the implication of the brother–sister relation serves as both attraction and prohibition, has been noted by several critics. See especially HARRY STONE, 'The Love Pattern in Dickens' Novels' in *Dickens the Craftsman*, ed. Robert B. Partlow Jr (Carbondale: Southern Illinois University Press, 1970); ALBERT J. GUERARD, *The Triumph of the Novel* (New York: Oxford University Press, 1976), p. 70. *Great Expectations* gives particular weight to the figure of the father as source of the law: Magwitch, assuming in different registers the role of father both to Estella and to Pip, becomes not a figure of authority so much as a principle of interdiction, of prohibition.

Postmodern

The term 'postmodern', which clearly plays off the concept of **'modernism'**, has acquired a wide range of connotations as an effective rallying point for a host of new departures in literary criticism. Generally they subsume some elements from Marxist, structuralist, rhetorical or reader-oriented approaches which are assimilated into their own distinctive principles.

The thrust of 'deconstruction', a term designating one of the major postmodern approaches to literature and philosophy, devolves from a suspicion of language, particularly its aptitude to carry unequivocal meanings. By means of close linguistic analysis the deconstructionists unmask a text as being in fact quite other than what it appears. Thus J. Hillis Miller entitles his study of Dickens' *Sketches by Boz* and *Oliver Twist* 'The Fiction of Realism', allying realism with a term suggestive of its non-existence. The essay, which first appeared in *Dickens Centennial Essays* (ed. Ada Nisbet and Blake Nevius, Berkeley and London: University of California Press, 1971), is a refutation of traditional readings which underline the closeness of Dickens' image of London to the actuality of his day. Miller maintains instead that the narration is essentially fictitious, and that this is revealed by the characteristic language, which is imaginative, metaphoric and figurative, and by its exposure of its own rhetorical devices and assumptions.

Like deconstruction, feminism seeks to reassess accepted knowledge, including uses of language, in order to uncover and revise the patriarchal biases and assumptions implicit in the hitherto normative, i.e. predominantly male readings. Feminism is a political label indicating support for the aims of the new women's movement which emerged in the late 1960s. It runs parallel to deconstruction in ferreting out the hidden agendas implicit in texts. In its political dimension feminism privileges gender, engaging in a style of criticism that necessarily allies the cultural with the literary. This is what Penny Boumelha does in her article 'Realism and the Ends of Feminism', a contribution to *Grafts: Feminist Cultural Criticism* (ed. Susan Sheridan, London and New York: Verso, 1988). She explores the potential of feminist readings in relation to George Eliot's novels, especially their endings, in which the options for the female protagonists are limited to marriage or death. She argues that these forms of closure not only replicate but even reinforce the poor opportunities for British middle-class women in the mid nineteenth century.

21   J. Hillis Miller on the Fiction of Realism*

. . . the illusion was reality itself.[1]

One important aspect of current literary criticism is the disintegration of
the paradigms of realism under the impact of structural linguistics and
the renewal of rhetoric.[2] If meaning in language rises not from the
reference of signs to something outside words but from differential
relations among the words themselves, if 'referent' and 'meaning' must
always be distinguished, then the notion of a literary text which is
validated by its one-to-one correspondence to some social, historical, or
psychological reality can no longer be taken for granted. No language is
purely mimetic or referential, not even the most utilitarian speech. The
specifically literary form of language, however, may be defined as a
structure of words which in one way or another calls attention to this
fact, while at the same time allowing for its own inevitable misreading as
a 'mirroring of reality.' 'The set (*Einstellung*) toward the MESSAGE as
such,' says Roman Jakobson, 'focus on the message for its own sake, is
the POETIC function of language.'[3] Realistic fiction is a special case of the
poetic function of language. Its peculiarity may be defined as the
reciprocal relation within it between the story narrated and the question
of what it means to narrate a story. One may say of realistic fiction what
Walter Benjamin says of Brecht's epic theater: its way of establishing the
set toward the message as such is 'to underline the relation of the
represented action to the action signified by the fact itself of
representation.'[4] This essay will attempt to test these generalizations by a
discussion of Dickens's *Sketches by Boz* and, more briefly, *Oliver Twist*.

At first sight the *Sketches by Boz* seem an unpromising text for such
study. They seem still rooted in the journalistic mode which was
Dickens's first way of writing as a parliamentary reporter.[5] The *Sketches*

---

* Reprinted from 'The Fiction of Realism: *Sketches by Boz, Oliver Twist*, and
Cruikshank's Illustrations' in *Dickens Centennial Essays*, ed. Ada Nisbet and Blake
Nevius (Berkeley: University of California Press, 1971), pp. 85–126.

are a representation in words of scenes, people, and ways of living which really existed in London in the eighteen-thirties. Here, even if nowhere else, Dickens seems to have been practicing a straightforward mimetic realism, especially in the section of the collected sequence called 'Scenes.' Here the reader may find vivid descriptions of many aspects of London life at the period of Victoria's accession, descriptions which have great value as 'social history.' There are sketches of old Scotland Yard, of Seven Dials, of Astley's, of Greenwich Fair, of Vauxhall Gardens, of omnibuses, cabs, coaches, and the people who run them, of Newgate Prison, pawnbrokers' shops, old clothes shops in Monmouth Street, of gin shops, private theaters, first of May celebrations, and so on. No one can doubt the 'photographic' accuracy of these descriptions. Dickens has obviously seen what he describes and reports it accurately with the good journalist's sharp eye for detail. Moreover, originals for many of the public figures alluded to in the *Sketches* or acquaintances used as models have been identified.[6]

The habitual narrative structure of the *Sketches* objectifies this journalistic model. The basic situation of the *Sketches* presents Boz as the 'speculative pedestrian' (*SB*, 190) wandering the streets of London. Boz is, like a good reporter, detached from what he sees in the sense of not being caught up in the life he witnesses, but this lack of involvement liberates him to see with great clarity and to record exactly what he sees. There is a good description of this way of being related to the world in a passage in the periodical version of 'The Prisoners' Van,' a passage suppressed in the collected *Sketches*. 'We have a most extraordinary partiality for lounging about the streets,' says Boz. 'Whenever we have an hour or two to spare, there is nothing we enjoy more than a little amateur vagrancy – walking up one street and down another, and staring into shop windows, and gazing about as if, instead of being on intimate terms with every shop and house in Holborn, the Strand, Fleet-street and Cheapside, the whole were an unknown region to our wandering mind.'[7] Boz looks at London as if he were a stranger in his own city. He has no business to be where he is, and therefore he is a 'wanderer,' and 'amateur vagrant.' He refers to himself here, as throughout, with the journalistic 'we,' which depersonalizes him, reduces him from a private man to a function, and at the same time suggests that he is divided into two consciousnesses. One is the public role of journalistic recorder who speaks not for himself but for the collective experience of all the dwellers in the city, for the universal truth which all know but do not know they know until it has been articulated for them by Boz. Such a truth is shared by all but is visible only to those who are disengaged from immediate involvement in the life of the city. Behind this collective self is Boz's other self, the private man behind the public role, who watches the journalist at work, somewhat self-

consciously. This deeper self, it may be, expresses his private experience
or private peculiarities covertly by way of the conventional mask.

Another text from the 'Scenes' will show the characteristically exact
notation of dress, behavior, time, and locale which Dickens's amateur
vagrant makes of what he sees. Roland Barthes has called attention to the
role of the 'irrelevant detail' in fiction or in history as a device for
establishing the authenticity of what is reported and for conveying 'l'effet
du réel.'[8] In such passages as the following the distinction between
'relevant' and 'irrelevant' detail seems in principle impossible to make.
The entire purpose of the passage is to tell the reader that such scenes do
in fact exist in the London streets on a Sunday afternoon and that Boz
has watched them with an eye on which nothing is lost, no detail
'irrelevant.' Each item is able by the fact of its existence to contribute to
Boz's amusement and to ours:

> Can any one fail to have noticed them in the streets on Sunday? And
> were there ever such harmless efforts at the grand and magnificent as
> the young fellows display! We walked down the Strand, a Sunday or
> two ago, behind a little group; and they furnished food for our
> amusement the whole way. They had come out of some part of the
> city; it was between three and four o'clock in the afternoon; and they
> were on their way to the Park. There were four of them, all arm-in-
> arm, with white kid gloves like so many bridegrooms, light trousers of
> unprecedented patterns, and coats for which the English language has
> yet no name – a kind of cross between a great-coat and a surtout, with
> the collar of the one, the skirts of the other, and pockets peculiar to
> themselves.
>
> Each of the gentlemen carried a thick stick, with a large tassel at the
> top, which he occasionally twirled gracefully round; and the whole
> four, by way of looking easy and unconcerned, were walking with a
> paralytic swagger irresistibly ludicrous. One of the party had a watch
> about the size and shape of a reasonable Ribstone pippin, jammed into
> his waistcoat-pocket, which he carefully compared with the clocks of
> St. Clement's and the New church, the illuminated clock at Exeter
> 'Change, the clock of St. Martin's Church, and the clock of the Horse
> Guards. When they at last arrived in St. James's Park, the member of
> the party who had the best-made boots on, hired a second chair
> expressly for his feet, and flung himself on this two-pennyworth of
> sylvan luxury with an air which levelled all distinctions between
> Brookes's and Snooks's, Crockford's and Bagnigge Wells
>
> (*SB*, 218–19).

The *Sketches by Boz* seem firmly attached to the social facts of London in
1836. As such, they are apparently fully open to analysis according to a

concept of interpretation which sets a solid reality on one hand and its mirroring in words on the other. The value of the *Sketches* is the exactness of the mirror's image. Such an analysis is confirmed by the rather slender tradition of critical comment on the *Sketches*. From the contemporary reviews down to the best recent essays they have been praised for their fidelity to the real. This critical line remains faithful to the linguistic doctrine of Plato's *Cratylus*, according to which 'the correct name indicates the nature of the thing.'[9] Things, in this case, as the critics note, are to be found especially in a region of lower middle class urban life which had not been much reflected before in fiction, in social history, or in journalism. This stratum of English life is that 'Every-Day Life and Every-Day People' of which the *Sketches* are said in their subtitle to be 'Illustrative.' If there is a fallacy in the concept of realism, criticism of the *Sketches* from 1836 to the present provides an excellent example of the fallacy at its most straightforward. Here it affirms itself in the sunlight with a clear conscience. Nowhere is there evidence of an uneasy sense that something might be wrong with the formulas of realism.

Dickens himself may be said to have initiated this tradition of criticism, not only with the subtitle but also with his claim in the original preface of February, 1836, that 'his object has been to present little pictures of life and manners as they really are.' As Kathleen Tillotson has observed, the early reviewers picked up this note and praised the *Sketches* for their 'startling fidelity,' for their power of 'bringing out the meaning and interest of objects which would altogether escape the observation of ordinary minds,' for their discovery of 'the romance, as it were, of real life.'[10] 'The *Sketches*,' says Mrs Tillotson, 'were acclaimed for their novelty and accuracy both in the kind of life observed, and the penetration of the observer accepting and transforming the commonplace . . . Throughout the reviews there is gratitude for the discovery of "every-day life" in neglected but immediately recognised pockets of urban and suburban society.'[11] The fullest contemporary statement of this interpretation of the *Sketches* is that made by John Forster in his *Life*. 'The observation shown throughout is nothing short of wonderful,' says Forster.

> Things are painted literally as they are. . . . It is a book that might have stood its ground, even if it had stood alone, as containing unusually truthful observation of a sort of life between the middle class and the low, which, having few attractions for bookish observers, was quite unhacknied ground. . . . It was a picture of every-day London at its best and worst, in its humours and enjoyments as well as its sufferings and sins, pervaded everywhere . . . with the absolute reality of the things depicted.[12]

One might expect Victorian accounts of the *Sketches* to be caught within

the Cratylean myth of representationalism. All Victorian criticism of
fiction, for the most part, remains enclosed within the formulations and
judgments of that myth. The only frequently expressed alternative was
the other form of representationalism which values a text for its accurate
mirroring of the feelings or subjective perspectives of its author.
Twentieth-century critics, however, might be expected to go beyond their
predecessors. Nevertheless, praise of the *Sketches* for their 'fidelity to
reality' persists with little change in the relatively sparse commentary the
book has received in our own day. Thea Holme, for example, in the
introduction to the Oxford Illustrated Edition of the *Sketches*, commends
Dickens for

> setting down . . . all the small events in the everyday life of common
> persons – bank clerks, shop assistants, omnibus drivers; laundresses,
> market women, and kidney-pie sellers: directing his powers of
> observation and description upon scenes and characters within the
> daily scope of any loiterer in London. . . . As an example of what is
> now called 'documentary' the *Sketches* deserve a unique place in
> literature. It has been pointed out elsewhere that more than half this
> volume's contents are facts: facts observed with an astonishing
> precision and wealth of detail
>
> (*SB*, vii, viii).

Mrs Tillotson uses the same kind of language as the nineteenth-century
reviewers to identify the quality of the *Sketches*. 'The tales and sketches
themselves,' she says, 'without annotation, give us the world which the
young Dickens saw.'[13] Angus Wilson, in his recent lively study of
Dickens, says of the *Sketches* that in them 'we see how a brilliant young
journalist's observation of London's movement is just on the point of
taking wings into imaginative art.'[14] An intelligent and sympathetic essay
on the *Sketches* by Robert Browning, to give a final example, is
constructed around the same assumptions. 'The London of the *Sketches*,'
says Browning, 'is not fictitious. . . . [Dickens] chronicles much that is
small in scale and dull-toned with such fidelity, that it is the distinction
of the *Sketches*, as it is that of Joyce's *Dubliners*, that the reader senses the
life of a whole city. . . . It is the first recommendation for this volume,
that in it [Dickens] gave such a lively account of what he saw and heard
in London . . . Dickens . . . felt the artist's primary need, to record.'[15]

The *Sketches by Boz*, in their apparent nature, in what Dickens said he
intended them to be, and in the traditional interpretation of them, seem
to offer little opportunity for a putting in question of realism. Moreover,
the theoretical schemas of a critic like Jakobson allow for the existence of
works of literature which refer outside themselves rather than remaining
reflexive. In Jakobson's list of the six functions of language the 'poetic'

function, in which language is focused on itself, exists side by side with what Jakobson calls 'a set (*Einstellung*) toward the referent, an orientation toward the CONTEXT – briefly the so-called REFERENTIAL, "denotative," "cognitive" function.'[16] Elsewhere in the same essay and at greater length in the influential discussion of two types of aphasia in *Fundamentals of Language*, Jakobson implies that there is a connection between this opposition of poetic and referential functions of language, on the one hand, and the distinction between two figures of speech, on the other. Metaphor is based on similarity and metonymy on contiguity. Poetry proper depends on metaphor, but realistic fiction defines people in terms of their contiguous environment. It favors metonymy over metaphor and the referential function of language over the set of language toward itself. Jakobson, it should be noted, allows for a complex relation between metonymy and metaphor, and for the use of both in poetry: 'Similarity superimposed on contiguity imparts to poetry its throughgoing [sic] symbolic, multiplex, polysemantic essence.'[17] In spite of this insight into the relation between the two tropes, however, he sees a tendency for language to split into two distinct regions, each governed by one of the 'gravitational poles' of these fundamental figures of speech:

> In manipulating these two kinds of connection (similarity and contiguity) in both their aspects (positional and semantic) – selecting, combining, and ranking them – an individual exhibits his personal style, his verbal predilections and preferences. . . . In poetry there are various motives which determine the choice between these alternants. The primacy of the metaphoric process in the literary schools of romanticism and symbolism has been repeatedly acknowledged, but it is still insufficiently realised that it is the predominance of metonymy which underlies and actually predetermines the so-called 'realistic' trend, which belongs to an intermediary stage between the decline of romanticism and the rise of symbolism and is opposed to both. Following the path of contiguous relationships, the realistic author metonymically digresses from the plot to the atmosphere and from the characters to the setting in space and time. He is fond of synecdochic details.[18]

Here is a clue which, while granting the approximate correctness of the traditional interpretation of the *Sketches by Boz*, may allow criticism to proceed beyond general statements about their 'faithful reproduction of the real.' Following this clue, it may be possible to identify how this fidelity is expressed in certain habits of language. In any case, the *Sketches* offer an excellent opportunity to test the validity of Jakobson's historical and linguistic schematizations. They were written during the time which he says marks the ascendancy of 'realism,' and they seem on other grounds to belong unquestionably in that pigeon-hole.

In spite of some youthful crudities and some self-conscious awkwardness of style the *Sketches by Boz* are a characteristic expression of Dickens's genius. Moreover, they contain all of Dickens's later work in embryo – the comedy, the sentimentality, the respect for the vitality of his characters, however foolish or limited they are, the habit of hyperbole, the admirable gift for striking linguistic transformations, the notion of an irresistible social determinism in which the urban environment causes the sad fate of the unlucky people living within it. The *Sketches* provide an excellent opportunity to watch the development of a great writer and to see his characteristic ways with words at the level of emergence, where they may be more easily identified. The full implications of the *Sketches* are only visible in the light of their relations to the later work of Dickens. They inevitably derive some of their meaning for a twentieth-century reader from the fact that, for example, he may encounter in 'The Hospital Patient' a preliminary sketch for the murder of Nancy in *Oliver Twist*. The *Sketches*, in spite of Dickens's well-known use of metaphor, are in fact based on a brilliant and consistent exploitation of what Jakobson calls 'the metonymical texture of realistic prose.'[19] Metonymy may be defined as a linguistic substitution in which a thing is named not directly but by way of something adjacent to it either temporally or spatially. Synecdoche, substituting part for whole, container for thing contained, attribute for substance, and so on, is an important subdivision of metonymy. In both cases the linguistic substitution is validated by an implied ontological link. Some relation of similarity or causality, it is suggested, actually exists in the real world between the thing and something adjacent to it.

If the *Sketches* are a work for the critic to explicate, searching for patterns dispersed in their multiplicity, London was for the young Dickens, in his disguise as Boz, also a set of signs, a text to interpret. The speculative pedestrian is faced at first not with a continuous narrative of the lives of London's people, not with the subjective state of these people at the present moment, and not even with people seen from the outside as appearance or spectacle. What he sees at first are things, human artifacts, streets, buildings, vehicles, objects in a pawnbroker's shop, old clothes in Monmouth Street. These objects are signs, present evidence of something absent. Boz sets himself the task of inferring from these things the life that is lived among them. Human beings are at first often seen as things among other things, more signs to decipher, present hints of that part of their lives which is past, future, or hidden.

The emblem for this confrontation of a collection of disconnected objects whose meaning is still to be discovered is the list. The many lists in the *Sketches* anticipate similar lists in Dickens's later novels, for example the description of the extraordinary things which tumble out of Mrs Jellyby's closet in *Bleak House*. In *Bleak House*, however, the contents

of Mrs Jellyby's closet are immediately 'readable' as evidence of her
quality as a wife and mother. Her irresponsibility has already been
encountered in other ways. In the *Sketches* the lists are often the starting
point of an act of interpretation which moves beyond them to the hidden
ways of life of which they are signs. The law of these lists is random
juxtaposition. They are not so much metonymic in themselves as the raw
material of metonymy, since there seems no meaningful connection
between any one object and those next to it. Boz's task is to discover
such connections, and at first the only metonymy involved seems to be
the synecdoche whereby such lists stand for the apparent disorder of
London as a whole. An admirable example of this motif is the description
of a 'broker's shop' in a slum neighborhood:

> Our readers must often have observed in some by-street, in a poor
> neighbourhood, a small dirty shop, exposing for sale the most
> extraordinary and confused jumble of old, worn-out, wretched articles,
> that can well be imagined. Our wonder at their ever having been
> bought, is only to be equalled by our astonishment at the idea of their
> ever being sold again. On a board, at the side of the door, are placed
> about twenty books – all odd volumes; and as many wine-glasses – all
> different patterns; several locks, an old earthen-ware pan, full of rusty
> keys; two or three gaudy chimney-ornaments – cracked, of course; the
> remains of a lustre, without any drops; a round frame like a capital O,
> which has once held a mirror; a flute, complete with the exception of
> the middle joint; a pair of curling-irons; and a tinder-box. In front of
> the shop window are ranged some half-dozen high-backed chairs, with
> spinal complaints and wasted legs; a corner cupboard; two or three
> very dark mahogany tables with flaps like mathematical problems;
> some pickle-jars, some surgeons' ditto, with gilt labels and without
> stoppers; an unframed portrait of some lady who flourished about the
> beginning of the thirteenth century, by an artist who never flourished
> at all; an incalculable host of miscellanies of every description,
> including bottles and cabinets, rags and bones, fenders and street-door
> knockers, fire-irons, wearing apparel and bedding, a hall-lamp, and a
> room-door
>
> (*SB*, 178–9, and see also pp. 189, 382–3 for additional lists).

Though these things were made by man and once expressed the quality
of human life, they are now broken, incomplete, useless, detached from
the environing context which gave them meaning, and thrown together
in pell-mell confusion. From such unlikely material Boz must put
together a coherent picture of London life. The Sketch from which the list
above is quoted observes that the articles in such shops differ from place
to place in the city and may be taken as trustworthy signs of the quality

of life in that part of London. 'Although the same heterogeneous mixture of things,' says Boz, 'will be found at all these places, it is curious to observe how truly and accurately some of the minor articles which are exposed for sale – articles of wearing apparel, for instance – mark the character of the neighborhood' (*SB*, 179). He goes on to give as examples the theatrical character of the things for sale in such shops in Drury Lane and Covent Garden, the nautical character of the things for sale in the shops in Ratcliff Highway, and the way the shops near the King's Bench Prison are full of things sold by the debtors imprisoned there:

> Dressing-cases and writing-desks, too old to pawn but too good to keep; guns, fishing-rods, musical instruments, all in the same condition; have first been sold, and the sacrifice has been but slightly felt. But hunger must be allayed, and what has already become a habit is easily resorted to, when an emergency arises. Light articles of clothing, first of the ruined man, then of his wife, at last of their children, even of the youngest, have been parted with, piecemeal. There they are, thrown carelessly together until a purchaser presents himself, old, and patched and repaired, it is true; but the make and materials tell of better days; and the older they are, the greater the misery and destitution of those whom they once adorned
>
> (*SB*, 181).

Here the literary strategy of the *Sketches* may be observed in little: first the scene, with its inanimate objects, then the people whose lives these objects are the signs, and finally the continuous narrative of their lives, which may be inferred from the traces of themselves they have left behind. Boz's work is analogous to that of a detective or archaeologist. From the bric-a-brac of a dead civilization he resurrects a whole culture, an unrecorded piece of history. This movement is recapitulated repeatedly. 'The Streets – Morning' (*SB*, 47–52),, for example, begins with the empty streets of London, an hour before sunrise, and as Boz watches they gradually fill with the life that is lived there. 'Shops and Their Tenants' (*SB*, 59–63), to give another example, begins with the description of a certain shop and then follows the history of its successive tenants as they may be guessed from changes in the outer appearance of the shop.

Perhaps the most striking example of this characteristic imaginative progression in the *Sketches* is the admirable 'Meditations in Monmouth Street' (*SB* 74–80). This is one of the best of the Sketches, a text already marked by the special qualities present in Dickens's mature work. The organising law of Boz's 'meditations' is given early in the Sketch:

> We love to walk among these extensive groves of the illustrious dead,
> and to indulge in the speculations to which they give rise; now fitting a
> deceased coat, then a dead pair of trousers, and anon the mortal
> remains of a gaudy waistcoat, upon some being of our own conjuring
> up, and endeavouring, from the shape and fashion of the garment
> itself, to bring its former owner before our mind's eye. We have gone
> on speculating in this way, until whole rows of coats have started from
> their pegs, and buttoned up, of their own accord, round the waists of
> imaginary wearers; lines of trousers have jumped down to meet them;
> waistcoats have almost burst with anxiety to put themselves on; and
> half an acre of shoes have suddenly found feet to fit them, and gone
> stumping down the street with a noise which has fairly awakened us
> from our pleasant reverie, and driven us slowly away, with a
> bewildered stare, an object of astonishment to the good people of
> Monmouth Street, and of no slight suspicion to the policemen at the
> opposite street corner
>
> (*SB*, 75).

Confronted with the clothes of the dead, Boz's speculations bring to life
in an instant the personages who once wore these clothes. The clothes
are metonymically equivalent to their absent wearers and give Boz access
to them. The life which properly belonged to the wearers is transferred to
the clothes. These leap up with an unnatural vitality to put themselves
on the ghostly owners conjured up by Boz's speculative imagination. The
fitting of the old clothes to mental images of their former owners begins
as a voluntary act. It is soon described as proceeding without
intervention by Boz. It becomes a spectacle rather than an act. The text
moves toward that personification of the inanimate which has often been
seen as one of the major sources of metaphor in Dickens's work:
'waistcoats have almost burst with anxiety to put themselves on.'[20] The
metonymic reciprocity between a person and his surroundings, his
clothes, furniture, house, and so on, is the basis for the metaphorical
substitutions so frequent in Dickens's fiction. For Dickens, metonymy is
the foundation and support of metaphor.[21] The passage quoted above
from the 'Meditations in Monmouth Street' moves not only to free Boz's
speculations from their voluntary basis but also to make them into a self-
generating reverie. As speculation becomes vision, quaint fancy becomes
grotesque hyperbole, and Boz witnesses the macabre ballet of whole
rows of coats, lines of trousers, and half an acre of shoes stomping
noisily off on their own accord. Finally the dream bursts of its own
excess, and Boz finds himself back to himself, self-consciously aware that
people are staring at his queer bewilderment. His return to himself gives
him a guilty feeling that he must have committed some crime for which

the policemen over the way may apprehend him as a danger to the community.

The initial description of the habitual progression of Boz's meditations in Monmouth Street is followed by a full-scale example of their operation on a particular occasion. From a row of old suits in a shop he identifies not only the person who must have worn them but his life story from his school-days to his death in banishment or on the gallows:

> We were occupied in this manner the other day, . . . when our eyes happened to alight on a few suits of clothes ranged outside a shop-window, which it immediately struck us, must at different periods have all belonged to, and been worn by, the same individual, and had now, by one of those strange conjunctions of circumstances which will occur sometimes, come to be exposed together for sale in the same shop. The idea seemed a fantastic one, and we looked at the clothes again with a firm determination not to be easily led away. No, we were right; the more we looked, the more we were convinced of the accuracy of our previous impression. There was the man's whole life written as legibly on those clothes, as if we had his autobiography engrossed on parchment before us
>
> (*SB*, 75).

The row of old suits is a legible text. Its reader is led first to the person who owned them, in a metonymic progression, and then on to the narrative of the man's life, given in this case, as in other similar cases in the *Sketches*, as a connected *récit*.

If a movement from things to people to stories is the habitual structural principle of the *Sketches*, the law which validates this movement is the assumption of a necessary similarity between a man, his environment, and the life he is forced to lead within that environment. As a man's surroundings are, so will his life be. This metonymic law functions implicitly everywhere, but it is presented explicitly in several striking formulations early in the *Sketches*. In one place Boz tells his readers that there is no reason to provide an analysis of a certain character's personality. An objective description of what he looked like and how he dressed will convey immediately his inner spiritual nature:

> We needn't tell you all this, however, for if you have an atom of observation, one glance at his sleek, knowing-looking head and face – his prim white neckerchief, with the wooden tie into which it has been regularly folded for twenty years past, merging by imperceptible degrees into a small-plaited shirt-frill – and his comfortable-looking form encased in a well-brushed suit of black – would give you a better

idea of his real character than a column of our poor description could
convey

(*SB*, 158–9).

In another Sketch the three-stage process is entered at the second stage,
and Boz's clairvoyant eye sees through to the life story of a solitary clerk
he glimpses in St James's Park, 'a tall, thin, pale person, in a black coat,
scanty grey trousers, little pinched-up gaiters, and brown beaver gloves'
(*SB*, 215). From the man's dress and behavior Boz can infer his whole
way of existence. He states for the reader the close reciprocity which
must exist between the two if his inferences are correct: 'There was
something in the man's manner and appearance which told us, we
fancied, his whole life, or rather his whole day, for a man of this sort has
no variety of days. We thought we almost saw the dingy little back office
into which he walks every morning . . .' (*SB*, 216). A detailed narration
of this man's day follows, including what he eats for dinner and the
amount he tips the waiter. In 'The New Year' Boz presents an elaborate
description of a party in the house opposite his own on the basis of the
fact that the house has green blinds. He knows the profession of the
master of the house by a glimpse of his clothes, by his way of walking,
and by means of those same green blinds: 'We can fancy one of these
parties, we think, as well as if we were duly dress-coated and pumped,
and had just been announced at the drawing-room door. . . . The master
of the house with the green blinds is in a public office; we know the fact
by the cut of his coat, the tie of his neckcloth, and the self-satisfaction of
his gait – the very green blinds themselves have a Somerset House air
about them' (*SB*, 226). A final succinct statement of the law of metonymy
on which the *Sketches* are built is given in the seventh Sketch:

> The various expressions of the human countenance afford a beautiful
> and interesting study, but there is something in the physiognomy of
> street-door knockers, almost as characteristic, and nearly as infallible.
> Whenever we visit a man for the first time, we contemplate the
> features of his knocker with the greatest curiosity, for we well know,
> that between the man and his knocker, there will inevitably be a
> greater or lesser degree of resemblance and sympathy
>
> (*SB*, 40).

Ex ungue lionem – as the whole beast may be conjured up from a single
claw, or as an archaeologist reconstructs a vanished civilization from a
few potsherds, so Boz can tell a man and all his life from even so small
and peripheral a part of him as his door knocker. The *Sketches* are
constructed around Boz's exercise of this power.

This law of metonymic correspondence underlies many other

characteristic linguistic procedures in the *Sketches*. Many begin with a generalization about a certain class of Londoners and then narrow down to a characteristic case. Mr John Dounce, for example, the hero of 'The Misplaced Attachment of Mr John Dounce' (*SB*, 244–9), is presented as one version of a whole class of Londoners, the 'steady old boys.' The part and the whole correspond, and John Dounce's nature and experiences seem determined by his membership in a class of which Boz could give many examples. Many of the characters in the *Sketches* are defined, in another form of metonymy, not as individual persons but as gestures, roles, or functions. One character says, 'Yes, I am the upper-boots.' He exists not as a man but as 'a voice from inside a velveteen case, with mother-of-pearl buttons' (*SB*, 408). The guests at a benefit, in another Sketch, are described not as people but as the drinks they have ordered: 'ninety-seven six-penn'orths of gin-and-water, thirty-two small glasses of brandy-and-water, five-and-twenty bottled ales, and forty-one neguses' (*SB*, 254). Here the part stands for the whole in a comic synecdoche which is a frequent stylistic resource in the later novels, as in the admirable metamorphosis of Sairey Gamp's husband, within her active imagination, into his wooden leg: 'And as to husbands, there's a wooden leg gone likeways home to its account, which in its constancy of walkin' into wine vaults, and never comin' out again till fetched by force, was quite as weak as flesh, if not weaker.'[22]

Metonymy provides a structuring principle for the *Sketches* in still another way. If each Sketch often recapitulates the progression from scene to person to narrative, the *Sketches* as a whole proceed through exactly this sequence. When Dickens collected the various texts from their random appearance over a period of three years in various periodicals, he rearranged the Sketches in a way which does not correspond to the chronological order of their original publication. The order finally adopted for the one-volume edition of 1839 and maintained in subsequent editions does match exactly, however, the sequence I have identified as appearing within the individual Sketches. First come a group of seven Sketches entitled 'Our Parish,' six of which had appeared originally as a connected series in a single periodical, the *Evening Chronicle*. The remaining Sketches are divided into three groups: 'Scenes,' 'Characters,' and 'Tales.'[23] This grouping seems clear evidence that Dickens had become to some degree aware of the principle which had governed his imagination during the composition of the *Sketches*. From scene to character to tale – the metonymic chain of substitutions could not be more clearly named. The *Sketches* when they were first collected were set side by side like the heterogeneous objects in a junk shop, but the final ordering reveals a significant relationship among them which was at first hidden but which can be revealed by their proper juxtaposition.

The clue taken from Roman Jakobson has seemingly sustained a vindication of the traditional description of the *Sketches* as realistic copying and an identification of the basic trope whereby that *mimesis* is performed. Moreover, it is easy to see how, in the case of the *Sketches*, the predominance of metonymy reinforces that deterministic vision of man's life which is often said to be an essential aspect of realistic fiction. One narrative pattern recurring in the *Sketches* is an apparently inescapable progression of the city dwellers step by step toward starvation, sickness, degradation, crime, depravity, suicide, or execution. A character caught in this progression is 'impelled by sheer necessity, down the precipice that [has] led him to a lingering death' (*SB*, 78). Such a sequence occurs in 'Our Next-Door Neighbour,' in 'The Pawnbroker's Shop,' in 'The Hospital Patient,' 'The Prisoners' Van,' and 'The Black Veil,' as the rather acerbic ending to a comic tale in 'A Passage in the Life of Mr Watkins Tottle,' and with melodramatic emphasis in the last Sketch, 'The Drunkard's Death.' There is a close relation between metonymy and this form of narrative. The story of a man's degeneration 'impelled by sheer necessity' constitutes a spreading out on the diachronic scale of the determinism implied synchronically in saying that each man is defined by what is around him. The Tales are often the temporal unfolding of what is initially affirmed pictorially, in the instant of juxtaposition within a Sketch. Three examples of this will bring into the open the implicit relation between spatial and temporal contiguity in the *Sketches*. The law of metonymic correspondence is presupposed as much in the narrative sequence of the Tales as in the interpretation of the Scenes and Characters from which these tales emerge. The scenes may present as a simultaneous tableau a progression which is achieved by a single individual only through a long period of his life. The presence in a single instant of more than one stage of such a progression strongly persuades the reader of the inevitability of the sequence.

One such scene is Boz's glimpse of two young girls, sisters, the elder defiant, the younger weeping bitterly, being taken from the Bow Street police station to the prisoners' van which will convey them to jail:

> These two girls had been thrown upon London streets, their vices and debauchery, by a sordid and rapacious mother. What the younger girl was then, the elder sister had been once; and what the elder then was, the younger must soon become. A melancholy prospect, but how surely to be realised; a tragic drama, but how often acted! . . . The progress of these girls in crime will be as rapid as the flight of pestilence

> (*SB*, 274).

Another such text makes explicit once more the way the physical objects Boz encounters in London contain folded up in themselves a multitude of tales. Again there appears the motif of the 'progress' frozen into a series of juxtaposed vignettes. The object contains, immobilized in an instant, the temporal history of the men and women who have used it: 'What an interesting book a hackney-coach might produce, if it could carry as much in its head as it does in its body! . . . How many stories might be related of the different people it had conveyed on matters of business or profit – pleasure or pain! And how many melancholy tales of the same people at different periods! The country-girl – the showy, over-dressed woman – the drunken prostitute! The raw apprentice – the dissipated spendthrift – the thief!' (*SB*, 84). The final example appears in 'The Pawnbroker's Shop.' Three women side by side in the shop constitute three stages from shabby genteel respectability to destitution and misery:

> Who shall say how soon these women may change places? The last has but two more stages – the hospital and the grave. How many females situated as her two companions are, and as she may have been once, have terminated the same wretched course, in the same wretched manner! One is already tracing her footsteps with frightful rapidity. How soon may the other follow her example! How many have done the same!
>
> (*SB*, 195).

Here are three excellent demonstrations of the metonymic basis of realistic narrative. Such narrative places in temporal sequence what can also be seen as spatially contiguous. The diachronic sequence has the same irresistible coercion as the synchronic law which says that between a man and his door knocker there will inevitably be some degree of resemblance and sympathy.

Tales like 'The Drunkard's Death,' in the final ordering of the *Sketches*, seem to emerge as linear narrative out of the static poses of the earlier Scenes and Characters. They also anticipate the grimmer side of Dickens's later fiction, for example the slow deaths of those destroyed by the Court of Chancery in *Bleak House*. Stories in this mode, however, by no means make up the majority of the Tales, nor of the briefer narratives interpolated in the earlier Sketches. Most of the Tales are comic or farcical stories. They anticipate more Sairey Gamp or Mr Pecksniff than the career of Jonas Chuzzlewit. The comic Tales are also anticipated in the more journalistic Scenes, for example in the admirable account of 'Aggerawatin Bill,' the omnibus cad (*SB*, 146–51), or in the description of the visit of a bourgeois family to Astley's (*SB*, 104–6). What interpretation of the comedy of the *Sketches* can be made?

To account for the comic aspect of the *Sketches* is one path (there are others) which leads to a recognition that the analysis of them so far undertaken here has been a good example of the way a literary text may contain the invitation to its radical misreading. We have been inveigled into taking as *mimesis* solidly based on an extra-literary world a work which is in fact fiction and which contains the linguistic clues allowing the reader to recognize that it is fiction. Moreover, this accounting for its status as literature takes place in a way especially appropriate to narrative fiction, by a reciprocity between the Scenes, Characters, and Tales themselves, and the implications of Dickens's 'representation' of them.

The theme of deception, play-acting, illusion, baseless convention pervades the *Sketches*, and Boz repeatedly performs what may be defined as an act of demystification. As a detached spectator he sees that the pretense is pretense and shows it as such to the reader, but for the most part the characters remain trapped in their illusions. This theme takes a number of different forms in the *Sketches*. One recurrent motif is the imitation of the upper class by the middle or lower class. Boz sees the speech, dress and behavior of the aristocracy as conventions based on no substantial worth. They are justified by no supernatural models, no 'divine right.' The apprentices of London, however, in 'Thoughts about People,' or the *nouveaux riches* of 'The Tuggses at Ramsgate,' take the shadow for the substance. The four apprentices who go out for a Sunday stroll adorned 'like so many bridegrooms' are said to be 'the faint reflection of higher lights.' In their good humor and innocent self-deception they seem to Boz 'more tolerable' than the aristocracy they imitate, 'precocious puppyism in the Quadrant, whiskered dandyism in Regent Street and Pall Mall, or gallantry in its dotage anywhere' (*SB*, 219). Mr Tuggs in 'The Tuggses at Ramsgate' is a London grocer who inherits a fortune and straightway leaves for Ramsgate. The story which ensues is the traditional one of the social climbers who are in their naiveté defrauded by a dishonest couple whom they take to be authentic members of the social class they wish to join. Mr Frederick Malderton, in 'Horatio Sparkins' was a young man 'who always dressed according to the fashions of the months; who went up the water twice a week in the season; and who actually had an intimate friend who once knew a gentleman who formerly lived in the Albany' (*SB*, 358). His family 'affected fashion, taste, and many other fooleries, in imitation of their betters, and had a very decided and becoming horror of anything which could, by possibility, be considered *low*' (*SB*, 356). The story turns on the way the Malderton family take Horatio Sparkins to be a nobleman in disguise and then discover that he is actually an assistant in a linen-draper's shop in the Tottenham Court Road.

If the theme of the inauthentic imitation by the lower middle class of an upper class without authenticity in itself runs through the *Sketches*, an even more pervasive theme is theatrical imitation as such. Critics from the earliest reviewers to present-day commentators have noted the importance of this in the *Sketches*. Dickens was already at this time of his life deeply involved in the theater, both as an amateur actor and as a novice playwright. During the period he was revising the *Sketches* he was at work on a burlesque, *O'Thello*, and on a farce, *The Strange Gentleman*, based on one of the Sketches, 'The Great Winglebury Duel.' The theater returns so often in the *Sketches* that London in this book comes to seem a place where everyone is in one way or another engaged not in productive work but in performing or witnessing scenic representations. They watch others pretend to be what they are not or play roles themselves. Certainly the attention paid to the theater and to musical performance is disproportionate. It constitutes a deformation in Boz's mirroring of the 'real' London. In spite of the importance drama undoubtedly had in the culture of early Victorian London, it seems unlikely that quite so large a proportion of its people were obsessed with it, involved in it in one way or another, or allowed their hair styles, attitudes, dress, speech, and gesture to be determined by it. The theatrical theme is also a good example of the way a topic frequently appears in the early journalistic Sketches and then is picked up as the background for a more frankly 'fictional' treatment in the Characters or Tales.

Among the Scenes is the admirable sketch of 'Astley's.' This includes not only a description of the circus part of the performance but also a reference to the farces and melodramas which accompany the circus and a description of the hangers-on around the stage-doors of minor theaters. Central in 'Greenwich Fair' is the description of 'Richardson's,' 'where you have a melodrama (with three murders and a ghost), a pantomime, a comic song, an overture, and some incidental music, all done in five-and-twenty minutes' (*SB*, 115). This is followed by an amusing paragraph describing the action of the melodrama. Next comes an important Sketch of 'Private Theatres,' then a description of 'Vauxhall Gardens by Day.' The theatrical or musical theme appears in several of the Characters: in 'The Mistaken Milliner: A Tale of Ambition,' which tells how a little milliner is persuaded to take voice lessons and then fails miserably at her first concert; in 'The Dancing Academy'; in the visit to the theater in 'Making a Night of It'; in the concert and vaudeville in the suburbs in 'Miss Evans and the Eagle.' Among the Tales there are musical performances aboard ship in 'The Steam Excursion' and a return to the theme of private theatricals in 'Mrs Joseph Porter.'

Throughout the *Sketches* characters are introduced whose lives are determined by the theater, for example a man seen 'lounging up Drury

Lane' in 'Shabby-Genteel People': 'The "harmonic meetings" at some fourth-rate public-house, or the purlieus of a private theatre, are his chosen haunts; he entertains a rooted antipathy to any kind of work, and is on familiar terms with several pantomime men at the large houses' (*SB*, 262–3). Another example is prefatory to a description of the brokers' shops in the neighborhood of Drury Lane and Covent Garden:

> This is essentially a theatrical neighbourhood. There is not a potboy in the vicinity who is not, to a greater or less extent, a dramatic character. The errand-boys and chandler's-shop-keepers' sons are all stage-struck: they 'gets up' plays in back kitchens hired for the purpose, and will stand before a shop-window for hours, contemplating a great staring portrait of Mr. Somebody or other, of the Royal Coburg Theatre, 'as he appeared in the character of Tongo the Denounced'. The consequence is, that there is not a marine-store shop in the neighbourhood, which does not exhibit for sale some faded articles of dramatic finery
>
> (*SB*, 179).

'All the minor theatres in London,' says Boz, 'especially the lowest, constitute the centre of a little stage-struck neighbourhood' (*SB*, 120).

The two most extended treatments of this theme of fascination by the drama are the descriptions of amateur theatricals in 'Private Theatres' and in the Tale called 'Mrs Joseph Porter.' A passage in the last paragraph of the periodical version of 'Astley's,' later omitted, anticipates the topic which is treated with great circumstantiality and verve in 'Private Theatres':

> It is to us matter of positive wonder and astonishment that the infectious disease commonly known by the name of 'stage-struck', has never been eradicated, unless people really believe that the privilege of wearing velvet and feathers for an hour or two at night, is sufficient compensation for a life of wretchedness and misery. It is stranger still that the denizens of attorneys' offices, merchants' counting-houses, haberdashers' shops, and coal sheds, should squander their own resources to enrich some wily vagabond by paying – actually paying, and dearly too – to make unmitigated and unqualified asses of themselves at a Private Theatre.[24]

'Mrs Joseph Porter' is probably based on 'Dickens's amateur production of *Clari* at Bentinck Street on 27 Apr. 1833; it may also bear some relation to his burlesque *O'Thello*, written about this time.'[25] The Tale describes an amateur performance of *Othello* by a Clapham family all 'infected with the mania for Private Theatricals' (*SB*, 421). From the near-slum areas

where the private theaters flourish to the well-to-do suburbs like
Clapham, from the edges of poverty to the upper middle class,[26] all Boz's
London seems to have caught the disease of theatrical representation.

The theater permeates the *Sketches* in still another way, a way that will
allow a more precise identification of its significance. If there are many
characters in the *Sketches* who are actually involved in the theater, the
theater is also one of Boz's major sources of metaphorical language. This
language is used to describe even those characters who have no direct
connection with the theater. Along with the people in Boz's London who
either play a role or watch others play one there are many other
characters who unwittingly behave, dress, or speak in ways that make
them like characters in a melodrama or farce. A pretty young lady, for
example, '[goes] through various . . . serio-pantomimic fascinations,
which forcibly [remind] Mr John Dounce of the first time he courted his
first wife' (*SB*, 248). Another character is shown 'standing up with his
arms a-kimbo, expressing defiance melodramatically' (*SB*, 269). Another
is 'one of those young men, who are in society what walking gentlemen
are on the stage, only infinitely worse skilled in his vocation than the
most indifferent artist' (*SB*, 278). This man wears 'a maroon-coloured
dress-coat, with a velvet collar and cuffs of the same tint – very like that
which usually invests the form of the distinguished unknown who
condescends to play the "swell" in the pantomime at "Richardson's
Show"' (*SB*, 281). Another person goes through 'an admirable bit of
serious pantomime' (*SB*, 279), speaks in 'a stage whisper' (*SB*, 282), and
appears later at a staircase window 'like the ghost of Queen Anne in the
tent scene in Richard' (*SB*, 306). Mr Septimus Hicks, in the same story,
speaks 'very tremulously, in a voice like a Punch with a cold' (*SB*, 285). A
few moments later he has an 'expression of countenance' more
discomposed than 'Hamlet's, when he sees his father's ghost' (*SB*, 285).
A maid dresses 'like a disguised Columbine' (*SB*, 295), and the 'manners
and appearance' of an Irishman '[remind] one of Orson' (*SB*, 298).
Another character bursts out of a back drawing-room 'like the dragon at
Astley's' (*SB*, 309). A series of such metaphors punctuate the Tale called
'Sentiment': a spoiled child is shown 'looking like a robber in a
melodrama, seen through a diminishing glass' (*SB*, 325), and his face
looks 'like a capital O in a red-lettered play-bill' (*SB*, 326). Boz makes self-
conscious use in this story of the language of advertisements for dramatic
performances: 'Preparations, to make use of theatrical phraseology, "on a
scale of magnitude never before attempted," were incessantly made' (*SB*,
327), and a group of 'fat mammas' look 'like the stout people who come
on in pantomimes for the sole purpose of being knocked down' (*SB*, 329).
In another story, 'The Bloomsbury Christening,' Mr Dumps speaks 'in a

voice like Desdemona with the pillow over her mouth' (*SB*, 478) and later rises from his chair 'like the ghost in Don Juan' (*SB*, 481).

Whenever Boz wants to find a picturesque way to describe one of his characters he is apt to use some simile or metaphor drawn from a range of theatrical reference extending all the way from Punch to *Hamlet*. The characters are not aware of the similarity of their gestures to those of pantomime, melodrama, or farce, but Boz is aware and makes his readers share his insight. Such metaphors present the characters as unwittingly imitative of something which exists in the social world shared by Dickens and his readers. This social reality, however, is openly factitious, illusory. Unconsciously theatrical gestures or speech are the signs not of a plenitude but of an absence. They have the hollowness of a mask. They refer not to the solidity of physical reality but to the fictions of a highly stylized theater. Such reference is one of the chief sources of comedy in the *Sketches*. This comedy presents people not as victims of coercive social 'forces,' as seems the case in stories like 'The Drunkard's Death,' but as consciously or unconsciously frauds. Character after character in the *Sketches* is shown pretending to be what he is not. A man in one story displays ostentatiously 'an immense key, which belonged to the street-door, but which, for the sake of appearances, occasionally did duty in an imaginary wine-cellar' (*SB*, 433). Another character looks like 'a bad "portrait of a gentleman" in the Somerset House exhibition' (*SB*, 369). Another person's face lights up with 'something like a bad imitation of animation' (*SB*, 438). A coach in the same story draws up before 'a cardboard-looking house with disguised chimneys, and a lawn like a large sheet of green letter-paper' (*SB*, 436). Everything in the *Sketches* seems to be what it is not, and Boz's chief work is not objective description but the uncovering of fraud.

The theme of disillusionment runs all through the *Sketches*, as in the description of the decay of May Day celebrations in 'The First of May,' or in Boz's confession that he is no longer enraptured by Astley's as he used to be and finds more interest in watching the audience than in watching the performance, or in that exercise in disenchantment, 'Vauxhall Gardens by Day':

We bent our steps to the firework-ground; there, at least, we should not be disappointed. We reached it, and stood rooted to the spot with mortification and astonishment. *That* the Moorish tower – that wooden shed with a door in the centre, and daubs of crimson and yellow all round, like a gigantic watch-case! *That* the place where night after night we had beheld the undaunted Mr. Blackmore make his terrific ascent, surrounded by flames of fire, and peals of artillery, and where the white garments of Madame Somebody (we forget even her name now), who nobly devoted her life to the manufacture of fireworks, had so often been seen fluttering in the wind, as she called up a red, blue, or parti-coloured light to illumine her temple!

(*SB*, 127).

Such an uncovering of the sordid reality behind a beguiling surface is the essential movement of the *Sketches*. The drama is important to Boz not because he is taken in by the theatrical, as are his characters, but because the theatrical metaphor expresses perfectly the process whereby Boz sees behind the scenes and leads his readers to see behind them too. Boz is the man who knows that behind the stage set is the cobwebby disorder backstage. Behind each mask he sees the shabby performer.

In this context it is possible to identify the somewhat surprising function in the *Sketches* of a character who anticipates Scrooge in hating children and dogs, and in refusing to participate in the social fictions which make life bearable for others. This bachelor figure, 'life-hater' as Robert Browning calls him,[27] is not so much rejected by Dickens in the two Sketches in which he appears ('Mr Minns and His Cousin' and 'The Bloomsbury Christening') as he is a surrogate for Boz himself. Like Boz he is a detached spectator able to see through the falseness of social life. Mr Minns is the point of view from which the reader sees the absurdity and vulgarity of the cousin's dinner party in his little cottage 'in the vicinity of Stamford Hill' (*SB*, 312), and Mr Nicodemus Dumps, who 'adored King Herod for his massacre of the innocents; and if he hated one thing more than another, it was a child' (*SB*, 467), is the reader's perspective in 'The Bloomsbury Christening.' Mr Dumps is granted the honor of using a style of metaphor peculiarly Boz's own. He describes the baby about to be christened as looking 'like one of those little carved representations that one sometimes sees blowing a trumpet on a tombstone' (*SB*, 476). When Boz himself describes the child's arm and fist as 'about the size and shape of the leg of a fowl cleanly picked' (*SB*, 479), it is clear that Boz (and Dickens) shared some of Dumps's distaste for babies and for the fuss that is made over them.

Boz's uncovering of the fictive nature of society by way of the metaphorical use of other fictions is not performed in the name of some possible authentic way of living. Each way of living imitates another way which is itself not solid or authentic. Each character lives as a sign referring not to substance but to another sign. This emphasis on play-acting and on the factitious calls the reader's attention to the fact that English society as a whole is based on arbitrary conventions, on the fictional ascription of value and significance to the stones, paper, glass, cloth of which the buildings, streets, clothes, and utensils of London are made. This giving of meaning is an act of interpretation creating a culture, generating those signs which Boz the speculative pedestrian must then interpret. Such ascription of meaning is not free. The imprisonment of the human spirit in its conferring of meaning is a fundamental theme of the *Sketches*. The collective creation of meaning and value is enclosed rigidly within conventions, modes of language, institutions, ways of behaving and judging, which have been inherited from the past. People in the *Sketches* are trapped not by social forces but by human fabrications already there within which they must live their lives. They live not in free creativity but as stale repetitions of what has gone before. The world of the *Sketches* is caught in the copying of what preceded it. Each new form is a paler imitation of the past. Each person is confined in the tawdry imitation of stale gestures. The reader of the *Sketches* receives a powerful sense not only of the comic vitality of Dickens's earliest creations, but of their enclosure, the narrowness of their lives, their spiritual poverty. They are pathetically without awareness that their cheapness is pathetic, hopelessly imprisoned within the cells of a fraudulent culture.

The comedy of the *Sketches* arises from the juxtaposition of Boz's knowledge of this situation against the blindness of the characters to it. They are blind either in the sense that they are not aware that their gestures have the stiff, conventional quality of pantomimic movements, or in the sense that they perform the imitation consciously but in the mistaken belief that what they are imitating has absolute value or substance, as the apprentices of London are beguiled by the dress and swagger of the Pall Mall dandies. The comedy of the *Sketches* depends on the innocence of the objects of our laughter and on the opposing presence of a spectator who sees the insubstantiality of the spectacle he beholds. At the same time Boz mimes the foolishness of the people he sees, creating it anew in a constant hyperbole which translates it into the linguistic acrobatics of his discourse. The pathos of Boz's characters lies in the fact that their spiritual energy is determined in its expressions by the objects within which they live, or rather by their acceptance of the meaning collectively ascribed by their culture to those objects. These objects are the residue of the culture they have inherited and have coercive force not as physical energies but as signs, habits of interpretation, forms. Such inherited forms constitute a world in which nothing is what it is, but everything is the arrow pointing towards something else. This world of the presence of an absence channels and confines the spirit in a metonymic determination of contained by container, vital energy by environment. In this sense the latter can indeed be taken by the attentive spectator as the index of the former. . . .

One way to see that the *Sketches* do put their own status in question is to return to the theatrical metaphors which appear in them so frequently. These work in a radically ambiguous way which contains in miniature the linguistic movement essential to the *Sketches*. This movement challenges the authenticity of what is represented while what is represented in its turn undermines the apparent solidity of the *Sketches* as an innocent act of representational mirroring. This reversal between two elements facing one another within the text is basic to the mode of existence of a work of literature and constitutes it as a literary use of language. In this fluctuation the figurative becomes the literal only to be transformed into the figurative again by a corresponding change of what it faces from the one into the other. In this subtle movement nothing moves but the interpretative act, but this movement may be stilled only at the peril of a necessary misreading. Such a hermeneutical wavering is like that egg mentioned by Yeats which turns inside out without breaking its shell, or it is like those Gestaltist diagrams which change configuration bewilderingly before the viewer's eyes. When Boz describes a character as having a 'melodramatic expression of horror' (*SB*, 397), or another character as 'going through a threatening piece of pantomime with [a] stick' (*SB*, 415), the first effect of this is to present a coolly analytical spectator confronting a real world whose factitiousness he uncovers by comparing it to the conventions of drama. In the second movement of the reader's interpretation, he recognizes that the characters have no existence outside the language Dickens has invented to describe them. Dickens has modeled them on the popular drama of his day. What had seemed 'realistic' comes to be seen as figurative, and the radically fictive quality of the *Sketches* as a whole comes into the open. Back and forth between these two interpretations the reader oscillates. Neither takes precedence over the other, but the meaning of the text is generated by the mirage of alternation between them.

When the reader has broken through to seeing local fragments of the text inside out, as it were, as well as outside in, then he recognizes that the *Sketches* from beginning to end are open to being read in this way. The *Sketches* are not *mimesis* of an externally existing reality, but the interpretation of that reality according to highly artificial schemas inherited from the past. They came into existence through the imposition of fictitious patterns rather than through the discovery of patterns 'really there.' Though this double reading of the *Sketches* would be valid whether it was asserted explicitly or not in the text, it happens that there are abundant clues informing the reader that the *Sketches* are fiction rather than *mimesis*. These clues identify the main sources of the fictional patterns according to which Boz interprets the appearances he confronts when he walks through London. One of these is the drama, as I have shown. The other two are the conventions of previous fiction and the conventions of graphic representation. There are almost as many explicit references to these last as to the theater. If people in the *Sketches* are often seen as like characters in a pantomime or melodrama, they are also often presented as like characters in a novel or in a print. A 'little coquette with a large bustle' looks 'like a French lithograph' (*SB*, 480). Another character 'with his white dress-stock, blue coat, bright buttons, and red watch-ribbon, strongly resemble[s] the portrait of that interesting but rash young gentleman, George Barnwell' (*SB*, 357), and a 'young gentleman with . . . green spectacles, in nankeen inexplicables, with a ditto waistcoat and bright buttons' is dressed 'like the pictures of Paul – not the saint, but he of Virginia notoriety' (*SB*, 392). The reference here is to the illustrations in *Paul et Virginie*. In another place a character is described as having 'looked something like a vignette to one of Richardson's novels, and [having] had a clean-cravatish formality of manner, and kitchen-pokerness of carriage, which Sir Charles Grandison himself might have envied' (*SB*, 431). In another Sketch there is an explicit reference to Hogarth, whom Dickens much admired and who is mentioned again in the preface of 1841 to *Oliver Twist*. In the latter, Hogarth is invoked as an excuse for the presentation of 'low' characters and is defined as 'the moralist, and censor of his age – in whose great works the times in which he lived, and the characters of every time, will never cease to be reflected' (*OT*, lxiv). In the *Sketches* Boz abandons the attempt to describe in language what could only be represented by a great artist like Hogarth: 'It would require the pencil of Hogarth to illustrate – our feeble pen is inadequate to describe – the expression which the countenances of Mr Calton and Mr Septimus Hicks respectively assumed, at this unexpected announcement' (*SB*, 289). The effect of this is to invite the reader to imagine the scene as if it were schematized according to the conventions of Hogarth's prints. If the reader has this reference in mind he may note, for example, that the juxtaposition of three women at different stages on the road to degradation in 'The Pawnbroker's Shop' is as much modeled on the eighteenth-century pictorial convention of the 'Progress' as it is on any observation of the real London of Dickens's day. The 'real London,' here, is presented according to forms borrowed from *A Harlot's Progress*.

In other Sketches Boz's imagination is controlled by literary rather than by theatrical or graphic conventions. In the examples already given of references to Richardson and to *Paul et Virginie* the allusion (significantly from the point of view of the interpretation I shall suggest of the relation between the *Sketches* and the illustrations for them by Cruikshank) is not to the texts of the novels but to their illustrations. These seem to have stuck in Dickens's mind as much as the stories themselves. There are, however, many explicit references to literary texts. The fare in a cab is 'as carefully boxed up behind two glazed calico curtains as any mysterious picture in any one of Mrs Radcliffe's castles' (*SB*, 471). There are several ironic references to the artificial conventions of fiction or journalism: 'Like those paragons of perfection, advertising footmen out of place, he was always "willing to make himself generally useful"' (*SB*, 382); 'Then, as standard novelists expressively inform us – "all was a blank!"' (*SB*,

270); 'We are not about to adopt the licence of novel-writers, and to let "years roll on"' (*SB*, 284); 'A troublesome form, and an arbitrary custom, however, prescribe that a story should have a conclusion, in addition to a commencement; we have therefore no alternative' (*SB*, 354); '"We will draw a veil," as novel-writers say, over the scene that ensued' (*SB*, 369). Even the name Boz, as Dickens later revealed, was an allusion to *The Vicar of Wakefield*. It was a corruption of 'Moses,' a name in the novel, and was the nickname Dickens gave to one of his younger brothers.

Side by side with the realistic way of seeing the *Sketches* as the discovery by Boz of true stories hidden behind the objects he encounters in his walks through London, there is another way which involves the same elements but with reverse polarity, as the ghost of the other way, its 'negative,' in which black becomes white, white black. To see the *Sketches* in this new way is to recognize that metonymy is as much a fiction as metaphor. Both are the assertion of a false identity or of a false causal connection. The metonymic associations which Boz makes are fancies rather than facts, impositions on the signs he sees of stock conventions, not mirroring but interpretation, which is to say, lie. A man's door-knocker is no necessary indication of his personality. It only seems so to the imagining mind of the inimitable Boz. An excellent example of this importation of the fictive into the real is the 'Meditations in Monmouth Street,' which seemed, according to my first reading of it, such a perfect case of the linguistic act whereby metonymy is employed as a decoding of the hidden significance of the real. The row of old clothes which Boz sees in Monmouth Street gives rise, however, to a wholly conventional narrative, the story of the idle apprentice. This story has many antecedents in eighteenth-century fiction, drama, and graphic representation. To remember this is to see that the theme in the *Sketches* of the irresistible coercion of social forces, the motif which seemed to be a fundamental part of their representation of urban life, is not 'truth' but literary fiction, perhaps no more than a sentimental lie. If the *Sketches* unmask their characters and show them to be living in terms of theatrical gestures, they also turn at crucial moments on their own conventions and expose these as fictions too. The stories which rise from the door-knockers, the old clothes, the objects in the pawnshop are Boz's inventions, not objective facts. Moreover, far from being the free creations of his imagination they are as much bound by forms inherited from the past as the gestures and speech of the characters within the *Sketches*. The movement from Scene to Character to Tale is not the metonymic process authenticating realistic representation but a movement deeper and deeper into the conventional, the concocted, the schematic.

Nor is Boz unaware of this. In several places he gives the reader the information he needs to free himself from a realistic interpretation of the

Sketches. To be so freed is to perceive that throughout the *Sketches*, in the phrase I have taken from 'The Drunkard's Death' as an epigraph for this essay, 'the illusion [is] reality itself' (*SB*, 493). In 'Meditations in Monmouth Street' Boz says, in a clause allowed to pass without question in my 'realistic' reading of this Sketch, that he fits the old clothes 'upon some being of [his] own conjuring up' (*SB*, 75). Later in the same Sketch, when Boz is in the midst of his invention of a new version of the story of the idle apprentice, he says, 'we felt . . . much sorrow when we saw, or fancied we saw – it makes no difference which – the change that began to take place now' (*SB*, 76). It makes no difference which because the seeing of Boz is all imaginary rather than real, made out of the whole cloth of those old suits. In another Sketch Boz says that 'the sudden moving of a taper' seen in the window of a hospital 'is enough to awaken a whole crowd of reflections' (*SB*, 240). He then proceeds to narrate the story of a girl beaten to death by her ruffian lover which anticipates the murder of Nancy by Sikes in *Oliver Twist*. In another place Boz demystifies his childhood enslavement to literary convention when he says: 'We remember, in our young days, a little sweep about our own age, with curly hair and white teeth, whom we devoutly and sincerely believed to be the lost son and heir of some illustrious personage' (*SB*, 171). To believe this was to be the victim of the fairy-tale patterns of children's literature, but the adult Boz has been disillusioned, or, at any rate, one part of his mind has been disillusioned. The other part used this same story of the workhouse son of the 'illustrious personage' as the basis of *Oliver Twist*. The *Sketches by Boz*, like *Oliver Twist*, express both the illusion and its deconstruction, just as the critic's interpretation of them must hover between realistic and figurative readings.

Perhaps the best example of a text explicitly calling attention to the fictive quality of the *Sketches* is a curious paragraph in which the failure of Boz's habitual processes of imagination brings into the open the laws by which it usually operates. Boz has been left alone in the parlor of 'an old, quiet, decent public-house' (*SB*, 235) near the City Road in the east of London:

> If we had followed the established precedent in all such instances, we should have fallen into a fit of musing, without delay. The ancient appearance of the room – the old panelling of the wall – the chimney blackened with smoke and age – would have carried us back a hundred years at least, and we should have gone dreaming on, until the pewter-pot on the table, or the little beer-chiller on the fire, had started into life, and addressed to us a long story of days gone by. But, by some means or other, we were not in a romantic humour; and

although we tried very hard to invest the furniture with vitality, it
remained perfectly unmoved, obstinate, and sullen

(*SB*, 239).

Here the inability of Boz's romantic imagination to follow the established
precedent brings to the surface the precariously fictive quality of that
imagination. The pewter pot and the little beer-chiller are characteristic
examples of utensils which in other Sketches are read as metonymic
signs of the life which has been lived in their vicinity. In their failure to
start into life there is a revelation of the fact that the vitality of such
objects does not belong in reality to them. It is invested in them by Boz,
and it is invested according to patterns of interpretation taken from
traditional literary forms. In such moments the *Sketches* make
problematical their mimetic function. In doing so they fulfill, in a way
appropriate to narrative fiction, the definition of literature as a use of
language which exposes its own rhetorical devices and assumptions.

This uncovering of the fictitiousness of the fictive is not performed,
however, in the name of some 'true' language for which a space is
cleared through the rejection of the fictive. Behind each fiction there is
another fiction, and this new fiction is sustained in its turn by the
counterpart phantom of a beguiling literal reading. Once more this is
easiest to see in its mirroring within the lives of the characters in the
Sketches. This mirroring corresponds rigorously to the mode of existence
of the *Sketches* themselves. In the *Sketches* the liberated characters are not
those who escape from conventional behavior. No one can escape.
Liberation is possible only to those who, like Aggerawatin Bill, the
omnibus cad, play their roles to the hilt, perform their part with such
abandon that this hyperbolic verve constitutes a kind of freedom. It is a
paradoxical freedom which both accepts the role (any action in the world
of the *Sketches* is a role of some sort) and, at the same time, reveals in the
excess with which the part is played that it is a part, that it could be
otherwise. Any behavior is incommensurate with the vitality which gives
energy to it. The heroes of the *Sketches* are such characters as Bill Barker,
the 'cad,' or his counterpart in the same Sketch, the red-cab-driver. The
latter knocks down a gentleman who protests the way he is treated, and
then 'call[s] the police to take himself into custody, with all the civility in
the world' (*SB*, 146).

Such admirable displays of deliberately outrageous behavior are exactly
parallel to the function of hyperbole in Dickens's own playing of the role
of Boz, the speculative pedestrian. In the incongruous metaphors, in the
pervasive facetious irony, in a constant play of language which calls
attention to its own clichés in ways which destroy their innocent
existence as nominal turns of language, Boz liberates himself in the only

way one can be liberated through language. He does not substitute true language for false, nor does he copy true models. Neither true language nor true models exist for Boz. Like Bill Barker, he must tell lies, employ fictions, in ways which expose the fact that they are lies. The use of clichés, in ways that reveal their reliance on metaphors which have come to be taken literally and which thereby have become the support of social fictions, contains this linguistic resource of the *Sketches* in miniature. An example is Boz's play with the phrase 'coming out' in 'The Mistaken Milliner: A Tale of Ambition':

> Now, 'coming out', either in acting, or singing, or society, or facetiousness, or anything else, is all very well, and remarkably pleasant to the individual principally concerned, if he or she can but manage to come out with a burst, and being out to keep out, and not go in again; but it does unfortunately happen that both consummations are extremely difficult to accomplish, and that the difficulties of getting out at all in the first instance, and if you surmount them, of keeping out in the second, are pretty much on a par, and no slight ones either – and so Miss Amelia Martin shortly discovered
>
> (*SB*, 254).

If the real world is a fiction and the reflection of it in literature a fiction too, what of the interpretation of the relation between them expressed by the critic? Can criticism formulate without equivocation the truth which the creative writer can only convey indirectly and in such a way that it will inevitably be misunderstood by his readers? No, the critic is caught in exactly the same predicament as the creative writer or as the man living in the real world. To formulate the relation between reader, text, and world assumed here will guard against misunderstanding what I have been saying as the return to a traditional polarity between seeing literature as realistic representation, on the one hand, and seeing it, on the other, as the creation of a self-contained subjective realm. The view of literary language I am presupposing would not see a work of literature as able ever to be self-contained, self-sustaining, hermetically sealed in its self-referential purity. A work of literature is rather a link in a chain of transformations and substitutions. To identify its ambiguous relation to the links in either direction is one way to articulate the incessant displacement of figurative by literal and of literal by figurative which takes place within a text in its transactions with the social world and with its readers. In one direction there is the social world which the *Sketches* 'describe.' This world is not a collection of hard facts. It is itself interpretation, based on other texts, of the matter of which London is made. In the other direction is the critic. His reading of the text, the connections he makes between one part of it and another, the pattern he establishes as his commentary on the whole, is interpretation in its turn. He asserts similarities and configurations which are not asserted as such in the text itself. He creates a pattern of meaning nowhere explicitly articulated. The fiction of the *Sketches* inserts itself as a text among other fictional texts, those within which the characters of the *Sketches* are shown to live. The critic's interpretation is fiction too. The *Sketches* are not a mirror of reality, but interpretation of interpretation, and the critic's discourse about the *Sketches* may be defined as interpretation of interpretation of interpretation. This chain of substitutions and transformations creates illusion out of illusion and the appearance of reality out of illusion, in a play of language without beginning, end, or extra linguistic foundation.

A glimpse of this reciprocity is provided by the story of the young Dickens's visit in his capacity as journalist to review a new farce at the Adelphi Theatre. The new play, he found, was a blatant plagiarism from one of his Sketches already published, 'The Bloomsbury Christening.' If his *Sketches* owed much to the theatrical part of the already existent culture, they entered themselves into that culture as one of its aspects. Dickens's interpretation of Victorian England is part of English history.

Now it is possible to see what is misleading in the formulation of Roman Jakobson which gave my interpretative journey its initial impetus. The distinction between romantic or symbolist poetry, based on metaphor, in which the set of language is toward itself, and 'realistic' texts, based on metonymy, in which the set of language tends to be 'primarily upon referent,'[28] cannot be made a diametrical opposition. Any literary text is both self-referential and extra-referential, or rather it is open to being not seen as the former and mistakenly taken as the latter. All language is figurative, displaced. All language is beside itself. There is no 'true' sign for the thing. Even proper names, as linguists and ethnologists have come to see, are figurative.[29] The true world, the hidden Logos, always slips away, is always a matter of somewhere else or of some other time. Both metonymy and metaphor are versions of the same 'fundamental of language,' the fiction of identity. The lie which says A equals B (metaphor) is no more 'poetic' than the lie which says A leads to B (metonymy). Both are naming one thing with the name of another, in a constant stepping aside which constitutes the life of language. Both metaphor and metonymy are open to a correct interpretation in which the figurative is seen as figurative. Both invite the misinterpretation which takes as substantial what are in fact only linguistic fictions. All poetry, however strongly based on metaphor, is liable to be read literally, and all realistic narrative, however metonymic in texture, is open to a correct figurative reading which sees it as fiction rather than *mimesis*. One might in fact argue that metonymic displacement, in its movement from presence to absence, is even more fundamental than metaphorical transference or superimposition. Metaphor could as easily be described as a special case of metonymy as metonymy a special case of metaphor. In any case, it is misleading to suggest that they are polar opposites, either as synchronic rhetorical fact giving rise to two distinct forms of literature or as the basis of literary history, for example the development from romanticism to realism to symbolism. All these historically located forms of literature are versions of the fundamental structure of a figurative language open to misreading as literal. All are open to similar procedures of corrent interpretation.

Notes

1. CHARLES DICKENS. *Sketches by Boz*, The Oxford Illustrated Dickens (London: Oxford University Press, 1966), p. 493. Further quotations from this text will be identified as *SB*, followed by the page number.

2. Among the scholars representing this development in criticism are Georges Blin, Roland Barthes, Jacques Derrida, Gilles Deleuze, Gérard Genette and Paul de Man. DERRIDA's 'The Double Session', in *Dissemination* (London: Athlone, 1981), pp. 173–286, and DE MAN's 'The Rhetoric of Blindness', *Blindness and Insight*, are particularly valuable for their formulations of the theoretical bases of such inquiries. HILLIS MILLER's *The Form of Victorian Fiction* (Notre Dame, Ind.: University of Notre Dame Press, 1968) is an attempt to make suggestions along these lines for nineteenth-century English novels.

3. 'Closing Statement: Linguistics and Poetics', *Style in Language*, ed. Thomas A. Sebeok (Cambridge, Mass.: MIT Press, 1966), p. 356.

4. Cited by Jean-Michel Rey from the *Essays on B. Brecht* in 'La Scène du texte', *Critique* **271** (Décembre 1969), p. 1068.

5. See JOHN BUTT and KATHLEEN TILLOTSON, '*Sketches by Boz*: Collection and Revision', *Dickens at Work* (London: Methuen, 1963), pp. 35–61; PHILIP COLLINS, 'A Dickens Bibliography', *The New Cambridge Bibliography of English Literature*, ed. George Watson, III (Cambridge: Cambridge University Press, 1969), cols 786–7; Appendix F, *The Pilgrim Edition of the Letters of Charles Dickens*, ed. M. House and G. Storey, I (Oxford: Oxford University Press, 1965) for detailed information about the writing of the *Sketches by Boz*, their publication in various periodicals, their revision and collection in 1836 in the two-volume *Sketches by Boz*, First and Second Series, published by Macrone, their further revision for the edition of 1839 in monthly parts published by Chapman and Hall and collected by them in the one-volume edition of 1839, and the final revision of 1850. Mrs Tillotson's essay (the preface of *Dickens at Work* says it is mainly hers) is especially valuable for its discussion of the process of revision which the *Sketches* underwent.

6. See *Dickens at Work*, pp. 46–8, 52–3, and the essays by W.J. CARLTON in *The Dickensian*, cited in Collins, *Bibliography*, col. 787.

7. Cited in *Dickens at Work*, p. 44.

8. In the essay of this title in *Communications*, XI (1968), pp. 84–9.

9. *The Dialogues of Plato*, trans. B. Jowett, 3rd edn, I (New York: Oxford University Press, 1892), p. 374.

10. Quoted in *Dickens at Work*, p. 37, from *Metropolitan Magazine* (March 1836), p. 77; *Examiner* (28 February 1836), p. 133; *Spectator* (20 February 1836), p. 183. See Collins, *Bibliography*, cols 786–7, for a fuller list of contemporary reviews, which were for the most part laudatory. Mrs Tillotson is right to say that the *Sketches by Boz* rather than *Pickwick Papers* were Dickens' first popular success as a writer.

11. *Dickens at Work*, p. 37.

12. *The Life of Charles Dickens*, Library Edition, revised, I (London, 1876), Book I, Section V. According to Collins, *Bibliography*, Forster is also the author of the review in the *Examiner* cited above.

13. *Dickens at Work*, p. 37.

14. *The World of Charles Dickens* (New York: Viking Press, 1970), p. 84.

15. 'Sketches by Boz', *Dickens and the Twentieth Century*, ed. John Gross and Gabriel Pearson (Toronto: University of Toronto Press, 1962). pp. 20, 21, 34.

16. *Style in Language*, p. 353.

17. *Ibid.*, p. 370.

18. ROMAN JAKOBSON and MORRIS HALLE, *Fundamentals of Language* (The Hague: Mouton, 1956), pp. 77–8.

19. *Style in Language*, p. 375.

20. For the seminal description of this aspect of Dickens' imagination, see DOROTHY VAN GHENT, 'The Dickens World: A View from Todgers's', *Sewanee Review*, LVIII (1950), 419–38.

21. GÉRARD GENETTE, in an excellent article, 'Métonymie chez Proust, ou la naissance du récit', *Poétique* 2 (1970), 156–73, published after Hillis Miller completed this study, has called attention to a similar founding of metaphor on metonymic assumptions in *À la Recherche du temps perdu*.

22. *Martin Chuzzlewit*, Chapter 40.

23. See *Dickens at Work*, pp. 41–3, 56–7, for a discussion of the ordering and re-ordering of the *Sketches* in the collected editions of 1836 and 1839.

24. Cited in *Dickens at Work*, p. 45.

25. *Ibid.*, p. 47.

26. The head of the family in 'Mrs Joseph Porter' is 'a stock-broker in especially comfortable circumstances' (*SB*, 421).

27. *Dickens and the Twentieth Century*, p. 28.

28. *Fundamentals of Language*, p. 81.

29. See JACQUES DERRIDA's discussion of the problematic of proper names in Lévi-Strauss's *Tristes tropiques*: 'The Battle of Proper Names', in *Of Grammatology* (Baltimore and London: The Johns Hopkins University Press, 1974), pp. 107–18, and see also ROLAND BARTHES, 'Proust et les noms', *To Honor Roman Jakobson* (The Hague: Mouton, 1967), pp. 150–8.

22   Penny Boumelha on Realism and Feminism*

What I hope to do, in this essay, is to mount a double argument: to engage with the debate over how nineteenth-century realism – taken for the moment to mark the recognition of an empirically associated set of texts – is to be theorised, and also to intervene in the question of the validity and the uses of interpretation for the feminist critic. Nineteenth-century realism has had a bad press in most developments in theory that fall under the broad heading of poststructuralism, and especially in those kinds of literary or cultural theory that are openly and self-consciously politically interested – and by these I mean, essentially, Marxism and feminism. The far-reaching suspicion of realist writing on the part of the theoretically inclined and its valorisation by the untheoretical both rest upon arguments that I want to oppose. It seems to me essential that we continue in feminist criticism to appropriate the texts and procedures of nineteenth-century realism, through which (or at least in full awareness of which) so many women, as writers and as readers, have found a way of instating themselves in the world.

And to appropriate requires us to interpret: interpretive reading, I would argue, can be an operation carried out not only *by* feminists but also *for* feminism. Feminism's necessary aim – the unmaking and remaking of knowledges, the refusal of singular perspective in the name of situated view – can work at the level of specificities: the appropriative critic can resist the arrest of meaning, contest the community policing of interpretation (even if it is true that everything we say will be taken down and may be used in evidence against us). It is the cultural and political uses to which texts can and will be put that must concern us; and feminist criticism at its best can illuminate and challenge those conditions that at once enable and circumscribe not only the work but also its social meanings. I recognise, however, that to speak, as I have done thus far, of 'appropriation' is to incite a critical activity that risks

---

* Reprinted from 'Realism and the Ends of Feminism' in *Grafts: Feminist Cultural Criticism*, ed. Susan Sheridan (New York: Verso, 1988), pp. 77–91.

reproducing the coercions of meaning characteristic of patriarchal interpretations of 'woman'. In the first place, it is obvious that, despite my own rhetorical singularity, there is no one feminism – there are feminisms. Then, too, texts are not feminine, of course, and still less female, but whereas the 'appropriation' of certain kinds of narrative may have a fine and sounding ring, a problematic element creeps in in the case of 'appropriating', say, *Clarissa*, or *Villette*, or *Jude the Obscure* – texts of the woman as victim and as writer, text as refusal to yield meaning. Perhaps what I am arguing for, then, would be better designated a technique of *ex*propriative reading, a critical mode that works to undo the ownership of the text by a consortium of patriarchal vested interests, not necessarily of specific interpretations, but of particular strategic aims and limits of interpretation.

The problem is that many, or most, politically orientated theories of realism have tended to argue (or on occasion to assume) that realist texts can only be read productively by contestatory or oppositional criticism in so far as they are disrupted by other modes of writing; that is, that we can only value a realist text for those moments when and where it shows the traces of other modes (whether those be chronologically prospective, as in the dislocations of early modernism, retrospective, as in half-repressed persistences of the Gothic, or simply lateral). This seems to me the constant underlying tenor of such critical positions, whether realism is seen as a set of properties or strategies inherent in the organisation of the text, or as an effect of reading. Clearly, I shall need to illustrate and substantiate this point by looking back at a couple of such critical proceedings.

One term that gained considerable currency, and which has proved particularly influential in discussions of nineteenth-century texts, is 'classic realism'. For proponents of this theory,[1] the idea of 'classic realism' is a critical tool with which to expose the bourgeois and humanistic epistemological bases of the 'great tradition' on which the most widely practised understandings of written narrative have long been predicated. Rather than addressing in a descriptive and categoric way the formal characteristics of realist texts, the 'classic realism' argument has aimed to show the political content built into their narrative tactics. In this argument, chief among the tactics of the classic realist or readerly text is a form of closure – not simply formal, but ideological – by which the reader is continually produced and addressed as a unified individual human subject, through such means as the convergence at a single and uniform ideological position of a set of hierarchised discourses of which one is always a controlling 'truth-voice'. The dissembling of fictionality and textuality, and a theory of language in which words correspond unproblematically to pre-existing referents in the world, are also held to be characteristic of classic realism, and to serve, by obscuring the written nature of the work, to consolidate such naturalising ideologies as the 'nature of things' or 'human nature'.

This concern with the political meanings of form seems to me entirely admirable; nevertheless, there are substantial difficulties with this particular theory. I shall be going on to some of them shortly, but let me make in passing the perhaps illicitly empirical point that the theory does not correspond to any actual text of the period that I can think of, though it identifies what might perhaps be called the aspirations of certain texts.

Another, and in some ways more sophisticated, version of a Marxist theory of realism is that to be found in the work of Ferrucio Rossi-Landi.[2] Rossi-Landi develops rigorously and explicitly an argument to be found in some form in many ideology-based accounts of realism. For him, 'realism' in literary discourse is constituted in its reception by a readership defined less as a collection of individuals than as a historically and socially determinate public; that is one reason why ideas of the 'realistic' have varied so much over time. Realism, he argues, is marked by the ease of reception which it encounters from such a public; as he puts it, the realist text 'encodes a message which is destined to be decoded by the public as representative of the dominant ideology'. The historical specificity of this idea of a public is, however, cancelled out by the notion of a textual destiny that circumvents that public. How, and by what agency, such a destiny can be imposed upon the text is unclear, just as the theory of 'classic realism' cannot explain how it is that a mode of reading can continue ahistorically to enforce itself upon both text and reader – or, indeed, how it is that, as critics or theorists, we see through – that is, resist – a mode of reading that enforces itself upon us as readers.

There is, in these theories, an odd and entirely unintended collusion between the theory and the political content it aims to indict: in each case, the interpretation concedes at once the total effectivity of the narrative strategies it identifies. The ideas of a predestined decoding (in Rossi-Landi) and of an inescapably unvarying subject-position produced by the interpellation of the text (in 'classic realism') appear to rule out any possibility of a counter-reading, let alone a plurality of reading. We can unknowingly accept or consciously reject, but the bourgeois affiliations of the text remain always and everywhere in place. We cannot read otherwise, cannot transform; and yet, surely, these are precisely the areas of textual theory in which feminist criticism has sought to install itself. Further, in the construction of such accounts of realism, the role of the 'dominant ideology' (itself a concept that has come under considerable attack within Marxism) or, for 'classic realism', of a readily identifiable set of class-interests means that the realist text can only be read as serving, more or less unambiguously, political values that we wish to contest; and this conclusion in turn would lock us into a static and troublingly unhistorical model in which realism emerges as always and everywhere reactionary and in which modernism, whether explicitly or by implication, comes to be seen as inherently progressive. These inferences, I think, are disturbing for feminism, not least because realism is the means by which so many nineteenth-century women writers staked a claim to speak of the public issues lying outside the constricted sphere of traditional feminist concerns.

If we accept, provisionally at least, the general map-cum-history of feminist criticism proposed by Toril Moi's *Sexual/Textual Politics*, then it is possible to find in both her Anglo-American and her French theoretical strains a central concern with realism.[3] The kind of 'images of women' criticism that is marked by its attempt to evaluate representations of women in texts according to their degree of correspondence to the experience of actual individual women quite clearly operates in only the most reflectionist model of realism, and, furthermore, in a form detached from any historical awareness, so that it often seeks to find in and through the work a set of attitudes (the author's or those of a vague 'society') for which the text can then be held responsible to contemporary feminism. I shall be coming back to this kind of feminist reading. More significantly, the useful work by the then Marxist-Feminist Literature Collective on women's writing around 1848[4] produces a line of argument rather like that of the Marxist theories I have outlined, if we transpose class interest into patriarchal ideologies and the interests of male dominance. Here, feminist protest and feminine desire are located only in the interstices of the realist text; to read a realist novel from this perspective is effectively to read only its disruptions and underminings. The realist strain or mode of such texts is posited as primarily a strategy of containment, an attempt at repressive coherence which serves the better to highlight the irruptions of Romanticism and the Gothic. There is at work here, to borrow Foucault's term, a kind of repressive hypothesis in the domain of textuality, by which potentially polymorphous radical forms are held in a precarious check by a reactionary mode that uncritically serves the social status quo.

A further perspective on this debate emerges from many of the uses of a Kristevan theory of the acquisition of language. Kristeva's alignment of the symbolic order of language with **phallocentrism**, and of the imperfectly repressed *chora* of the pre-linguistic pulsional semiotic with the pre-Oedipal phase of mother-identification, lends itself to a privileging of avant-gardist or modernist writing. It is there that Kristevan feminism finds the site of a mother-identified semiotic writing, a writing that constitutes itself always as marginal to and subversive of the symbolic order of language. In most critical uses of Kristevan theory that I know, realist writing is taken as that which is to be disrupted because it serves a form of social organisation that feminists contest. Once again, as with another kind of feminist attention to realist texts, a dichotomy is established between two kinds of writing, in a way that assigns fixed textual–political connotations to each.

But all of these arguments commence with the same manoeuvre: the collapse into and on to one another of realism as an epistemolgy and realism as a mode of writing. By a conceptual sleight of hand, a critical practice that values the second is made complicit with the first. Yet it is patently not the case that only bourgeois humanists or misogynistic reactionaries continue to enjoy and to find fruitful the work of, say, George Eliot, and certainly I at least would not wish to suggest that this should become the case. Again, the argument against realism, if I may call it that, frequently rests upon an assumption that it is characterised by an inability or a refusal to know itself as writing; illusionism, a kind of wilful self-blindness destined to induce in its reader a reciprocal self-blindness, is often held to be realism's major ideological tactic. But the social meanings of forms, while determinate, are not determined by the ideologies and interests of the moment of their production alone; they are dynamic, constantly reproduced and reformulated by continuing literary and critical processes that are themselves always in process and contestation. I do not wish to argue for an atomised universe of individualised reader response, nor for a rapturous instability of polysemy; on the other hand, it is surely too simple to see publics as directly representative or expressive of single, homogeneous class, gender and racial positions.

Over against these kinds of arguments, I want to propose that a feminist reading of any text, whether it is by a woman or a man, needs to know and accept that it is an appropriation of the work in the name of (a) feminism, rather than a revelation of its intrinsic meaning, even if that meaning be ideologically or socially defined. In that case, a feminist reading is a reading made for ourselves by the needs and interests of contemporary feminism, but it must be grounded in an awareness of the historical and formal possibilities of writing and reading if it is genuinely to explore the relation between the work and the society that produces it and its reading; and that seems to me an essential task of feminist cultural criticism. After all, feminist criticism has always worked on the basis of positing another possibility of relationship between reader and text than that of mutual reflection; its modes of reading have been to oppose, to appropriate for another understanding, to read against the grain. It would be futile to argue for, say, a rehabilitation of realism as inherently progressive, in some Lukácsian downgrading of modernism; I want, rather, to refuse the overly simple opposition of these or any other modes, and to suggest that we should not read realism only as a failure to be or to become another mode. Realist texts can be read by and for feminism, not in a flatly mimetic sense but as they enact in both their coherences and their incoherences the struggle between their representation and its own limits and incompletions.

George Eliot has often been cited as a prime example in the accounts of realism I have been discussing, as she is for instance in Belsey's version of the 'classic realism' argument, so that if illusionism, controlling truth-voices, unproblematic reproductions of the dominant ideology and wilful suppression of textuality are to be found anywhere, we might not unreasonably expect to find them in her writing. The ways in which Eliot's work is realist – if not 'classically' – are evident enough, and in any event have been widely discussed in criticism of her, though even here, of course, it should be remembered that she also wrote such things as the profoundly non-realist, typological 'half' of *Daniel Deronda* the story *The Lifted Veil* which draws on the Gothic to show how Latimer's 'visions' of the soul and nature of woman in fact produce their own confirmation in his wife, and other works that do not altogether fill the realist bill.[5] The ways in which Eliot transgresses the boundaries of the 'classic realist' mould also deserve some attention, however. There is, for example, the obviousness of voice and of a narrator's presence in much of her writing. *The Mill on the Floss*, after all, begins by establishing its narrator as immersed in dream and memory; this opening does not initiate what Belsey calls 'a privileged, historic narration which is the source of coherence of the story as a whole'.[6] There are, too, those chapters in *Adam Bede* and *The Mill*, often read simply as manifestos of realism, in which the narrative is interrupted with a discussion of the principles on which it is constructed and organised – hardly an illusionist device.

Then again, the epigrams and moral axioms, snatches of verse and apparent extracts from dramas that Eliot wrote as epigraphs to the chapters of some of her novels flagrantly advertise the texuality of the work and its unsettling relation to the putative authority of other texts, as well as suggesting the range of other possible genres and modes in which the work could have been conceived. In the case of *Felix Holt*, this adumbration of alternative discourses and genres reaches beyond the confines of the novel itself into Eliot's political journalism (the article 'Felix Holt's Address to Working Men'). Within that novel, it virtually constitutes itself into a plot: the world of 'the poets' and reading as parable, of tragedy and 'fine stories' associated with the introductory coachman-storyteller and with Mrs Transome is displaced by Esther, 'critic of words' and associate ('affiliate', indeed, in the novel's transposition of literary genealogies into family relationships) of the independent chapel-goers, for whom reading is precisely commentary and dissent. In the space of only about fifteen pages in the novel, Esther discusses and is discussed in relation to ballad heroines, tragic heroes, genteel comedy, the want of romance and the renunciation of utopias. Esther's schooling in realism, in opting for the 'middling lot' of typicality (not the '*via media* of indifference' also evoked in the novel), enacts and argues the novel's case for its own mode. Even the naming of the heroine can be related to this intertextual self-definition: where Charlotte Brontë's *Villette* uses the actress Vashti (and her biblical prototype) to figure the inflammatory but self-dooming spectacle of the woman artist, Eliot's *Felix Holt* counters with its figure of Esther and her biblical prototype.

In the Bible story[7] – I believe it is tactfully customary at this point to add 'you will recall' – Esther succeeds Vashti as wife to Ahasuerus; Vashti is displaced for her refusal to display herself as a spectacle of beauty for his assembled male guests, whereas Esther, orphaned and not beautiful, manages to achieve her ends by cont·   ·tercession with her king-husband. The political implications of this story may not be inspiring for feminists, but it, too, has its place in the claim Eliot is staking for realism in the novel's considerations of reading and writing. The point of remarking such elements here is not to insist upon a non-realist or proto-modernist Eliot to stand in the place of the Aunt Sally of classic realism, but to suggest how, even as she stayed largely within the conventions of nineteenth-century realism, Eliot's writing was able to explore its limits, subject its idea of representation to scrutiny and question its practices. That is to say, her practice of realism contains its own elements of self-referentiality even in its claim to mimetic reference.

I want now to go on to use this question of realism as a basis for examining the assumptions implicit in some of the feminist critiques of Eliot's fiction. Eliot has long occupied a privileged, if problematic, place in feminist criticism. The reasons for her pre-eminence are not hard to find; they include her unchallenged place in the great collection of set texts we have come to call the canon, the formidable figure she seems to have been personally, her rare combination of passion and wit, her frequent refusal of the consolations of romance. And yet she has also proved frustrating – even enraging – to some feminists. The reasons for their anger can fairly readily be demonstrated, and some of them conceded without dissent. Eliot displays the injustices and abuses that press upon the lives of her women and then seems to refuse the logic of the insight offered by her own texts, apparently resolving the conflict between romantic, individualist rebellion and the power of community morality all too easily in favour of the latter. She may deplore the restricted lives of her heroines, but she appears to celebrate the morality of martyrdom to which they give rise; Elaine Showalter has commented with as much asperity as aptness that she 'elevates suffering into a female career'.[8] Again, she shows her women to be capable of intellectual and social achievement and aspiration, but offers them no field in which to exercise these abilities, consigning heroines finally for the most part only to death or to marriage. Most offensive of all, for some, is Eliot's refusal to bestow upon her heroines the opportunities that she so fully and joyously seized for herself; for Kate Millett, Eliot 'lived the revolution . . . but did not write of it'.[9] The whole tenor of such criticism is summed up in this comment by Jenni Calder: 'Sadly, and it is a radical criticism of George Eliot, she does not commit herself fully to the energies and aspirations she lets loose in these women. Does she not cheat them, and cheat us, ultimately, in allowing them so little?'[10]

This is a serious question and a sad catalogue of complaints, but I doubt whether the critique they frame is in fact a radical one. All of these critiques originate from and exemplify broadly the same kind of criticism, long dominant within English and American feminism at least, that leans heavily upon the presupposed ability of the reader – always, I think, a female reader – to recognise on the basis of her own uproblematised experience the 'authenticity' (or lack of it) in the work under discussion. Evidently, such a naively reflectionist model of realism drastically reduces the scope of texts it can address; that is one reason why Eliot, so closely identified with realism, has figured so largely in this kind of criticism, and it is also the reason why those aspects of her work that escape or question the mimetic have often met with a blank rejection or a puzzled inadequacy of response. But more pertinently for my purposes, this kind of criticism runs into serious theoretical problems even in its address to elements of realism. It tends on the one hand to approach novels for their sociological content – for their depiction of the injustices and abuses suffered by women – but on the other hand it contains a strongly prescriptive strain in its insistence on looking for positive role-models with whom contemporary feminists might expect to identify. The resulting requirement of fantasy heroines in realist textual environments places anachronistic and unanswerable demands upon the possibilities of writing mid-nineteenth-century realism.

The problem is often raised most acutely by fictional endings. Realism, bounded more or less by its project of representing in some typical form the real conditions of social existence, has tended to reduce the options for its female protagonists to either marriage or death. Of course, the virtual interchangeability of the two is itself telling. The kind of feminist readings I have just been discussing (which come from what is, perhaps unfortunately, the strain of feminism from which realist texts have received their most detailed readings) have been apt to see both these forms of closure as not simply representing but reproducing – enforcing, even – the impoverished opportunities that the social order of nineteenth-century Britain afforded actual historical women of the middle class. That is, they have tended to see a final marriage as a cop-out and a final death as a victimisation of the heroine. Yet, at the same time, they work with a moralised version of genre that sees fantasy or romance as unworthy and evasive. A critical double-bind is thus established by which virtually all novels written before the contemporary expansion of both women's opportunities and feminist theory must be judged and found wanting. However, if we look at the endings of realist novels – whether marriage, death, or some other form – in formal and ideological terms rather than these anachronistically mimetic ones, they will often yield more interesting results for feminist criticism than the failure to provide positive role-models or the paucity of social opportunities. The necessity of an ending, after all, is one of the ways in which any fiction, however involuntary, flaunts its textuality. Novels are obliged to end, and therefore to end abruptly, the novel must always have the last word. The endings of the realist text often push to the point of stark visibility the struggle of a self-styled truthful representation to reduce into some form of textual closure those 'truths' of women's desire or aspiration or articulateness that it has itself displayed.

It is in the light, then, of this double concern – to read the work for feminism and to situate it within its generic and historical constraints – that I should like to discuss the endings of some of Eliot's novels. I begin with *The Mill on the Floss*. I am not concerned to establish that Eliot was or was not a feminist (though I do not mean to say that that is a question without interest), but rather to examine the ways in which the novel's focus upon a strong female protagonist troubles its form and brings it up against the limits of its own theoretical project. The novel sets out as a *Bildungsroman*, a form that characteristically concerns itself with the growth of a male protagonist. That this form becomes problematic when it centres upon a girl rapidly becomes easy to see; after all, *Bildung* – culture, education – is the very thing most bitterly denied the novel's heroine. The form of the *Bildungsroman* has built into it the requirement and affirmation of the values of autonomy and self-definition – values by no means always considered appropriate for women. It is an almost generically individualistic fable of identity, whose considerable appeal to Victorian readers depended partly upon its confirmation of the integrity and coherence of the individual over time, and in this it posits character rather than social determination as the motive force of its narrative development. Eliot's project, by contrast, is to show, through the device of compared and contrasted brother and sister, how powerfully forces and expectations not generated within the individual character determine the growth of Tom and Maggie. This central contrast is obviously an effective vehicle for feminist commentary, one that will be taken up again by several of the more polemical women writers of the 1880s and 1890s.

It is Maggie alone, though, who increasingly becomes the protagonist of the novel as the children are progressively separated by education and puberty (*Bildung* and sexuality, the poles of the novel). The violence of the collision between the ideological underpinnings of the form and the range of possibilities for the fictional heroine becomes evident in the ardour of Maggie's espousal of Thomas à Kempis and the renunciation of the self. Of course, this novel of the growth of the individual self is caught in its own trap, and Maggie's self-abnegation must inevitably reveal itself to be an inverted form of the self-affirmation that the *Bildungsroman* demands. Feminine self-suppression and heroic self-affirmation enter into contradiction with one another, and the result has been diagnosed by some character-orientated critics as masochism. But as Maggie grows into adulthood, another problem becomes pressing: within the conventions of realism, the novel can offer Maggie – or the middle-class woman in general – no vocation, no meaningful work to match that of the *gebildete* male protagonist. We are back at the crossroads: marriage or death. It is here that Eliot's refusal of romance comes into play. The paltriness of the temptation provided by Stephen Guest, the unsatisfactory nature of the romantic escapade (Maggie's is a sexual fall only by the rules of community interpretation), enact all over again the restriction of the opportunities available to her. It is sufficient to rule out the possibility of marriage, however, and only death presents itself as a conclusion. It is important, though, that Maggie does not, for example, gently expire from one of those quasi-symbolic brain fevers so apt in this period to strike down heroines with brain enough to become enfevered. Instead, she is at once vindicated and annihilated by the flood which, however well-laid the clues of imagery and rhetoric may be, strikes the reader each time anew as sudden, arbitrary. This ending to the novel has occasioned a great deal of commentary and interpretation, often based on disappointment. It has been seen, by feminists among others, as evasive, abrupt, improbable. The reunion with Tom that the flood effects has likewise been deplored as sentimental, undeserved by him, too transparently a wish-fulfilment of Eliot's longing to overcome the disapproval of her own brother. For some feminist critics, the ending has combined sell-out (reconciliation with the oppressive brother) with victimisation (sacrifice of the woman). But the plot ending is not necessarily the destiny of the text – it may be only its destination. There is more to be said about Maggie's death (as there will be about Dorothea's marriage) than simply that it happens.

And, indeed, quite a lot more has been said. A large and varied range of interpretations of the events of the flood has been offered: in my own and other people's readings, it has figured as (among others) a revenge murder of Tom; a narrator's murder of Maggie; the destruction of the restrictive community; the fulfilment of an incest fantasy; regression to a prepubertal age without sexual difference; the re-emergence of catastrophic theories of evolution as a series of creations; the reconciliation of male and female elements; anal rage (in this classically Freudian reading, the 'dark masses' floating in the river are, of course, faeces); the projection of Maggie's impulses towards martyrdom and heroism on to the forces of nature; and a moment of sexual release, the 'little death' of orgasm mimicked by the larger death.[11] Any or all of these interpretations might be acceptable. But more important, I think, is the sheer excess of the text over such interpretations, the flagrantly fantasised and contrived nature of the ending. It acknowledges and makes unusually visible the formal-cum-ideological impasse that the novel has reached by virtue of its concentration on the development of a woman for whom no meaningful future – no 'end' in its other sense – can be imagined. It breaks out of this impasse only by sweeping the novel out of the realist mode altogether. The irreconcilable contradictions of ideology and form bring the novel hard up against the very limits of its own realism, and the flood that crashed through those barriers submerges the world of history (and of mimetic realism) along with St Ogg's, bringing with it the victory of symbol, legend, fantasy. This, it seems to me, is the most exciting feminist point to be made about *The Mill on the Floss*: the dammed-up energy created by the frustrated ambitions and desires, intellectual and sexual, of the woman is so powerful that it cannot be contained with the forms of mimesis: the repressed and thwarted potential of Maggie conjures into being that destructive, vengeful, triumphant flood. The ending confers upon Maggie those possibilities of heroism that will be withheld from Dorothea and Gwendolen, but there is an ideological price to be paid, as Gillian Beer has argued: 'The subversive vehemence of Maggie's fate both releases from the bonds of social realism, and yet neutralises its own commentary by allowing her, and so us, the plenitude which is nowhere available in her society.'[12] It is the only occasion in these major novels when Eliot will console us with such fantasied plenitude for the narrow, unjust, oppressive world that social realism has to depict.

Middlemarch explicitly eschews such transcendence by the individual. The novel repeatedly cautions against the consolatory illusions of egotism, and it enacts through its metaphors of web, stream and connective tissue as much as through its plot the imbrication of the individual character in its social medium. It is a novel in which simplifying and synthetic hypotheses of interconnectedness – Casaubon's *Key to All Mythologies*, Lydgate's search for the 'primitive tissue', Bulstrode's version of Providence – are satirised by the baldly material and frankly melodramatic connections established at the level of plot, by money, parentage, shared acts committed in the past – by inheritance, that is, in all its forms.[13] *Middlemarch* uses a relentlessly materialist vocabulary of health and disease, microscope and lens, inheritance and debt in its analyses of feeling and moral quality. The effect is partly to unsettle character, in its more traditional conception, as the engine driving the plot, and partly to frustrate romantic individualist notions of heroism. True, Dorothea is a belated St Theresa, with no order to found; but it is also true that by the end of the novel she is only one of 'many Dorotheas'. Typicality is pre-eminent over singularity in this text.

It has by now become unnecessary to point out the elements of explicit

or implicit feminist protest in the novel: its depiction of what Elaine
Showalter has called 'The woman's text in *Middlemarch* . . . the fall of
Dorothea'.[14] Nevertheless, it is worth looking once more at the ending
that the novel offers its heroine. In a sense, it is conventional enough,
certainly more conventional than Maggie's flood. The 'Finale' chapter,
with its more or less direct address to the reader and its closing tour of
the marriages, seems reminiscent of the tidying-up operations at the end
of a Jane Austen novel, a closed ending if ever there was one. And yet,
the conventionality and the tidiness are somewhat undercut by the
acknowledgement of the reader's probable discontent, through the
opinions of Sir James Chettam and of local gossip. But the reader is pre-
emptively rebuked as well as being the object of sympathy:

> Many who knew her, thought it a pity that so substantive and rare a
> creature should have been absorbed into the life of another, and be
> only known in a certain circle as a wife and mother. But no-one stated
> exactly what else that was in her power she ought rather to have done
> – not even Sir James Chettam, who went no further than the negative
> prescription that she ought not to have married Will Ladislaw.[15]

In this 'negative prescription', of course, Sir James prefigures many
subsequent critics. The comment stresses the absence of alternatives 'in
her power', but if Dorothea cannot have power, she can at least have
Will. The pun is embedded in the novel itself, and surely to some effect
in a work where wills are otherwise associated with patriarchal authority,
with the 'dead hand' of law, prohibition and patrimony. Dorothea must
give up her inheritance in order to marry Ladislaw: that is, she must defy
the will of the father–husband in order to choose a new Will for herself.
In this there is some parallel with Ladislaw himself; descended from
rebellious women, negating the primacy of origin by 'prefer[ring] not to
know the source of the Nile', Will too has renounced what is for him a
birthright rather than a right of marriage, a (nonetheless conditional)
inheritance from Casaubon. In this double refusal of the weight of the
'dead hand' of patriarchal precedence, there are distinct hints of what a
later feminist, the short-story writer George Egerton, will call 'the
Regeneration of Two', a new imagining of relations between women and
men.[16]

Felix Holt has already effected a compromise version of this kind of
ending. Esther, in that novel, refuses most (though not quite all) of her
inheritance, but only the better to reinstate patrilineage and true
paternity: the novel closes with the image of the 'young Felix' whose
inheritance is not of money but of 'science' – indeed, of 'more science
than his father'.[17] In bringing together Esther and Felix, the novel
operates a curious interaction of class and gender determinations: Felix,

the novel's representative of working-classness (who, incidentally, is a skilled artisan in a home-based trade, watch- and clock-making, and therefore by no means typical of the industrialised working class of the period), is underwritten in his political conservatism by his familial origins. It is precisely because he stands by his 'own people' that his politics are endorsed by the narrative, just as it is precisely because he comes from outside the class for which he presumes to speak that Harold Transome is (politically) illegitimate. Esther, on the other hand, is validated by her passage from 'fine lady' to wife of Felix by her refusal of determination by inheritance and the law. Again, despite the explicit conservatism of the novel (which I do not wish to make invisible), this representation of genealogies and affiliations brings with it a potentially radical questioning of the 'family relations' of literary history: who fathered, who should or can father, the texts of the woman, of dissent, of what passes here for radicalism? Are such texts legitimate or illegitimate? Can they be 'fathered' by George Eliot?

In *Daniel Deronda*, of course, the search for an origin, a determination, leads not to the father, but to the rejecting artist–mother whose privileging of her own needs and ambitions frees Daniel, and with him Gwendolen, for their forms of indeterminacy. Daniel's decision to commit himself to the struggle to establish a Jewish state in the East produces an open ending; the fact that it has been 'closed' for us by history should not obscure the uncertainty that it embodied in its own time. Equally, it suggests that the gestures realism makes towards history can be prescient as well as mimetic. Daniel, then, as male protagonist and bearer of the novel's title for his name, is allowed an open ending, a discontinuity that nevertheless, in its typological form, commits him to at least some new form of patrilineage. On the other hand, the novel's female protagonist, Gwendolen, must confront an ending more radically open in its indeterminacy – an ending that so far has not been closed for feminism by history. The novel imagines nothing, and therefore leaves open everything, for her. Gwendolen, in a final letter to Daniel, writes: 'I have remembered your words – that I may live to be one of the best of women, who makes others glad they were born. I do not yet see how that can be.'[18] We do not have to subscribe to the ethics of Daniel's faith, nor indeed to his authority as mentor and judge of the 'best of women', to find in those words an affirmation of hope, of visionary possibility ('I do not *yet* see') as well as an acknowledgement of limitation. In these words, with their avowal of the unimaginable nature of such transformations, we can read for feminism the importance of Eliot's testing of the potentialities and limits of the realist mode for the representation of the desires and aspirations of women. In the ambivalent fantasy of Maggie's extinction and transcendence, in the equally ambivalent acquiescence of Dorothea's commonplace fate, and in the frank uncertainty of Gwendolen's future, Eliot's endings bring into fiction the collision of the unsatisfied, perhaps even illimitable, desire of her heroines with the restricted possibilites of the world as it could be imagined by realism. It is in this sense (not, I know, her own) that I should like to end with Virginia Woolf's comment on Eliot's heroines; they are, for her, the transcription of a women's consciousness that 'seems in them to have brimmed and overflowed and uttered a demand for something – they know not what'.[19] Eliot's endings bear witness to the struggles of her realism to imagine, to bring within the grasp of representation, that 'something', even as it concedes that it 'knows not what'.

Notes

Parts of this essay have previously appeared in 'George Eliot and the End of Realism' in Sue Roe (ed.), *Women Reading Women Writing*, Brighton, 1987.

1. This concept is most explicitly and conveniently set out in Catherine Belsey, *Critical Practice* (London, 1980), pp. 67–84, 112–17.

2. Both the reference and the translation here are borrowed from John Frow, *Marxism and Literary History* (Oxford, 1986), p. 102.

3. TORIL MOI, *Sexual/Textual Politics: Feminist Literary Theory* (London, 1985).

4. Marxist–Feminist Literature Collective, 'Women's Writing: "Jane Eyre", "Shirley", "Villette", "Aurora Leigh"' in Francis Barker *et al.*, (eds), *1848: The Sociology of Literature. Proceedings of the Essex Conference on the Sociology of Literature, July 1977* (University of Essex, 1978), pp. 185–206.

5. This has, of course, been remarked elsewhere, and *The Lifted Veil*, in particular, has received critical attention: see, for instance, SANDRA M. GILBERT and SUSAN GUBAR, *The Madwoman in the Attic: The Woman Writer and the Nineteenth-Century Literary Imagination* (New Haven, 1979), pp. 443–77.

6. *Critical Practice*, pp. 71–2.

7. Esther, in particular i, ii and v.

8. ELAINE SHOWALTER, *A Literature of Their Own: British Women Novelists from Brontë to Lessing* (London, 1978), p. 125.

9. KATE MILLET, *Sexual Politics* (London, 1972), p. 139.

10. JENNI CALDER, *Women and Marriage in Victorian Fiction* (London, 1976), p. 158. Also drawn upon in this paragraph is Zelda Austen, 'Why Feminist Critics Are Angry with George Eliot', *College English* 37, 1976, pp. 549–61; PATRICIA MEYER SPACKS, *The Female Imagination: A Literary and Psychological Investigation of Women's Writing* (London, 1976), pp. 45–7; and LEE R. EDWARDS, 'Women, Energy and *Middlemarch*', *Massachusetts Review* 13, 1972.

11. In this brief conspectus, Boumelha draws on discussions of the ending in critical works mentioned elsewhere in these notes, and on: GILLIAN BEER,

'Beyond Determinism: George Eliot and Virginia Woolf' in Mary Jacobus (ed.), *Women Writing and Writing About Women* (London, 1979), pp. 80–99; LAURA COMER EMERY, *George Eliot's Creative Conflict: The Other Side of Silence* (London, 1976), pp. 5–54; JOHN GOODE, ' "The Affections Clad with Knowldege": Woman's Duty and the Public Life', *Literature and History* 9, 1983, pp. 38–51; MARY JACOBUS, 'The Question of Language: Men of Maxims and *The Mill on the Floss*' in Elizabeth Abel (ed.), *Writing and Sexual Difference* (Brighton, 1982), pp. 37–52; JANE MCDONNELL, ' "Perfect Goodness" or "The Wider Life": *The Mill on the Floss* as *Bildungsroman*', *Genre* 15, 1982, pp. 379–402; JOHN P. MCGOWAN, 'The Turn of George Eliot's Realism', *NCF* 35, 1980, pp. 171–92; JUDITH LOWDER NEWTON, *Women, Power, and Subversion: Social Strategies in British Fiction, 1778–1860* (Athens, Ga., 1981) pp. 125–57; DIANNE F. SADOFF, *Monsters of Affection: Dickens, Eliot and Brontë on Fatherhood* (London, 1982), pp. 65–118.

12. GILLIAN BEER, *George Eliot* (Brighton, 1986), p. 104.

13. Cf. LEO BERSANI, *A Future for Astyanax: Character and Desire in Literature*, (Boston, Mass., 1976), pp. 63–6.

14. ELAINE SHOWALTER, 'The Greening of Sister George', *Nineteenth Century Fiction* 35, 1980, p. 306.

15. *Middlemarch*, ed. W.J. Harvey (Harmondsworth, 1965), p. 894.

16. GEORGE EGERTON, 'The Regeneration of Two' in her *Discords* (London, 1894; rptd, with *Keynotes*, London 1983), pp. 163–253.

17. *Felix Holt, The Radical*, ed. Peter Coveney, (Harmondsworth, 1972), p. 606.

18. *Daniel Deronda*, ed. Barbara Hardy (Harmondsworth, 1967), p. 882. Cf. Lyn Pykett, 'Typology and the End(s) of History in *Daniel Deronda*', *Literature and History* 9, 1983, pp. 65–6.

19. VIRGINIA WOOLF, 'George Eliot' in *Virginia Woolf: Women and Writing*, Intro. Michèle Barrett (London, 1979), p. 159.

Glossary

ADDRESSEE The receiver of a message.

ADDRESSOR The sender of a message.

ALEATORY Dependent upon chance, luck, or an uncertain outcome.

ANAPHORA Deliberate repetitions of a word or phrase at the beginning of several successive verses, clauses, or paragraphs.

ANAGRAMMATISATION Turning into an anagram, i.e. a word or phrase formed by reordering the letters of another word or phrase.

ANTHROPOCENTRIC Regarding human beings as the central fact or final aim of the universe; interpreting reality exclusively in terms of human values and experiences.

ANTHROPOMORPHIC Attributing human motivations, characteristics or behaviour to inanimate objects, animals or natural phenomena.

ASMODEUS Prince of demons in jewish demonology; particularly associated with sensuality. In *El Diablo conjuelo* by Guevara, Asmodeus is a devil who can lift the roof off Madrid houses in order to reveal what is going on inside.

BATESON, GREGORY (1904–80) Cultural anthropologist who worked on Balinese families and on communications theory; *Mind and Nature* (1979) and *Studies in Symbolism and Cultural Communication* (1980) are among his most important works.

BILDUNGSROMAN A German term, now naturalised into English, to denote a novel that traces a young person's development.

BREMOND, CLAUDE (1929–) French literary critic, author of *Logique du récit* (1973; *Logic of Narrative*).

CATACHRESIS The wrong use, misapplication of a word, especially by a mixing of metaphors.

CHEVREUL, EUGÈNE (1786–1889) French chemist whose theory of colours inspired the Impressionists.

CODE Set of conventional signals used in transmitting messages by e.g. flags, telegraph, heliograph; adopted by the structuralists as a term to denote recurrent patterns in a text to be combined by readers into a system of meanings.

COMÉDIE LARMOYANTE Sentimental, tear-jerking eighteenth-century type of comedy.

COMMODIFICATION A Marxist term to denote a materialistic approach to objects and ideas.

DECONSTRUCTION Devolves primarily from the work of the French philosopher Jacques Derrida, especially from three of his early books, all published in France in 1967 and translated into English as *Speech and Phenomena* (1973), *Of Grammatology* (1974) and *Writing and Difference* (1978). Deconstruction opens up texts by examining the nature of the structure which the text reflects and upholds, and in particular by highlighting the margins, limits, ambiguities and traces associated with such a structure.

DENOTATION Act or process of assigning a meaning to a term; often signifies a specific meaning as distinct from connotation, which encompasses also the associations evoked by the term.

DIACHRONIC Considering phenomena as they occur or develop through time.

DISCOURSE Originally a speech, lecture or written treatise; now used for any verbal expression in speech or writing.

DOXA A generally held opinion, common sense. Used by Barthes in *S/Z* to suggest the conformism against which Barthes's ideal reader reacts.

EPISTEMOLOGY The theory of the basis and methods of knowledge.

FEMINISM The doctrine that advocates and demands for women the same rights granted to men, as in political and economic opportunities and status; in literary criticism a protest against sex-coded and gender-inflected approaches, identifying the distortions of male readings and providing corrective counter-readings.

FIGURATIVE Using figures of speech, not literal; having a symbolical or metaphorical connotation; abounding in figures of speech.

FREUD, SIGMUND (1856–1939) Austrian neurologist whose investigations into neuroses, hysteria and dreams as outlets of the unconscious parts of the mind led to the evolution of the therapeutic method of psychoanalysis, popularly known as 'the talking cure', for patients are encouraged to free associate and so to fathom the sources of their problems.

GENETTE, GÉRARD (1930–) French literary critic who applied the principles of structuralism to Proust's *Remembrance of Things Past* in *Narrative Discourse* (1980); also *Narrative Discourse Revisited* (1988).

GREIMAS, ALGIRDAS JULIEN (1917–) A Russian, currently at the French National Research Centre, interested primarily in semantics; has explored his structuralist approach to the matter of meaning in *Sémantique structurale* (1966; *Structural Semantics*) and in *Du Sens* (1970; *On Meaning*).

HERMENEUTICS The science and methodology of interpretation, originally of the Bible, now of any text.

HUMANIST Concerned with the study of human beings; in literary criticism the approach that envisages texts as a reflection of a social reality of their time and place, and examines how human lives are portrayed in their social context.

IDEALISM Often taken as the opposite to materialism or realism; the conception of the universe which regards the mind as the ultimate reality, and ideas as the only objects of perception.

IDIOLECT Speech of an individual, considered as a linguistic pattern unique among speakers of that language or dialect.

INTERTEXTUALITY The theory that texts consist of interwoven allusions to previous texts.

ISOTOPISM Term derived from physics; an isotope is one of two or more atoms, the nuclei of which have the same number of protons but different numbers of neutrons.

KIERKEGAARD, SØREN (1813–55) Danish thinker who wrote on philosophical, psychological and literary topics, including such concepts as irony and anxiety.

LÉVI-STRAUSS, CLAUDE (1908–) Belgian anthropologist who provided decisive models for the structuralists in the years after the Second World War in his studies of the relationships of human beings to their linguistic and social structures.

LOCUS AMOENUS Latin for 'pleasant place'; a literary topos.

LUCAS, DR PROSPER Published 1842–50 two immense volumes on heredity which Emile Zola consulted for the design of his series of novels about the Rougon-Macquart family.

MARXISM The political and economic ideas of Karl Marx (1818–83) and Friedrich Engels (1829–95) as developed into a system of thought that gives class struggle a primary role in leading society from bourgeois rule under capitalism to a socialist society and thence to communism; in literary criticism an interpretation of texts in the light of this view.

METAPHOR Figure of speech in which a word or phrase is used to denote or describe something entirely different from the object, idea, action or quality which it primarily and usually expresses, thus suggesting a resemblance or analogy.

METONYMY Figure of speech which consists of putting the name of one thing for another, the substituted word expressing an object or idea closely associated with that for which it stands; substitution based on the principle of contiguity.

MIMESIS Imitation of nature in art and literature; mimicry.

MODERNISM A term that denotes, roughly, post-1918 writing, often characterised by a consciousness of historical discontinuity, a sense of alienation, loss and despair.

MONOSEMESIS Singularity of meaning.

OBJECTIFY Term used by phenomenologists to denote the process whereby readers come to grasp a text.

ONOMASTIC Of or pertaining to a name or names.

PARATAXIS Use or arrangement of successive clauses, etc. without connecting words.

PHALLOCENTRISM centring on the phallus, the emblem of (alleged?) male dominance over women.

PHENOMENOLOGY The study of all possible appearances in human experience, during which considerations of objective reality and of purely subjective response are temporarily left out of account.

PIAGET, JEAN (1896–1980) Swiss psychologist who worked mainly on child development, especially the perceptions of time and space; *Structuralism* (1968, trans. 1970).

POLYSEMY Multiplicity of meanings; adjective: POLYSEMANTIC.

POSTMODERN Literally, postdating the Modernist movement in literature that began roughly after the First World War; more commonly it denotes critical approaches such as deconstruction and feminism that came into the forefront after the structuralist revolution of the 1960s and 1970s.

PRAGUE SCHOOL A group of linguists in Prague in the 1930s, including Roman Jakobson, an émigré from Russia; they saw language as an ultimately coherent structure, and analysed the variety of functions it fulfils in communication; successors to the Russian formalists and forerunners of the structuralists.

PROPP, VLADIMIR (1895–1970) Russian linguist and folklorist who devised an influential taxonomy of narrative plots in *Morphology of the Folk-Tale* (1958).

READER-ORIENTED A type of criticism that envisages readers as active participants in the construction of the text.

RECEIVER Structuralist term for reader; also RECIPIENT

REFERENTIAL The adjective pertaining to referentiality, i.e. the act of making reference to an extraneous world believed to exist independently outside the realm of the fiction; the REFERENT is the object to which reference is made.

REPRESENTATION The act of representing, i.e. depicting, portraying, bringing to mind; a portrait, graphic reproduction.

REPRODUCTION That which is reproduced, a representation, an image, counterpart.

RHETORICAL Pertaining to the art of persuasive speech or writing; concerned with structure, cadence and style.

RUSSIAN FORMALISTS The Moscow Linguistic Circle, founded 1915, and the Petrograd Society for the Study of Poetic Language, founded 1916, whose members included Boris Eichenbaum, Roman Jakobson, Viktor Shklovsky, Boris Tomasjevsky, Juri Tynyanov; had a renewed impact after Todorov's translation of their work in 1965 as *Théorie de la littérature*; practised a morphological approach to literature, and were interested in the differentiation of literary from ordinary language, specifically literariness, i.e. what makes a text a work of literature, what devices and techniques are agents of literariness; major source of structuralism.

SELF-REFLEXIVE Used of a fiction that embraces within its parameters reflections on the act of writing, and that therefore clearly announces itself as a piece of writing.

SEMANTICS Branch of linguistic study which deals with the development of meaning.

SEMIOSIS The process of attaching significations to signs.

SEMIOTICS The study of signs and their role in the formation of significations.

SENDER Structuralist term for author or narrating voice.

SIGN The combination of a signifier and a signified.

SIGNIFIED The thing or concept denoted by a signifier.

SIGNIFIER The word or term that denotes a signified.

STRUCTURALISM Literary school emanating from Paris in the 1960s and 1970s, but originating earlier in Russian Formalism and the Prague School; sees texts as self-contained systems governed by artifice in construction, and arising not from reference to any externally postulated reality but rather out of inter- and intratextual allusions.

STURM UND DRANG Literally: Storm and Stress; a German literary movement of about 1770–90, whose essence was rebellion and renewal.

SUPERSTRUCTURE Used by Marxists to denote the ideational institutions of a society as distinct from the processes and direct social relations of material production.

SYLLOGISTIC Pertaining to or resembling a syllogism, i.e. a form of deductive reasoning consisting of a major premise, a minor premise and a conclusion.

SYNCHRONIC Studying phenomena without consideration of historical sequence or data.

SYNECDOCHE Figure of speech in which a part is used to imply a whole.

SYNTAGM(A) A rule-governed sequence of two or more units of the same type; originally applied by Saussure to sounds and grammatical entities, and subsequently expanded to include narrational types such as the performative (relating to tests and struggles), the contractual (pertaining to the establishment and infringement of contracts) and disjunctional (involving various kinds of movement and displacements).

TODOROV, TZVETAN (1939–) Literary critic currently Director of the French National Research Centre; *The Fantastic: A Structural Approach to a Literary Genre* (1968, trans. 1975); *The Poetics of Prose* (1971, trans. 1977).

VERISIMILITUDE Quality of appearing to be true, plausible, lifelike without necessarily claiming to be a direct imitation; related to the French neoclassical concept of *vraisemblance* in drama.

VRAISEMBLABLE Likely, probable, credible.

Notes on Authors

AUERBACH, ERICH (1892–1957) Professor of Romance Philology at Marburg University, Germany; forced to retire by Nazi laws in 1935; refugee at Turkish State University, Istanbul, where he wrote *Mimesis* (1946); emigrated to USA 1947, and joined French Department at Yale University in 1950.

BALZAC, HONORÉ DE (1799–1850) moved to Paris from his native Tours as a young man to study law, but instead took to writing novels; extraordinarily prolific output, including *Eugénie Grandet* (1833), *Le Père Goriot* (1834), *Le Lys dans la vallée* (1836), *César Birotteau* (1837), *Les Illusions perdues* (1837), *Le Curé de village* (1840), *Les Paysans* (1844), *La Cousine Bette* (1847), *Le Cousin Pons* (1848), etc. gathered into *La Comédie humaine*, a cycle intended to portray all aspects of French society.

BARTHES, ROLAND (1915–1980) a highly versatile and innovative French literary critic, who championed structuralism in the 1960s and 1970s and also explored various other areas such as semiotics, fashion and photography; works include *Le Degré zéro de l'écriture* (1953: *Writing Degree Zero*, 1967); *Critique et vérité* (1966; *Criticism and Truth*, 1987); *Système de la mode* (1967; *The Fashion System*, 1983); *L'Empire des signes* (1970; *Empire of Signs*, 1982); *S/Z* (1970; English, 1974); *Mythologies* (1970; *Mythologies*, 1972); *Nouveaux essais critiques* (1972; *New Critical Essays*, 1980); *Le Plaisir du texte* (1973; *The Pleasure of the Text*, 1977); *Roland Barthes par Roland Barthes* (1975; *Roland Barthes by Roland Barthes*, 1977).

BERSANI, LEO (1931–) Professor of French and Comparative Literature at the University of California at Berkeley; *Marcel Proust* (1965); *Balzac to Beckett: Center and Circumference in French Fiction* (1970); *A Future for Astyanax: Character and Desire in Literature* (1976); *Baudelaire and Freud* (1979); *The Death of Stéphane Mallarmé* (1981).

BOUMELHA, PENNY (1950–) teaches at the University of Western Australia; *Thomas Hardy: Sexual Ideology and Narrative Form* (1982); *Charlotte Brontë* (1990); participant in 'Feminism and the Humanities' at the Humanities Research Centre, Australian National University (1986).

BROOKS, PETER (1938–) Professor of French and Comparative Literature at Yale University and Director of Whitney Humanities Center; *The Novel of Worldliness* (1969); *The Melodramatic Imagination* (1976); *Reading for the Plot* (1984).

DURANTY, EDMOND (1833–1880) journalist and minor novelist; edited *Réalisme* 1856–57.

Notes on Authors

ELIOT, GEORGE (Mary Ann Evans) (1819–1880) leading English novelist; *Scenes from Clerical Life* (1858); *Adam Bede* (1859); *The Mill on the Floss* (1860); *Silas Marner* (1861); *Middlemarch* (1872); *Daniel Deronda* (1876).

FLAUBERT, GUSTAVE (1821–1880) leading French novelist; *Madame Bovary* (1857); *Salammbô* (1862); *L'Education sentimentale* (1869); *Trois contes* (1877); *Bouvard et Pécuchet* (1881).

ISER, WOLFGANG (1926–) German critic who teaches at the University of Konstanz and also at the University of California at Irvine; *The Implied Reader: Patterns of Prose Communication from Bunyan to Beckett* (1972; English, 1974); *The Act of Reading: A Theory of Aesthetic Response* (1976; English, 1978); *Prospecting: From Reader Response to Literary Anthropology* (1989).

JAMES, HENRY (1843–1916) major American novelist who migrated to England; *The American* (1877); *The Europeans* (1878); *Daisy Miller* (1879); *The Portrait of a Lady* (1881); *The Bostonians* (1886); *The Princess Casamassima* (1888); *The Tragic Muse* (1890); *The Figure in the Carpet* (1896); *The Spoils of Poynton* (1897); *What Maisie Knew* (1897); *The Turn of the Screw* (1898); *The Awkward Age* (1899); *The Wings of the Dove* (1902); *The Ambassadors* (1903); *The Golden Bowl* (1904); *The Art of Fiction* (1884).

LEWES, HENRY (1817–1878) English critic and thinker; *The Life of Goethe* (1855); *Physiology of Common Life* (1859–60); *Problems of Life and Mind* (1874–79); *Physical Basis of Mind* (1877).

LODGE, DAVID (1935–) Professor of English at the University of Birmingham and novelist; *The Language of Fiction* (1966); *The Modes of Modern Writing: Metaphor, Metonymy, and the Typology of Literature* (1977); *Working with Structuralism* (1981). Novels include *Changing Places* (1979); *Small World* (1984) and *Nice Work* (1988).

LUKÁCS, GEORG (1885–1971) Hungarian Marxist critic; *Theory of the Novel* (1920; English, 1971); *History and Class Consciousness* (1923; English, 1971); *The Historical Novel* (1937; English, 1962); *Studies in European Realism* (1935–9; English, 1950).

MACHEREY, PIERRE (1938–) French philosopher and literary critic who teaches at the Sorbonne in Paris; *Pour une Théorie de la production littéraire* (1966; *A Theory of Literary Production*, 1978).

MAUPASSANT, GUY DE (1850–93) French novelist and short story writer; *La Maison Tellier* (1881); *Une Vie* (1883); *Bel Ami* (1885); *Le Horla* (1887); *Pierre et Jean* (1888); *Fort comme la mort* (1889).

MILLER, JOSEPH HILLIS (1928–) American critic associated with deconstructionism at Yale, now teaches at the University of California at Irvine; *The Disappearance of God: Five Nineteenth Century Writers* (1963); *Fiction and Repetition* (1982); *The Linguistic Moment: From Wordsworth to Stevens* (1985); *The Ethics of Reading* (1986).

WALTON, KENDALL L. (1939–) American philosopher of aesthetics who teaches at the University of Michigan; *Mimesis as Make-Believe: On the Foundations of the Representational Arts* (1990).

WATT, IAN (1917–) English critic who has taught in Great Britain and in the United States, now at Stanford University; *The Rise of the Novel* (1957); *Conrad in the Nineteenth Century* (1979).

Further Reading

Modern Literary Theory, ed. Ann Jefferson and David Robey, 2nd edn, London: Batsford, 1986. A superb, comprehensible introduction to the entire field, including essays on 'Russian Formalism' by Ann Jefferson (pp. 24–45); 'Modern linguistics and the language of literature' by David Robey (pp. 46–73); 'Structuralism and post-structuralism' by Ann Jefferson (pp. 92–121); 'Reading and interpretation' by Ian Maclean (pp. 122–44); 'Modern psychoanalytic criticism' by Elizabeth Wright (pp. 145–65); 'Marxist literary theories' by David Forgacs (pp. 166–203; and 'Feminist literary criticism' by Toril Moi (pp. 204–21). Suggestions for additional reading are appended to each chapter.

Contemporary views and reviews

ALLOTT MIRIAM (ed) *Novelists on the Novel* (London: Routledge & Kegan Paul, 1959). Section II, 'The Novel as a Portrait of Life' (pp. 59–84), presents a series of extracts from many novelists' views.

BECKER, GEORGE (ed) *Documents of Modern Literary Realism* (Princeton: Princeton University Press, 1963). A wide-ranging collection of contemporary views and reviews.

Humanist

HEMMINGS, F.W.J. (ed). *The Age of Realism* (Harmondsworth: Penguin, 1974). An informative collection of essays on realism in Russia, France, Germany, Spain, Portugal and Italy, prefaced by a socio-historical introduction. An excellent starting point.

LEVINE, GEORGE 'Realism Reconsidered', in *The Theory of the Novel*, ed. John Halperin (London and New York: Oxford University Press, 1974), pp. 233–56. A succinct argument for the view that 'Fiction is fiction is fiction'.

LEVINE, GEORGE *The Realistic Imagination: English Fiction from 'Frankenstein' to 'Lady Chatterley'* (Chicago: University of Chicago Press, 1981). An important reassessment of the role of imagination in realistic fiction.

LEVIN, HARRY T., *The Gates of Horn: Five French Realists*. (London and New York: Oxford University Press, 1963). The second chapter, 'Romance and Realism' (pp. 24–88), offers an elegant account of the conjunction between social forces and literary factors in the formation of realism; followed by illuminating sections on Stendhal, Balzac, Flaubert, Zola and Proust.

NOCHLIN, LINDA *Realism* (Harmondsworth: Penguin, 1971). A probing analysis of realism in the visual arts.

STERN, J.P. *On Realism* (London and Boston: Routledge & Kegan Paul, 1973). A difficult but deeply thoughtful book.

WILLIAMS, D.A. (ed) *The Monster in the Mirror* (London: Oxford University Press, 1978). An interesting collection of essays, especially Cecil Jenkins, 'Realism and the Novel Form' (pp. 1–15), and D.A. Williams, 'The Practice of Realism' (pp. 257–79).

Marxist

EAGLETON, TERRY *Criticism and Ideology* (London: Verso, 1975). Addresses the relationship of criticism and ideology, with special reference to Marxist materialism.

EAGLETON, TERRY *Marxism and Literary Criticism* (Berkeley and London: University of California Press, 1976). An introduction to the field; on Lukács, see pp. 20–31.

JAMESON, FREDRIC, *Marxism and Form* (Princeton: Princeton University Press, 1971). A sophisticated analysis; on Lukács, see pp. 195–201.

LICHTHEIM, GEORG *Lukács* (London: Fontana/Collins, 1970). A biographical and critical overview of Lukács' work.

WILLIAMS, RAYMOND *Marxism and Literature* (Oxford: Oxford University Press, 1977). Discusses the impact of Marxism on literary criticism.

Structuralist

BARTHES, ROLAND *S/Z*, trans. Richard Miller (New York: Hill & Wang, 1974). A revolutionary treatment of Balzac's story *Sarrasine*.

BARTHES, ROLAND 'Introduction to the Structuralist Analysis of Narrative' in *Image – Music – Text*, trans. Stephen Heath (New York: Hill & Wang, 1977), pp. 79–124.

CULLER, JONATHAN *Structuralist Poetics* (London: Routledge & Kegan Paul, 1975). An account of the linguistic foundations of structuralism and of its implications for the study of literature.

DEGEORGE, RICHARD and FERNANDE (eds). *The Structuralists* (Garden City, New York: Doubleday, 1972). A useful anthology of structuralist approaches.

Realism

HAWKES, TERENCE *Structuralism and Semiotics* (London: Methuen, 1976). A sound and accessible introduction.

JAMESON, FREDRIC *The Prison-House of Language* (Princeton: Princeton University Press, 1972). A critical account of Russian formalism and of structuralism.

TANNER, TONY, *Adultery in the Novel* (Baltimore and London: Johns Hopkins University Press, 1979). Chapter 4 (pp. 233–367) offers an intriguing reading of Flaubert's *Madame Bovary*.

Rhetorical

AUSTIN, J.L. *Sense and Sensibilia* (Oxford: Clarendon Press, 1962). Chapter VII (pp. 62–77) on the meanings of 'realism'.

BOOTH, WAYNE C. *The Rhetoric of Fiction* (Chicago: University of Chicago Press, 1961). The fundamental book on the rhetorical approach to fiction.

FOWLER, ROGER *Linguistics and the Novel* (London: Methuen, 1977). A fine introduction to the linguistic aspects of fiction.

Reader-oriented

FREUND, ELIZABETH *The Return of the Reader* (London and New York: Methuen, 1987). An excellent survey of various forms of reader-oriented criticism.

ISER, WOLFGANG *The Implied Reader: Patterns of Communication from Bunyan to Beckett* (Baltimore and London: Johns Hopkins University Press, 1974). A largely practical experiment in reader-oriented criticism.

ISER, WOLFGANG *The Act of Reading* (Baltimore and London: Johns Hopkins University Press, 1978). A theoretical exposition.

RIFFATERRE, MICHAEL *Fictional Truth* (Baltimore and London: Johns Hopkins University Press, 1990). Argues, especially in the Introduction (pp. xii–xix) and in Chapter 2 (pp. 29–52), that it is readers who actualise texts, and that they do so by discovering the signs of its fictionality.

WALTON, KENDALL L. *Mimesis as Make-Believe* (Cambridge, Mass.: Harvard University Press, 1990). A demanding but rewarding consideration of the foundations of representation in the visual arts as well as in literature.

Psychoanalytic

BROOKS, PETER 'Freud's Masterplot', Chapter 4 (pp. 90–112) of *Reading for the Plot* (New York: Vintage, 1984) for a conceptualisation of Brooks's method.

FELMAN, SHOSHANA 'Turning the Screw of Interpretation' in *Literature and Psychoanalysis* FELMAN, SHOSHANA ed, (Baltimore and London: Johns Hopkins

University Press, 1977), pp. 94–207. A bold, psychoanalytically based, deconstructive reading of Henry James's *The Turn of the Screw*.

MILLER, D.A. *Narrative and its Discontents* (Princeton: Princeton University Press, 1981). A Freudian approach to plot dynamics.

ROBERT, MARTHE *The Origins of the Novel*, trans. Sacha Rabinovitch (Bloomington: Indiana University Press, 1980). Explores an intriguing Freudian hypothesis about the origins of narration.

WRIGHT, ELIZABETH *Psychoanalytic Criticism: Theory in Practice* (London and New York: Methuen, 1984). Gives a discerning overview of the spectrum of psychoanalytic approaches.

Postmodern

CULLER, JONATHAN *On Deconstruction: Theory and Criticism after Structuralism* (Ithaca and London: Cornell University Press, 1982). An exposition of various trends in post-structuralist criticism, including feminism.

GREENE, GAYLE and KAHN, COPPÉLIA *Making a Difference: Feminist Literary Criticism* (eds) (London and New York: Methuen, 1985). A varied collection of essays in feminist criticism.

MOI, TORIL *Sexual/Textual Politics: Feminist Literary Theory* (London: Methuen, 1985). A probing, essential study.

NORRIS, CHRISTOPHER *Deconstruction* (London and New York: Methuen, 1982). The best brief introduction.

SCHOR, NAOMI *Breaking the Chain: Women, Theory, and French Realist Fiction* (New York: Columbia University Press, 1985). Feminist readings of French realist texts.

Index

Index